GERARD MANLEY HOPKINS

GERARD MANLEY HOPKINS

(1844–1889)

A Study of Poetic Idiosyncrasy in Relation to Poetic Tradition

BY

W. H. GARDNER

WITH A FOREWORD BY

GERARD HOPKINS

Volume I

"Every true poet, I thought, must be original and originality a condition of poetic genius; so that each poet is like a species in nature (not an *individuum genericum* or *specificum*) and can never recur. That nothing should be old or borrowed however cannot be."

(G. M. H., *Further Letters*, p. 222.)

NEW HAVEN
YALE UNIVERSITY PRESS
1948

First published in England 1944
First published in U.S.A. 1948

TO

FATHER JAMES P. O'DONOHOE, S.J.

THIS VOLUME IS AFFECTIONATELY
DEDICATED

MADE AND PRINTED IN GREAT BRITAIN BY
MORRISON AND GIBB LTD., LONDON AND EDINBURGH

PREFACE

THE shape and presentation of the following study have been affected by the World War. My serious work on Hopkins began ten years ago and was originally determined by two desires: first, to produce a book which would enable others to follow, with profit, my own efforts to understand this puzzling and strangely exhilarating poet—to share, in fact, my own growing admiration for his rare individual qualities; second, to cover my chosen ground with such thoroughness that my work would satisfy university requirements as a thesis for a doctorate in Philosophy.

Having succeeded in the latter aim, I was soon to be thwarted in my main project; for owing to the paper shortage, my book, as it stood, was declared to be too bulky for immediate publication. This rebuff, however, proved (or rather I hope *will* prove) to be salutary: it gave me time to ponder a criticism made by Professor H. B. Charlton—a stricture which confirmed my own feeling—namely, that I had not said all I wanted to say about Hopkins. I realized that my commentary, especially upon some of the mature poems, had been unduly constricted by academic and other self-imposed conditions. It became obvious to me that in order to complete my plan and do justice to my project I should be obliged to overflow the limits of a single volume.

Eventually the sympathetic co-operation of my publishers made it possible for me to split my book into two parts; it was decided that I should present, in the first and larger volume, such matter as might be more readily appreciated in these dour and distracted times, and leave for a second and later volume those chapters which, though indispensable to a broad and satisfying treatment of this poet's work, were not absolutely essential to an unbiased, intelligent approach. These deferred chapters will include a full account of the early poems and influences, of the poet's reading and critical opinions; and, above all, my attempt to determine the influence of the Greek, Latin, Welsh, and Teutonic traditions upon his idiosyncratic and at the same time eclectic genius. I propose also to add to this complementary volume some matured appreciations of the greater post-*Deutschland* poems, especially those which have perforce received only partial or incidental treatment in the following pages. I understand, moreover, that in the present centenary year some fresh biographical facts may come to light; and such material, utilized during the period of delay imposed by war-time conditions, would enable me to give the maximum cogency to my final estimate of Hopkins's achievement and status as a poet. [Actually, my second volume, augmented by further studies of the poets background, mature poems, and musical interests, has proved to be the larger of the two.—1948.]

Though fifty-four years have passed since his death, only twenty-five have elapsed since his poetry was first given to the world. Hence no apology is due for this new study of his work; for, although he has enjoyed for at least ten years what may be described as a 'vogue', and has been rendered belated homage in some highly stimulating critiques, his brilliant, provocative genius has so far been honoured in no adequately comprehensive treatise. We have been given many subjective opinions but relatively few objective facts. The *Letters* (in three volumes) and the *Note-books*, so ably edited by Professor C. C. Abbott and Mr. Humphry House respectively, are of course, after the *Poems*, our chief sources of authentic literary data; but even Professor Abbott, in the 'Introduction' to his first volume, proves to be a somewhat biased commentator. It is indeed hard to find a single critic who has made any bold attempt to examine either the poetry or the life in all their many aspects. Admittedly, I myself have used biographical facts only when they were relevant to critical exposition; nor would I invite for my completed survey that pretentious epithet 'definitive'. I have tried, however, to achieve a balanced conspectus, and to present a solid factual basis for every subjective judgment.

My main purpose is clearly indicated in the sub-title: it is, in effect, to show that Hopkins, at first sight so odd, eccentric, even revolutionary in the matters of style and rhythm, is actually and eminently as legitimate an offspring of the great European poetic tradition as any English poet before him; it is also to show that Hopkins, like the greater poet Shakespeare, appeals successfully to different levels of understanding. There is, in his verse, a primitive quality, a certain primary poetic meaning, which goes home at once; on the other hand, his subtle overtones and obliquities, his richly varied rhythms, his elaborately poeticized theology and philosophy, his deeper probings into sensory and intellectual experience—these are qualities to be fully appreciated only by those readers who know something of the great traditions in which he was nurtured—in which moreover, as scholar and priest, he was both 'curious' and learned. It is this ability, first to attract and then to hold our attention, that will ensure for him a permanent place among the English poets. The principle of Truth in Christianity and the principle of Beauty in Æschylus and Shakespeare—these, as I hope to prove, are the twin anchors above which he will "ride time like riding a river", resisting all the currents and eddies of taste and fashion.

My grateful acknowledgments to those who have helped in the shaping of the present volume must begin with a citation from a poet and critic I have always admired—the late Harold Monro. It was in 1931 that his phrase, "the magnificent Gerard Manley Hopkins", seemed to me to crystallize the memorable quality in certain lines which rang in my head :

"The grey lawns cold, where gold, where quickgold lies. . . ."

"Didst fettle for the great grey drayhorse his bright and battering sandal."

For me the first Hopkinsian allurement was mainly poetical ; there was something numinous and mystical too, perhaps, but the initial appeal was certainly not theological or ethical. I soon realized, however, that I should not go far in a serious study of this poet unless I learnt more about his beliefs and the Jesuit way of life. To this end I approached the Rector of Manresa House, the Jesuit Novitiate at Roehampton, and through his courteous introduction I gained an esteemed friend and mentor : Father James P. O'Donohoe, S.J., though 'emeritus', was still young enough in mind to be deeply interested in Hopkins's poetry, and anxious for someone to write what he facetiously called a 'crib' to the more obscure passages.

Many were the delightful hours we spent reading Hopkins together, and the inspiration afforded by Father O'Donohoe's wide knowledge and kindly character enabled me to overcome many initial difficulties. The immediate outcome of these readings was the appearance of my essay on *The Wreck of the Deutschland*, and here I must thank the English Association and Mr. Herbert Read, editor of *Essays and Studies* (vol. xxi. 1935)—the former for kindly permitting me to incorporate my article in the present volume, the latter for his interest and encouragement.

Through Father O'Donohoe I met Mr. Francis Brand, then

a Jesuit at Campion Hall and an enthusiastic student of Duns Scotus. From him I learnt much about the Subtle Doctor, his texts and his commentators, and I cordially repeat here the acknowledgment I made at the beginning of my essay, " Hopkins and Duns Scotus ", which was printed by Dr. F. R. Leavis in *Scrutiny* (June 1936). Other members of the Society of Jesus to whom I am indebted are Father Martin C. D'Arcy, Rector of Campion Hall, who graciously afforded me facilities for examining the considerable batch of MSS. in his keeping; Mr. Vincent Turner, who advised me on some knotty points of philosophy; the Editor of *The Month* and Father Geoffrey Bliss, who have kindly allowed me to include in the present volume the latter's reconstructions of two of Hopkins's unfinished poems.

For permission to inspect the poet's MSS. and private papers at Amen House; for advice and facilities cheerfully and readily granted at all times, and above all for his generous appreciation of my work in progress and completed, I tender my sincere thanks to Mr. Gerard Hopkins. It is through him, and by the courtesy of the Oxford University Press and the poet's relatives, that I am allowed to quote freely from the published *Poems*, *Letters* and *Note-books*, and also from many unpublished papers. Further, it was Mr. Gerard Hopkins who introduced me to Mrs. Robert Bridges; by her I was entertained most hospitably at Chilswell House and kindly permitted to inspect, copy and quote from the invaluable MS. 'A', her husband's own collection of Hopkins's autograph poems.

Probably every writer is aware of an imponderable debt to certain friends whose tastes agree with his own and from whose conversation he has derived the stimulus of criticism and encouragement; such friends, in my case, are my past and present colleagues, Mr. C. J. A. Hill, B.A., and Mr. E. L. Hillman, B.A. Again, for some incisive criticism and useful advice in the initial stages of my work I wish to record my indebtedness to the late Miss Gertrude Hollingworth, M.A.

For permission to quote at length from copyright material I am obliged to Mr. Wilfred Meynell for Francis Thompson's sonnet, "To a Child" (*Poems*, vol. ii.); to Faber & Faber Ltd. and Mr. Herbert Read for " Day's Affirmation ", from *Poems, 1914–1934*; To Joiner & Steele Ltd. and Mr. Monk Gibbon for the sonnet " To Gerard Manley Hopkins ", and parts of others from *Seventeen Sonnets*; to Gerald Duckworth & Co. Ltd. for extracts from C. M. Doughty's *Dawn in Britain*; to the Editor of

The Listener and the author for Mr. T. H. White's "A Dray Horse"; to Mrs. Austin Duncan-Jones and the Cambridge University Press for many excerpts from *The Poetry of Gerard Manley Hopkins* (1933).

As regards the many other shorter extracts from copyright prose and verse which I have ventured to quote for purposes of criticism and comment, I trust that the authors (if alive) and publishers concerned will accept this general acknowledgment of my indebtedness.

W. H. GARDNER.

EAST SHEEN, SURREY,
1944.

PREFACE TO THE SECOND EDITION

THE generous welcome accorded to the first edition of this volume has induced me to reissue it without major alterations. In respectful reply to certain of my critics, I must reaffirm that every chapter, as it stands, is integral to my comprehensive plan as it is enunciated in the sub-title. I do not claim that the comparative morphology and prosodic analyses of Chapter III are capable of bringing home poetic beauty to those who are quite incapable of receiving it directly from the poems; I do claim, however, that this chapter is necessary to show how far Hopkins departed from conventional practice, to reveal the system behind his apparent wantonness, to clarify, intensify, and (in a critical sense) to authenticate that beauty which is, or should be, spontaneously perceived through the ear. Similarly Chapters VI and VII provide historical and critical data which are relevant to my purpose: the impact of such a poet as Hopkins upon his own and the immediately succeeding generation forms an episode in literary history from which something useful may always be learnt.

Some score of minor emendations have been made *passim*; the most important is on p. 26, where I have rectified a regrettable misunderstanding of Father Christopher Devlin's views on the Scotist theory of knowledge.

In all footnote and other references to the *Poems*, I have thought it advisable, for the present, to retain the numbering of the Second Edition (1930). For the convenience of those readers who will have access only to the Third Edition (1947) I have given, in Appendix F of Volume II, a table to facilitate reference.

W. H. G.

June 1947.

CONTENTS

Reproduction by kind permission of the Oxford University Press.

FOREWORD

THE publication of this, the first of Dr. Gardner's two volumes, falls in the year that holds the hundredth anniversary of the birth of Gerard Manley Hopkins, who was born, not as is generally supposed in June, but in July 1844, at 4.15 a.m. on the 28th day of that month. It has been remarked already by more than one writer that the celebration of his centenary has produced in many minds a sense of curious shock. It is surprising, it is almost disconcerting, to find that a writer so often hailed as 'modern' should, in the prosaic annals of chronology, turn out to be so ancient. I have a particular and personal reason for responding uncomfortably to the jarring impact of that reminder. To realize, when still at an encouraging distance from extreme senility, that one's uncle was born a century ago is an experience not wholly delightful. True, I never did, never could have, set eyes upon my father's eldest brother, since I was born several years after his death, but, for all that, so extended a bridge across the expanse of time sounds unpleasantly solid and resonant beneath my feet. It is strangely borne in upon the mind of one who fondly thinks himself the contemporary of Mr. Eliot that, as the result of some odd transference, he seems to be within almost visible distance of Mr. Southey. But there is comfort in the thought that the recognition has been shared by others who have not the same selfish reasons for dismay: that for the critic as well as for the nephew the passage of those hundred years is embarrassing and scarcely credible. For the 'modernity' of Father Hopkins has been the note struck by every admiring commentator of the last twenty-five years. It has rung out with a vibrant iteration which has threatened, at times, to drown a deeper and more lovely music. Nor is it hard to understand why that single aspect of a superb body of work should, for so long, have been obsessive.

The *Collected Poems* were published for the first time in 1918. They struck at a generation wearied by war and conscious, perhaps to excess, that it was standing on the threshold of a new age. There was a widespread feeling that English poetry had withdrawn into the limpid smoothness of a minor backwater. Regularity and melody, it was held, had become facile and academic. A new manner was in the making, and it sought a master. To ears eager for novelty this new voice, calling across the Victorian wastes, was especially welcome. But it was hardly to be expected that it should be set to the credit side of a century which was already drawing narrowly into a vista of contempt. With acclamation Hopkins was co-opted into the shining company of the post-war years, and for a long time his manner, that did "so rinse and wring the ear," kept many indifferent if not actually hostile to the profound sources of his inspiration. It was all very natural, but some of its effects were unfortunate. Much writing about him was superficial and not wholly comprehending. Silly things were said about his vocation, still sillier, perhaps, about his dearest friend, Bridges, who had nursed and tended the treasure of his verse, and was now shown in scarce recognizable and diabolic colours. It was time that serious and balanced thought should be given to the subject, and in the work of Professor Abbott, Mr. House, Dr. Pick and Dr. Gardner a more responsible attitude has found expression.

Hopkins the poet deserves to be more than the mere starting-point for subjective reverie. There is a great deal in his work that demands, and repays, careful examination. But the critic who would do justice to this urgent voice and complicated mind must be more than usually well equipped—more than usually sensitive to language, curious in matters of rhythm, sympathetic to theological and metaphysic implications, patient with obscurities which, though rarely deliberate, are always fundamental. There was room for exegesis even more than for appreciation, and future students of the Hopkins Canon will owe an inexhaustible debt of gratitude to Dr. Gardner's long and meticulous labours. His two volumes are models of informed appraisal. He has gone deeply into difficult problems. Many have realized, for instance, that Duns Scotus exercised an overwhelming influence upon my uncle's mind, but few have troubled to sound that Schoolman's difficult depths. But how important it is for the writer on Hopkins to do so, Dr. Gardner, acknowledging the help given him by such students as Father O'Donohoe and Mr. Francis Brand, has made very clear. The demonstration of the extent to which the Scotist philosophy bears upon the hard difficulties of "inscape" and "instress" alone marks his book as being a first-class contribution to literary analysis and constructive interpretation. In his study, too, of Hopkins's prosodic erudition and metric pattern he has given lucid and much-needed help to those who have found the Author's own Preface in the 1918 edition of the *Poems* a hindrance rather than a guide to understanding. The most obvious intricacies of that arabesque have found, too frequently, their imitators, and it was time that an attempt should be made to trace and establish the nature of the intellectual articulation which underlies it.

There is little hope now that much of value remains undiscovered with which to amplify the body of the poet's work. A few letters may still come to light, but that any poems can still be found is extremely improbable. Nor has careful search succeeded in bringing to light more than a few scraps of musical exercises. These have been printed, but of the large-scale choral work which Father Hopkins projected and upon which he said, at the end of his life, that he had embarked, nothing exists. This fact gives rise to a disappointment which is likely to remain unassuaged. Of his drawings a number were included in the volumes of Letters and Note-Books, but a great many more exist. Their publication is one of the only major tasks remaining for those who would make available the rich variety of his production. It might worthily have illustrated his hundredth anniversary. But war-time stringencies and conditions have made impossible an enterprise which needs unrationed resources of the highest quality. It is to be hoped that when paper and typographical skill are to be had once more for the asking, the series of sketch-books happily preserved will be printed. For my uncle's drawings were no minor hobby, no careless splashing in pleasant but unimportant shallows. They are the partial expression of a vision of the material world which was an essential part of his genius. There is, in the best of them, a fierce intensity of contemplation which tears at " inscape " with an almost relentless fervour, and sets the chosen trees, clouds and waterscapes in a hushed expectancy of gaze.

But his work, in the main, has been finally collected and presented. Nothing could have marked more happily this centenary year than the publication of Dr. Gardner's volumes. They will remain an essential part of the equipment needed by every student of Hopkins, and, as criticism, will take a high place in the long and honourable line of English literary scholarship.

GERARD HOPKINS.

9 South Parks Road,
Oxford,
June 1944.

CHAPTER I

THE TWO VOCATIONS

THE work of every poet is naturally influenced by the main events and changing conditions of his daily life; and though it is the weakness of some modern critics to exaggerate or distort that influence, a purely literary and scholastic criticism, which made no attempt to relate the work to the man and the man to his environment, would inevitably fall short of the whole truth.

The outward events in the life of Gerard Manley Hopkins were never spectacular. Except for one major crisis, when he shocked and wounded his parents and academic seniors by entering the Roman Catholic Church, his relatively short stay of forty-five years left nothing for popular biographers to intensify and romanticize—nothing like the love-letters of Keats, the domestic tragedy of Shelley, or the drug-inspired dereliction of Francis Thompson. From the psychological and psycho-pathological points of view, his life-story is profoundly interesting; yet the general trend of his career has been obliquely summed up in one of his own sonnets:

> " But be the war within, the brand we wield
> Unseen, the heroic breast not outward-steeled,
> Earth hears no hurtle then of fiercest fray." [1]

The " years and years of world without event " in Hopkins's life were not, indeed, filled up with a task so humdrum and humble as that of St. Alphonsus; yet his peculiar situation rendered the task of maintaining a high standard of spiritual detachment and integrity an even more difficult one for him. Living the comparatively cloistered life of a Jesuit priest, he was at the same time in close intellectual contact with men like Robert Bridges, R. W. Dixon and Coventry Patmore, two of whom, though in some ways his inferiors, had achieved a considerable reputation in that art towards which Hopkins himself was strongly drawn. The story of his life presents, from one angle, the tragic conflict of a man torn between two vocations

[1] *Poems of Gerard Manley Hopkins* (1918), No. 49. (All references in the following pages will be to the Second Edition of 1930.)

—the religious and the artistic-creative (for the impulses of his creative sensibility were not confined to poetry); from another angle it presents the heroic struggle of a man who is so completely dedicated to one profession that he deliberately sacrifices another possible and in some ways more exciting profession because he is sure that God wills it to be so.

Here, therefore, is occasion for serious disagreement among critics—a problem in discrimination and emphasis which may divide Catholic and non-Catholic readers for all time. Broadly stated, the decision of the former will be that the life of Father Hopkins is a great example, that his poetry is the breath and finer spirit of all knowledge because its direct inspiration is the knowledge of God; the decision of the latter will be that the life of Hopkins involved a tragic mistake, that his poetry was saved precariously from the ruins of a purpose which was not altogether in harmony with the man's psychic individuality.

An attempt to elucidate this problem will not be the main purpose of this book and its sequel; it will, however, be a necessary *part* of that purpose, which is to present a complete account of a highly idiosyncratic body of poetry as it is seen against a wide background of poetic tradition. Unless the man behind and *in* the poetry is reasonably well understood, the poetry itself must remain partially obscure. On the other hand, when once the religious problem has been rendered less opaque by a careful study of the poet's beliefs, philosophical presuppositions and frank confessions in the *Letters*, much that formerly appeared difficult and incongruous will prove to be both lucid and logical.

Born in 1844 at Stratford, Essex, Hopkins was brought up in a home where simple piety and practical endeavour on the one hand and varied artistic culture on the other fostered from the beginning both the *character* and the *personality* of the boy. We adopt these terms (with due definition) as convenient symbols to indicate a natural dichotomy of being which in Hopkins was particularly marked—two strains in the man which *tend* to pull in opposite directions.[1] Character we define as the stamp imposed upon the individual by tradition and moral training; it may also be desired and self-imposed, and in any case it is maintained by an effort of the will. By personality we mean the

[1] Cf. Mr. Herbert Read's use of the terms in *Form in Modern Poetry* (1932), chap. ii. With Mr. Read's thesis that *character* necessarily thwarts *personality* we do not agree: the case of Hopkins does not support his contention.

free or comparatively untrammelled psychic individuality, that complex of native faculties, " wild and self-instressed ", which find their highest expression in great works of art. Character results when the mind and the passions are subjected to a strict regulative principle : personality, though eclectic and assimilative in all directions, tends to be guided only by the inner law of its own being. Yet in a subject like Hopkins, just as the character is partly determined by the individual will, so the personality is restrained and guided by the secondary force of character.

Hopkins's father (Consul-General of the Hawaiian Islands to Great Britain) combined practical efficiency with something of a poet's vision ; [1] his mother " gave to her son her gentle nature and love for metaphysical speculation ".[2] This literary turn in the father stimulated the poetic proclivities of Gerard. Yet the Consul-General did not bequeath to his son enough practical efficiency to make him a successful man of action. As a parish priest in Liverpool and Glasgow Hopkins was unhappy : his physique could not cope with the heavy duties ; his sensitive nature was oppressed by the vice and squalor. As a teacher in Jesuit school and university, he was not unsuccessful, but was always over-conscientious, worried and constrained. " Never ", said a Dublin contemporary, " was a squarer man in a rounder hole ".[3]

Similarly, the gentle nature inherited from the mother did not exclude a vein of stubborness. In an epigram dated August 1864 he confessed that pride was the vice for which he felt least antipathy.[4] He made it a fixed rule never to quarrel, but he could always express his opinions on moral and aesthetic matters with a vigour and independence which made no concessions to sentimentality.

The Hopkins family, in which there were seven younger children, was deeply interested in the visual arts, and all were to some extent accomplished in painting and music. Arthur, a younger brother, eventually became a professional painter, and Gerard himself, after his sixth year, received lessons in music and drawing from an aunt who was both musician and portrait-painter. As a draughtsman he made rapid progress, and by his

[1] See *Letters of G. M. H. to Robert Bridges* (1935), pp. 56–7. (Hereafter, *Letters*, vol. i.)

[2] *Life of G.M.H.* (1930), by G. F. Lahey, S.J., p. 1. (Hereafter, *Life* (Lahey).)

[3] *A Note on Hopkins's Religious Life*, by Humphry House. (*New Verse*, No. 14 (April 1935), p. 3.)

[4] *Note-books* (1937), p. 28.

twentieth year had developed a strength and delicacy of line, together with a feeling for internal pattern, which very few mere amateurs can ever achieve. In 1863 he was admiring Millais and sending his friend Baillie some sketches " in a Ruskinese point of view ".[1] His affinity with Ruskin is again revealed in his love and knowledge of architecture and in the nature-description and word painting of his Journal.[2]

His interest in music increased with the years. Those critics who blame his religious vocation almost exclusively for the smallness of his poetic output and for his pathetic inability to finish so many projected prose works would do well to consider the hours he must have spent on Egyptology and the rudiments of musical composition. As he himself realized (unfortunately without profiting thereby), the production of a large body of work of the highest excellence in any of the arts demands undivided concentration. His musical studies were not wasted, for they profoundly influenced his conception of poetic rhythm ; but his real artistic *forte* lay in poetry, not in music.

In 1854 he was sent to the Cholmondley Grammar School, Highgate. Here his precocious command of language and unusual sensibility won him the School Poetry Prize on two occasions, the first in his sixteenth year, the second in his eighteenth ; these prize poems will be discussed later in relation to his other early verses.[3] It is more significant to remark here that while his personality (in every sense of the word) was making a deep impression upon all who knew him, there were also clear indications of the developing character.

Observing that nearly all the people around him " consumed more liquids than was good for them ", he resolved to prove his theory by drinking nothing for a week. The result was that he collapsed at drill ; but when this feat of abstinence was doubted by a master, a schoolfellow exclaimed : " *He* tell a lie ? Why, he would sooner die ".[4] So early appeared that moral scrupulosity which played so large a part in his attitude to life and poetry.

In October 1863 he went up to Balliol College, Oxford, with an exhibition. During the next four years he read Classics ; but the influence of the celebrated Regius Professor and Broad Churchman, Jowett, was not so decisive as the example and

[1] *Further Letters of G. M. H.* (1938), p. 55.
[2] *Note-books*, pp. 105–217.
[3] In Vol. II. of the present work (chap. i.).
[4] *Life* (Lahey), p. 6.

aura of Cardinal Newman, who was then at the Oratory. We have also to reckon with the undoubted but not clearly defined impact of Walter Pater upon a pupil so avid of aesthetic doctrine as Hopkins. Although no letters survive, the two men maintained a warm friendship for many years.

Among his more intimate friends at this time were Robert Bridges,[1] with whom he construed Greek and discussed poetry; the scholarly and sceptical A. W. M. Baillie,[2] with whom he corresponded for the rest of his life; and Digby Mackworth Dolben,[1] the young religious enthusiast for whom Hopkins conceived a high admiration and whose premature death by drowning affected him deeply. Other friends like Garrett, Macfarlane, and Addis were all devout Anglo-Catholics, and contributed to the religious atmosphere which had pervaded Oxford since the advent of the Tractarians.

Hopkins himself was taking life very seriously. As a student he was, says Bridges:

> "so punctilious about the text, and so enjoyed loitering over the difficulties, that I foresaw we should never get through." [3]

This 'fascination of what's difficult' remained with Hopkins all his life; it appeared also at this time in his strict self-discipline. His diaries [4] contain a scrupulous record of his youthful misdemeanours and even sins, the words being deleted with pencil as, presumably, they were confessed and forgiven. During Lent, 1866, he wrote:

> "No pudding on Sundays. No tea except to keep one awake, and then without sugar. . . . Not to sit in armchairs except I can work in no other way. Ash Wednesday and Good Friday bread and water." [5]

The same year he was received into the Catholic Church, and in 1867 graduated with a 'first' in Classical 'Greats.'

Both Liddon and Pusey (to whom Hopkins had formerly 'confessed') tried hard to dissuade him from his religious purpose, the former with gentle pleas, the latter with some asperity. But Hopkins was not to be shaken; and his letter to Newman soon after is typical of the man who had as much to do with the

[1] See *Letters,* vol. i. p. 1, notes 2, 3 and 5.
[2] See *Further Letters,* B. [3] *Life* (Lahey), p. 18.
[4] Now in the possession of Campion Hall, Oxford.
[5] *Note-books,* p. 53.

writing of the *Poems* as the virtuoso and experimenter with daring new theories of rhythm :

> " I have been up at Oxford just long enough to have heard from my father and mother in return for my letter announcing my conversion. Their answers are terrible : I cannot read them twice. If you will pray for them and me just now I shall be deeply thankful." [1]

Throughout these four years of study and spiritual unrest Hopkins had been intermittently occupied with verse-writing. His preoccupation with religion is revealed in " poems of a very Catholic character ", most of them being abortive—the " beginnings of things, ruins and wrecks ", as he called them. His mind was also exercised by general aesthetic principles. There is a comment of 1864, made after a reading of Matthew Arnold on *The literary influence of Academies*, which is interesting in view of his later development :

> " I am coming to think much of taste myself, good taste and moderation, I who have sinned against them so much. But there is a prestige about them which is indescribable." [2]

The potential artist enjoys himself in a Platonic dialogue (possibly written for Walter Pater), *On the Origin of Beauty*.[3] In this graceful but again unfinished composition Hopkins advances two theories which have important bearings upon his later poetry : the first, that beauty consists in the judicious blending of regularity with variety, evenness with oddness, is not original but is maintained with freshness and point throughout a lengthy examination of a horse-chestnut leaf ; [4] the second, with more originality, distinguishes two kinds of beauty—*diatonic* and *chromatic* :

> " The diatonic scale, you know, leaves out, the chromatic puts in, the half notes."

As applied to poetry, *diatonic* includes Parallelism in all its forms, whereas under the head of *chromatic*

> " come emphasis, expression (in the sense it has in Music), tone, intensity, climax, and so on."

[1] *Further Letters*, pp. 253–7 and p. 19.
[2] *Ibid.* p. 74.
[3] Dated, May 12, 1865.
[4] For an account of his preoccupation with visual beauty at this time, see *Further Letters*, p. 55.

Emphasis and intensity, he admits, may be given abruptly, and so belong to diatonism ; " perhaps tone or expression best give the field of chromatic beauty ".

On the Origin of Beauty almost certainly owes something to Hopkins's intercourse with Pater.[1] Unfortunately, the allusions to Pater in the *Letters* contain no references at all to his writings or to those aspects of his work with which Hopkins must have been in sympathy. What those aspects were we can deduce from the poet's own utterances—presuppositions and tenets which, if not entirely due to Pater, must have been strengthened by his teaching and example.

Pater was indeed only five years older than Hopkins himself ; and had published little of importance before the essay on Winckelmann, of 1867 ; but it may be assumed that many of his ideas had already been formed, or were still in the exciting process of germination, at the time when Hopkins was his pupil. Pater's intense feeling for Hellenic and Renaissance art and humanism would attract the aesthete in Hopkins but repel the Catholic. The ideas and sentiment expressed in the famous Conclusion to *The Renaissance* (written in 1868, omitted in the second edition as " it might possibly mislead young men ", but later restored) might have been given at least a tentative expression by the tutor Hopkins knew ; but at no time would Hopkins have said bluntly that " we are all under sentence of death with a sort of indefinite reprieve ", and consequently that the true wisdom in living is to gather up in art and song the ecstasy of one's passing moments. " Of such wisdom ", says Pater,

> " the poetic passion, the desire of beauty, the love of art for art's sake, has most. For art comes to you proposing frankly to give nothing but the highest quality to your moments as they pass and simply for those moments' sake." [2]

Such a doctrine is, as we shall see, opposed to the mature Hopkins's more profound reconciliation of aesthetics and ethics. Yet there is a lecture note of 1873–4 [3] which is remarkably like a passage in *The School of Giorgione* (1873), in which Pater says that the mere matter of a poem or painting is nothing without the

[1] In *Note-books*, p. xxiii., Mr. Humphry House says : " I have seen a suggestion somewhere that the dialogue was written for Walter Pater."

[2] *The Renaissance* (ed. of 1910), p. 239.

[3] Quoted in full in Vol. II. chap. ii. of the present work.

form and handling, and that the form or mode of handling should become an end in itself, should penetrate every part of the matter.[1] Meaning, says Hopkins, is essential to poetry "only as an element necessary to support and employ the shape which is contemplated for its own sake". But this merely states that a beautiful form, pattern, design is necessary to distinguish poetry from prose or inferior verse; it still admits the corollary that the higher the matter the greater is the poetry.

Hopkins has other interesting points of contact with Pater—resemblances which may have been due as much to manifold influences working simultaneously upon two rare and not dissimilar natures as to any direct intercourse between the two men.

The idea expressed in the Platonic dialogue, that beauty is enhanced by a note of strangeness, goes back beyond Bacon to Aristotle. It is paralleled also in Pater's words at the beginning of his essay on the poetry of Michelangelo; moreover, Pater's definition of the 'Michelangelesque' in art is strikingly illustrated in the mature poetry of Hopkins:

> "A certain strangeness, something of the blossoming of the aloe, is indeed an element in all true works of art: that they shall excite or surprise us is indispensable . . . and this strangeness must be sweet also—a lovely strangeness."

Pater found in Michelangelo what most good critics have found in Hopkins:

> "Sweetness and strength, pleasure with surprise, an energy of conception which seems at every moment to break through all the conditions of comely form, recovering, touch by touch, a loveliness found usually only in the simplest natural things—*ex forti dulcedo*." [2]

Again, few English poets have been actuated so powerfully and consistently as Hopkins was by the principle enunciated in Pater's "*All art constantly aspires towards the condition of music*". In Hopkins, as in Mallarmé, we discern this great *Anders-streben*, the partial alienation of the art of poetry from its own limitations in order to achieve "a perfect identification of matter and form".[3]

When Pater speaks of "the charm of *ascêsis*, of the austere and serious girding of the loins in youth",[4] we think as readily

[1] *Op cit.*, p. 135.
[2] *Ibid.* p. 73.
[3] *Ibid.* pp. 133–5.
[4] *Ibid.* Preface, p. xiii.

of Hopkins as of Flaubert. Indeed, Pater himself achieved in prose what Hopkins achieved in poetry—a triumph of contradictions. Pater's plea, in the essay on Style, for the patient and arduous removal of all surplusage did not preclude the idea of rich ornamentation, an " honourable artifice " ; he did not sacrifice the *nuance* to lucidity. Like Hopkins, he stressed the labour, the delightful sense of difficulty overcome, the full artistic pleasure of elaborate workmanship. Lastly, the whole complex of Hopkins's poetic style is a justification of Pater's belief, " at this late day ", in the value of eclecticism.

Among Hopkins's undergraduate essays there is but one other noteworthy passage ; on the subject of *Health and Decay in Art*, he says :

> " Perfection is dangerous because it is deceptive. Art slips back while bearing, in its distribution of tone, or harmony, the look of high civilization towards barbarism. Recovery must be by a breaking up, a violence, such as was the Preraphaelite school." [1]

This proves that the violence of his own later innovations in poetic style had a conscious or at least a sub-conscious rational basis.

In 1867 Hopkins was teaching at the Oratory, and telling Baillie that he hoped the work would not take up too much time as he wanted to read " almost everything that has ever been written ".[2] Yet he was soon to realize that such an ambition, like an earlier one, was doomed to disappointment. The next year he writes :

> " You know I once wanted to be a painter. But even if I could I would not, I think, now, for the fact is that the higher and more attractive parts of the art put a strain upon the passions which I should think it unsafe to encounter." [3]

This fear of temptation, of emotional excitement, is significant. Had he not already been conscious of his religious vocation, such a confession would have seemed an unworthy shrinking from life. Three months later he had decided to enter the Society of Jesus.

[1] Quoted by kind permission of the Rector of Campion Hall, Oxford.

[2] *Further Letters*, p. 81.

[3] *Ibid.* p. 84. Cf. Wordsworth's reason for not writing love-poems : " they would be too passionate ".

Newman begged Hopkins not to call the Jesuit discipline hard as it would get him to heaven.[1] After two years, when he had proceeded from the novitiate at Roehampton to Stonyhurst for his course in philosophy and mathematics, he wrote to Baillie in a different strain :

> " The life here though it is hard is God's will for me as I most intimately know, which is more than violets knee-deep." [2]

For a time the active *personality* has been almost completely subjected to the passive *character* ; yet the immediate result was to prove less disastrous than the present-day fear of ' repression ' might lead us to expect. What threatened to be a serious dislocation was to become in many ways a successful coalition of energies.

For comparisons we must go to that great age of faith and genius—the seventeenth century. With Hopkins, as to a less marked degree with Donne, Herbert and Vaughan, the very willingness of that ultimate self-surrender opened up a loophole of escape for the personality, so that the very act of renunciation could be at the same time a bold statement of self-possession—that is, of poetic idiosyncrasy :

> " As when the heart says, sighing to be approved,
> *O, could I love !* and stops, God writeth, *Loved.*"
> (Herbert's *A True Hymn.*)

Similarly Donne, who had cried :

> " Batter my heart, three-personed God,"

could say to his friend, Mr. Tilman, who had taken orders :

> " Thou, whose diviner soul hath caused thee now
> To put thy hand unto the holy plough, . . . [3]
> What bring'st thou home with thee ? how is thy mind
> Affected since the vintage ? Dost thou find
> New thoughts and stirrings in thee ? and, as steel
> Touched with a loadstone, dost new motions feel ? "

Hopkins also was to feel new stirrings and magnetic re-orientations : as the needle of character moved to the south of

[1] *Further Letters*, p. 261, C 11. [2] *Ibid.* p. 88.

[3] Hopkins used this image of the plough in *The Windhover* and in a letter to Dixon (*Letters*, vol. ii. p. 88).

scholastic and monastic Christianity, the pointer of personality slewed round to the bleak north of such uncompromising technique as :

> " What life half lifts the latch of,
> What hell stalks towards the snatch of,
> Your offering, with despatch, of ! " [1]

To trace the development of the poet in Hopkins we turn first of all not to the Early Poems but to the prose of his early diaries.[2] Those descriptions of landscape and cloudscape jotted down during a tour of Switzerland in 1868, just before he joined the Jesuits, proclaim a lusty, almost hedonistic sensibility. The observation is direct, the expression spontaneous and individual. With the eye of a Ruskin, and the same power of using words as pigments, he glances from heaven to earth, noting the varied forms and changing moods of nature and recording every significant detail. The artist, moreover, is merged in the metaphysician. In the vagaries of shape and colour presented by hills, clouds, glaciers and trees he discerns a recondite pattern—" species or individually-distinctive beauty " [3]—for which he coins the name " inscape " ; and the *sensation* of inscape (or, indeed, of any vivid mental image) is called " stress " or " instress ".

Instress is nowhere specifically defined ; but the two terms, *instress* and *inscape*, are used together for the first time in some early notes on Parmenides. Speaking of that philosopher's " great text " concerning τὸ ἐόν and τὸ μὴ ἐόν, and " a little over-defining his meaning ", Hopkins says :

> " Perhaps . . . it means that all things are upheld by instress and are meaningless without it. . . . His feeling for instress, for the flush and foredrawn, and for inscape is most striking, and from this one can understand Plato's reverence for him as the great father of Realism." [4]

Hopkins's interpretations of Parmenides are tinged with Christian predilection ; and here " instress " seems to imply a supernatural force which binds in, bounds, the finite One. It is in effect, for Hopkins, the hand of God upon His creation—the vividness and completeness of the Divine Concept, in which nothing, ultimately, is ' extended ' or ' unforedrawn '. Hence

[1] *Poems*, No. 24.
[2] *Note-books*, p. 105 *et seqq.*
[3] *Further Letters*, p. 225.
[4] *Note-books*, p. 98.

about six years later the rudely arched timber-frames of a barn at Roehampton could prompt him to write :

> " I thought how sadly beauty of inscape was unknown and buried away from simple people and yet how near at hand it was if they had eyes to see it and it could be called out everywhere again." [1]

The perception of *inscape* is marked simultaneously, as a rule, by a flow of *instress*, as though the individual beholder becomes mystically one with the Whole. The word *instress* is used in a bewildering variety of contexts, but its combined epistemological and mystical value is brought out in the following :

> " I saw the inscape . . . freshly, as if my eye were still growing, though with a companion the eye and the ear are for the most part shut and instress cannot come." [2]

As in mysticism, solitude and concentration are preliminary to the act of ' illumination ', the inflow of supersensuous ' knowledge '. The word *instress* is also used later in a frankly theological sense to describe an access of Divine grace—" instressing the affective will ".[3]

In the Journal we see how a deliberate act of contemplation seems to produce a purely subjective revelation :

> " But such a lovely damasking in the sky to-day I never felt before. The blue was charged with simple instress." [4]

There is a true and a false " instress of nature ", for as he says elsewhere, " When you look hard at a thing it seems to look hard at you " ; yet only by constantly refreshing the mind by looking hard and long in this way can you " remember or believe how deep the inscape in things is ".[5]

This habit of grafting new words on the language for the purpose of expressing urgent personal concepts goes to prove that whereas in a Keble or a Newman the poetic form is deliberately adopted as a medium for the religious character, in Hopkins the religious outlook seems to be attained, or at least maintained, through the medium of direct poetic apprehension—

[1] *Note-books,* p. 161 (June 19, 1872). [2] *Ibid.* p. 171.

[3] " Comments on the Spiritual Exercises of St. Ignatius Loyola " (*Note-books,* p. 325). Cf. *The Wreck of the Deutschland,* stanza 5, line 7.

[4] *Note-books,* p. 143.

[5] *Ibid.* p. 140. An imperfect form of inscape he calls " idiom " (pp. 128–9).

seems indeed at times to be the culminating phase of poetic experience. Moreover, the impassioned observations in the Journal increase our understanding not only of the imagination which could turn to Sprung Rhythm and other new verse-modes, but also of the intellect which turned to religion for philosophic assurance :

> ". . . some ashes growing in a beautifully clustered 'bouquet', the inward bend of the left-hand stem being partly real, partly apparent, and helped by τύχῃ τέχνην στερχούσῃ." [1]

This artless art of fortuitous combinations in nature, coupled with the poet's intense enjoyment of similar though contrived effects in music and architecture, anticipates the more flexible rhythms in his own poetry. As music and poetic rhythm were to him 'fluid architecture', so architecture was 'frozen music'.

> ". . . little curled ends of some corbels in the nave are freakishly turned each a different way . . . the scroll of open tracery, the flight or spirit of which it is impossible not to feel." [2]

And again, in the Lady-chapel of Ely Cathedral :

> "The all-powerfulness of instress in mode and the immediateness of its effect are very remarkable" [3]—

words which express accurately our own thought on first reading *The Wreck of the Deutschland.*

We cannot leave the Journal without noting other evidences of the developing personality. There is the sensuous poet's aptitude for the precise word, the *nuance*, the musical phrase, the simple yet fire-new analogy. We read of "*bright-plucked* water swaying in a pail" (p. 106), of thunder "musical and like gongs and rolling in great *floors* of sound" (p. 112), of "little *walking* wavelets edged with *fine eyebrow crispings*" (p. 114). All the senses are enlisted, and the resultant impression has the vividness and colour of reality, as in the bold synaesthesia of :

> "But this sober grey darkness and pale light was happily broken through by the orange of the pealing of Mitton bells." [4]

Yet the visual image, the vision of the painter, is everywhere predominant. "Stars twirling brilliantly" [5] remind us of Van

[1] *Note-books*, p. 112. Cf. p. 173 : "All the world is full of inscape and chance left free to act falls into an order as well as purpose". To perceive this is to have a feeling for the "flush and foredrawn".

[2] *Ibid.* pp. 117–8. [3] *Ibid.* p. 119. [4] *Ibid.* p. 158. [5] *Ibid.* p. 110.

Gogh, and there is, indeed, a real affinity with this painter in the whole conception of "instressed" landscape. In *Further Letters* (p. 50) there is reproduced a pencil-drawing of "Shanklin, Isle of Wight, 1866", which consists of an unfinished study of trees in a cleft or chine. Here the feeling of cosmic energy in natural growth, and the bold stylization of the foliage in the foreground, are an almost exact anticipation of the peculiar vision and technique of Van Gogh. Hopkins was justified in writing to his brother, twenty-two years later :

> "That drawing appears to me unique in its kind : it is a pity it is not finished, which is only a few days' more work." [1]

The quality which Hopkins always hoped to find in both painter and nature-poet was "searchingness". The searching eye is directed into a mass of detail to discover the *inscape*, and in this respect inscape resembles what Mr. Clive Bell and other admirers of modern French painting have called "significant form". There is this difference, however—that to Hopkins the fine execution of selected detail (whether in words, lines or pigments) was always as important as it was to a Pre-Raphaelite painter.[2] His early preoccupation with visual form will be brought out by a comparison between the pencil-sketch called "Waves. Study from the cliff above, Freshwater Gate" and the following piece of excellent descriptive prose :

> "About all the turns of the scaping from the break and flooding of the wave I have not yet satisfied myself. The shores are swimming and the eyes have before them a region of milky surf, but it is hard for them to unpack the huddling and gnarls of the water and law out the shapes and the sequence of the running ; I catch, however, the looped or forked wisp made by every big pebble the backwater runs over—if it were clear and smooth there would be a network from their overlapping, such as can in fact be seen on smooth sand after the tide is out— ; then I saw it run browner, the foam dwindling and twitched into long chains of suds, while the strength of the backdraught shrugged the stones together and clocked them one against another." [3]

The alertness of the ear in "clocked" is matched by the acuity of eye and mind which produced "huddling" and

[1] *Further Letters*, pp. 50–51.

[2] Cf. *Letters*, vol. ii. (June 30, 1886), p. 135 : "I agree to Whistler's striking genius —feeling for what I call *inscape* (the very soul of art) ; but then his execution is so negligent, unpardonably so sometimes. . . ." Yet the Pre-Raphaelites Millais and Holman Hunt were found to be wanting in *instress* and *inscape* (*Note-books*, pp. 192, 193, 197).

[3] *Note-books*, pp. 164–5.

SHANKLIN, ISLE OF WIGHT, 1866

(*Pencil Drawing by G. M. H.*)

(*opposite p.* 14)

" shrugged ". And here perhaps is another reason why Hopkins did not persevere to become a painter, if only an amateur painter ; to one so in love with movement and sound as well as visible shape only the *progressive* arts were fully satisfying. The limitations of painting and sculpture, their very stillness and dumbness, would have oppressed him ; he would have been plagued by all the nightingales of nature and art.

The auditory inscape and rhetorical verve which Hopkins desiderated in the *Letters* and achieved in his poetry is already suggested in the prose of the Journal—in the " long *dribble bubble-strings* " of the receding wave, in " a tree *rubbing and ruffling* with the water at the neck just above the fall ".[1] Similar alliterative doublets are " threads and thrums ", " balk or bolt ", " flix or fleece ", " rincing or riddling ". The poetry is again anticipated in the habit of repeating certain words, dwelling on particular aspects and sensations which denote salient points in experience and are the *leit-motifs* of this poet's peculiar vision ; and these expressions usually emphasize the richness and intricate variety of natural forms : *laced*, *dappled*, *crisped*, *wimpled*, *fretted*, *quained*, *pied* and *brindled*. Such perceptions and the images based upon them are what Dr. I. A. Richards has called " points of relative stability in the drift of experience ", a means of orientation.[2] With Hopkins, however, as we shall now see, the main point of stability and the final orientation were determined as much by Catholic theology as by poetic sensibility.

Two years before beginning the Journal, Hopkins had come so completely under the influence of the Augustinian and Franciscan rules of conduct as to write a poem, the beautiful *Habit of Perfection*,[3] in which he raises for himself a lofty ideal of asceticism and devotion :

> " Shape nothing, lips ; be lovely-dumb . . .
>
> O feel-of-primrose hands, O feet
> That want the yield of plushy sward,
> But you shall walk the golden street
> And you unhouse and house the Lord."

The *personality* is bowed in homage to the desired *character*, but is far from being suppressed : as with George Herbert, the very gesture of submission is idiosyncratic. If Hopkins did not attain

[1] *Note-books*, pp. 202 and 111.

[2] *Principles of Literary Criticism*, p. 295. For the development of this subject, see below, chap. v.

[3] *Poems*, No. 3 (1866).

the full renunciation of sensuous delight in the world around him it was because he realized that not Catholicism or even the Jesuit discipline demanded such a sacrifice; that the talent lodged with him should not remain useless but should be used, as it was used, for the glory of God.

On his entering the Society of Jesus in the autumn of 1868, Hopkins applied himself to the cultivation of that disciplined and selfless character which is the principal aim of the *Spiritual Exercises*, the text-book written by the sixteenth-century founder of the Society, St. Ignatius Loyola. Some knowledge of this book, which Hopkins worked through once every year and upon which he wrote part of a commentary, is indispensable to a just appreciation of the doctrine and philosophy which underlie his poetry.

The *Exercises* are intended to encourage right powers of "election": they direct a man "first of all to choose his state of life in view of God and salvation solely; secondly, when his state of life is fixed, to order the details of his daily conduct on the same principle". The editor we are quoting adds the warning: "To carry this out will be found to involve much overcoming of oneself".[1]

We find, therefore, that "election" and self-sacrifice are major themes in the life and work of Hopkins. If there is one thing common to all great poets it is an almost exclusive devotion to their art. But for a Jesuit priest such an extravocational interest or "inordinate attachment" would be fatal to duty and a perfect spirituality: hence the founder's repeated exhortations to *indiferencia* (detachment),[2] in which Hopkins meekly acquiesced. In a letter to Dixon (1878), he says:

> "What [verses] I had written I burnt before I became a Jesuit and resolved to write no more, as not belonging to my profession, unless it were by the wish of my superiors."[3]

During the following seven years' silence, part of which was spent at St. Beuno's, North Wales, he began to learn Welsh, "but not with very pure intentions perhaps".[4] Confiding in his rector, he was discouraged—"unless it were purely for labouring among the Welsh". Hopkins saw that it was not so, but later resolved to make the conversion of Wales his sole aim.

[1] Edition of 1915, by Joseph Rickaby, S.J., whom Hopkins knew at St. Beuno's in 1874 (*Note-books*, pp. 213–4).

[2] *Spiritual Exercises*, ed. *cit.*, "Principle and Foundation", p. 18. Also pp. 166–7.

[3] *Letters*, vol. ii. p. 14.

[4] *Note-books*, p. 210.

He soon found, however, that the inscape of Welsh poetry was an insidious lure ; after weighing his purpose by the Ignatian rules of election,[1] he decided to give it up. His simultaneous abandonment of Welsh and music aggravated a mood of dejection which was then upon him ; but as time proved, his legitimate connexion with both was by no means at an end.

In assessing the profound influence of his religious life upon his poetry, we must give due weight to that section of the *Exercises* which is called " Particular Examen ".[2] This deals with a rigorous method of daily self-scrutiny to rid the soul of sin. Important too, for an understanding of the later sonnets, is the Ignatian account of " consolation " and " desolation ", the former being " any inward joy that calls and attracts to heavenly things and to the salvation of the soul ", the latter being " a darkening of the soul, trouble of mind, movement to base and worldly things, restlessness . . . moving to distrust, loss of hope . . . when the soul feels thoroughly apathetic, tepid, sad and as it were separated from her Creator and Lord." [3]

Modern psycho-pathology can no doubt trace the immediate causes of many such states, but it cannot explain away their spiritual significance. If all disturbing spiritual aspirations and depressions could be ' conditioned ' out of existence, so that we all lived like the decently regulated animals so dear to Walt Whitman, the value of Hopkins's poetry would disappear. But not anticipating such a calamity, we now consider the facts in the light of universally accepted values. " Desolation ", then, is by no means incompatible with the highest religious ecstasies, even with mysticism. As St. Teresa says in her autobiography, " Every virtue, even faith itself, was then suspended in me ". But the question as to how far Hopkins's poetry is the expression of mystical experience must be deferred until we have examined the later sonnets in their proper setting.[4]

It is natural that the intense meditation and contemplation induced by the *Spiritual Exercises* should influence the poetic imagination.[5] Many of Hopkins's mature poems are spontaneous yet conscious illustrations of the Jesuit ideal, vivid personal commentaries on certain passages in the Ignatian rule. The sestet of *The Soldier*,[6] for instance, was inspired by the

[1] *Spiritual Exercises*, pp. 149–60.
[2] *Op cit.* pp. 52–6.
[3] *Op. cit.* pp. 68–9.
[4] See below, chap. vi. pp. 226–8.
[5] A Jesuit ' meditates ' on a *truth* or body of truths ; he ' contemplates ' a scene in the life of Christ.
[6] *Poems*, No. 39.

Ignatian analogy between a great temporal king and the spiritual King, Christ :[1]

> " Mark Christ our King. He knows war, served this soldiering through. . . ."

Again, in his " Contemplation to obtain Love ", St. Ignatius says that the religious aspirant, imitating Christ, should give everything he possesses back to God : " Take, O Lord, and receive all my liberty, my memory, my understanding, and all my will. Give me your love and grace, because that is enough for me ".[2] That is a momentous vow for a poet to make—a hard sacrifice for one conscious of rare individual powers. Only by an earnest and profound reconciliation of the claims of body and soul, imagination and spirit, could such a man find ease in the otherwise too rigorous bonds of moral duty. We have already quoted from *Morning Midday and Evening Sacrifice* ; and the same theme of renunciation is treated with even greater boldness and originality in *The Golden Echo.*[3]

The principle of " detachment " also profoundly modified Hopkins's conception of Beauty. This subject, examined in the Platonic dialogue from the purely philosophic or neutral point of view, is now regarded from a Christian standpoint. In his mature poems, Hopkins examines the claims of what Keats and Bridges called " the principle of Beauty in all things ". To Keats, as to Pater and the Aesthetes, Beauty was single and good—it was Truth. To Hopkins it was two-fold—" mortal beauty " and " immortal (or supernatural) beauty ". Thus the effect or *instress* of beauty was equivocal ; Hopkins saw that beauty could be either an insidious attraction towards the lower levels of being or a constant admonition to the higher. It all depended upon the state of the receptive mind, the character. On the analogy of the sensitive soul's response to the transient and relative beauty of this world, the Christian, by a definite motion of the will towards ' the highest spiritual poverty ', aspires to the permanent and absolute Beauty of the supernatural world—union with God in the Beatific Vision :

> " Immortal beauty is death with duty," [4]

as Hopkins says in his patriotic song.

[1] *Spiritual Exercises,* ed. *cit.*, " Kingdom of Christ ", p. 77 *et seqq.*
[2] *Ibid.* p. 209.
[3] *Poems,* Nos. 24 and 36.
[4] *Poems,* No. 59 (dated 1885).

The enjoyment of beauty is a sacrament, and the implied obligation is an act of sacrifice, the controlling of the sensibility by the disciplined will : " Give beauty back . . . back to God, beauty's self and beauty's giver ".[1]

In a later poem, *To what serves Mortal Beauty ?* [2] Hopkins faces the danger of over-indulgence, and asks : " What do then ? how meet beauty ? " The answer is an attempt to bridge the gap between the transient and the permanent, to reconcile the poet with his impulse of acceptance and the priest with his doctrine of detachment :

> " Merely meet it ; own
> Home-at-heart, heaven's sweet gift ; then leave, let that alone.
> Yea, wish that though, wish all, God's better beauty, grace."

Recognition of this ethical function of beauty leads to an understanding of its metaphysical significance ; it helps us to appreciate those poems in which direct sensuous enjoyment of natural beauty induces a doctrinal, dogmatic or quasi-mystical consummation—the spiritual exegesis of nature's parable : we mean the early nature sonnets, *God's Grandeur*, *The Starlight Night*, *Spring*, etc.[3] On the other hand, failure to grasp or sympathize with the poet's metaphysic leads to an attitude of misconception, as in the following :

> " The sensuous insistency with which, in these sonnets, earth and air are claimed for Christ is to my sense taut and artificial, suggesting a profound emotional dislocation, with the ensuing desolation of *Carrion Comfort* as its inevitable counterpart." [4]

This view is sincere, typical, and up to a point understandable. Its last phrase, however, is merely a euphemistic way of saying that Hopkins was the victim of self-deception, that the poet ' dragged in ' the name of Christ simply to mollify the conscience of the priest.

To a non-Christian, the repeated introduction of Christ as a kind of poetic and pantheistic symbol may well appear " taut and artificial " ; but that is no reason for saying that the frequency of this *motif* betokens a " profound emotional dislocation " in a sincere believer like Hopkins. The implication behind the criticism is that *Carrion Comfort* points to a loss or weakening of faith ; but unless the *Letters* and *Note-books* are

[1] *The Golden Echo.* [2] *Poems*, No. 38. [3] Nos. 7, 8, 9, 14.

[4] Mr. Basil de Selincourt in a review of the *Letters* (*The Observer*, January 20, 1935).

grossly disingenuous, such a position is now quite untenable. To a fellow-Christian, the Christ-symbol indicates rather a profound and spontaneous unification of the intellect and the senses, that mystical fusion of the Many and the One which is at the root of a large number of conversions to the religious attitude and mode of life. As we know from his criticisms of Keats and Whitman, Hopkins was not satisfied with a poetry that rested in the senses and the emotions alone ; he desired intellectual satisfaction as well—that unity and completeness which for him theism alone could provide. Theism dressed not only his days but his thoughts about man and the universe " to a dexterous and starlight order " ; and the nature sonnets are evidence not of emotional dislocation but of *his* discovery of a philosophic faith about which he could say, with confidence and joy : " On this principle hang the heavens and the earth ".[1]

To Hopkins, external nature was a sublime theophany. In his own words :

> " God's utterance of Himself in Himself is God the Word, outside Himself is this world. *This world then is word, expression, news of God.* Therefore its end, its purpose, its purport, its meaning is God, and its life or work to name and praise Him." [2]

So that when the poet writes :

> " I walk, I lift up, I lift up heart, eyes
> Down all that glory in the heavens to glean our Saviour ",

we hear not a suggestion of neurosis but rather the note of peace and certainty—the " ecstasy " which Dr. Richards once said Hopkins " failed to reach ".[3]

For most Englishmen, perhaps, Christ stands to-day for an ideal (or Utopian) code of morals ; and to those for whom the supernatural foundation of the Faith has lost much of its reality, any connexion between a code of morals and a mystical vision of Nature must seem arbitrary and suspect. Yet the phenomenon was known and recognized in the primitive Church and is found in later metaphysical poetry. The metaphorical assimilation of natural beauty and moral, spiritual good caused Hopkins

[1] For the Catholic and Jesuit (and hence Hopkins's) concept of " the grandeur of theism ", see *Mirage and Truth*, by M. C. D'Arcy, S.J., p. 89.

[2] *Life* (Lahey), p. 124 (epigraph).

[3] *The Dial* (Chicago), September 19, 1926.

to declare *St. Patrick's Breastplate* [1] " one of the most remarkable compositions of man " [2] :

". . . I bind unto myself to-day
The virtues of the star-lit heaven,
The glorious sun's life-giving ray,
The whiteness of the moon at even,
The flashing of the lightning free,
The whirling wind's tempestuous shocks,
The stable earth, the deep salt sea,
Around the old eternal rocks."

Something even nearer to Hopkins's concept is found in Wordsworth's *Tintern Abbey* ; speaking of the tranquil restoration of remembered, assimilated beauty, he says :

" feelings too
Of unremembered pleasure : such perhaps
As have no slight or trivial influence
On that best portion of a good man's life,
His little, nameless, unremembered acts
Of kindness and of love."

From this it is but a step to Hopkins's comment in the Journal :

" I do not think I have ever seen anything more beautiful than the bluebell I have been looking at. *I know the beauty of our Lord by it.*" [3]

It would have been possible for Hopkins to arrive at this metaphysical fusion of God the Word and nature without the aid of specific external suggestion ; though that suggestion might have come from a number of very early sources, such as the more spiritual forms of pantheism. It is most probable, however, that a direct stimulus came from the Schoolman, Duns Scotus, whose profound influence we must now examine.

Scotus taught that God the Son " personifies " nature ; yet a pantheistic heresy is carefully avoided, since although He is *in* the world, He is not *of* it. The Franciscan school, to which Scotus belonged, was not so chary of pantheistic implications as were the Dominicans, whose great spokesman was St. Thomas Aquinas. The Franciscans stressed the nearness of God, the pervading spirit of Love, and like St. Francis himself they cordially greeted the ' image ' or ' vestige ' of God in all created things, animate and inanimate. In this respect, Hopkins too

[1] Ascribed to St. Patrick, *circa* 372–466. (Tr. of Mrs. C. F. Alexander.)
[2] *Letters*, vol. i. p. 232.
[3] *Note-books*, p. 134 (May 1870).

resembled St. Francis ; he also had much in common with the speculative mysticism of the Seraphic Doctor, St. Bonaventure, and of the Subtle Doctor, Duns Scotus. Hence the gleaning of Christ from " the glory of the heavens ", the wafting Him out of " lovely-asunder starlight ", and the seeing in distant hills of His " world-wielding shoulder "—all these conceptions were to Hopkins much more than poetic fancies : they were metaphysical realities, just as Scotus himself was :

" Of realty the rarest-veinèd unraveller ".[1]

Hopkins first came upon Scotus when holiday-making at Douglas, Isle of Man, in 1872 :

> " At this time I had first begun to get hold of the copy of Scotus on the Sentences in the Baddely library and was flush with a new stroke of enthusiasm. It may come to nothing or it may be a mercy from God. But just then when I took in any inscape of the sky or sea I thought of Scotus." [2]

To demonstrate clearly the influence of this Schoolman on the poetry of Hopkins we must give some account of three of his chief doctrines—his metaphysical formalism, his intuitionalism, and his voluntarism. On all these questions Scotism differs from Thomism, the system taught by the Jesuit theologians. The divergence is especially marked in their respective principles of individuation ; and since the *instress* of singularity is a recurrent theme in Hopkins, we shall begin by seeing how, according to Scotus, the individual nature is determined.

Every finite being is composed of *ens et carentia* [3] : the intrinsic degree of each thing is its lack of infinity in every natural activity, and the same intrinsic degree in several activities will connect all those activities and make them one individual nature by giving them the same direction.[4] The Scotist principle of individuation embraces the celebrated and subtle *distinctio formalis a parte rei* or formal distinction between the individual nature and the specific or common nature (e.g. *humanitas*). That last formal determination, or *ultima realitas entis*, which restricts

[1] *Poems*, No. 20.

[2] *Note-books*, p. 161. Scotus's great commentary on the *Sentences* of Peter Lombard is called *Opus Oxoniense* (vols. viii. to xxi. in the Paris reprint of Wadding's edition, 1891–5). Cf. *Letters*, vol i. p. 31 (Feb. 1875) : " After all I can, at all events a little, read Duns Scotus, and I care for him more even than Aristotle and more *pace tua* than a dozen Hegels."

[3] *Opus Oxoniense*, I, dist. 8, q. 2.

[4] *Ibid.* I, dist. 2, q. 2.

the specific form and completes it, is called by Scotus *haecceitas* ('thisness').[1] But *essentia creaturae est sua dependentia ad Deum*: underlying individuality and the specific nature is the universal Nature (a concept ultimately mystical rather than metaphysical), which expresses the unity of all created things.

All created substances, says Scotus, are immediately active, and not merely, as Aquinas says, *mediantibus accidentibus*. (For Aquinas the principle of individuation is *materia signata quantitate* or 'quantified matter', and matter is the principle of passivity; but the Scotist *haecceitas*, with its multiplicity of metaphysical elements called *formalitates*,[2] is an extension of the Aristotelian Form, and Form is the active principle.) Individuality then is the direction given to natural activities by the *haecceitas*: it is the real relation between the creature and God.

Hopkins seized with delight on the Scotist principle of individuation, as we know from those poems in which he makes the activity of a thing a special element in that thing's being. First, in *Henry Purcell* (1879)[3]:

> "It is the forgèd feature finds me; it is the rehearsal
> Of own, of abrupt self there so thrusts on, so throngs the ear."

The great storm-fowl, to which Purcell is compared, "but meaning motion fans fresh our wits with wonder"; and so also do the Windhover ("the achieve of!") and Harry Ploughman ("Harry bends—look!").[4] Even more explicit is No. 34:

> "Each mortal thing does one thing and the same:
> Deals out that being indoors each one dwells;
> Selves—goes itself; *myself* it speaks and spells,
> Crying *Whát I dó is mé: for thát I cáme*."

The stress on *What* (instead of on *Crying*) is 'Scotist' as well as rhythmical.

But Hopkins is chiefly concerned with the finite being which has the richest individuality, nature's "clearest-selvèd spark" —man:

> "Our law says: Love what are | Love's worthiest, were all known;
> World's loveliest—men's selves. Self | flashes off frame and face."[5]

[1] *Opus Oxoniense*, II, dist. 3; *Quaestiones supra Libros Metaphysicos*, IV, q. 2, n. 24 and VII, q. 19, n. 8. The word *haecceitas* occurs only in *Qu. Lib. Met.*, VII, q. 13.

[2] See de Wulf; *History of Medieval Philosophy*, vol. ii. p. 72 *et seqq.*

[3] *Poems*, No. 21. [4] *Ibid.* Nos. 12 and 43. [5] *Poems*, No. 38.

Physical attributes are subordinate aspects of the total *haecceitas*, which in rational beings is the spring of all action and is therefore identified with the Will.[1] It is the Will, and not the Intellect, which ' possesses ' a loved object. Intellect is related to the specific, common nature of man ; whereas Will is the expression of individuality. Another important point on which Scotus differs from Aquinas is that the former lays greater emphasis upon the freedom of the Will[2] : in spite of God's essential co-operation in our every action, we are free to choose the objects of our love, the objects we would possess, our τέλος.[3] Thus in each man there is the individual element—*haecceitas*, Will, spring of action ; and exerting a constant pressure on the Will is the fact that his intellectual and animal nature is really, though mysteriously, united to all men, and indeed to all creation.[4]

A striking expression of quasi-mystical sympathy or intuitive love-knowledge is found in the poem called *Brothers* ; and a more melancholy aspect of the universal Nature—that of decay and mortality—is dealt with in *Spring and Fall*, and again in the Journal when, on seeing some ash trees cut down, Hopkins writes :

> " there came at that moment a great pang and I wished to die and not to see the inscapes of the world destroyed any more." [5]

Such hyperaesthesia reminds us of that curious case in Hardy's novel, *The Woodlanders*, where the death of a tree actually causes

[1] " Vital activities cannot be reduced to the plasticity of the body in which they manifest themselves. *They denote a superior perfection.* That is why, in addition to the form of materiality, *every organism has a vital form.*" (de Wulf, *op. cit.* p. 80.)

[2] But Verweyn warns us, " dass die Freiheitslehre der beiden Scholastiker nicht als ein Gegensatz zwischen Determinismus und Indeterminismus charakterisiert werden darf. . . ." The truth is stated by Fonsgrive : ". . . le dominicain met l'accent sur l'intelligence et le franciscain le met sur la volonté sans que ni pour l'un ni pour l'autre l'intime synergie des deux facultés soit détruite ". (See *La Philosophie du B. Duns Scot.*, by E. Longpré (Paris, 1924), p. 195, n. 2 and 4.) Nevertheless to Longpré (an acknowledged authority) : " Philosophe de la volonté, certes le Docteur Franciscain l'est incomparablement." (*Op. cit.* p. 227.)

[3] " Hereby, I may tell you, hangs a very profound question treated by Duns Scotus, who shows that freedom is compatible with necessity." (*Letters*, vol. i. p. 169.) Hopkins himself treats the question of freedom and personality in his *Comments on the Spiritual Exercises* (*Note-books*, pp. 322–37). Speaking of " moral pitch ", " pitch of the will " and " pitch of being ", he concludes by asking (p. 328) : " Is not this pitch or whatever we call it then the same as Scotus's *ecceitas* (sic) ? " (*Ecceità* is the Italian form of *haecceitas*, or ' haecceity,' as it is frequently written.)

[4] As de Wulf says : " L'indéterminisme de Scot a été faussement interprété par ceux qui font de la décision volontaire un acte capricieux et irrational. En réalite la volition, quoique libre, est raisonnée." (Longpré, *loc. cit.*)

[5] *Note-books* (April 8, 1873), p. 174.

the death of a man. But to turn again from the universal Nature to the specific nature of man, Hopkins's preoccupation with *haecceitas* as the key to *humanitas* is well illustrated in the introductory rubric to the Purcell sonnet :

> " The poet wishes well to the divine genius of Purcell and praises him that, whereas other musicians have given utterance to the moods of man's mind, he has, beyond that, uttered the notes and very make and species of man as created both in him and in all men generally." [1]

To Hopkins's statement of 1872, that whenever he took in an inscape of sea or sky he thought of Scotus, we may now add the following of 1879 :

> " But as air, melody, is what strikes me most of all in music, and design in painting, so design, pattern, or what I am in the habit of calling *inscape* is what I above all aim at in poetry. Now it is the virtue of design, pattern or inscape to be distinctive. . ." [2]

His own nature had led him to attach great importance to individuality in things, to personality in men, and this predilection had been intensified by Scotus. There is an anecdote of the poet's Stonyhurst days, when an amazed gardener saw him walking round and round a stone on the path and scrutinizing it curiously from all angles ; and even that action might have been inspired by the Schoolman : *necesse est per aliquid positivum intrinsecum huic lapidi.*[3] Scotus, moreover, laid great stress on the fact of self-consciousness ; and Hopkins too says :

> " Nothing else in nature comes near this unspeakable stress of pitch, distinctiveness, and selving, this selfbeing of my own." [4]

But distinctiveness or idiosyncrasy in itself can have no metaphysical or moral value unless it is, as in the system of Scotus, a valuable link in the ontological argument ; for then, as Hopkins says, " to be determined and distinctive is a perfection, either self-bestowed or bestowed from without ".[5]

Fr. C. Devlin, S.J., has shown[6] that Hopkins's inspirational view of poetic creation, with its concepts of *inscape* and *instress,*

[1] *Poems,* No. 21.
[2] *Letters,* vol. i. p. 66.
[3] *Opus Oxoniense,* II, dist. 3, q. 2, n. 4.
[4] *Comments on the Spiritual Exercises.* (*Note-books,* p. 309.)
[5] *Ibid.* (*Note-books,* p. 312.)
[6] In his valuable article, *Hopkins and Duns Scotus,* in *New Verse,* No. 14 (April 1935), pp. 13–4.

roughly corresponds to the Scotist doctrine that the " first act " of knowledge is a confused intuition, a union of sense and intellect in which the mind is conscious of the Object as a living, concrete Nature. This intuition is then contracted by the senses to a " particular glimpse " or " most proper appearance " (*species specialissima*), which is our nearest *living* approach to the Singular. According to de Wulf, however, Scotus does not separate the intuition from the vision of the Singular :

> " Careful to secure for the understanding the immediate perception of individual reality, Scotus allows, in addition to the abstract and universal knowledge which is *distinct*, a preliminary intuitive knowledge representing a concrete and singular thing in a confused manner (*species specialissima*). This concept of the singular arises at the first contact of the intelligence with that outside it, and is formed simultaneously with the sense knowledge of an object." [2]

It is in the " second act " (conation) that knowledge proceeds from the concrete and particular to the abstract and universal. Not until the first sense-knowledge has been dwelt on by the abstractive mind does the significance of the particular as a key to the universal, the reality of *being* in all its richness of intelligibility, become known. Hopkins probably identified the Scotist special concept of the singular with his own private concept of *inscape* (though the latter has a relatively narrow aesthetic connotation) and the *primum actum* with his own experience of primary *instress* ; for just as instress may be passively received from a perfect inscape, so an inscape or idea may be

[1] *Op. Ox.*, I, dist. 3, q. 6, n. 14 ; and II, 3. 2 : " Prima intellectio est naturae." Also *Quaestiones supra Libros Metaphysicos*, VII. 15.

[2] " Totus ordo confuse concipiendi prior est comparando ad totum ordinem distincte concipiendi. . . . Primum actualiter cognitum confuse est species specialissima cuius singulare fortius et primo movet sensum sive sit audibile sive visibile sive tangibile. Quodcumque enim individuum fortius movet sensum, eius species primo cognita est cognitione confusa. Et hoc, supposito, quod singulare est in debita proportione praesens sensui." (*Op. Ox.*, I, dist. 3, q. 2, n. 4.) Cf. Longpré, *op. cit.* p. 38. de Wulf continues : " Is it not in harmony with the logic of the system that this intuitive contact of the mind should precede the reflective contact ? There is in the individual being perceived by our senses an internal wealth of entities apart from the work of the mind. Our concepts adapt themselves to these, and are intuitive resemblances of the real. Thanks to this concept of the singular, the understanding enters into direct relation with the extramental world, and perceives existing in their particular state those elements of reality represented in a universal state by ' distinct ' knowledge. Thus the objectivity of intellectual knowledge is accentuated and linked up with the existing and actual world even more than in St. Thomas." (*Op. cit.* vol. ii. p. 81, § 316.)

actively "instressed" by the intelligence which is trying to "law out the shapes" and give permanent logical form, in a picture or poem, to knowledge acquired through the senses.

To Hopkins, therefore, an inscape was something more than a delightful sensory impression : it was an insight, by Divine grace, into the ultimate reality—seeing the "pattern, air, melody" in things from, as it were, God's side.[1] Scotus offered the poet an aesthetic sanction and the priest a moral justification for his inordinate attachment to poetry and the other arts. That is perhaps why Scotus so swayed his spirits to peace. Moreover, the very multiplicity of individualities in the created universe was in itself a proof of God's infinity. This idea is expressed in the sonnet already quoted (No. 34), in which we see the most complete and successful union of the poet and the Scotist :

> "Í say móre : the just man justices ;
> Keeps gráce : thát keeps all his goings graces ;
> Acts in God's eye what in God's eye he is—
> Chríst—for Christ plays in ten thousand places,
> Lovely in limbs, and lovely in eyes not his
> To the Father through the features of men's faces."

God the Son assumes *all* Nature ; hence the individual, intrinsic degree of Christ sums up the degrees of all men. The whole sonnet is a poetic statement of the Scotist concept that individual substances, according to the metaphysical richness of their being, make up one vast hierarchy with God as their summit.[2]

Hopkins saw in Scotism a noble tribute to the dignity of man. It was natural that a poet as sensuous as Keats should esteem above all other philosophers the one who emphasized the greater importance of the concrete over the abstractions of the mind, and who stressed the close relation between activity and substance ; equally natural that an anthropophile as great as Wordsworth himself should share the Scotist conviction that humanity is too noble a thing to be a mere lump of clay acted upon by outside forces : *Oportet dignificare naturam humanam quantum possibile.* He would agree with Scotus that by the Aristotelian doctrine that free will is an imperfection and by

[1] Cf. Mr. Devlin, *loc. cit.* p. 13 (bottom) *et seq.*

[2] de Wulf, p. 72. Cf. *Note-books*, p. 332 : "That is Christ playing at me and me playing at Christ, only that it is no play but truth ; That is Christ *being me* and me being Christ." See also *ibid.* p. 335, lines 1–10.

the Thomistic that the will is a passive faculty—*valde vilificaretur natura humana*! Man must use his freedom of choice to perfect his individual nature "where it fails", to give the whole being its true direction Godwards:

"Doff darkness, homing nature knows the rest—"[1]

This brings us naturally to the main thesis of the unfinished poem, *On a piece of music* (No. 67), the distinction between "the good" and "the right", between mortal beauty and supernatural beauty. Ostensibly the theme is the freedom which music and (by analogy) architecture enjoy from the sphere of moral values; but its implications are wider and deeper:

"How all's to one thing wrought!
The members, how they sit!"

The work of art, perfect in inscape and outscape, reminds us of the τυχῆς τέχνην στερχούσης of the ash trees. It is an immediate spontaneous activity of the individual nature, or, to return to a more normal phraseology, a faithful expression of personality. But personality involves separation: the artist works by laws of his own fashioning; as Bacon says: "He must do it by a kind of felicity (as a musician that maketh an excellent air in music), and not by rule".[2]

"Nor angel insight can
Learn how the heart is hence:
Since all the make of man
Is law's indifference."

Distinctive natural beauty is good; but the moral theme has entered with the word "heart". That this word symbolizes man's attitude to Divine law we know from a passage about the nun in *The Wreck of the Deutschland*:

"Ah! there was heart right!
There was single eye!"[3]

We cannot probe another's secret. Each man is alone with God. Man is a wayward creature, "unteachably after evil"; waywardness, aloofness, or distinctiveness in genius is "good" but

[1] *Poems*, No. 27. Cf. Duns Scotus (*Opus Ox.* IV, dist. 49, q. 10, n. 2, xxi. 318): "natura non potest remanere natura quin inclinetur ad suam perfectionem . . ." (Longpré, p. 69.)

[2] *Of Beauty*.

[3] Stanza 29.

not necessarily " right ". By a volitional ' act of love ' man's works must be directed Godwards :

> " What makes the man and what
> The man within that makes :
> Ask whom he serves or not
> Serves and what side he takes."

Hopkins may have believed that music, as an art, " is purely abstract, ideal, unconnected with reality and life ", and that such an expression as " the high moral tone of Beethoven's work " is meaningless. Yet one critic, misapplying a phrase in the *Letters*,[1] supposes that Hopkins, as poet, " wished to achieve the pure art, morally neutral,[2] in which such interests as corybantic, sadistic images, etc., without being suppressed, can be controlled and philosophically employed ".[2] Undoubtedly Hopkins wished his aesthetic and moral motives to be formally combined as base and acid are in a salt ; but any latter-day suggestion that poetry should be innocent of, or ' unsullied ' by, moral considerations would have been repudiated with vigour. In an early letter he says :

> " With regard to morality it is true no doubt ἁπλῶς that any subject may be chosen for its art value alone. . . . The question however is the practical effect, and is of course one of degree . . . it is impossible not personally to form an opinion against the morality of a writer like Swinburne . . . one thinks e.g. *Othello* should be called innocent, Ovid immoral. . . ." [3]

It is a serious mistake to regard Hopkins as a ' modernist ' with a veneer of Victorian piety. When he called himself a " blackguard ", as he frequently did, he was expressing a deeper dissatisfaction with his own shortcomings than the complacent majority could ever feel. When he said that Walt Whitman's mind was more like his own " than any other man's living " [4] he was signalizing a resemblance in personality or ' individual degree ' which made both adopt nearer-to-prose rhythms to express a " furious and devouring love of nature ".[5] But when he added : " As Whitman is a very great scoundrel that is not a pleasant confession ", he was deploring Whitman's great song

[1] " But I grant that the Greek mythology is very susceptible of fine treatment, allegorical treatment for instance. . . . No wonder : the moral evil is got rid of and the pure art, morally neutral and artistically so rich, remains and can be even turned to moral uses." (*Letters*, vol. ii. p. 147.)

[2] *New Verse*, No. 14 (April 1935), p. 22.

[3] *Further Letters*, pp. 81–2.

[4] *Letters*, vol. i. p. 155.

[5] Mr. Madge in *New Verse* (*cit.*), p. 17.

about his indifference to the true regulative principle—the Catholic Church: "good" (or *natural* beauty) "grows wild and wide . . .

> "But *right* must seek a side
> And choose for chieftain one." (Stanza 4.)[1]

The author of the *Song of Myself* had certainly chosen a chieftain; but his name was not Christ: it was Whitman—or Demos. Therefore although he, like the composer or the architect, "made known the music of his mind":

> "Yet here he had but shown
> His ruder-rounded rind.
>
> Not free in this because
> His powers seemed free to play:
> He swept what scope he was
> To sweep and must obey."

Hopkins is tackling the "profound question treated by Scotus"; he is trying to reconcile freedom and necessity in artistic creation. Robert Bridges, not realizing, apparently, the ethical significance of this poem, takes the stanza just quoted as the key to the whole:

> "No. 67 is the draft of what appears to be an attempt to explain how an artist has not free will in his creation. He works out his own nature instinctively as he happens to be made, and is irresponsible for the result."[2]

Omit the last clause and this interpretation is true up to the point where the artist brings the will-guided intelligence to bear upon the *speciem* or "glimpse" of Nature which he has taken in: he is not responsible for his peculiar mental pattern or "inscape", but he is responsible for its spiritual orientation. So long as the work of a Swinburne or a Whitman was "morally neutral", the Jesuit might have said:

> "Therefore this masterhood,
> This piece of perfect song,
> This fault-not-found-with good
> Is neither right nor wrong."

Unless the artist (no matter what his medium) accepts responsibility for all the moral implications of his work and gives beauty

[1] Stanza 7 in Third Edition. [2] *Poems of G. M. H.*, p. 99.

"back to God", that work can have no more immortal, supernatural beauty:

> "than red or blue,
> No more than Re and Mi,
> Or sweet the golden glue
> That's built for by the bee."

The whole poem is a token of the remarkable scrupulosity and consistency shown by Hopkins the priest towards the art and concomitant interests of Hopkins the poet. Corroboration of the above exegesis will be found in that other admirable fragment, *On the Portrait of Two Beautiful Young People* (No. 54). Stanza 7 is almost an epitome of the Scotist concept of the *haecceitas*, the "moral pitch" of the Self, as expressed in the Will:

> "Man lives that list, that leaning in the will
> No wisdom can forecast by gauge or guess,
> The selfless self of self, most strange, most still,
> Fast furled and all foredrawn to No or Yes."[1]

But in stanza 5, allegiance to the right regulative principle is clearly stated as the *sine qua non* of a disciplined will:

> "Where lies your landmark, seamark, or soul's star?
> There's none but truth can stead you. Christ is truth."

To this poet, truth is not Beauty or any other vague, subjective concept, but simply Christ. Moreover, the very richness of Personality's regalia may prove a greater attraction to the Devil: "favoured make and mind" and

> "that most in you earnest eye
> May but call on your banes to more carouse.
> Worst will the best."

[1] The "self of self" is the supposit, the Self, the *ultima realitas entis*, which is clothed with a nature to form a complete personality. It is called "selfless" because it is "prior to nature", upon which it depends for its manifestation in being; it is "fast furled" and secret, for although its pitch of action is free, its destiny has been "foredrawn" by God: hence its full potentialities are unknown even to the person himself. (See *Comments on the Spiritual Exercises*, *loc. cit.* p. 322.)

There is an interesting application of this quatrain in chap. viii. of *Practical Criticism*, to which it stands as epigraph. Dr. I. A. Richards is saying that the final acceptance or rejection of a poem is an act of the will, a decision of the total personality: "The personality stands balanced between the particular experience which is the realized poem and the whole fabric of its past experiences and developed habits of mind. What is being settled is whether this new experience can or cannot be taken into the fabric with advantage" (p. 303). Substitute *real* action for the vicarious action of a poem and that is what Hopkins meant.

The worst moral diseases attack the finest spirits ; and *corruptio optimi pessima.* Of no less a spirit than Whitman or Goethe this Jesuit would have asked, indeed *did* ask :

> " What worm was here
> To have havoc-pocked so, see, the hung-heavenward
> boughs ? "

The logical conclusion to the above arguments would be a full exposition of the thought-content and emotional implications of *The Windhover*, that great poem in which we find at once a subliminal conflict and a profound reconciliation of those elements in the man which we have been examining—personality and character, the poet and the priest. But this exposition entails a discussion on imagery and diction which must be held over till a later chapter. It is enough to say here that the poem describes a state of equilibrium, the precarious and sensitive poise maintained between the two vocations during the greater part of his life.

The appeasement and resignation expressed in this poem were not absolutely decisive. Yet up to 1885, when *Carrion Comfort* was written " in blood ", Hopkins's work cannot as a whole be called unhappy. Many of these poems—*Henry Purcell*, *Brothers*, *The Blessed Virgin*, etc., are as much the consummation of pure joy as any in the language. In *Spelt from Sibyl's Leaves*, however, we hear harsh repercussions of the ' particular examen ' :

> " Let life, waned ; ah, let life wind
> Off her once skeined stained veined variety upon all on two
> spools . . .
> . . . black, white ; right, wrong ; " [1]

There, no doubt, is the dislocation which some critics have deplored—that the rich variety of such a poet's intellect, imagination and potential experience should be levelled down to this stern ' dichotomy of right and wrong '. Yet if we discount the moral aspect and consider only the poetry, can it truthfully be said that his cry of " Oúr tale, O oúr oracle ! " is justified ?—that the poet's " dapple " is really at an end ?—that his valuable personality is quite steeped, pashed and dismembered in the larger unit of the Jesuit discipline ? The answer is in the poem itself : diction, rhythm, imagery, organization of experience—all are new, individual.

[1] No. 32.

An interesting pendant to *The Windhover* is the sonnet *In Honour of St. Alphonsus Rodriguez* (1888). Despite its objective theme, it is, one feels, strongly subjective, and goes to prove that Hopkins's loyalty to the regulative principle had moulted no essential feather up to the year before his death. Like *The Windhover*, the poem deals (explicitly this time) with the " unseen war within the heroic breast " of the humble, plodding servant of Christ : and the note of triumph is unmistakable :

> " Yet God that hews mountain and continent . . .
> *Could crowd career with conquest* while there went
> Those years and years by of world without event
> That in Majorca Alfonso watched the door." [1]

As with King Lear, this projection of the self into another was a kind of relief. The hurtle of the poet's own " fiercest fray " we hear in the sonnets Nos. 40, 41, and 45. Yet commentators on the so-called tragedy of Hopkins's whole life (Dr. I. A. Richards, for example) are so anxious to give full weight to these utterances that they ignore the psychological significance of first-rate poems of quite a different outlook. *Harry Ploughman* (1887) and the incomplete *Epithalamion* (1888) are both joyous products of the unimpeded personality. (There is no need to discover a pathological symptom in the violent physical action of the former or in the missing nuptial exegesis of the latter.) Moreover, to anyone who can entertain even only the smallest wistful hope of Immortality, *That Nature is a Heraclitean Fire* (1888) must surely present as perfect a collaboration of priest and poet as *The Windhover*.

How far the ill-health and depression so frequently mentioned in the *Letters* [2] were due to thwarted physical impulses would be a dangerous matter for speculation by one who is not a trained neuropathologist. It is certain, however, that many of the later sonnets are concerned with the poet's struggle to live in accordance with the Ignatian rule. " One step ", says a commentator on the *Exercises*, " is patience and meekness under affronts ". Touching the former virtue, Hopkins laments :

> " Patience, hard thing ! the hard thing but to pray,
> But bid for, Patience is ! " [3]

[1] St. Alphonsus was " a laybrother of our Order, who for forty years acted as hall-porter to the College of Palma in Majorca ; he was, it is believed, much favoured by God with heavenly lights and much persecuted by evil spirits." (*Letters*, vol. i. pp. 292–3.)

[2] See *Letters*, vol. i. pp. 28, 33, 84, 211, and numerous references *passim*.

[3] *Poems*, No. 46.

3

And that his " elected silence ", whether as patriot, priest, poet, or plain man, could at times prove almost unbearably irksome we learn from No. 44. In this he may be uttering a repressed desire to write a political tract on the relations between England and Ireland, a diatribe against Gladstone or the Fenians, or perhaps merely to speak his mind freely to those about him.[1] But to some ears the sestet vibrates with a deeper, more tragic note, which hints at something more personal and essential than a sporadic patriotism or what Dr. Richards somewhat curiously calls " self-consciousness ".[2]

No doubt Hopkins suffered greatly ; yet he had been prepared for periods of dejection and disillusion by the *Spiritual Exercises*, in which moods of desolation are minutely described and dogmatically accounted for.[3] In the words of Father J. Keating, S.J. :

> " Whatever experiences are reflected in the four or five ' terrible sonnets ', so full of spiritual ' desolation ', so expressive of ' the dark night of the soul ', that those close to Christ are at times privileged to pass through, they cannot have been due to a mere sense of failure and frustration, still less to doubt as to whether he had chosen aright." [4]

We may cite in corroboration Hopkins's own words : " I have never wavered in my vocation, but I have not lived up to it ".[5] And as for suffering, he had explicitly stated, in 1869, that suffering, nobly endured, was a mark of special grace :

> " What suffering she had ! . . . But sufferings falling on such a person as your sister was, are to be looked on as the marks of God's particular love, and this is truer the more exceptional they are." [6]

Yet those who maintain that much of his trouble was due to unsatisfied creative impulses have no mean evidence to go on. There is first the significant passage in a letter of 1885, in which he regrets his inability to carry out one of his literary projects (a work on metre) in spite of the fact that neither time nor encouragement by his Superior had been lacking : " it kills me to be time's eunuch and never to

[1] See *Letters*, vol. i. p. 131 : " I am a very great patriot ". Also *Further Letters*, pp. 110, 114, 139, 146, etc., for his opinion of Gladstone and Home Rule.

[2] In *The Dial*, Sept. 19, 1926.

[3] See *Rules for the Discernment of Spirits*, First Week, Fourth Rule.

[4] *The Month*, July 1935.

[5] *Letters*, vol. ii. p. 88.

[6] *Letters*, vol. i. p. 25. Cf. *The Wreck of the Deutschland* (1875–6), stanza 22.

beget "[1]; and frustration could hardly be more articulate than in No. 50, from its cry:

> "Why do sinners' ways prosper? and why must
> Disappointment all I endeavour end?"

to the poignant re-assertion of:

> ". . . birds build—but not I build; no, but strain,
> Time's eunuch, and not breed one work that wakes."

Nevertheless, his vocation was not altogether uncongenial to his muse: "I find within my professional experience now a good deal of matter to write on".[2] He had leisure, but was either too conscientious or too jaded to make full use of it. His projected "great ode on Edmund Campion, S.J." had to be abandoned because his life in Liverpool and Glasgow was "a slavery of mind and heart".[3] His extreme sensitiveness manifested itself also in a curious vacillation between confidence in his own powers and an almost unmanly diffidence. But it was not in poetry only that his vein refused to flow:

> "Unhappily I cannot produce anything at all, not only the luxuries like poetry, but the duties almost of my position, its natural outcome—like scientific works. . . . Nothing comes: I am a eunuch—but it is for the kingdom of God's sake."[4]

The mortification expressed in the sonnets 44 and 50 is intensified in the acute anhedonia and spiritual dyspepsia of No. 45:

> "I am gall, I am heartburn. God's most deep decree
> Bitter would have me taste. My taste was me . . .
> Selfyeast of spirit a dull dough sours. . . ."

The active personality has not been perfectly assimilated by the passive religious character. "Selfyeast of spirit" suggests the individual (and Scotist) vital principle, the psychic individuality, rather than the immortal soul of the Christian, which strives to annihilate the Self either in works of charity or in a perfect union with its Creator.[5] Yet the souring of the personality and

[1] *Letters*, vol. i. p. 222; cf. vol. ii. pp. 88 and 108.

[2] *Ibid.* p. 86. Cf. *Poems*, Nos. 27, 29, 30, etc.

[3] *Ibid.* pp. 135–6. Cf. vol. ii. p. 97.

[4] *Ibid.* p. 270; "if finished, will it pass the censors? . . . will the *Classical Review* or any magazine take it?"

[5] Cf. "Man's mounting spirit" in *The Caged Skylark* (1877). Here we have the Augustinian view of the body cumbering the spirit.

the consequent loss of inspiration is *like* the death of the soul; it is a foretaste of perdition:

> "I see
> The lost are like this, and their scourge to be
> As I am mine, their sweating selves; but worse."

—the mere husks of men, without vision or hope. Contrast this with the Scotist ecstasy of No. 34—" Selves, goes itself; *myself* it speaks and spells ". Now, " What I do is me " seems to have become " What I cannot do is what I want to be ". The last two words of the poem, placed in emphatic isolation, must not be misread; they safeguard the priest's sincerity, for with a sudden twist the poet diverts our attention from himself to what without some saving grace he would become. As in *Carrion Comfort*, having groaned " I can no more ", he immediately cries " I can ". Yet when he remonstrates with God, or attributes the bitter taste of himself to " God's most deep decree " (" baffling ban "), he seems to confess that the mortification he endures is very much more than the voluntary mortification of the patient ascetic. The complaint we hear seems to come from a personality which is prevented by ill-health, overwork, and psychological inhibition from reaching its full stature.

Despite the fact that Hopkins frequently disclaimed any desire for poetic fame, and was in all sincerity willing to leave his poetry " entirely to be disposed of by obedience ",[1] it is probable that Father Keating and other religious apologists have underestimated the agonies of failure and frustration which creative genius, without any religious complications, can undergo; they seem to have ignored the neuroses which may be caused when powerful instincts and impulses are repressed or imperfectly satisfied. But this qualification does not invalidate their belief in the supernatural origin and purpose of Hopkins's desolations. Such experiences have been regarded by many serious thinkers as a phenomenon worthy of consideration in any complete study of man. Admit the possibility, and it follows that God's purpose with the spirit, as with the body, might well disclose itself in ways that are clearly explainable in the light of psychology and physiology.

To sum up, whether the cry of anguish in the later sonnets was due to mutilation or to probation, the gain to poetry, on the

[1] See *Letters*, vol. i. pp. 133, 283; vol. ii. pp. 28, 93, 150. But contrast i. 231; ii. 6.

whole, outweighs the loss. Had Hopkins been physically stronger, less devout, less sensitive, less neurotic, we should have had more poems but not the ones we now treasure. His output was restricted but at the same time intensified—allotropized from graphite to diamond (what R. W. Dixon called " the terrible crystal " [1]) in the stringency of his " bleak asceticism ". Being one of those described by William James as needing " some austerity, wintry negativity, roughness and danger to be mixed in to produce the sense of an existence with character, texture and power ",[2] his moral fastidiousness, in union with his ritualistic sensualism, had valuable repercussions in the rigours and splendours of his poetic style. On the other hand, the religious life probably fostered that unsophisticated, intuitive approach to nature, life and language which, as Vico said, is an essential condition of the true ' original ' poet.

Yet no single term or antinomy will suffice to describe his complex and versatile personality. He was at once *naïf* and learned, intuitionalist and intellectual. With a leaning, on one side of his nature, towards mysticism,[3] he was on the other side as rational and forthright in his approach to reality as Dr. Johnson. Boldly independent in Art and Metaphysics, he was always, in Religion, the humble child of Authority. So far, however, from " whirling dizzily in a spiritual vacuum ",[4] the personality of Hopkins found in its delimited experience a medium of considerable resistance through which it could at times beat up to heights unattempted before in English poetry.

[1] *Letters*, vol. ii. p. 80. [2] *Varieties of Religious Experience*, p. 298.

[3] See below, chapter vi.

[4] Mr. Middleton Murry, *Aspects of Literature* (1920).

CHAPTER II

"THE WRECK OF THE *DEUTSCHLAND*"

THE poem we are about to examine, the first and longest of those written in Hopkins's mature style, presents more problems than any other great ode of equal length in the language. We therefore propose to treat it separately, partly because it stands at the beginning of the author's career as a poet of undoubted genius (and the labour spent on it, as Bridges said, "served to establish the poet's prosody and perhaps his diction"), and partly because it has been widely misunderstood, unwisely depreciated, and too frequently denied the rank and importance which it fully deserves in its own right.

The fact that a disastrous shipwreck should occasion a new mode in English poetry is not so remarkable as the personal circumstances which led to the writing of the poem. Having for seven years regarded poetry for poetry's sake as "unprofessional", Hopkins was now, at the age of thirty-one, reading theology at St. Beuno's College, North Wales. In his own words:

> "When in the winter of '75 the *Deutschland* was wrecked in the mouth of the Thames and five Franciscan nuns, exiles from Germany by the Falck Laws, aboard of her were drowned I was affected by the account and happening to say so to my rector he said that he wished some one would write a poem on the subject. On this hint I set to work and, though my hand was out at first, produced one. I had long had haunting my ear the echo of a new rhythm, which now I realized on paper." [1]

As we shall see more fully in a later part of the present work,[2] he had first tried out a new stress-metre in the revised version of *St. Dorothea*, about which he had written to Bridges on August 7, 1868:

> "I hope you will master the peculiar beat I have introduced into *St. Dorothea*. The development is mine but the beat is in Shakespere—e.g.
>
> 'Whý should thís desert be?'—and
>
> 'Thoú for whóm Jóve would swear'—where the rest of the lines are eight-syllabled or seven-syllabled." [3]

[1] *Letters*, vol. ii. p. 14. [2] Chapter i. of Volume II.

[3] *Letters*, vol. i. p. 24.

But *The Deutschland* contained many more startling innovations than the earlier poem, and it is not surprising that the immediate fate of this amazing *tour de force* was not happy :

> " I had to mark the stresses in blue chalk, and this . . . and a great many more oddnesses could not but dismay an editor's eye, so that when I offered it to our magazine, the *Month*, though at first they accepted it, after a time they withdrew and dared not print it." [1]

It is important to realize at once that although Hopkins speaks here of " oddnesses ", he at no period of his life (and certainly not in the heat of composition) regarded his innovations as really odd. When, a year later, he sent the poem to his friend Bridges, the latter was not pleased with it, called it " presumptuous jugglery ", and suggested alterations. But Hopkins would not hear of it :

> " I cannot think of altering anything. Why shd. I? I do not write for the public. You are my public and I hope to convert you." [2]

Bridges refused to read the poem again " for any money " ; but Hopkins remonstrated with him :

> " You would have got more weathered to the style and its features—not really odd. . . . When a new thing, such as my ventures in the *Deutschland* are, is presented us our first criticisms are not our truest, best, most homefelt, or most lasting, but what come easiest on the instant. They are barbarous and like what the ignorant and the ruck say. This was so with you." [3]

The future Laureate's first thoughts on this poem are described as bilge-water, " vulgar mudbottom and common sewage " ; so that we are left in no doubt that Hopkins was both sincere and constant in the technical and artistic decisions he had taken ; indeed, the constancy was proved by the almost immediate writing of another " shipwreck " piece in the same manner, *The Loss of the Eurydice*.[4]

In his notes to the *Poems*, Bridges calls *The Deutschland* " a great metrical experiment " ; and this putting of the emphasis upon the prosodic aspect has been echoed by later critics. A great experiment the poem certainly was ; but one of our main objects

[1] *Letters*, vol. ii. p. 15. [2] *Ibid.* vol. i. p. 46. [3] *Ibid.* vol. i. p. 50.

[4] In the same letter Hopkins says : " I enclose you my *Eurydice*, which the *Month* refused. Write no bilgewater about it . . . which being short and easy please read more than once."

is to show that the work is considerably more than a mere experiment. Bridges was probably more deeply impressed with its essential poetry than his recorded words would seem to indicate ; but the fact that the poem was distasteful to him " in both subject and treatment " (he was always repelled by the " full-blooded Roman theology ") [1] prevented him from seeing all its poetic merits, and this attitude of Bridges, together with certain other editorial comments in the standard edition of the poems, is likely for some time yet to create an unfavourable prejudice in many readers.

To most people at present, as to Bridges, *The Wreck of the Deutschland* is nothing less than " a great dragon folded in the gate to forbid all entrance " ; [2] and indeed new readers will at any time be well advised to make their approach to Hopkins through the comparatively simple anthology pieces, like *Pied Beauty* and *The Starlight Night.* Yet there is no truth in the damaging implication that *The Deutschland* is more than legitimately difficult to appreciate either as " new rhythm " or as pure poetry. No single work illustrates more remarkably the truth of the statement that, from the literary standpoint, it is not what a poem *says* that matters, but what it *is.* Admittedly there are stanzas from which the thought is not easily disentangled. Yet even in these dark places the flower of poetry will still be found blooming—surprising felicities of rhythm, diction, imagery. Moreover, this poet's darkness is worth more than many another poet's daylight. It is, with few exceptions, always the midnight which is charged with the mysteries of veiled luminaries and budding morrows—" splendid obscurities ". Coleridge has said that poetry gives most pleasure when only generally understood ; and there are difficult passages in this poem which, by their sheer magic, almost induce us to condone superficial reading. Hopkins himself says, in a letter to Bridges :

> " Granted that it needs study and is obscure, for indeed I was not over-desirous that the meaning of all should be quite clear, at least unmistakeable, you might . . . have nevertheless read it so that lines and stanzas should be left in the memory and superficial impressions deepened, and have liked some without exhausting all." [3]

To-day that seems a very reasonable stipulation, and is borne out by our own experience. Good poetry, however, will

[1] See his *Memoir of D. M. Dolben* (Oxford Univ. Press).
[2] *Poems*, p. 104.
[3] *Letters*, vol. i. p. 50.

always stand the test of intellectual analysis,[1] and in this poem, stanzas like Nos. 4 and 27 will yield further delight when the mind has assimilated and organized the more recondite thoughts and images.

In later chapters it will be necessary to trace the growth of " sprung " and " counterpointed " rhythms in Hopkins's mind and practice, and at the same time to point out, in greater detail, obvious influences and corroborative traditional parallels.[2] Our immediate purpose will be to take up the challenge thrown down by Bridges and overcome the " dragon " in a bold frontal attack, presenting just so much prosodic information as will be necessary for a first intelligent and sympathetic reading of the poem. The original autograph manuscript, with its marked stresses and other signs to assist the reader (or rather performer) has unfortunately been lost ; and even had it not been, typographical considerations would have rendered the printing of that unconventional notation obnoxious to most people. Indeed, Hopkins himself, though he continued to use signs until 1887 or later, was inclined to agree with Bridges that they were undesirable—" a confession of unintelligibility ".[3] At this late day, however, we know enough about his intentions to understand his rhythms, and in due course criticism and education will, we hope, make the question of stress-marks and signs superfluous.

The explanation of the " new rhythm " given in the Author's Preface to the *Poems* (written in 1883, or not much later) is excellent as far as it goes, but to obtain a fuller light we must supplement it with certain passages in the *Letters*. To approach the poem and its rhythm solely from the prosodic standpoint is, however, a mistaken attitude. The " new rhythm ", as it turned out, was not merely a new kind of metre ; it included, as we shall see, a new and effective fusion of rhythm and texture or tone-values. But as the consideration of rhythm as a system of scansion seems to have been uppermost in the poet's mind, we will begin with this aspect of the work.

[1] This statement is made in full cognizance of A. E. Housman's well-known position : " That is nonsense ; but it is ravishing poetry " (*The Name and Nature of Poetry*, p. 41). Meaning is always part of the greatest poetry.

[2] See Chapter III. ; an historical survey of the development of sprung rhythm will be included in Vol. II.

[3] Cf. *Letters*, vol. i. p. 189 : " You were right to leave out the marks : they were not consistent for one thing, and are always offensive. Still there must be some ". Cf. also p. 265.

Sprung Rhythm was called a *rhythm* and not a *metre* in order to avoid confusion with standard English syllabic metres, in which the verse is normally measured by the number of syllables. Nevertheless, the element of time, as in music, is not absent from Sprung Rhythm, which is virtually a stress-metre derived from a number of sources, literary and otherwise. Greek melic verse and the rhythms of " all but the most regular music " were certainly powerful influences ; [1] but the two most immediate indigenous sources were the " irregular " choruses of Milton's *Samson Agonistes*, and the free rhythms of popular jingles and nursery rhymes. Sprung Rhythm, moreover, is closely akin to the rhythms of ordinary speech.

Hopkins was probably the first to discover that the choruses in *Samson Agonistes*, so far from being capriciously irregular, were built up on a carefully calculated system of " counterpoint ", or reversed feet.[2] Here he saw the possibility of development, and the direction of this development was determined by the freedom and vigour of such a popular cadence as " *Díng, dóng, béll,* Pússy's ín the wéll ; *Whó pút* her ín ? Líttle Jóhnny Thín, etc.".[3] This he calls a simple form of Sprung Rhythm, and similar effects are to be found in Shakespeare, Coleridge (*Christabel*), Campbell (*The Battle of the Baltic*), Tennyson (" Break, break, break "), Arnold and others. It is significant that the nursery rhyme quoted above is ' pointed ' in accordance with its musical setting, which gives a stronger stress to the first " in " than it would normally receive in ordinary speech. This suggests also a comparison between Sprung Rhythm and the ' pointing ' of the Psalms in Anglican church services.[4] The mode of singing is that a certain number of words (varying from one or two to as many as twenty) are intoned on one note, and then follow several others in strict time. By this means, verses of entirely different length as regards number of words are accommodated within the melodic flow of the single or

[1] See Vol. II. chaps. ii. and iii. of the present work.

[2] See *Milton's Prosody*, by Robert Bridges (Clarendon Press, 1921), p. 51, footnote.

[3] *Letters*, vol. ii. p. 14.

[4] This comparison was first suggested by Mr. C. K. Ogden in his Editorial to *Psyche*, vol. xvi. (1936). In this useful discussion of Sprung Rhythm, Mr. Ogden also points out the probable influence of Hebrew metre on Hopkins. In Hebrew verse " the accentuation, the rhythmic beat dominates everything ", so that it is immaterial " whether one, two, or three syllables intervene between the consecutive beats " Incidentally, it was in February 1875 that Hopkins wrote : " Hebrew is part of our curriculum ". (*Letters*, vol. i. p. 31.)

double chant. The essential difference is that in Sprung Rhythm, 'time' is never completely disregarded.

The primary rule of Sprung Rhythm is that "*one stress makes one foot, no matter how many or how few the syllables*":

> "I should add that the word 'sprung' means something like abrupt, and applies only by rights where one stress follows another running, without syllable between." [1]

Thus from a healthy fusion of artificial and popular elements arose the bold, varied and sustained Sprung Rhythm of *The Deutschland.* Hopkins adds:

> "I do not of course claim to have invented *sprung rhythms* but only *sprung rhythm* . . . what I do in the *Deutschland* is to enfranchise them as a regular and permanent principle of scansion." [2]

In maintaining that his rhythm was based on "a better and more natural principle than the ordinary system, much more flexible and capable of much greater effects",[3] he says, in a letter to Bridges:

> "Why do I employ sprung rhythm at all? Because it is the nearest to the rhythm of prose, that is the native and natural rhythm of speech, the least forced, the most rhetorical and emphatic of all possible rhythms, combining, as it seems to me, markedness of rhythm—that is rhythm's self—and naturalness of expression—for why, if it is forcible in prose to say 'lashed ⁚ rod' am I obliged to weaken this in verse, which ought to be something stronger, not weaker, into 'lashed birch-rod' or something?" [4]

This combined naturalness and markedness of expression we have found it convenient to refer to hereafter as "expressional rhythm"; the term subsumes what Hopkins himself calls "imitative rhythm",[5] but signifies more precisely a vital fusion of the internal rhythm of thought-and-emotion and the external rhythm of sounds.

The verse of this poem must be scanned in feet of from one to four syllables, regularly, and for particular effects any number of weak or "slack" syllables may be used. The stress falls upon the first (or only) syllable in each foot; also, the metre of each line takes up immediately that of the one before, so that "the scanning runs on without a break from the beginning, say, of a

[1] *Letters*, vol. ii. p. 23. [2] *Ibid.* vol. i. p. 45. [3] *Ibid.* vol. ii. pp. 14–15.

[4] *Ibid.*, vol. i. p. 46. The great colon between "lashed" and "rod" indicates that both words are fully stressed, i.e., *láshed ród.*

[5] E.g. in *The Eurydice*: "Then a lurch forward, frigate and men": "I don't see the difficulty about the 'lurch forward' . . . which is imitative as usual. . . ." (*Letters*, vol. i. p. 52.)

stanza to the end, and all the stanza is one long strain, though written in lines asunder".[1] A final and necessary condition (one that Hopkins was constantly repeating) is that this verse is "less to be read than heard": Sprung Rhythm is an "oratorical" rhythm.[2]

Before we illustrate the scansion a word must be said about the eight-line stanza employed.[3] In the whole of Part I (stanzas 1–10), the number of stresses in the stanza is, by lines, 2–3–4–3–5–5–4–6; and these line-lengths are indicated by the manner of the indenting. In Part II, however, the first line of every stanza has three stresses, and in the first edition of the *Poems* (1918) this change was shown by the alignment of the manuscript:

> "Ínto the snów she swéeps,
> Húrling the háven behínd,
> *The Déutschland*, on Súnday; and só the sky kéeps
> For the ínfinite aír is unkínd . . ."

In the second edition (1930), and all subsequent impressions, this quantitative pattern is technically (but not aesthetically) impaired by the indenting of the first line, as in Part I:

> "Ínto the snóws she swéeps
> Húrling the háven behínd . . ."

so that many readers of the second edition have not been aware, or have not been certain, that the first lines in Part II had one more stress than those of Part I. In this chapter, therefore, we shall restore the alignment of the first edition, which is prosodically exact and true to the poet's intention.

The poem was probably begun with the second stanza in Part II (No. 12),[4] and the scansion here presents no difficulty:

> "On ⁝ Sáturday saíled from Brémen,
> Américan-óutward-bóund,
> Take séttler and séamen, tell mén with wómen,
> Two húndred sóuls in the róund—
> O Fáther, not under thý féathers nor éver as guéssing
> The góal was a shóal, of a fóurth the dóom to be drówned;
> Yet díd the dárk side of the báy of thy bléssing
> Not váult them, the míllions of róunds of thy mércy not réeve
> even thém in?"

[1] *Poems*, Author's Preface, p. 4.
[2] *Letters*, vol. i. p. 46.
[3] See Mr. C. K. Ogden, *op. cit.* p. 13.
[4] *Letters*, vol. i. p. 44.

The most frequent cause of uncertainty in the stressing throughout the poem is the juxtaposition of two long or strong syllables which seem at first to be equally important. An example in the above stanza is " dark side " ; but here both the meaning and the alliteration (with " did ") award the stress to " dark ", while " side " has the strength of a secondary stress (" dárk sìde "). The effect is to give weight and solemnity, like the classical spondee, and we have counted twenty-five other examples in this poem.[1]

The first stanza of Part I, though one of the most beautiful, is not easy to scan.[2] The first line is " rove over " :

> " Thóu màstering mé
> Gòd ! gíver of bréath and bréad ;
> Wórld's stránd, swáy of the séa ;
> Lórd of líving and déad ;
> Thou hast bóund bónes and véins in me, fástened me flésh,
> And áfter it álmost únmade, whát with dréad,
> Thy dóing : and dóst thou tóuch me afrésh ?
> Óver agáin I féel thy fínger and fínd thée." [3]

In line 1, " Thou " stands in natural opposition to " me ", though in actual recitation " *mast*ering " and " God ! " carry almost as much emphasis as the syllables which mark the rhythmic beat.

An extreme example of monosyllabic feet is the last line of stanza 11 :

> " The ⁝ sóur | scýthe | crínge, and the | bléar | sháre | cóme."

Of such feet Hopkins says :

> " . . . one syllable has not only the stress of its accent but also the slack which another word would throw on one or more additional syllables, though here that may perhaps be latent, *as though the slack syllables had been absorbed.*"

[1] See Appendix A.

[2] See *Psyche* (1936), *loc. cit.* p. 13. The scansion given by Mr. Cecil Day Lewis is obviously incorrect.

[3] MS. " A " shows an earlier, less satisfactory version of lines 1 and 2 :

> " God mastering me
> Giver of breath and bread . . ."

Line 6 is worded and stressed thus :

> " And áfter it at tímes almóst unmáde me with dréad . . ."

This stressing of " almóst unmáde " is intolerable.

This " easily felt principle of *equal strengths* " [1] applies also to the polysyllabic feet, as in :

> " The appealing of the | Passion is | tenderer in | prayer
> apart : " (Stanza 27.)
> " Let him easter in us, be a | dayspring to the | dimness of us,
> be a | crimson-cresseted | east," (Stanza 35.)

The structure of the elaborate stanza is not materially altered by these eccentric feet ; they indicate merely a change of tempo : " The feet are assumed to be equally long or strong, and their seeming inequality is made up by pause or stressing." [2] It follows that the " paeonic " and longer feet must be pronounced more quickly than the shorter ones if the metrical pattern is to be preserved. But this does not imply an uncomely gabbling : as in the application of the musical terms *rallentando* and *accelerando*, the time-rule is slightly flexible, and can at suitable moments be extended or diminished without injury to the formal proportions. In the MS. " A " version of *The Sea and the Skylark*, Hopkins actually wrote :

> " *Rallentando.*
> To man's last dust, drain fast towards man's first slime." [3]

In *The Deutschland* he might well have written (stanza 31) :

> " *Accelerando.*
>
> No not uncomforted : lovely-felicitous Providence,
> Finger of a tender of, O of a feathery delicacy, the breast
> of the
> Maiden could obey so, be a bell to, ring of it, and
> Startle the poor sheep back ! is the shipwrack then a harvest,
> does tempest carry the grain for thee ? "

In a valuable note prefixed to the poem in MS. " A ",[4] the poet explains how the *length* and *strength* of the stressed syllables affect the reading of a passage like the above. When, he says, more than one syllable goes to the beat, then if the beating

[1] *Letters*, vol. ii. p. 22.
[2] *Poems*, Author's Preface, p. 5.
[3] *Ibid.* No. 11, line 14.
[4] The note is in the handwriting of Bridges, but the wording is so characteristic of Hopkins that it must be either a copy of his autograph or a carefully remembered report of his spoken words. We quote by kind permission of Mrs. Robert Bridges.

syllable is of its nature long, the stress laid on it must be stronger the greater the number of syllables belonging to it, "the voice treading and dwelling; but if on the contrary it is by nature light, then the greater the number of syllables belonging to it the less is the stress to be laid on it, the voice passing flyingly over all the syllables of the foot and in some manner distributing among them all the stress of the one beat". The question as to which syllables are strong and which light must, he says, be left for the ear to decide; but as an example he takes the line:

> "Fínger of a ténder of, Ó of a féathery délicacy, the breast
> of the . . ."

> "The first two beats are very strong and the more the voice dwells on them the more it fetches out the strength of the syllables they rest upon; the next two beats are very light and escaping, and the last, as well as those which follow in the next line, are of a mean strength, such as suits narrative. And so throughout let the stress be made to fetch out both the strength of the syllables and the meaning and feeling of the words."

In his use of Sprung Rhythm, therefore, we see how far Hopkins went in the process of forcing versification out of its regular syllabic rut; with what deliberate, sensitive, and thorough calculation he tried to endow it with some of the variety and flexibility of both musical rhythms and speech rhythms without loss of central architectonic control.

We have so far examined only one aspect of the poet's "new rhythm"—that dealing with stress and measure. In a letter to Bridges he says:

> "But as air, melody, is what strikes me most of all in music, and design in painting, so design, pattern . . . is what I above all aim at in poetry." [1]

This pattern he achieves by building up a seemingly precious yet entirely organic system of tone-values. Alliteration, assonance, partial assonance, interior rhyme and subtle vocalic "scales" are all employed not merely as ornamental devices but as definite structural modes in the making of a complex expressional rhythm. Their employment is not regular and monotonous as it would be if determined by a prearranged and inviolable tone-pattern. Alliteration in Hopkins, for instance, is

[1] *Poems*, pp. 96–97.

used with far greater imaginative purpose than in either Langland or Swinburne. In *The Deutschland*, alliteration and other phonal correspondences (“ certain chimes, suggested by the Welsh poetry I had been reading—what they call *cynghanedd* ”) [1] are used in conjunction with a free, creative handling of syntax as a means of giving emphasis to the rhythm,—intensity, colour, and precision to the diction. The unit of variation is the “ musical phrase ” rather than the line or stanza, and the result is a unique poetic design, a verbal tapestry of brilliant texture.

We may now illustrate the poet’s preoccupation with expressional rhythm by quoting in full the first stanza in Part II :

“ ‘ Sóme fínd me a swórd ; sóme
The flánge and the ráil ; fláme
Fáng, or flóod ’ goes Déath on drúm,
And stórms búgle his fáme.
But wé dréam we are róoted in éarth—Dúst !
Flésh fálls within síght of us, wé, though our flówer the sáme,
Wáve with the méadow, forgét that there múst
The sóur scýthe crínge, and the bléar sháre cóme.”

The powerful, cumulative effect is produced by the judicious placing of pauses and alliterative consonants (*f*lange, *f*lame ; *f*ang, *f*lood ; *D*eath, *d*rum). Great emphasis is given to “ some ” at the end of line 1 and “ flame ” in line 2 by means of the pause, or silent syllable, before each. What a pregnant statement is “ Dust ! ” at the end of line 5 ! How apt is the alliterative link with “ dream ” !

Again, in stanza 18, having told us how the brave nun rose like a prophetess above the tumult of the wreck, the poet breaks out with :

“ Ah, tóuched in your bówer of bóne
Are you ! túrned for an éxquisite smárt
Have you ! máke words bréak from me hére all alóne
Do you !—móther of béing in me, héart.”

No rhythmic device could be more natural than the overflow in these lines. As with a sob, each line stumbles and falters over the threshold of the next, and the regularity of this encroachment sets up a vertical cross-current of pure expressional rhythm without disturbing the basic metre.

[1] *Letters*, vol. ii. p. 15. The influence of Welsh poetry on Hopkins is treated exhaustively in Vol. II. chap. iii. of the present work.

Now contrast the agitation of the above passage with the restrained rhythm of the following :

> " Jésu, héart's líght,
> Jésu, máid's són,
> Whát was the féast fóllowed the níght
> Thou hadst glóry of thís nún ?—" [1]

Such hushed and reverential invocations should indeed be so retarded. So, too, even grammar should yield to more important considerations, and the expulsion of the relative pronoun after " feast " (Hopkins had no use for the colourless, otiose word) definitely improves the cadence.

A further device for varying the rhythm is the use of trisyllabic run-on rhymes in the very next stanza (No. 31) :

> " Well, shé has thée for the páin, for the
> Pátience ; but píty of the rést of them !
> Héart, go and bléed at a bítterer véin for the
> Cómfortless únconféssed of them—" [2]

The rhymes in lines 1 and 3 are not mere factitious ornament. Wishing to dispense with the final pause (the passage is *accelerando*), the poet uses them as a substitute to mark the metrical divisions ; so that in reading, while we are primarily conscious of the speech-rhythm, we are conscious also of the metre. It should be noted how the pause at " pain ", in the midst of the first rhyme-group, produces a drag, a sense of effort : the rhythm is " imitative as usual ".

Lastly, the variety of rhythmic resources in this poem is no less apparent in the six-stress lines which terminate the stanzas. A typical or ' average ' line would be that in stanza 6 :

> " And hére the fáithful wáver, the fáithless fáble and míss."

But for the rest of these " alexandrines ", no two are metrically identical, and in rhythmic flexibility they show an extraordinary range. In a line like :

> " To flásh from the fláme to the fláme then, tówer from the
> gráce to the gráce," [3]

we have a typical loping Swinburnean movement (with what seems also to be a share of that poet's peculiar vagueness) ; but

[1] Stanza 30. [2] " She " is the nun ; " thee " is Christ. [3] Stanza 3.

this precise effect is never repeated. The poem is perhaps unique in the way it gives us a spice of one poet here and a flavour of some other poet there, yet never degenerates into pastiche. Never for a moment does it lose its own individuality.

The Bridges "dragon", we submit, is now tamed. The poem is no longer to be regarded as a "metrical experiment" but as a metrical accomplishment, a masterpiece of poetic rhythm. We may now proceed to an examination of its content.

The argument falls conveniently into four sections or movements, which may be briefly summarized as follows:

(1) Proem: Meditation on the mystery of God's infinite power as contrasted with Man's creeping subservience; dissolution of the physical life counteracted by the gift of grace through Christ; the mystic "stress" exerted on the human soul by Natura Benigna and Natura Maligna; this sensitivity to divine admonition attributed to the Crucifixion, with which the present disaster is implicitly identified; invocation to God to master his rebellious creature either by slow intuitive, or sudden and violent, apocalypse. (Stanzas 1–10.)

(2) Dramatic description of the wreck and attendant circumstances. (Stanzas 11–17.)

(3) The behaviour of the heroic nun; tentative analysis of her motives; her act ultimately attributed to prophetic inspiration and the faith which creates faith. (Stanzas 18–31.)

(4) Return to the theme of the Proem: reconciliation to God's Will; faith in a benign if inscrutable Purpose heightened to a triumphant hymn of adoration; Assumption of the nun as a second Virgin; plea for intercession on behalf of English heretics. (Stanzas 32–35.)

In handling this complex theme Hopkins was not uninfluenced by the method of Pindar.[1] But as a Christian poem, and again as an impassioned, subjective treatment of an ostensibly objective matter, *The Wreck of The Deutschland* may in some ways be compared to Donne's *Anniversaries*. In each work an external event supplies the initial inspiration, the *motif* and the broad framework of circumstance, while the poet's own religious

[1] Cf. *Letters*, vol. i. p. 49: "*The Deutschland* would be more generally interesting if there were more wreck and less discourse, I know, but still it is an ode and not primarily a narrative. There is some narrative in Pindar, but the principal business is lyrical."

fervour, 'mysticism', or (if you will) poetic numinosity, supply the emotional tone and the more profound thoughts and images. In each poem it is this imaginative fusion of the impersonal and the personal, the accidental and the fundamental, the particular and the universal, which gives the intellectual content a piquancy equalled only by the sustained beauty of the verbal incantation.

Part the First describes with great poignancy the feelings and thoughts of a deeply religious man after he has recovered from the first shock of a disaster in which the innocent and the brave have suffered and perished. In the opening invocation to God, "Lord of living and dead", bountiful in creation yet stern and terrible in mastering his rebellious creature, Man, we are made to feel that the poet's first emotions were painful and disturbing; we perceive that there has been a mental struggle, in which the problem of evil and the Christian doctrine of Divine Love and Omnipotence have been with difficulty reconciled by reason and faith. The problem of evil, which has rightly been called "the great theoretical difficulty for a religious view of the world", may with equal justice be accepted as "a necessary factor in the emergence of the religious attitude"[1]; and with this paradox the mind of Hopkins was always deeply engaged. But whatever may have been the precise nature of the first mental conflict, it is certain that he had recovered the tranquillity of faith before he began the poem. His Catholic theology (like the earlier Platonism) conceived God as the All-Good, who, as such, could not be held directly responsible for evil; but whereas the Platonist explained disaster as being the work of Necessity (that seeming power of resistance in the material world which prevents the perfect representation of the Divine Thought), the Schoolmen accepted it as a mystery, a negative attribute of the good, a force without which the various forms of moral virtue could not flourish. This might not be "the best of all possible worlds", but it was the one which God, for his own good reasons, had chosen to create.

One is reminded of Shelley's powerful rendering of the Platonic conception:

> ". . . the One Spirit's plastic stress
> Sweeps through the dull dense world . . .
> Torturing th'unwilling dross that checks its flight
> To its own likeness . . ."[2]

[1] See *The Idea of God*, by W. R. Matthews. [2] *Adonais*, 381–4.

words which Hopkins may have remembered, for without participating in Shelley's pantheism he uses the word "stress" in a similar sense many times in *The Deutschland* and elsewhere. Indeed, a sound and satisfying reading of the more abstract passages in the poem depends largely upon the accuracy with which we interpret certain words and phrases that are used in a specific or somewhat arbitrary sense—arbitrary, that is, in respect of current usage, but in their application always harking back to their origins. "Stress" is such a word; "horror of height", "laced", "spell", "grace", "pressure", and "principle" are others, all occurring in the first four stanzas. As one critic has finely and tersely expressed it, the wreck that Hopkins describes "is both occasion and symbol. He realizes it so vividly that he is in it; and it is at the same time in him".[1]

> "I díd say yés
> O at líghtning and láshed ród;
> Thou héardst me trúer than tóngue conféss
> Thy térror, O Chríst, O Gód;"[2]

That perhaps may be taken as sympathetic participation in the "occasion"—the terrors of the storm; yet the "lightning and lashed rod", together with the undeniably personal nature of the confession which follows, would seem to indicate that the poet's mind was possessed rather by a poignant phase in the evolution of his own soul:

> "Thou knówest the wálls, áltar and hóur and níght:
> The swóon of a héart that the swéep and the húrl of thee tród
> Hárd dówn with a hórror of héight:"[2]

Perhaps it was an occasion in the early stages of his novitiate; perhaps a later period of desolation: certainly an experience not unlike that of Francis Thompson in *The Hound of Heaven*. These images of physical terror are the symbols of the spiritual storm—the cataclysm in which every argument and lust of the physical being was finally (as he thought) submerged. The last bristling resistance of his mortal nature was trodden "hard down" with the horror incident to a full realization of Man's subservience in relation to God's incalculable range and altitude.

[1] Dr. F. R. Leavis in *New Bearings in English Poetry* (1932), p. 176.
[2] Stanza 2.

The phrase "horror of height" could refer only to some such state of authentic quasi-mystical perception. We are at first reminded of Francis Thompson's *Dread of Height*; but there is no real resemblance. Thompson's dread is a kind of spiritual vertigo induced by an almost sensual indulgence in the golden love-feasts of the high banquet-hall, and the consequent fear:

> "Lest like a weary girl I fall
> From clasping love so high."[1]

But the emotions of Hopkins are no such indulgence. The sensation of being a languid Gulliver in the hands of a divine Brobdingnagian of unknown intentions is one in which many mystics have luxuriated. Hopkins, however, never ceased to be a rational man. He may almost be said to struggle with the Holy Ghost as with an incubus: the pangs of surrender are physical no less than spiritual; his midriff is astrain, his whole being is "laced" with the terrific "stress" of Pentecostal fire.[2] His pursuit and capture was more like a paralysing nightmare than Thompson's was; for whereas the latter:

> ". . . was sore adread
> Lest, having Him, I must have naught beside,"

Hopkins seems to have had no alternative but complete destruction:

> "The frówn of his fáce
> Befóre me, the húrtle of héll
> Behínd, whère, whére was a, whére was a pláce?"

Incidentally, with what success do the repetitions in this last line convey the sensation of panic—the last effort, perhaps, of the "unwilling dross" in Hopkins to escape from God's "plastic

[1] *Poems*, vol. ii. p. 19 (Burns Oates and Washbourne).

[2] It is interesting to compare this stanza (2) with the sonnet *Carrion Comfort* (No. 40), written approximately ten years later. The images of physical assault are repeated: the victim feels the same desire to escape, this time from Despair ("me frantic to avoid thee and flee"). The whole sestet might, indeed, refer to the same occasion as that described so cryptically in *The Deutschland*. Christ himself is the "hero" whose "heaven-handling" flung the wretch down, trod upon him; and in the last lines the identity of Despair is explicit:

> "That night, that year
> Of now done darkness, I wretch lay wrestling with (my God!) my God."

stress ". Then, to show how the soul's surrender to God is paradoxically its only means of deliverance :

" I whírled out wíngs thàt⁀spéll [1]
And fléd with a flíng of the héart to the héart of the Hóst."

By an apt image the heart is compared to a homing pigeon :

" My héart, but yóu were dóvewinged, Í can téll,
Cárrier-wítted, I am bóld to bóast,
To flásh from the fláme to the fláme then, tówer from the
gráce to the gráce."

The unusually evocative quality of the diction throughout the poem is well illustrated in this stanza (No. 3). With words like " spell " and " Host ", the supra-logical connotations and accidental associations reinforce the literal meaning. This evocativeness makes itself felt not only in passages where the imagery is clear-cut and precise, but also in places where the total effect is vague and somewhat blurred, as in the last line of this same stanza. Some knowledge of the theological conception of grace is perhaps necessary for a proper understanding of the last image ; yet the mind open to suggestion will probably respond without recourse to St. Teresa or St. John of the Cross. If we allot the first flame to retributive lightning, the second may well be the symbol of the Holy Ghost ; and once the soul is delivered from the fear of imminent destruction it may well " tower ", like Shakespeare's falcon, to its " pride of place ", that exalted state of mystic contemplation whence evils and temptations become easy prey.[2] A greater precision in expressing these theological concepts would have added nothing to the poetic vigour of the line ; indeed, a certain vagueness is inseparable

[1] The word " spell " in this context is a characteristic instance of Hopkins's disregard for the temporary inconvenience caused to his reader by seemingly wanton ambiguities. At first we are not sure whether " spell " is verb or noun, or whether " that " is relative pronoun or demonstrative adjective. But on a second reading it becomes clear that only the latter functions supply the required sense, " spell " then signifying one of a series of short periods of arduous pain or labour ; and " *that* spell " was obviously the last of the series—the crisis. (See also stanza 4, where " proffer " is a noun, and " O unteachably after evil ", in stanza 18, where " after " has verbal force.)

[2] Cf. *Note-books*, p. 332 : " For grace is any action, activity, on God's part by which, in creating or after creating, he carries the creature to or towards the end of its being which is its self-sacrifice to God and its salvation ". Cf. also *ibid.* p. 337 : " Elevating [grace], which lifts the receiver from one cleave of being to another . . ."

from all attempts to describe those ineffable experiences which, for want of a better word, we must call *mystical* or *quasi-mystical.*[1] Moreover, in Hopkins we have always to reckon with the powerful urgency of the rhythm, which is a definite stimulus to imaginative effort.

Nothing but such "majestic instancy" would ever carry the average reader through the many superficial difficulties of the next stanza (No. 4), with its swift transition from one metaphysical [2] image to another :

> "I am sóft síft
> In an hóurglass—át the wáll
> Fást, but míned with a mótion, a dríft,
> And it crówds and it cómbs to the fáll ;"

Consideration of the mystic way of spiritual salvation has led naturally to this reflection on the steady dissolution of the physical life. The rhythmic felicity of this quatrain is enhanced by the manner of the indenting. The slight uncertainty in the metre of the second line is fitting ; and as we gradually become aware that the sand is dropping away down the centre, how the rhythm gathers up speed and a fateful regularity ! Then comes a change of metaphor :

> "I stéady as a wáter in a wéll, to a póise, to a páne,
> But róped with, álways, áll the way dówn from the táll
> Félls or flánks of the vóel, a véin
> Of the góspel próffer, a préssure, a prínciple, Chríst's gíft." [3]

The hour-glass, small homely object, apt symbol of the less important physical being, is suddenly abandoned in favour of larger symbols which express the simultaneous recovery and reinforcement of the essential spiritual life ; yet there is just

[1] Cf. Wicksteed (*Dante and Aquinas*, p. 40) : "Unless the mystic speaks in consciously inadequate symbols, he finds that every phrase he utters recognizes restrictions and implies limitations which his sense of the infinite has transcended and rejected".

[2] We use "metaphysical", not in the Johnsonian sense of "conceited", but as implying a certain refinement and complexity of thought—an ecstasy of intellectual parturition as we find it in Shakespeare and Donne. A new emotion seems to be engendered by the mental process itself. Here, moreover, the philosophical connotation is quite relevant.

[3] The first image may have been suggested to Hopkins by the well in the grounds of St. Beuno's College, where the poem was written. Not far from the College is a hill called The Moel ("bare hill"), of which Hopkins's word, *voel*, is a mutated form.

enough resemblance between the forms and movements of the two sets of objects to allow the subjective thought to jump, like an electric current, from one to the other. The dichotomy of being, from the religious point of view, has never been more tersely or more poignantly expressed.

Having dealt with the ritualistic and theological modes of revelation, the poet proceeds, in stanza 5, to express that mystical illumination which is due to direct contact with the mystery and beauty of nature :

> " I kíss my hánd
> To the stárs, lóvely-asúnder
> Stárlight, wáfting him óut of it ; ánd
> Glów, glóry in thúnder ; "

Once more the audible rhythm and the mental images are perfectly assimilated. The metre allows the utmost liberty to the speech-rhythm without loss of compactness. The overflow from " lovely-asunder " to " starlight " imparts an *élan* ; the pause before (and after) " and " in the final clause fittingly ushers in the more solemn and sonorous thought. But line 7 ends with two characteristic and cryptic words :

> " Since though he is under the world's splendour and wonder,
> His mýstery múst be instréssed, stréssed ; "[1]

" Instressed " is, of course, an intensive form of the *leit motif*, " stress " ; and " stress ", which occurs twice in the next stanza, conveys the idea of supernatural overmastering influence accompanied by a sudden inrush of revelation [2] : it seems to imply (as, indeed, Scotus does) that our knowledge of the Divine Nature depends less upon the faculty of reason than upon those direct manifestations of Himself to the soul of man which God pleases to make :

> " For I gréet him the dáys I méet him, and bléss when I
> únderstánd."

[1] The allocation of stresses in this line is from MS. " A ".

[2] Cf. the second stanza in the fragment No. 73 :

> " What I know of thee I bless
> As acknowledging thy stress
> On my being, and as seeing
> Something of thy holiness."

Or, as in stanza 1 :

> " Óver agaín I féel thy fínger and fínd theé." [1]

The repetition of " stressed " after the stronger and more precise " instressed " is at first puzzling ; but this is not mere expletive. If " instressed " signifies (to put it crudely) " driven home ", forcibly borne in upon the mind made receptive by humility and faith, it implies also, as elsewhere in Hopkins, that the mind is not passive ; it can (and here it *must*) dwell upon, focus, and try to " law out " its own concept ; [2] " stressed " adds to this the general idea of emphasis, underlining, as though the poet is putting all the weight of personal experience behind his assertion.

Bridges condemned the whole line as " unpoetic "—an effort to force emotion into a theological channel.[3] Not all readers will agree with him. Two words so integral to the poetry of the whole do not spoil a mellifluous stanza, and the numinous emotion is so universal as to place it outside theology altogether. In any case, " force " is not a happy word to apply to feelings so obviously spontaneous and sincere as those of Hopkins.

The same may be said of the next two stanzas (6 and 7), which are in some respects the most difficult, and the most important, in the whole poem. They are doctrinal, yet a course of theology is not indispensable for their elucidation.

In stanza 5 the poet has said that Man's reactions to the beauty and variety of nature produce an intuition of the Divine goodness and power ; but he proceeds to qualify this by adding that the deeper significance of God's purpose, the awful mystery of His being, is not always revealed easily and continuously in this way ; it is often brought home to us with a certain stunning violence, like the dint of a hammer on white-hot iron :

> " With an ánvil-díng
> And with fíre in him fórge thy wíll." [4]

[1] Cf. *Note-books,* p. 337 : " This is truly God's finger touching the very vein of personality ". See also *ibid.* p. 332, and *Letters,* vol. ii. p. 93.

[2] Cf. *Note-books,* p. 349 : " This song of Lucifer's was a dwelling on his own beauty, an instressing of his own inscape ". Also *ibid.* pp. 310, 312 and 321.

[3] *Poems,* p. 96 (Preface to Notes).

[4] Cf. stanza 10 :

> " Whéther at ónce as ónce at a crásh Pául,"

and *Note-books,* p. 335 : " Now . . . it is true that God can raise anyone from any pitch of will and being however low to one in which he shall be gracious and consenting to God and in St. Paul's case wonderfully did so . . ."

This rare emotional stress, spiritual illumination, is brought about not by mere disaster, mere horror, but rather by those contingencies wherein the intensity of human suffering is heightened by and contrasted with the innocence and fortitude of the victims. In the case of *The Deutschland*, the poet is shaken with horror and admiration—suppressed, bewildered resentment against the Power which could permit such apparent injustice, and gratitude to that same Power for the noble virtues evoked. Hence he instinctively relates the victim's experience to that of Christ.[1] Like the theologian, he is unable to explain contingent evil on purely rational grounds ; he therefore follows the " list " of his emotions, and recovers his mental equilibrium by adopting the faith that God's purpose in Man can be fulfilled only by a continuous process of suffering and redemption :

> " Nót out of his bliss
> Spríngs the stréss félt
> Nor fírst from héaven (and féw know thís)
> Swíngs the stróke déalt—"

Is it not natural, then, that " here the faithful (that is, *some* of the faithful) waver ", and that the " faithless " who, in spite of Plato, seek to explain ultimate realities by ratiocination only, should " fable and miss " ?

This supernatural stress, therefore, is a truth that predominates, " rides time like riding a river ", floats buoyantly on the stream that bears all other truths away, and derives ultimately from Christ's Passion and the bitter-sweet sensations engendered by that apocalypse. Such profound emotions had been " felt before " (witness the death of Socrates), but Christ's Passion was the culmination, the ' discharge ' into the world of a new ethic —the concept that self-sacrifice is the fundamental principle of perfection.

At this point, Hopkins identifies the external drama of events with the internal drama of his own mental and emotional states. This he does not explicitly, but by a tacit, almost unconscious allusion to a certain important resemblance between Christ, the five nuns, and himself—namely, the fact that they had all dedicated their lives to the service of others, to a vocation

[1] Cf. *Letters*, vol. i. p. 188 : ". . . nor is it any mystery that a just man should be crucified, but that God should, fascinates—with the interest of awe, of pity, of shame, of every harrowing feeling ".

fraught with hardship, danger, and disappointment.[1] The more explicit statement is in stanza 22:

> "Five! the finding and sake
> And cipher of suffering Christ.
> Mark, the mark is of mán's máke
> And the word of it Sacrificed."

This, in turn, leads on to the contemplation of a similar sacrifice in St. Francis:

> "Joy fall to thee, father Francis,
> Drawn to the life that died;"

Again, in stanza 27, we have what is ostensibly a conjecture concerning the facts of the "tall" nun's life—facts that would explain her call to Christ to "come quickly":

> "Nó, but it was nót thése.
> The jading and jar of the cart,
> Time's tásking, it is fáthers that ásking for eáse
> Of the sodden-with-its-sorrowing heart."

Yet at the same time we are reminded of other instances of the same divine despair—Christ's lamentation over Jerusalem, his last cry: "My God, my God, why hast thou forsaken me?" and also of Hopkins's own agonized utterances in the last sonnets.[2]

The above exegesis of the more obscure implications of stanza 6 has been carried out, we believe, in the light of common knowledge and common sense. Many readers without either Thomist or Scotist theology might have interpreted the lines as follows: "God's direct influence is felt only through the benign aspects of nature: the malign aspects, the seemingly malicious scourging of Man by "stars and storms", all forms of misadventure which strike the guilty into appalled silence and flush all sympathetic hearts with almost insupportable pity—these are

[1] In a letter to Dixon (? July 3, 1886) this vocational relationship with Christ is stated very frankly: "Above all Christ our Lord: his career was cut short . . . he was doomed to succeed by failure; his plans were baffled, his hopes dashed, and his work was done by being broken off undone. However much he understood all this he found it an intolerable grief to submit to it."

[2] E.g. *Poems*, No. 50:

> ". . . why must
> Disappointment all I endeavour end?"

According to Bridges, Hopkins "was not considered publicly successful in his profession". (*Poets of the Century*, 1906; ed. Miles, vol. vii. p. 180.)

not directly the work of God." Believing in an omnipotent God, Hopkins could not have attached any importance to the Platonic "Necessity", which postulates a stubborn resistance to God's power in the material world; but he certainly believed that human malignity prevented the smooth working out of the Divine Will. He throws out a far from ambiguous hint that human error and cruelty, if not absolutely the *cause* of the *Deutschland* disaster, at least stand terribly rebuked by it. How else are we to interpret the words

> "Nor first from heaven (and few know this)
> Swińgs the stróke deált—"[1]

and

> "Wring thy rebel, dogged in den,
> Man's málice, with wrecking and storm . . ."[2]

and the final plea, in stanza 10:

> "Make mercy in all of us . . ."?

Was not Saul made merciful after his sudden conversion? Perhaps one may suggest, without irreverence, that above the tumult of the sinking *Deutschland* the poet hears the voice of God: "Falck, Falck, why persecutest thou me?"

Against this reading, however, we have to consider the significance of certain words in stanza 21:

> ". . . but thou art above, thou Orion of light;
> Thy unchancelling poising palms were weighing the worth,
> Thou martyr-master:"

So God was, after all, the Prime Mover; he was the Hunter, who beat these nuns from their monastic covert in Germany so that their faith and fortitude might be tested by ordeal and death. The poet accepts the scourge of heaven with complete faith in ultimate beatitude—"the heaven-haven of the Reward":

> "He was to cure the extremity where he had cast her;
> Dó, dèal, lórd it with líving and deád;"[3]

We see then that the storm is "both occasion and symbol" inasmuch as it excites and finally subdues the inner conflict. It subdues the conflict because it brings conviction of supernatural control; yet it is only the sensitive heart of the potential

[1] Stanza 6. [2] Stanza 9. [3] Stanza 28.

martyr (" hard at bay ", stabbed awake, " trodden hard down with the sweep and hurl of God's dark descending ") which feels the " divine stress " and can utter spontaneously the cry of the stricken Saul : " Who art thou, Lord ? " and " What wilt thou have me to do ? " In stanza 8 this point is enforced by the elaborate yet perfectly apt image of the " lush-kept, plush-capped sloe ", which bursts in the mouth and flushes the whole man with its " sour or sweet " (or both !) nectar. Early or late (and there is a special grace or authenticity in a late conversion), men come to acknowledge the divinity of Christ : either " first ", by a subjective realization of the divine principle underlying " the world's splendour and wonder " ; or " last ", in extremity, having been driven into acquiescence, forced to crouch before the thunder-throne. But Hopkins would rather all men should yield readily to the gentler, more sensuous persuasions :

" Or ráther, ráther then stéaling as Spríng
Through him, mélt him but máster him stíll." [1]

It would seem by this last line, however, that he regards both experiences, the " sweet " and the " bitter ", as essential to the true poise and discipline of the human soul ; for he is constantly reiterating the paradox of God's simultaneous exercise of mastery and mercy, austerity and love :

" Father and fondler of heart thou hast wrung :
Hast thy dark descending, and most art merciful then." [2]

Part the Second of our poem plunges quickly into the description of the actual wreck. The poet follows closely the contemporary newspaper accounts of the disaster ; yet his style never lapses into the prosaic, and the combined ideality and realism of the word-painting is hardly to be matched in English literature. The style varies from the almost (though not quite) colloquial ease of the beginning :

" On Saturday sailed from Bremen,
American-outward-bound,
Take settler and seamen, tell men with women,
Two hundred souls in the round—"

[1] Stanza 10. Cf. the sonnet called *Spring* (*Poems*, No. 9).

[2] Cf. the close of *In the Valley of the Elwy* (No. 16) :

" Complete thy creature dear O where it fails,
Being mighty a master, being a father and fond."

It is in this sense that the lesson of the *Book of Job* is completed by the teachings of Christ.

to the elaborate, ' stylized ' manner of

" Wíry and whìte-fíery and whírlwind-swìvelled snów
Spins to the wídow-máking unchilding unfathering deeps."

Between these extremes we have a passage in which the words arrange themselves naturally in the non-logical, inverted order of rapid, excited speech—a device which recalls the spontaneous vigour of the old ballad or folk-song :

" Ínto the snów she swéeps,
Hurling the haven behind,
The Deutschland on Sunday . . ."

" Sitting Eastnortheast, in cursed quarter, the wind."

An even greater excitement, an almost hysterical breathlessness of dramatic narration is achieved in stanza 28, where the frantic efforts of the drowning to save themselves, and the poet's attempt to evoke and express the vision of the nun, are merged in a striking aposiopesis :

" But hów shall I . . . máke me róom there :
Reach me a . . . Fancy, come faster—
Strike you the sight of it ? look at it loom there,
Thing that she . . . there then ! the Master," [1]

All this, however, falls easily within the bounds of poetic tradition. But we know of no precedent for the following passage, in which, by means of a more than Shakespearian ellipsis, the terror and confusion of that " unshapeable shock night " are represented, with what literally approaches the speed of thought, in a series of cinematographic " shots " :

" They fóught with Gód's cóld—
And they could not and fell to the deck
(Crúshed them) or wáter (and drówned them) or rólled
With the sea-romp over the wreck."

It is difficult to do justice to the power and fitness of these lines—the dash of the waves, the physical agony, the brute callousness of nature, which both rhythm and diction suggest.

[1] The poet was quick to perceive the analogy of Simon Peter, who saw Christ walking on the water ; hence, probably, the allusion to the apostle in the next stanza (29).

One of the greatest merits of this poem is the effective use of contrast. We have already considered the varieties of rhythm employed; but this variety extends also to visual and intellectual conceptions. Vivid and moving as it is, the description of the wreck is not overdone; the agony is not drawn out, but is relieved by brief flashes of passionate but always optimistic reflection on the spiritual issues involved. One example is stanza 18, the beginning of which we have already quoted; and in stanza 21, after having recorded the malignity of nature—

> "Súrf, snòw, ríver and éarth
> Gnáshed:"

the poet derives consolation from his faith in God's hidden purpose, and in the last line gives his emotion a tender, symbolic utterance in images which recall the sincere, decorative manner of a Veneto, a Mantegna, or a Botticelli:

> "Storm-flákes were scróll-leaved flówers, lily-shówers—sweet
> héaven was astréw in them."

In the next two stanzas (22 and 23) we have an amazing "metaphysical" digression—a musical fantasy, like a piece of elaborate ornamentation by Mozart, on the fortuitously mystical theme of Five. We say "fortuitously", because if there had been only *four* nuns to lament, or if they had chanced to be Benedictines instead of Franciscans, the charm could not have been wound up. Yet can we blame the poet for making the most of his opportunities? So superheated by passion is the furnace of his mind that he can take this apparently pinchbeck material, melt it down, and then reforge it into images of pure gold. The secret of this Midas-touch lies in the imaginative power and suggestiveness of the poet's diction, which in these two stanzas (as, indeed, everywhere) will repay the closest scrutiny. But although this kind of virtuosity will never appeal to all types of reader, there are and always will be many who will find in it a delicacy, a pathos, and a unifying harmony which more than justify the means employed. Neither Donne nor Crashaw has shown greater skill in that intellectual alchemy which transmutes the factitious into the fundamental.

A last example of effective contrast is the pure 'skyscape'

painting of stanza 26—the concrete image which symbolizes the joys of Paradise :

> " For how to the heart's cheering
> The down-dugged ground-hugged grey
> Hovers off, the jay-blue heavens appearing
> Of pied and peeled May !
> Blue-beating and hoary-glow height ; or night, still higher,
> With belled fire and the moth-soft Milky Way,"

Here, as always, we note the unexpected words. There is one epithet only, " pied ", which might have been used by some earlier writer ; yet all the rest are completely justified by their truth and beauty.[1]

The last section of the poem (stanzas 31 to 35) deals with the poet's final reconciliation to the ways of God. Hopkins believed that the nun's heroic mien brought comfort and faith to the last moments of the doomed voyagers :

> ". . . lovely-felicitous Providence
> . . . is the shipwrack then a harvest . . . ? "

God's sovereignty he " admires ", and is grateful for His mercy. He regards the nun as a type of martyr and her vision of Christ as a second mystic advent :

> " But here was heart-throe, birth of a brain,"

for

> " Not a doomsday dazzle in his coming, nor dark as he came ;
> Kind, but royally reclaiming his own : "

All of which makes it difficult to agree absolutely with Mr. Herbert Read, who has expressed the opinion that *The Wreck of the Deutschland* is a poem " of contrition, fear, and submission, rather than of the love of God ".[2] It is true that all these elements are present, although the " contrition " is vicarious rather than personal, and the " fear " is not imcompatible with the love of God : yet there seems to be a flouting of evidence

[1] " Moth-soft " anticipates both the " moth-like stars " of W. B. Yeats and the " mothy and warm " evening of Hardy's *Afterthought*. The magnificent " belled fire ' is not unlike Mr. Blunden's " bell-like evening when the may's in bloom " (*Almswomen*). The beauty of " down-dugged " is not that of convention, but of " inscape ", perfect fitness.

[2] *New Verse*, No. 1, 1933.

in the implication that this love of God, which the Catholic faith enjoins, is absent from the poem.

> "Beyónd sáying swéet, past télling of tóngue . . ."

and

> ". . . bút be‿adóred, bút be‿adóred Kíng." [1]

are surely not insincere and empty catchwords. Admittedly the first ten stanzas foreshadow the inner conflict and gloom of the last "terrible" sonnets; and Canon Dixon found in the poem "elements of deep distress" which made him read it with "less excited delight" than that with which he read the other poems.[2] But the phrases "terrible pathos" and "terrible crystal", which Dixon so aptly applied to Hopkins's poems (and which Mr. Read quotes with special reference to *The Deutschland*), are true only in so far as they emphasize the sincerity and concentrated passion with which Hopkins depicts the tragedy of the human situation—a tragedy which, however enigmatic it may appear in the later sonnets, is explicitly stated in this poem to be only apparent. A more cogent piece of evidence in support of Mr. Read's view is, perhaps, certain lines in *The Loss of the Eurydice*, written nearly three years later (1878):

> "The Eurydice—it concerned thee, O Lord:"

and also

> "Deeply surely I need to deplore it,
> Wondering how my master bore it," [3]

—which might be taken as a veiled rebuke to the Deity. Yet the last three stanzas of the poem contradict even these. It must be allowed that in *The Deutschland* the faith Hopkins evinces is that of one who has replied in the affirmative to Francis Thompson's question:

> "Is my gloom, after all,
> Shade of his hand outstretched caressingly?" [4]

Concerning *The Deutschland*, Hopkins's first great poem, possibly his masterpiece, it is important in the interests of art, religion, and the poet's character to recognize the fact that he could achieve poetry of a high, if not of the very highest, order in the

[1] Stanzas 9 and 10.
[2] *Letters*, vol. ii. p. 80.
[3] Lines 1 and 97–8.
[4] *The Hound of Heaven*.

5

expression of a definite belief, which may be accurately epitomized in the words of Duns Scotus : " Deus nihil potest velle, nisi sicut est volendum." This faith is implicit throughout and culminates in the triumphant concluding stanza, in which the poet, apostrophizing the dead nun, desires her to intercede for those who remain outside the faith in Britain :

" Our Kíng back, oh, upon Énglish sóuls ! "

And the note of canorous optimism reaches its climax in the last two lines, which resemble the finale of a Bach fugue or a Beethoven symphony. Loaded almost beyond the limit of their metrical capacity, their passion seems to expend itself in the heavily accented rhythm of a protracted roll of drums :

" Príde, ròse, prínce, héro of ús, hìgh-príest,
Our héarts' chàrity's héarth's fíre, our thóughts' chìvalry's
throńg's Lórd."

Never before or since have we seen such a row of genitives ; a fact which might condemn it in prose, but not in poetry.

The whole question of beliefs and doctrine in poetry has in recent years received exhaustive treatment at the hands of Dr. I. A. Richards,[1] who points out that in these days, when (as agnostics put it) " so many beliefs are breaking up ", the question as to how much sectarian doctrine may legitimately be incorporated in a poem becomes more urgent than ever before. Consciously or unconsciously, the poet aims at expressing universal experience in terms of his own experience ; and as certain beliefs and doctrines form an integral part of that personal experience—are, as it were, the rough-hewn symbols of it—we should be as illogical in denying him the use of these materials as in denying him the common symbols of language. But naturally the poet will draw upon all such recondite or controversial matters at his own risk : the farther he goes in that direction the fewer will be his followers,[2] the harder will he find it to achieve universality. And what is this universality, so dear to critics of the classical school ? There is a universality in Gray's *Elegy*, a universality in *Lycidas*, a universality in the *De Rerum Natura*, a universality in the *Paradiso* ; but it is from the more difficult of these poems that we deduce the higher aesthetic criterion. In other words,

[1] See *Principles of Literary Criticism* and *Practical Criticism*.
[2] Unless, of course, he has the power to make converts.

the poet may make whatever demands he likes upon our knowledge, sympathy, credulity, so long as he is able to transform common objects with passion, create a semblance of authority, and (should his doctrine be unacceptable) bring about not so much " a willing suspension of disbelief " as a desire to extract from him that which is more fundamental (if not, necessarily, more valuable) than any belief—the secret of his peculiar attitude and personality.

Apart from temporary ambiguities, unusual coinages, and syntactical audacities (all of which provide a healthy and stimulating resistance to the mind), the main cause of obscurity and difficulty in *The Deutschland* is the presence of either esoteric or inadequately articulated doctrine. Frequently Hopkins is doing no more than follow the example of Dante and Milton at their most lucid, as for instance, when familiar and illuminating words from the Scriptures are quoted or woven deftly into the fabric of the poem. The last two lines of stanza 26 :

> " What by your measure is the heaven of desire,
> The treasure never eyesight got, nor was ever guessed what
> for the hearing ? "

are an adaptation of 1 Cor. ii. 9. Again, in stanza 29 we have :

> " Ah ! there was a heart right,
> There was single eye ! "

in which the phrase " single eye " is taken from St. Matthew vi. 22. Occasionally we find a piece of doctrine which could arouse the intended response only in a certain type of Catholic reader :

> " The appealing of the Passion is tenderer in prayer apart." [1]

But the sensitive unbeliever is immediately swept on by the sheer pagan splendour of the next lines :

> " Other, I gather, in measure her mind's
> Burden, in wind's burly and beat of endragonèd seas."

Dr. Richards has said that when a poem is completely successful such elements of doctrine and belief as are present do not obtrude themselves upon the reader's consciousness ; whenever

[1] Stanza 27.

they do we cease to be reading poetry and for the nonce are reading theology, political history or what not. That is often true, though the Plimsoll line of such obtrusion must vary considerably from one person to another. But there is one passage in *The Deutschland* where many will be pulled up with a jolt, stung into resistance or resentment as their minds are jerked suddenly from pure poetry to theological polemic :

> " But Gertrude, lily, and Luther are two of a town,
> Chríst's líly and beast of the wáste wóod : " [1]

Yet is it not well done? The allusion to St. Gertrude [2] (the German Benedictine mystic of Eisleben, Luther's birthplace) is not adventitious. Hopkins has just called Deutschland " double a desperate name " : it is the name of the unfortunate ship and also of the country which exiled the five nuns. He then says that the same country and town may produce two entirely different types of person ; it has always been so, since

> " Abel is Cain's brother and breasts they have sucked the
> same."

The introduction of St. Gertrude is what would be called nowadays a " private " reference or image ; yet when we know that her prayers contain a devotion *On the Passion of Our Lord*, a theme of intrinsic importance in the poem, we realize that there was, for Hopkins, a strong emotional link between Gertrude and the nuns. Moreover, the symbolism of the " beast " and the " waste wood ", with its ominous echo of Jeremiah and Dante, is at least effective.[3] Above all, the passage does not leap out of its context : in style and rhythm the stanza is in harmony with the rest of the poem. We may perhaps compare it to the famous diatribe in *Lycidas*—by some condemned as the one " false note ", by others praised as a *locus classicus* of successfully poeticized doctrine.

There can be no doubt that Hopkins, despite a complete absence of unqualified praise from other people, retained a great faith in the value of his poem ; so that when he admits, in a letter to Bridges, that " There are some immaturities in it

[1] Stanza 20.

[2] Born *c.* 1256, died *c.* 1302. She anticipated the ' modern ' Catholic devotion to the Sacred Heart of Jesus. Hopkins mentions her in his fragmentary sermon *On the Sacred Heart* (June 26, 1881). See *Note-books*, p. 295.

[3] *Jeremiah*, v. 6 ; *Inferno*, Canto 1.

I should never be guilty of now ",[1] we have to remember his peculiar position, and resist the temptation to pick on this or that as one of the " immaturities " in question. There are few, if any, passages in this poem which will strike *every* responsible critic as being faulty or immature.

When all allowances have been made, however, it will be found that *The Wreck of The Deutschland* has a completeness, an intellectual and emotional unity, a subtlety and variety of verbal orchestration which are unique not only in English but also, we believe, in the literature of the world. It is essentially a poem to be read aloud ; but like a sonata, it demands not a little interpretive skill. Its qualities are not to be gauged in one or two hasty, possibly peevish, readings. It is tart wine, but it mellows with keeping. The majority of sensitive readers will probably experience at first a mixture of attraction and repulsion. They will be attracted by what Father Lahey has called " the many marvellous lines which spangle the whole poem "—an unfortunate saying, which gives an erroneous impression of mere accidental and extrinsic felicity ; they will be repelled by the strangeness of its individual style. It is by now generally recognized, however, that familiarity with Hopkins's style dispels much of the strangeness without destroying the value of his innovation. The infinite variety of *The Deutschland* is in some measure due to its difficulty. As we re-read the poem, we are continually surprised by new aspects of its poetry, but we do not exhaust its intellectual possibilities. In Dixon's words, it is " enormously powerful ". It takes possession of the mind, fascinates, puzzles, exasperates, allures and recaptures it once again. Some may be, indeed have been, disturbed by the fervent irrationalities of its Trinitarianism and Marianism, its so-called martyrolatry and saint-worship ; they may, at first, resent the insidious persuasiveness of its appeal ; but they will probably be forced to agree with Longinus that it is not to persuasion but to ecstasy that passages of extraordinary genius carry the hearer. To the ardent Catholic the poem must always stand as one of the loftiest expressions of both the central problem and the crowning glory of his creed—the problem of tragedy and the triumph of faith. To others it will perhaps rather suggest the tragedy of faith and the triumph of pure poetry. There are

[1] *Letters*, vol. i. p. 119. Cf. *loc. cit.*—" I agree that the *Eurydice* shews more mastery in art, still I think the best lines in the *Deutschland* are better than the best in the other ". We cannot agree with this preference for the art of the *Eurydice*.

things in this poem which will never please the prejudiced, the occasional, the superficial and the uninformed reader. Moreover there will, perhaps, always be some people of taste and judgment who, like Robert Bridges, will be unable to pronounce it uniformly successful. Yet with an ever-growing number of serious students of literature it will undoubtedly take the rank it deserves beside the *Nativity Ode*, *Lycidas*, *Intimations of Immortality*, and *The Hound of Heaven*.

CHAPTER III

SONNET MORPHOLOGY

HOPKINS's most significant contribution to English verse morphology consisted in a number of variations played upon the traditional Petrarchan or Italian sonnet-form. The success of Wordsworth and Keats as sonneteers, together with the growing interest in the Shakespearian sequence, gave rise, in the nineteenth century, to a spate of sonnets ; and by 1883 sonneteering had become so common that Dixon was forced to write :

> " I wish the present run, or rather rush, upon the sonnet were over. It is a bore to see the inevitable ' regular structure ' week after week in all the ' cultured ' organs, the fifth verse forever virtuously turning the others, as it were, inside out." [1]

Hopkins must have felt a similar dissatisfaction at least six years earlier ; but his astute perception of the inherent fitness and beauty of the Petrarchan sonnet led him not to abandon the form but rather to develop its latent possibilities.

Such a representative collection as William Sharp's *Sonnets of the Century* (1888) shows an easy preponderance of poems which adhere fairly strictly to the Italian formula. The minor Victorians (Sharp, Lang, Lee-Hamilton and many more) were all expert imitative craftsmen, and the sonnet, besides providing a fascinating literary exercise, had the salutary effect of restraining a facile romanticism and the floods of what Hopkins might have described as a thin " Parnassian " garrulity.[2] With all but a few poets, such as Mrs. Browning and the Rossettis, Milton's trumpet had become a thin pipe playing a graceful academic tune ; at the same time, nearly all the respectable Petrarchan sonnets written within the last hundred years contrive to reflect and re-echo, with persistent faithfulness, the sonnet styles of the earlier masters—Milton, Wordsworth, and Keats, while some have been content to reproduce the pale, sentimental manner of William Lisle Bowles.

The Elizabethan or Shakespearian type has proved even more difficult to write well without obtrusive echoes of Shakespeare. The ghosts of memorable sonnets are hard to lay, and the reason

[1] *Letters*, vol. ii. p. 110. [2] See *Further Letters*, p. 69 ; also below, p. 80.

was once stated by Mr. T. S. Eliot. To create a form, he said, was not merely to invent a shape, a rhyme or a rhythm. It was also the realization of the whole appropriate content of that rhyme or rhythm. The sonnet of Shakespeare was not merely such and such a pattern, but a precise way of thinking and feeling.

For this reason Meredith was acting wisely when, in *Modern Love* (1862), he avoided undesirable echoes of Petrarch and his imitators by eschewing the Italian sonnet-form and building up a new sixteen-line stanza which was sufficiently like and sufficiently unlike the original medium of love-poetry to give piquancy to his new matter. Similarly, Wilfred Scawen Blunt varied the Shakespearian pattern in *The Mockery of Love*.

Perfect proof of the soundness of Mr. Eliot's dictum is provided by Francis Thompson. Here was a poet who, when his style was moulding itself organically from within, was as strongly individual as Crashaw. Yet if we take a line from one of his sonnets—

"When from the blossoms of the noiseful day",

we hear at once a distinct reminiscence of Shakespearian cadence:

"When to the sessions of sweet silent thought."

And does not the *whole* of the following sonnet by the same poet reproduce the master—Shakespeare's peculiar way of thinking and feeling?—

"Whenas my Life shall time with funeral tread
The heavy death-drum of the beaten hours,
Following, sole mourner, mine own manhood dead,
Poor forgot corse, where not a maid strows flowers;
When I you love am no more I you love,
But go with unsubservient feet, behold
Your dear face through changed eyes, all grim change
  prove;—
A new man, mockèd with misname of old;
When shamed love keeps his ruined lodging, elf!
When, cerémented in mouldering memory,
Myself is hearsèd underneath myself,
And I am but the monument of me:—
  O, to that tomb be tender then, which bears
  Only the name of him it sepulchres!"[1]

[1] "To a Child" (*Poems*, vol. ii.).

Consciously or unconsciously, diction, syntax and imagery have been made to conform to that rhythm which is the life-blood of this particular poetic body. We note the usual parallelism, the characteristic repetition (with or without variation) in lines 5, 7 and 11. Words and phrases like *funeral tread*, *misname of old*, *ceremented*, *monument of me*, etc., are all integral to the manner of Shakespeare's elegiac sonnets: it was obviously not Thompson's aim 'to infuse a new spirit into the old form without destroying its identity'.

Thompson's sonnet was probably written in the decade following Hopkins's death; it is, however, relevant to this discussion as showing what Hopkins might have been doing with the sonnet had he not taken elaborate precautions to avoid such unmistakable derivation and echo. As it was, his efforts to redeem the sonnet from a cramping standardization were not appreciated by those who should have been best qualified to judge them. When his friend Dixon tried to get some of Hopkins's work into a sonnet-anthology, published in 1882 by Hall Caine, the latter was prevented from discovering an important new poet by his theoretical presuppositions. In a letter to Bridges, Hopkins says:

> "Mr. Hall Caine is not going to print me, because the purpose of his work is to 'demonstrate the impossibility of improving upon the acknowledged structure whether as to rhyme scheme or measure'. Poor soul, he writes to me as to a she-bear robbed of her cubs. . . . To support himself he showed some of my sonnets to a 'critic of utmost eminence'; who thought with him." [1]

The 'critic' may have been Rossetti, Matthew Arnold or Watts-Dunton; but whoever it was, in the eyes of critical orthodoxy Hopkins the sonneteer was still-born and decent-buried in 1882. His fine (and prophetic) independence of spirit in this matter is shown in a remark to Bridges:

> "*Persuade* Hall Caine to put in my *Andromeda*! Absit." [2]

The conservatism of the nineteenth century attitude towards legitimate themes and forms in poetry was nowhere more manifest than in their belief about the inviolable nature of the Sonnet. A concise statement of this belief is contained in the Introduction to Sharp's *Sonnets of the Century* (1888)—

[1] *Letters*, vol. i. p. 128. [2] *Ibid.* vol. i. p. 132.

a rationale which was and still is widely regarded as authoritative and final.[1]

The rules there enumerated are well known, and although Hopkins had already broken many of them with remarkable results, one is bound to admit that the rules were deduced with sound Aristotelian logic from the best works of the few great sonneteers. The fallacy, however, in all such rules is in the assumption that there is no genuine poetic impulse, no strikingly new thought, imagery, diction and rhythm which cannot, by patient art, be forged into the standard pattern.

Sharp starts off with a good principle: he admits that

> "the mould is a very secondary matter compared with the substance that renders it vital, and . . . a fine poem in not altogether the best form is infinitely better than a poor or feeble one in a flawless structure."

Yet when he turns from a just appreciation of the Shakespearian form to consider the sonnets of Drummond, he makes the inconsistent statement that this poet's "essential" weakness was his inability to adopt any pure mould:

> "His sonnets may be regarded as English bastards of Italian parentage or as Italian refugees disguised in a semi-insular costume."[2]

But Drummond's attempt to weld the two standard forms into a third which would be more personal yet still a sonnet was not *prima facie* an "essential" weakness. Neither was the Spenserian mould the *primary* cause of Spenser's relative failure as a sonneteer. Drummond was a worthy precursor of Hopkins in the religious sonnet, but his essential weakness was indicated by Jonson: he "smelled of the schools"; he was often imitative, stiff in movement, lacking the master-touch. Again, Sharp virtually condemns as "bastard" the form of sonnet used by Blanco White in his famous *Night and Death*[3]; yet in a note to the poem he echoes the praise of Coleridge and pronounces it one of the noblest sonnets in any language.[4]

According to Sharp, there can be only three genuine sonnet types: (1) the Petrarchan or Natural Sonnet; (2) the English or Shakespearian; (3) the Miltonic (any Sonnet, whether the

[1] The purpose of the collection was to show "how much of the poetic thought of our own time has been cast in the mould of the sonnet, and how worthy that mould is of the honour". (*Introduction*, p. xxviii.)

[2] *Loc. cit.* p. lxi. [3] *Ibid.* p. lxiii. [4] *Ibid.* p. 332.

Petrarchan or Shakespearian mould, with unbroken continuity, metrically or otherwise, in its presentation).[1] In the wide scope thus afforded, he continues, no poet can with justice complain of too rigid limitations. Such objection-making as Hopkins's practice had already exemplified could be neatly rebuffed with the words adapted by Capel Lofft from Menzini :

> " No Procrustes has obliged you to be lopped to the measure of this bed ; Parnassus will not be in ruins even if you should not publish a sonnet."

Later, Sharp sets out " the ten absolutely essential rules for a good sonnet ".[2] The very first rule is the only one that Hopkins persistently broke as a matter of principle : *I. The sonnet must consist of fourteen decasyllabic lines.* There are also three other clauses (parts of Rules IV, V, and VII) which, even if he knew them, did not prevent Hopkins from " doing otherwise " or at least seeming to do so. The first of these, that " no terminal should also occur in any portion of any other line in the same system ", has been so freely honoured in the breach by Wordsworth, Keats, Rossetti and others that we are hardly shocked when Hopkins infringes it six times in one sonnet. Judging by Sharp's comment on certain " unpleasing assonantal relations " in three of Keats's sonnets, the clotted consonancies and vowel-chimes in Hopkins would have been met with an even stronger reproof than this :

> " These are genuine discords, and those who are unable to perceive them simply prove their deficiency in ear." [3]

The other two clauses, the one condemning " obscurity " and the other recommending " reticence ", are of doubtful validity, since neither term admits of precise definition ; hence their application, in the last resort, is a matter of personal caprice. If we accept the standard of lucidity set by the average Victorian sonneteer, then *The Windhover*, *Henry Purcell* and many other of Hopkins's so-called sonnets are, as sonnets, defective. The combination (desiderated by Sharp) of amplitude and reticence in expression is even harder to assess without personal predilection. *Carrion Comfort* and *Harry Ploughman*, *Hurrahing in Harvest* and *Felix Randal*, these are certainly " ample " in expression ; but are they also reticent ? Have they the " essential qualities " of dignity and repose ? Whatever we may think to-day, the

[1] *Loc. cit.* p. lxvi. [2] *Ibid.* p. lxxix. [3] *Ibid.* p. lxix.

school of Hall Caine and William Sharp would undoubtedly have demurred.

Returning to the question of pure form, we see that the canonization in Sonnet Law first of the English three-quatrains-and-a-couplet and then of Milton's disregard of the Italian *rima chiusa* and regular *volta* was merely a matter of time. Yet where passionate loyalties are involved, heresy continues to rankle. Milton's practice of running the octave into the sestet was condemned by Mark Pattison, who said that Milton thereby "missed the very end and aim of the Petrarchan scheme".[1] A similar attitude was taken up fifty years later by that sonnet-legislator *par excellence*, T. W. H. Crosland. In his book, *The English Sonnet* (1917), Crosland points out that Milton wrote only one formally perfect Petrarchan sonnet—*To Mr. H. Lawes*. Crosland, however, was such a rigid formalist that he was no more able than Pattison to perceive that Milton eschewed the regular *volta* in nine sonnets out of eighteen from a desire to achieve perfection in a different way. Having said that the "turn" in the middle of the eighth line of *On His Blindness* could easily be corrected (that is, shifted to its proper position at the end of the line), Crosland imputes the "blemish" to the fact that Milton

> "suffered from that grave infirmity of sonnet poets, namely, a disposition to the tolerance of purely formal or technical lapses in their own work."[2]

Actually, Milton must have realized the great effectiveness of the *volta*; but his deviation from the regular quatrain and tercet rhythm was a "lapse" in keeping with his great contribution to sonnet-music—the fresh, varied and passionate rhythm given to his verse by a free use of *vers enjambés* or "over-rove" lines. Wordsworth deemed the new form worthy of imitation; and although Hopkins wrote only one purely Miltonic sonnet (No. 50), three of his experiments in an expanded sonnet-form (Nos. 32, 42 and 48) follow the Miltonic principle—and not without success.

Crosland's critical dogmatism must be examined in some detail, since it represents the 'climate' of academic opinion into which Bridges was loth to precipitate his friend's poetry and into which Hopkins's sonnets (or sonnetal poems) were posthumously born in 1918.

[1] *Loc. cit.* p. lxii. [2] *The English Sonnet* (edn. of 1926), p. 38.

The highest poetry in English, we are told, has been written only in the decasyllabic line, a measure which owes its existence to the sonnet.[1] Any poem not written in decasyllables is not a sonnet,[2] and we must infer that Hopkins's appropriation of that term was a mistake. In a chapter called *Sonnet Legislation*, Crosland reacts against the eighteen alternatives given by Sharp for the rhyme-scheme of the sestet, and lays down the law, once for all, that only the two schemes used by Petrarch "are tolerable":

> "Deviation from the octet rule is *absolutely impermissible*. Deviations from the sestet rule are undesirable and when they run to couplets, final or otherwise, *altogether vicious*." [3]

We are to deduce therefore *a priori* and on metrical grounds that *The Windhover*, the *Heraclitean Fire* and *Spelt from Sibyl's Leaves* are not "the highest poetry"; that *The Starlight Night* and eight other sonnets are seriously vitiated in their sestets; and that Hopkins's sonnet-technique as a whole was (to use this critic's favourite expression) "past praying for".

Crosland regrets that it is, at present, impossible to formulate impeccable rules for every verse-form. But with the sonnet we know exactly how we stand:

> "For the Sonnet, on the other hand, the legislation is fixed, established, stable and unassailable. The observance of it means perfection; any breaking away from it means imperfection." [4]

Such morphological moralizing militates against the early acceptance of any poet who is genuinely original.[5] Admittedly, the Petrarchan sonnet-form, with its elaborate metrical, phonal, linguistic and psychological restrictions, is an ideal and powerful instrument, and in the hands of the right poet will at any time lead to one kind of perfection; but to say that any infringement of or deliberate breaking away from one or more of the rules must inevitably lead to imperfection is to ignore the diversity of human genius; it also presumes too much upon the supposed autonomy of *matter* on the one hand and *form* on the other.

[1] *The English Sonnet* (edn. of 1926), p. 30, Rule 15. Cf. p. 17: "Sublimity in English climbs on decasyllables".

[2] *Ibid.* p. 71. [3] *Ibid.* p. 39. [4] *Ibid.* pp. 46–7.

[5] Even Shakespeare knew this wagging of the legislative forefinger, for in one sonnet he speaks of

> "art made tongue-tied by authority
> And folly doctor-like controlling skill." (Sonnet lxvi.

Even Crosland admits, somewhat illogically, that the sonnet should have in it something which

> "Comes not by casting in a formal mould
> But from its own divine vitality"[1];

for the final word, however, we may go to Courthope, the apostle of "Law in Taste"[2]:

> "To attempt to confine the liberties of the poet by any *a priori* system of critical legislation is, as I have said more than once, worse than useless. Genius must be left to find out the law for itself."

It would be more accurate to say, perhaps, that genius must find out that *peculiar modification of the law* which best suits its own idiosyncrasy. That, as we shall see, is what Hopkins did with the traditional Sonnet.

Among Crosland's fixed and unassailable rules are the following:

> "Full pauses should never be employed after the first word in a line, or at the end of the first, second, third, fifth, sixth or seventh line of the octet, or at the end of the first or fifth line of the sestet."[3]

Hopkins, too, was an ascetic in poetry; but he preferred to choose his own modes of restraint and constriction. In his sonnets full pauses are to be found in all the places enumerated above, and some of his finest effects have been produced by breaking the rhythm at what were traditionally regarded as the most sensitive positions: it is noteworthy, moreover, that Hopkins, being also a theorist, was more aware of this sensitiveness in the verse than most other poets, with whom it is largely a matter of instinct or imitation.

His many sectional pauses after the first word or syllable are unprecedented in the English sonnet:

> "It gathers to a greatness, like the ooze of oil
> Crushed." (No. 7.)

> "Brute beauty and valour and act, oh, air, pride, plume here
> Buckle!" (No. 12.)

> "But tell me, child, your choice; what shall I buy
> You?—" (No. 39.)

[1] Wordsworth. [2] *Life in Poetry: Law in Taste* (1901), p. 283. [3] *Ibid.* p. 73.

"Cheer whom though? the hero whose heaven-handling
flung me, fóot tród
Me?" (No. 40.)[1]

These abrupt pauses and nervous rhythms are all part of a style and handling which contravene yet another established sonnet convention; as Crosland puts it in his seventeenth rule:

> "A sonnet must not be dramatic or exclamatory in its diction; it must not be overburdened with interrogative lines or sentences. . . ."[2]

Yet *Carrion Comfort*, which in its major and minor systems is a longer Petrarchan sonnet, contains as many as nine interrogations; and in spite of the "technical lapse", the poem is held by good critics to touch the sublime. Again, *The Starlight Night* is deservedly a popular anthology poem; yet its regular Petrarchan octave is a series of ten exclamations, while the sestet begins with five more.

In the same sonnet we note the irregular final pauses in lines 7 and 9; and Crosland's rule is again broken in line 5 of *Spring* and line 13 of *To what serves Mortal Beauty?* and "Thou art indeed just, Lord" (No. 50).

Sonnet Legislation of the above kind does not inhibit the true poet; it actually helps him by providing a standard, a criterion. But the dogmatism of the legislator tends to enslave the minds of many critics and readers to what Dr. I. A. Richards has called "technical presuppositions". We have said that Hopkins the sonneteer was buried in 1882; and even before he was disinterred and found to be skippingly alive in 1918, one critic had unwittingly done his best to keep him underground by announcing, in 1917:

> "*Mannered* sonnets are defective sonnets, even when, as is rarely the case, the manner is the poet's own."[3]

Hopkins, we suppose, must be classed as a "mannered" poet. He called the majority of his poems "sonnets" and thereby challenged comparison with the great masters of the Italian sonnet-form in English—Milton, Wordsworth, Keats, Rossetti and Mrs. Browning. Yet there would still be no harm in saying of Hopkins's sonnets, as we have heard it said of Shakespeare's: "They are not sonnets, but they are rare poems". The danger of Legislation becomes apparent when we hear: "Quite good,

[1] For other examples, see *Poems*, Nos. 11, 14, 25, 32, 39, 40 (line 9), 42, 44, 46, 47, 48, 50, 69. [2] *The English Sonnet*, p. 75. [3] Crosland, *loc. cit.* p. 97.

but not completely successful ; because after all, they are not *true* sonnets" ; or even the extreme view (encouraged in the less sensitive by Crosland's uncompromising formalism) : "What presumption, to call these sonnets ! "

We now pass on to a more detailed account of Hopkins's handling of the sonnet form. He broke away from certain regular sonnet-habits because the force of his own personality and inspiration demanded a greater freedom in both rhythm and diction. His was the passion that searches out, discovers and lays hold of the forms pre-ordained for its utterance ; but as he was different from all poets before him, so the form he ultimately adopted had to be different. Moreover, knowing "the fascination of what's difficult", he knew also the tedium of what has become easy through long practice. We are forced to believe, for instance, that the majority of Wordsworth's less interesting sonnets were produced with a fatal facility, like the portraits of Kneller.

In criticizing one of Dixon's sonnets, Hopkins remarks on

> "a certain stiffness, as the majority of Wordsworth's have, great sonneteer as he was ; but he wrote in 'Parnassian', that is the language and style of poetry mastered and at command but employed without any fresh inspiration." [1]

Certainly a great deal of Wordsworth, Coleridge, Shelley, Tennyson, Morris, Bridges and others is written in this 'Parnassian', and well over eighty per cent. of the sonnets written within the last fifty years are buckramed with the same style.

But although Hopkins disregarded many minor restrictions, he by no means rejected the essentials of sonnet form : he had, indeed, a passion for mathematically precise literary classifications which would impress any of the academic legislators.

The proportion of octave to sestet in the Italian sonnet was to him an absolute canon of perfection :

> "Now it seems to me that this division is the real characteristic of the sonnet, and what is not so marked off and moreover has not the octave again divided into quatrains is not to be called a sonnet at all. For in the cipher 14 there is no mystery, and if one does not know or avail oneself of the opportunities which it affords it is a pedantic encumbrance and not an advantage. The equation of the best sonnet is
>
> $(4+4)+(3+3)=2\cdot4+2\cdot3=2(4+3)=2\cdot7=14.$" [2]

[1] *Letters*, vol. ii. p. 72. [2] *Ibid.* vol. ii. p. 71.

This line of figures itself looks like a pedantic encumbrance; but the point Hopkins wishes to stress—the proportion of octave to sestet and the most effective subdivision of each part—is one in which he is in complete agreement with all the legislators. On the same grounds he justifies the Shakespearian form :

> " I recognize stricter and looser forms than the Shakespearian sonnet though it is a sonnet only *in genere* and not one if by sonnet you mean the Italian sonnet, which is the sonnet proper—but this is a question of names only—the Shakespearian sonnet is a very beautiful and effective species of composition in the kind. But then, though simpler, it is as strict, regular, and specific as the sonnet proper. Moreover it has the division into the parts 8+6, at all events 4+4+4+2." [1]

As we should expect from one whose most cherished aesthetic principle was that of *harmony in variety*, Hopkins esteems the sonnet proper as

> " one of the works of art of which the equation or construction is unsymmetrical in the shape $x+y=a$, where x and y are unequal in some simple ratio, as 2 : 1, 3 : 2, 4 : 3 : perhaps it would be better to say $mx+nx=a$."

He then refers to St. Augustine of Hippo's treatise *De Musica*, in which similar unsymmetrical proportions are worked out for the Hexameter and Ionic Trimeter. Some further analogies from pure music lead up to an interesting dogma :

> " I could show, if there were time, that it would be impracticable to have a ratio of the sort required with numbers higher than 4 and 3. Neither would 4 : 2 do, for it would return to 2 : 1, which is too simple."

Two further advantages of the sonnet proper are : (1) it is divided symmetrically into multiples of two, as all effects taking place in time tend to be ; and (2) it links together, first two even or symmetrical quatrains and then two uneven or unsymmetrical tercets.

On the rhyme-scheme Hopkins is equally emphatic :

> " And even the rhymes . . . I could shew are founded on a principle of nature and cannot be altered without loss of effect. But when one goes so far as to run the rhymes of the octet into the sestet a downright prolapsus or hernia takes place and the sonnet is crippled for life." [2]

[1] *Loc. cit.*

[2] *Loc. cit.* Dixon comments : " You demonstrate the regular form to be the most beautiful. . . ." (P. 80.)

Dixon pointed out that Surrey and Spenser had not merely imitated the Italian sonnet, but had tried to

> " have in English something like it : i.e. doing in English what it did in Italian, but yet not the same." [1]

This induced Hopkins to put his finger on what he considered the main weakness of the English sonnet, and thereby to prepare the critic's mind for his own peculiar innovation : this weakness was the very feature which Sharp and Crosland considered to be so characteristic and vital—the regular decasyllabic line :

> " The main reason why the sonnet has never been so effective in England as in Italy I believe to be this : it is not so long as the Italian sonnet ; it is not long enough. . . ." [2]

Such iconoclasm has to be supported by an analogy from architecture : in the Doric order, the Parthenon is the standard of perfection ; its proportions are the *typical* proportions :

> " But if a building is raised on a notably larger scale it will be found that these proportions . . . must be changed or the Order abandoned. Now if the Italian sonnet is one of the most successful forms of composition known, as it is reckoned to be, its proportions, inward and outward, must be pretty near perfection."

But although the English " sonnet proper " conforms to the Italian type in all other respects, the English decasyllable is shorter than the Italian *endecasillabo*, not by one syllable only, but frequently by three or four, owing to the slurring of final and initial vowels. Hopkins quotes :

> " Non ha l'ottimo⁀artista⁀alcun concetto
> Che⁀un marmor solo⁀in se non circonscriva."

> " Each line has two elisions and a heavy ending, or 13 syllables, although only 11 count in the scanning."

Actually, there are plenty of lines with fourteen or fifteen syllables, as this from Petrarch :

> E le braccia e le mani e i piedi e il viso.[3]

Hopkins also remarks that in the Italian the syllables themselves are longer :

> " We have seldom such a delay in the voice as is given to the syllable by doubled letters (as ' *o*ttimo ' and ' conc*e*tto ') or even by two or more consonants (as ' art*i*sta ' and ' c*i*rconscriva ') of any sort, read as Italians read."

[1] *Loc. cit.*, p. 80. [2] *Loc. cit.*, p. 85 *et seqq.* [3] *In Morte di M. Laura*, No. 24.

The English sonnet as a whole therefore suffers from a want "not of comparative but of absolute length". Perhaps, he adds, the proportion of the Italian to the English is 4 : 3 or 3 : 2—

> "The English sonnet is then in comparison with the Italian short, light, tripping and trifling." [1]

Many will protest angrily against the last epithet: it is too strong, or even absurd when we remember the dignity and weight of the best of Shakespeare, Milton and Wordsworth in this kind. Nevertheless, Hopkins has some justification for saying that this lightness in the English sonnet "has been instinctively felt". When the poet has not taken adequate measures to avoid it, the fastidious ear must often have noticed the weakness of lines which contain too many short or lightly stressed syllables, and which have in consequence less than five rhetorical stresses. Wordsworth undoubtedly is, as Hopkins pointed out, inclined to be somewhat light in his versification:

> "To level with the dust a noble horde,
> A bróthérhood of vénerable trées."

Again, the first line of Byron's noble sonnet—

> "Eternal Spirit of the chainless mind"—[2]

has only three long syllables to restrain the speed of the other seven; and Meredith's

> "The army of unalterable law" [3]

is so light as to be virtually only an accentual trimeter.

Hopkins allows that in the best English sonnets this defect of "lightness" is countered or overcome by various devices:

> ". . . by the mere gravity of the thought, which compels a longer dwelling on the words, as in Wordsworth . . . by inversion and a periodic construction . . . there is a good deal of this in Bridges' sonnets; or by breaks and pauses, as
>
> 'Captain or colonel or knight-at-arms'
>
> or by many monosyllables, as
>
> 'Both them I serve and of their train am I':
>
> this is common with τοὺς περὶ Swinburne; or by the weight of the syllables themselves, strong or circumflexed and so on, as may be remarked in Gray's sonnet, an exquisite piece of art, whatever Wordsworth may say.
>
> 'In vain to me the smiling mornings shine—' [4]"

[1] *Loc. cit.* p. 86.
[2] *On the Castle of Chillon.*
[3] *Lucifer in Starlight.*
[4] See Preface to the *Lyrical Ballads* (1800).

He might have noted also that Shakespeare's lines are seldom light, owing to his skilful use of packed or heavily charged verses —well imitated in Francis Thompson's

> " Your dear face through changed eyes, all grim change
> prove "

with its three long vowels and six diphthongs.

Both the weakness and the various remedies have been recognized by all the best legislators ; but Hopkins's minute examination of these points is important as showing that when he rejected the ' iambic ' decasyllable in favour of his own counterpointed, outriding and sprung rhythms, he did so not in ignorant caprice but in the full knowledge of what he was doing. He wanted the maximum length and weight of the Italian sonnet and also, in order to escape the " Parnassian " rut, enough syllabic elbow-room to create his own diction, texture and rhythmic pattern.

Hopkins came to the conclusion that the mechanical difficulty of " lightness " could best be overcome by a mechanical remedy :

> " none, I think, meets it so well as these ' outriding ' feet I sometimes myself employ, for they more than equal the Italian elisions and make the whole sonnet rather longer, if anything, than the Italian is. Alexandrine lines (used throughout) have the same effect." [1]

These outriding half feet or hangers, we are told in the *Author's Preface* (page 5), are marked " by a loop underneath them, and plenty of them will be found ". They are to be found, however, only in the manuscripts, for without the help of the nether loop the reader who has not made a careful study of the poet's theory will stand little chance of distinguishing accurately between an outride and an ordinary foot in ' falling ' rhythm. Ignorance of the true nature of the outride has not prevented readers of fine ear from attaining an adequate grasp of the poet's rhythmical intentions ; but a more precise and widespread knowledge of those intentions will remove many misunderstandings and make the reading of Hopkins less difficult and discouraging at the outset.

Outrides first appear in *God's Grandeur* and three other sonnets of 1877. *Hurrahing in Harvest* has the following note :

> " Sonnet (sprung and outriding rhythm. Take notice that the outriding feet are not to be confused with dactyls or paeons

[1] *Letters*, vol. ii. p. 87.

though sometimes the line might be scanned either way. *The strong syllable in an outriding foot has always a great stress and after the outrider follows a short pause.* The paeon is easier and more flowing)." [1]

Turning to MS. "B", from which the text is taken, we read :

> "Summer énds now ; now, bárbarous in béauty, the stóoks arise
> Aróund ; up abóve, what wínd-walks ! what lóvely behávіour
> Of sílk-sack clóuds ! . . ."

We have marked the stresses in order to show how the outride affects the rhythm of the whole line. It is convenient here to consider the rhythm as 'rising', so that the looped half-foot *follows* the regular foot. Thus the "great stress" on the first syllable of "barbarous" is natural, but the "short pause" after the outride would hardly be suspected without the notation. In the next line, however, the pause after "walks" is as natural as the double stress on "wind".

On referring to the *Preface*, we find that *hangers* or *outrides* are given as the second of two licences natural to sprung rhythm, the other being "rests, as in music". The outride is defined as

> "one, two, or three slack syllables added to a foot and not counted in the nominal scanning. They are so called because they seem to hang below the line or ride forward or backward from it in another dimension than the line itself, according to a principle needless to explain here." [2]

Now the nominal scanning of the lines quoted above can be heard when they are read aloud *without* the looped syllables. When the latter are restored, moreover, we can surely feel

[1] *Poems*, p. 107.

[2] *Poems*, p. 4. A hint as to the "principle" which Hopkins finds needless to explain and also as to the origin of the word "hanger" as an alternative for outride may perhaps be discovered in a *Journal* jotting on the τύχῃ τέχνην στέρχουσα of natural inscape in trees. After a fall of snow, he says : "The limes, elms and Turkey oaks it crisped beautifully as with young leaf. Looking at the elms from underneath, you saw every wave in every twig . . . and to the *hangers* and flying sprays it restored, to the eye, the inscapes they had lost". (*Note-books*, p. 130.)

These analogous uses of the word "hanger" are typical of Hopkins's fondness for relating architectural to natural forms (e.g. *ibid.* pp. 109 and 146) ; and the freedom and "barbarous" beauty of his own verse rhythms suggest a comparison with just such a tree-scape as that we have quoted. Metrical "hangers", like flying buttresses, are both functional and decorative.

how they ride off from the line or hang below the line while still remaining part of it. On this principle, the otherwise obscure rhythm of the last line of this sonnet can be thus elucidated :

" The heárt réars wíngs bóld and bólder
And húrls (for him,) O hálf hurls éarth (for him) óff under his féet." [1]

Despite its name, the outride, in its simplest form, is not an entirely new thing in English verse. It is more than probable that Hopkins drew the first idea of it from Shakespeare or Milton. In a letter to Dixon (Oct. 5, 1878), he says that outriding feet are found " in Shakespeare's later plays, but as a licence, whereas mine are rather calculated effects ". Abbott notes the frequency with which an extra syllable is added before a pause ; it is usually at the end of the second foot :

" For míne own sáfeties ; you máy be ríghtly júst "
(*Mac.*, IV. iii. 30),

but sometimes at the end of the third or fourth foot :

" For góodness dáres not chéck thee ; wear thóu thy wróngs "
(*ibid.* IV. iii. 33) ;

" With áll my hónours ón my bróther : whereón "
(*Tempest*, I. ii. 127).[2]

Again, under the headling " Apparent and Doubtful Alexandrines ",[3] Abbott quotes from both early and late plays a number of lines in which the redundant syllables are explained as being slurred, contracted, or entirely omitted in pronunciation :

" Were rích and hónourable ; besídes the géntlemén "
(*Two Gent.* III. i. 64).

[1] This sonnet has three other outrides :

" Rapturous love's greeting of réaler, of róunder replíes ? " (Line 8.)

" And the azurous hung hílls are his wórld-wíelding shóulder." (Line 9.)

[2] *Shakespearian Grammar* (1874), p. 331, § 454. Cf. *Milton's Prosody*, p. 6, where Bridges shows the frequency of the " mid-verse extra-metrical " syllable in the early Shakespearian work—*Comus* : " And as I past I wor*shipt* : if that you seek " (302), etc.

[3] *Op. cit.* pp. 397–401.

Here the last word might have been pronounced " genmen " ; but a similar explanation could hardly be adduced for

" For ínequálity : but lét your réason sérve "
(*Meas. for Meas.*, V. i. 65) ;

" Cálls her a nónpareil ; I néver sáw a wóman "
(*Tempest*, III. ii. 108).

Although in his *Preface* Hopkins admits outrides in sprung rhythm, he intended them originally to be an addition to counterpoint rhythm only. In 1877 he wrote :

> " There are no outriding feet in the *Deutschland*. An outriding foot is, by a sort of contradiction, a recognized extra-metrical effect. It is, and is not, a part of the metre ; not part of it, not being counted, but part of it by producing a calculated effect which tells in the general success. But the long, e.g. seven-syllabied, feet of the *Deutschland* are strictly metrical. Outriding feet belong to counterpointed verse, which supposes a well-known and unmistakable or unforgettable standard rhythm : the *Deutschland* is not counterpointed ; counterpoint is excluded by sprung rhythm. But in some of my sonnets I have mingled the two systems : this is the most delicate and difficult business of all." [1]

Hopkins wished to preserve a clear distinction between sprung and counterpointed rhythm. While the former was admirably suited to a long and richly varied ode like *The Deutschland*, he was at first chary about introducing poly- and mono-syllabic feet into an organism so delicately balanced as the Italian sonnet-form—feeling, perhaps, that much of the grace, dignity and repose peculiar to the form would be lost. But as his technical mastery increased, he was led naturally into innovations and complexities which, as we shall see, gave a perennial freshness to his work.

Plain counterpoint arises when " reversal is repeated in two feet running, especially to include the sensitive second foot ". It is illustrated in two lines of Hopkins's first mature sonnet, *God's Grandeur* : here, as almost everywhere else in the MSS., the reversed feet are marked by " twirls " :

" The world is charged with the grandeur of God . . ."

" Generations have trod, have trod, have trod . . ." [2]

[1] *Letters*, vol. i. p. 45. Incidentally, we have found nothing longer than a six-syllabled foot in *The Deutschland* : " Fínger of a ténder of, Ō of a féathery délicacy . . ." (Stanza 31.)

[2] MS. " A ". In his *Preface* (p. 5), Hopkins has mistakenly put ⌒ for ⌒. The sign ⌒ is described in the *Harry Ploughman* MS. " B " as a " quiver or circumflexion, making one syllable nearly two " (e.g. " soared " " curls ").

Without the notation in the first line, the poet's rhythmical intention would be far from obvious. The same guidance was proffered, perhaps wisely, at the opening of *In the Valley of the Elwy* :

" I remember a house where all were good . . ."

and in lines 3 and 4 of No. 50. Yet once we have grasped the principle of counterpoint and can " supply mentally the conventionally fixed form at the time when we are actually reading another one ",[1] the twirls are no longer necessary in the text and may be safely confined to the expositions of the prosodist.

The relation of the outride to counterpoint rhythm is thus described by the poet :

> ". . . by means of ' outrides ' . . . you will find in some of my sonnets and elsewhere I secure a strong effect of double rhythm, of a second movement in the verse besides the primary and essential one, and this comes to the same thing or serves the same purpose as counterpointing by reversed accents as in Milton." [2]

This function of the outriding half-foot in setting up a counter-rhythm may be seen also in Shakespeare :

" Is not so estimable, profitable neither "
(*Merch. of Venice*, I. iii. 167).

" With all prerogative ; hence his ambition growing "
(*Tempest*, I. ii. 105).

This effect in Hopkins is illustrated by the following lines from *Duns Scotus's Oxford* :

" Ónce encóunter in, here cóped and póisèd pówers ; "
" RíValled ínsight, be ríval Ítaly or Greéce ; " [3]

In each line, after the outride, there is a perceptible change from ' falling ' to ' rising ' rhythm.

As will be seen from the transcription given below of the full MS. notation of certain sonnets, Hopkins was not always consistent in his marking of outrides. While most of the nether

[1] *Letters*, vol. ii. p. 41. [2] *Ibid.* vol. i. p. 41.
[3] MS. " B ". The latter line is equivalent to

" Rivalled insight, be rival, etc."

loops do not materially alter our own spontaneous rhythmical interpretation of the line, there are some syllables unlooped which are metrically identical with others that carry the notation ; such a dubious distinction is in the sonnet just quoted :

> " Of réalty the rárest-véinèd unrráveller ; a nót "

Why is not the last syncopated syllable of " unraveller " an outride also ? The alliteration puts a great stress on the syllable " -rav- ", and the semi-colon after this word has far more realty than the theoretical pause after the marked outride.

The easiest way for the reader to master the outride without the aid of notation is to study its use in the one poem in which it is employed with positional regularity. Of *The Bugler's First Communion* Hopkins says :

> " There is an outride between the 3rd. and 4th. foot of the fourth line of each stanza." [1]

This fourth line has five stresses, and in nine of the twelve stanzas the outride is quite easily detected ; e.g.—

> " Sháres their bést gifts súrely, fall hów things wíll),"
>
> " Bréathing blóom of a chástity in mánsex fíne."
>
> " An oúr day's Gód's own Gálahad. Though thís child's dríft."

In three lines, however, the inevitable whimsy appears, and the post-outride pause (if theory holds) is a matter of subtle expressional reading :

> " Low-látched in léaf-light hóusel his too húge godhéad."
>
> " Híes héadstrong to its wéllbeing of a self-wíse self-wíll ! " [2]

Slight pauses after both these outrides *could* be justified ; but many people would prefer a different reading—a pause after " wellbeing ", for instance.

This poet's desire to increase the length of the sonnet-line, to give the maximum variety to its rhythm and at the same time to help the struggling reader over all the new metrical

[1] *Poems*, p. 109, No. 23.

[2] MS. " B ". The scansion of the last line of the poem, together with other problems of the outride, are dealt with below in Appendix B (p. 284).

stiles, caused him to invent other marks which may as well be examined at once.

In conjunction with the outride, we find the " hurried foot ", which is indicated by a musical phrase-mark. Harry Ploughman,

" Though as a beechbole firm, finds his, as at a rollcall, rank . . .

" He leans to it, Harry bends, look. Back, elbow, and liquid waîst
In him all quaîl to the wallowing o' the plough : " [1]

The metre of this poem is described as " very heavily loaded sprung rhythm ",[2] and the three- and four-syllabled hurried feet (or rather, hurried slack syllables, for the stress is not included in the phrasing) are obviously intended to be pronounced in the time normally allowed for two syllables—not theoretically and approximately only, as with the paeons and longer feet of *The Deutschland*, but with a precision which is at once metronomic and realistic.[3] Yet in the second hurried foot, the ideal enunciation is physically unattainable. We can hear it mentally, however, and even the best we can do rhetorically still suggests the roll of the drum as the company dresses by the right. The next hurried foot shows the same perversity of ignoring the comma ; but the effect of excited utterance is both colloquial and poetically satisfying. Yet would the line be less satisfying if another outride had been substituted for the hurried foot ?—

" He leans to it, Harry bends, look. . . ."

The rhythm of the line is strong and beautiful without any notation at all ; for in this poem, as almost everywhere in music, some latitude of interpretation may be safely allowed.

Besides the loops illustrated above, Hopkins used also the shorter ⌒, which " slurs " two syllables into one, as in the Italian *endecasillabo* :

" Those years and years by of world without event
That in Majorca Alfonso watched the door." [4]

More useful, though by no means indispensable, is the bracketing of two adjacent syllables by the mark ⌐¬, which means that " though one has and the other has not the metrical stress, in the recitation-stress they are to be about equal " ; it occurs eleven

[1] MS. " A ". See the facsimile opposite p. 262 of *Letters*, vol. i. [2] *Poems*, p. 116.
[3] See note on facsimile of *Harry Ploughman* (*loc. cit.*). [4] *Poems*, No. 49.

times in *To what serves Mortal Beauty* and five times in *Tom's Garland*, e.g.:

> "Our law says: Love what are | love's worthiest, were all known;
> World's loveliest—men's selves. Self | . . ."[1]

This sonnet in alexandrines (No. 38) is described as "Common rhythm highly stressed"; and as in No. 42, the stressing of syllables which would normally be light gives rhetorical weight to the philosophic argument. The principle, however, is implicit in Shakespeare's

> "Shall Time's best jewel from Time's chest lie hid?
> Or what strong hand can hold his swift foot back,"[2]

and in Francis Thompson's

> "Your dear face through changed eyes, all grim change prove";[3]

but few English poets (and those rarely) have used the device so skilfully as Hopkins in making the semantic rhythm (the rhythm of thought, meaning) break across the metrical pattern —a kind of counterpoint which, as we shall show in our next volume, was common in the Greek choric poetry.

Of the other marks used by Hopkins the most interesting is the pause (⌒), as illustrated in the *Harry Ploughman* MS. This, we are told, does not differ much from the strong stress (^), for with both the syllable thus dwelt on or prolonged "need not have the metrical stress." Now in his placing of these metrical stresses Hopkins is sometimes so oddly perverse that we can well understand the desire and ultimate decision of Bridges to omit from the printed text all but the very few which seemed absolutely essential. The fourth line of *Harry Ploughman* runs:

> "Héad and fóot, shôuldér and shánk—"

This must mean that the second syllable in "shoulder" is not to be elided but is to be given a certain prominence, as in the rifleman's command, "Shóuld-ér . . . árms!" But the metrical stress, "marked in doubtful cases only" often *creates* a doubt by standing over the most unlikely syllables. In the same poem we read:

> "And features ín flesh whát deed he each must do—"

and

> "Them—broad ín bluffhíde his frówning féet lashed!"

[1] See *Letters,* vol. ii. p. 129. [2] Sonnet LXV. [3] See sonnet quoted above.

Yet because we may prefer (as Bridges did) a more natural and facile reading of these lines, putting our metrical stress on "flesh", "deed", and "bluff-", it would be foolish to conclude too hastily that the poet's own scansion was mere aberration and eccentricity. The tendency of modern speech is to slur or muffle the preposition, a practice which is unsympathetic to poetry, where every word should have its significance. Moreover, Hopkins probably did not intend the natural vigorous speech-rhythm to be entirely suppressed: that, indeed, would be quite contrary to his general theory and practice. He wanted a subtle compromise, in which the reader hears the counterpoint of two rhythms (the metrical and the oratorical) while giving a full sonority to every word. This is what Hopkins means by calling the rhythm "very heavily loaded": the coefficient of stress, as it were, is higher than in other poetry, and more degrees of variation are to be registered.

Failure to understand this, together with an inability to perceive the poet's true meaning, has led one critic to condemn Hopkins's stress-marks at the end of *The Lantern out of Doors*:

> "Christ minds; Christ's interest, what to avow or amend
> There, éyes them, heart wánts, care háunts, foot fóllows kínd,
> Their ránsom, théir rescue, ánd first, fást, last fríend."

Mr. Louis MacNeice (having erroneously placed the stress on "foot" instead of on "follows") comments thus:

> "These are strong and effective lines, but Hopkins's notation makes them vicious. Merely through sticking to his fetish of five stresses per line, he (a) goes miles away from his admired rhythms of ordinary speech, and (b) (which matters more) slurs over, as unstressed, words—'heart', 'care', 'rescue', 'first', 'last'—which, both for their sound-value and their meaning, *ought not* to be slurred over." [1]

Mr. MacNeice's animadversion is, to our mind, painfully slipshod. Passing over the singular view that to preserve the traditional five-stress verse of the sonnet is a fetish, we assert that here Hopkins goes no further from ordinary speech-rhythms than a packed rhetorical poetry legitimately *may* go; that the unstressed words mentioned by Mr. MacNeice are not, in reading aloud, "slurred over" at all, but are given at least seven-eighths of the weight given to the stressed syllables; and that the stresses

[1] *Modern Poetry* (1938), p. 124.

on " their " and " and " in line 3 can be justified as pointing the precise meaning that Hopkins wished to convey.

The question of the pentameter with heavy unstressed syllables has been authoritatively treated by Bridges [1]; Milton's

> " Rocks, cáves, lakes, féns, bogs, déns and shádes of déath "

(ii. 621) is to be read, he says, as here accented :

> " and if the heavy syllables between these accents are themselves stressed, then the accented syllables will, by the enforcing of the voice-tone, be able to subordinate them."

In Hopkins's second line, the first word is to be treated as an outride (" aménd there ") ; and apart from this peculiarity, the spondaic movement of the line is not unfamiliar to readers of Shakespeare and Donne.

In the last line, the stressing of " their " instead of " rescue " is at first sight odd ; but this " enforcing of voice-tone " on " their " while not obscuring the strong sense-relation between " ransom," and " rescue ", introduces an additional overtone of meaning—the idea that Christ died even for those attractive strangers, half-friends and fleeting acquaintances, many of whom, in their pagan self-sufficiency, are (alas !) indifferent to the proffered salvation. So far from eschewing speech-rhythm, Hopkins seems to be adopting the accent of popular oratory : " Workers, this is your *chance* ; this is *your* opportunity, if only, etc." Yet since he is writing a sonnet in Standard Rhythm, he contrives to make the line scan as an ' iambic ' decasyllable by the elision of the second syllable of " rescue " before the rhetorically emphatic " ând ". Nevertheless, the fact that Hopkins intended the word " rescue " to be given its full weight in recitation is proved by the notation in the earlier MS. " A " version :

> " Their ransom, their rescue, and first, fast. . ."

Here the third foot " réscue, and ", is reversed, " rescue " taking the stress which MS. " B " gives to " and " ; this may be rationalized in conventional prosody as

— –́ | ˘ –́ | –́ — | — –́ | — –́

or, if the quantities are suspect,

˘ –́ | ˘ –́ | –́ ˘ | ˘ –́ | ˘ –́

[1] *Milton's Prosody*, p. 40.

Of the two notations, that printed by Bridges from B is the more satisfactory, provided the natural accent of "rescue" is not suppressed.

Pace Mr. MacNeice, no poet ever took such elaborate precautions as Hopkins to ensure that important words should not be "slurred over". In a note attached to the early MS. "A" version of *The Starlight Night*, he says:

> "To be read . . . slowly, strongly marking the rhythm and *fetching out the syllables*."

This process of "fetching out" is strikingly illustrated by the notation of the first copy of *Walking by the Sea*:[1]

> "Left hand off land I hear the lark ascend
> With rash-fresh more, repair of skein and score,
> Race wild reel round, crisp, coil, deal down to floor
> And spill music till there's none left to spend."[2]

The circumflexions and the pause both indicate an abnormal lengthening of long syllables, while the upright accents, equivalent to staccato dots in music, show that fourteen consecutive syllables (including the whole of one line) are to be pronounced with a crisp and almost equal emphasis.

Hopkins used altogether in the various MSS. some twenty-one different recitation marks.[3] His self-justification for so much unconventional ingenuity is as follows:

> "My meaning surely *ought* to appear of itself; but in a language like English, and in an age of it like the present, written

[1] MS. "A". The revised version, in B, with the title *The Sea and the Skylark*, is the one printed (*Poems*, No. 11).

[2] The mark ∞, on "music", is a variant of ∽=reversed foot.

[3] They are as follows:

(*a*) *Heavy stress* (metrical): ˝ and ̏ ; ∨ (*Echoes*, MS. "A").
(non-metrical): ∧ ; > ; "AND" (No. 12).

(*b*) *Normal stress* (metrical): ´ and ` ("heard stress" and "dumb stress" marked by • and ₒ below the syllable—No. 42); a "great colon" before the stressed syllable (⁚) in sprung rhythm only; ∽ (reversed foot).
(non-metrical): ˈ (=crisply or staccato).

(*c*) *Lengthening*: ⌒ (dwell); ∽ (circumflexion).

(*d*) *Phrasing*: ⌐¬ (equal recitation-stress); ⌒ (elision and linked rhyme); ‿ (outride); ⁀ (hurried foot).

(*e*) *Rest*: | (caesural mark in alexandrines); . . (.) (hiatus, as in Nos. 32 and 36; hiatus without dots in No. 26).

(*f*) *Direction*: "rallentando" written three times: No. 8, second half of line 9; No. 11, line 14; No. 14, second half of line 4.

words are really matter open and indifferent to the receiving of different and alternative verse-forms, some of which the reader cannot possibly be sure are meant unless they are marked for him. Besides, metrical marks are for the performer and such marks are proper in every art." [1]

Yet the fact that so many of his stress-marks overlap in function, while others are nowhere precisely defined, proves that he never really perfected his system of metrical notation. In 1883 he wrote to Bridges :

> " You were right to leave out the marks : they were not consistent for one thing and are always offensive. Still there must be some. Either I must invent a notation applied throughout as in music or else I must only mark where the reader is likely to mistake, and for the present this is what I shall do." [2]

The MS. of *Harry Ploughman* shows that in 1887 he had not abandoned the idea of working out a complete notation ; indeed, some of the metrical marks here would seem to many readers redundant. We must candidly admit two facts : first, that some of Hopkins's most successful rhythms are not based entirely upon speech-rhythm but are a highly artificial fusing of speech-rhythm and *musical* rhythm—that is, the rhythm of sung or chanted words ; second, that whereas some of the marks, like those indicating stress, outrides and hurried feet, do actually save the reader's time by clarifying the rhythm at once,[3] other marks, like the " dwell " and " circumflexion ", impart a touch of affectation by underlining the obvious or by overdoing the expressiveness already inherent in the choice and ordering of the words.

Still, the omission from the printed text of almost all the notation is not altogether satisfactory : the reader should have the means of discovering the poet's precise intentions. To this end a compromise might still be effected by the inclusion of a more complete and scholarly Introduction—a " grammar " of the poet's rhythm, containing well chosen examples of the manuscript notation.

By the various means described above, Hopkins aimed at extending the English sonnet to the size of the Italian or even of the French. Sometimes he went far beyond his prototypes ; at other times (as in *Andromeda*) he is content with a form which

[1] *Letters*, vol. i. p. 265. [2] *Ibid.* p. 189. Cf. p. 215.

[3] Cf. " I cannot identify with certainty a single outride in *Felix Randal* ". (Reviewer in *The New Statesman*, March 15, 1919.) See below, p. 216.

is in the aggregate a bare five syllables longer than the most regular English type. But taken as a whole, the sonnet-form in Hopkins's hands is brimful like a lake after heavy rains: we plumb its maximum depth. By "fundamental brain-work", he succeeded in making the sonnet not only a new but a bigger thing, a more significant poetic unit.

It has been frequently stated by critics that Hopkins, towards the end of his life, was purifying his style and stabilizing his rhythm: indeed, he himself said that he hoped to attain a "more Miltonic balance". In the words of Mr. Charles Williams:

> "His poetic tricks, his mannerisms, his explorations in the technique of verse, are not in the earlier poems and they are disappearing from the later. Had he lived, those tricks might have seemed to us no more than the incidental excitements of a developing genius." [1]

That statement (with its undefined condemnation in the word "tricks") does less than justice to the sincerity and technical achievement of Hopkins's middle mature period; it also ignores the bold experimentation of poems written on the very eve of his death. We cannot agree with the implied opinion that the sonnets written, say, between 1879 and 1885 are in some way deficient as poetry; are interesting merely as tentative, transitional exercises.

Actually, no other poet has rung so many various and intrinsically beautiful changes on the fundamental sonnet-form. The tragic and intensely personal subjects of the later sonnets of desolation give them a greater significance in the eyes of many readers; but the sonnets of the middle period (including the masterly *Sibyl's Leaves*) deserve to be honoured with equal attention in any thorough survey of the poet's technical development. To such a chronological classification we now proceed.

Hopkins's sonnets fall into certain time-groups which correspond roughly with the main types of sonnet-form which he either adopted or invented. They do not correspond exactly, because the poet was never static: he was forever trying new methods, shifting the emphasis, lengthening or shortening the line, distending or compressing the musical and semantic phrase to meet the changing demands of matter and mood.

[1] *Poems of G. M. H., Introduction,* p. xvi. Cf. *ibid.* p. 99.

The first period and group comprises the eight sonnets written about the year 1865. In our next volume these will be discussed as poetry, but they are relevant here since they demonstrate the fact that Hopkins began his work as a sonneteer by faithfully copying the best models. The first four sonnets (Type A) are Miltonic in structure.[1] They follow the original Italian rhyme-scheme, including that arrangement for the sestet which Rossetti and Sharp considered the most satisfactory (C–D–C–D–C–D).

In the next two sonnets, those addressed *To Oxford* (Type B), the *volta* is observed ; but in the two that follow (*Easter Communion* and " See how Spring opens ") the division into octave and sestet is, apart from the rhymes, merely typographical. These 'prentice sonnets waver between Petrarch and Milton in the matter of form, while the diction owes much to Shakespeare and Drayton.

The second period (Type C) begins with *God's Grandeur* and includes all the sonnets of the year 1877 with the exception of *The Windhover* (No. 12) and the next three poems. At this time, Hopkins begins to append to each poem a short note describing its rhythm, and the six sonnets of Type C are all in Standard Rhythm with varying proportions of counterpointed and sprung elements. The word " opened " in the metrical description of No. 8 is obscure ; but it probably epitomizes the phrase " opening with sprung leadings " in No. 9, and refers to the downright sprung rhythm of the first line of both octave and sestet ; yet three of the four " openings " in Nos. 9 and 10 would normally be called ' trochaic catalectic '.

In *The Sea and the Skylark* (No. 11) and *In the Valle of the Elwv* (No. 16) we come to " that most delicate and difficult business of all ".–standard rhythm, in parts sprung and in others counterpointed (Type C_1). These prosodic facts, however, do not force undue difficulties upon the reader who has already caught the movement of the four preceding sonnets. The third line of No. 16 does, indeed, admit of two scansions :

(1) " Cómfort | ing sméll | bréathed at | very⁀ént | éring "
(2) " Cómforting | sméll | bréathed at | véry | énterîng " ;

but in spite of the unstressed rhyme-syllable in the latter, this ' sprung ' reading is to be preferred as being more natural and, in expressing a spontaneous delight, more imitative.

[1] *Note-books*, pp. 42–4.

The poems of Type C contain only one example of the outride, and that is an entirely anomalous double hanger (or, more probably, an oversight) in line 3 of No. 7 :

" It gathers to a greatness, like the ooze of oil . . ." [1]

In the four sonnets of Type D, however (Nos. 12, 14, 15 and 20) both the paeonic foot and the outride are freely used. The sonnet-mould received its first considerable stretching in the muscular proportions of *The Windhover*, which is the crowning masterpiece of the second period.

Never before had the canonical and " essential " iambic decasyllable been subjected to such a racking as in

" kíng-
dom of dáylight's dáuphin, dapple-dáwn-drawn Fálcon, in
his ríding . . ."

Never had it been expanded by heating and then suddenly contracted by cooling as in :

" As a skáte's heel sweeps smóoth on a bów-bend : the húrl
and glíding
Rebúffed the bíg wínd. My heárt in híding . . ."

The rhythm is described as " Falling paeonic, sprung and outriding ". Hopkins must have meant what he said ; and since the outrides are clearly marked on both A and B manuscript, it follows that the scansion of this sonnet given by Father Lahey in the *Life* (p. 103) is not an accurate guide to the poet's intention. Having called the first line " a regular iambic pentameter rove over " (as though the metre were counterpointed only), he describes the first four syllables of the next line (" -dom of daylight's ") as a first paeon—a scansion which ignores both stress and quantity. Not only does he omit the two outrides in this line, but on another page he gives, as an " admirable example " of the outride, the words *dapple-dawn-drawn Falcon, in his*—a phrase which does not conform to either definition or notation.[2] Against line 8 he writes " Hangers ", when in fact not one outride is indicated in his scansion or in the MSS.

[1] MS. " A ". [2] P. 94.

The following notation and metrical reading are derived from a collation of the MSS.[1] :

"I caught this morning morning's minion, king-
    dom of daylight's dauphin, dapple-dawn-drawn Falcon,
        in his riding
  Of the rolling level underneath him steady air, and
    striding
High there, how he rung upon the rein of a wimpling wing
In his ecstasy! then off, off forth on swing,
  As a skate's heel sweeps smooth on a bow-bend : the hurl
    and gliding
  Rebuffed the big wind. My heart in hiding
Stirred for a bird,—the achieve of, the mastery of the thing!

Brute beauty and valour and act, oh, air, pride, plume, here
  Buckle! AND the fire that breaks from thee then, a
    billion
Times told lovelier, more dangerous, O my chevalier!
  No wonder of it : sheer plod makes plough down sillion
Shine, and blue-bleak embers, ah my dear,
  Fall, gall themselves, and gash gold-vermilion."

This scansion could be further simplified by ignoring the outrides—that is, by treating each one as part of a paeon or dactyl. Even as it stands, it does away with Father Lahey's multiplicity of terms—Rocking Feet, Hypermetric, Catalectic, Second Paeonic; for although Hopkins himself admits 'rocking' feet in sprung rhythm[2] (and the 'rocking' foot is a pleasing variation of the 'falling' or 'rising' foot), yet the idea seems to be precluded by the more important conception of "rove-over" lines, a device which ensures organic continuity and a cumulative rhythm.

A very curious expedient was the writing of 'AND' in capitals (line 10). This could only be to point out that although

[1] A and B. Only the eight outrides marked *below* the syllables are from the MSS. Two others (lines 4 and 6), together with the mark ⌐¬ in four places, seem both logical and useful. > is from MS. "A".

[2] Author's *Preface*, p. 1.

the word counts in the scansion merely as a slack syllable, in the actual reading aloud it must be pronounced with speed and stress ; by this means the poet hoodwinks the academic exciseman and slips in what is virtually a six-stress line under cover of a pentameter. And does not the sense justify this liberty ?

The metrical form of *The Windhover* is continued, though with less daring and *élan*, in *Hurrahing in Harvest*, *The Caged Skylark*, and in the first sonnet of the poet's third period of sonnet activity—*Duns Scotus's Oxford* (1879). But the second period produced yet another interesting and successful experiment—the Curtal Sonnet (Type E). *Pied Beauty* (1877) and *Peace* (1879) are the only two finished specimens of this charming form, which is

> " constructed in proportions resembling those of the sonnet proper, namely 6+4 instead of 8+6, with however a half-line tailpiece (so that the equation is rather $\frac{12}{2}+\frac{9}{2}=\frac{21}{2}=10\frac{1}{2}$) ".[1]

What is the mystery of $10\frac{1}{2}$? The only danger in its fascinating irrelevance is that some people may suppose that Hopkins is all the time working to learned theory instead of just opening his heart and being a poet.

Pied Beauty is written in five-stress lines[2] ; whereas *Peace*, being in alexandrines and showing a slight variation in the rhyme scheme of the last four lines, constitutes a new type (E_1). The Curtal Sonnet is a perfect medium for the expression of a lyrical impulse which is intellectually too slight to fill up the normal sonnet-mould.

The poet's tendency, in *The Windhover*, to stretch the five-stress line into an alexandrine made it almost inevitable that he should, in his third sonnet-period (1879–81), use the six-stress line throughout.

Actually there have been very few alexandrine sonnets in English ; until the last fifty years, the measure had always been considered alien to the spirit and form of the language. As a recent writer on the sonnet says :

> " Sidney gives us the form at its best, but a comparison with his own five-foot sonnets shows the unsuitability of the French form to the English language. Concentration of language is lost in a line normally too long for the divisions of English poetic language, and the invariable end-pause, and the break in the middle of each line, destroy the flexibility of movement which is so powerful a source of expression." [3]

[1] Author's *Preface*, p. 6.

[2] The unfinished *Ash-boughs* (No. 56) is also a Curtal Sonnet in five-stress lines.

[3] *The English Sonnet*, by Enid Hamer, p. xlvi. She includes one sonnet by Hopkins (*Poems*, No. 50).

It is surely remarkable that as late as 1936 an anthologist who knows Hopkins's work should pronounce Sidney the best exponent of this form, and then proceed to depreciate the form for all the inherent weaknesses that Hopkins so triumphantly avoids. Although he evinced, like Whitman, "a preference for the alexandrine",[1] Hopkins was fully aware of its disadvantages: "That metre, unless much broken as I do by outrides, is very tedious"[2]; "and to vary the division, the phrasing, successfully, and for long, is a most difficult matter". Common blank verse, he says, will naturally fall into variable divisions, "whereas the equal division of the alexandrine is first poor and then nearly invariable. Nevertheless I have grappled with this".[3]

Let us first see how Sidney does not grapple with it:

> "Those looks, whose beams my joy, whose motion is delight,
> That face whose lecture shows what perfect beauty is,
> That presence which doth give dark hearts a living light,
> That grace which Venus weeps that she herself did miss . . ."[4]

—and then turn to the MS. "A" reading of *Henry Purcell*:

> "Have fair ⁚ fallen, O fair, ⁚ fair have fallen, so dear
> To me, so arch-especial a spirit as heaves in Henry Purcell,
> An age is now since passed, since parted; with the reversal
> Of the outward sentence low lays him, listed to a heresy, here.
> Not mood in him nor meaning, proud fire or sacred fear,
> Or love or pity or all that sweet notes not his might nursle:
> Ít is the fórgèd féature | fínds mé; it is the rehéarsal
> Of own, of abrupt ⁚ self there so thrusts on, so throngs
> the ear.
>
> Let him oh! with his air of angels then lift me, lay me!
> only I'll
> Have an eye to the sakes of him, quaint moonmarks, to
> his pelted plumage under
> Wings: so some great stormfowl, whenever he has walked
> his while
> The thunder-purple seabeach plumèd purple-of-thunder,
> If a wuthering of his palmy snow-pinions scatter a colossal
> smile
> Off him, but meaning motion fans fresh our wits with
> wonder."

[1] *Letters*, vol. i. p. 157.
[2] *Ibid.* p. 80.
[3] *Ibid.* p. 203.
[4] Quoted by Enid Hamer, *loc. cit.*

The " great colons " placed between juxtaposed stressed syllables, the seventeen outrides, two elisions, and single hurried foot all serve to elucidate the rhythm : in the one line where any doubt could remain (line 7) we have marked the stresses and caesura.

The next sonnet in this class (Type F) is *Felix Randal* (1880). Its almost conversational rhythm, matching the homely diction of the octave at least, is worked up without strain and with a peculiar felicity into a sounding rhetorical climax ; yet the movement of this strong and natural rhythm is not readily perceived without the aid of its fifteen outrides :

> " Félix Rándal the fárrier, | O he is déad then ? my dúty áll
> éndéd,
> Who have wátched his móuld of mán, | big-bóned and
> hárdy-hándsome
> Píning, píning, till tíme when | réason rámbled in it ánd
> some
> Fátal fóur disórders, | fléshed there, áll conténded ?
>
> Síckness bróke him. Impátient | he cúrsed at fírst, but
> ménded
> Béing anóinted and áll ; | though a héavenlier héart begán
> some
> Mónths éarlier, since Í hád | our swéet repríeve and ránsom
> Téndered to him. Áh well, God rést him | áll road éver he
> offénded !
>
> This séeing the síck endéars them | tó us, us tóo it endéars.
> My tóngue had táught thee cómfort, | tóuch had quénched
> thy téars,
> Thy téars that tóuched my héart, child, | Félix, poor Félix
> Rándal ;
>
> How fár from thén fórethought of, | all thý more bóisterous
> yéars,
> When thóu at the rándom grim fórge, | pówerful amídst
> péers,
> Didst féttle for the gréat grey dráyhorse | his bríght and
> báttering sándal ! " [1]

[1] All the outrides are from MS. " A ", except the second in each of lines 1 and 3, which are from B and H respectively.

The remaining sonnets of Type F all belong to the year 1885: they are—*To What Serves Mortal Beauty?*, (*The Soldier*), and, greatest of all (*Carrion Comfort*). These again have something of the spasmodic, impulsive style of inspired conversation—a rhythm which seems rugged until the second or third repetition of a whole quatrain or tercet reveals the underlying harmony of thought to thought and stress to stress. In No. 38, the printing of the caesural mark removes any possible ambiguity from the fairly straightforward Common Rhythm; but in No. 40 the omission of both outrides and caesural marks must put a considerable strain upon the average reader's sense of rhythm. Here is the present writer's stressing of the last five lines:

> "Nay in áll that toíl, that coíl, | sínce (seems) I kíssed the
> ród,
> Hánd rather, my héart, lo! lapped stréngth, | stole jóy,
> would láugh, chéer.
> Cheer whóm though? the héro whose héaven-handling |
> flúng me, fóot tród
> Me? or mé that fóught him? O whích one? | is it éach
> one? That níght, that yéar
> Of nów done dárkness I wrétch | lay wréstling with (mý
> God!) my Gód."

In all three sonnets, the skill with which Hopkins avoids the weakness of the mid-line break by placing the caesural pause between closely related syllables [1] and obviates the "invariable end-pause" by a rapid over-reaving from line to line should dispel once for all any legislator's qualms about the suitability of this sonnet-form to the English language.

After *Henry Purcell* we find Hopkins alternating between the earlier conventional sonnet-types and even more daring experiments in augmented forms. The next three (all of the year 1879) [2] are in Common or Standard Rhythm, one being regular and two counterpointed.

[1] E.g. the MS. (H) of (*The Soldier*) begins:

> "Yes, whý do we áll, séeing of a sóldier, bléss him? bless
> Our rédcoats, óur tars? Bóth | thêse béing, the gréater párt. . ."

[2] *Andromeda* (No. 25), *The Candle Indoors*, and *The Handsome Heart*. The last was re-written in alexandrines (MS. "A").

Of the first, *Andromeda*, Hopkins wrote :

> " I endeavoured in it a more Miltonic plainness and severity then I have anywhere else. I cannot say it has turned out severe, still less plain, but it seems almost free from quaintness and in aiming at one excellence I may have hit another." [1]

Metrically this sonnet goes right back to Type A ; yet its effect is utterly different. The mature poet's skilful use of long and weighted syllables (" doomed dragon's food ") together with strong yet delicate phrasing, which, like the phonal texture, is less Miltonic than Welsh, certainly justifies his claim to " another kind of excellence ".

This form (Type A_1) is repeated only twice—in *Ribblesdale* (1882) and *St. Alphonsus Rodriguez* (1888). In the latter, Hopkins was again deliberately curbing his idiosyncrasy, but this time to satisfy the expectations of others :

> " I ask your opinion of a sonnet written to order. . . . The sonnet (I say it snorting) aims at being intelligible." [2]

The result of this unwilling self-discipline is even more remarkable than before. In the poet's own comment on the sestet—" It is, so far as I can see, both exact and pregnant " [3]—we have the clue to an important change which was taking place in his later sonnets : he was to aim more and more at exactness and pregnancy of statement, and to this end many of the earlier textural exuberances were to be discarded. Yet this change was not absolute, and as far as it went it was not in the poet's own eyes a discrediting of his earlier manner. He never wrote anything more pregnant than parts of *The Deutschland* and the whole of *The Windhover*, and in some of his later " sonnets " he managed to combine pregnancy with the extreme of virtuosity and musical elaboration.

His next innovation was a sonnet in eight-stress lines (Type G). In *Spelt from Sibyl's Leaves*, however, the ringing trochees of *Locksley Hall* have been broken and varied by almost as many mono-, tri-, and quadrisyllabic feet, by frequent over-reaving and anacrusis. Hopkins was probably right in pronouncing it " the longest sonnet ever written " ; though many a latter-day Bentley would shake his head and say : It is a very powerful poem, but it is not a sonnet.

[1] *Letters*, vol. i. p. 87. [2] *Ibid*. p. 293. [3] *Ibid*. p. 297.

This work, we are told,

> " is, as living art should be, made for performance . . . not reading with the eye but loud, leisurely, poetical (not rhetorical) recitation, with long rests, long dwells on the rhyme and other marked syllables, and so on. This sonnet should be almost sung : it is most carefully timed in *tempo rubato*." [1]

These directions, we submit, are extremely helpful and should be printed with the text or in the Notes. Like the *Deutschland* and the *Echoes*, this sonnet is a task for the sensitive virtuoso in the art of verse speaking, and the *rubato* effect allows of individual interpretations within the broad march of a pulsing but not facile cumulative rhythm. The whole poem, moreover, shows a complete disregard for " Miltonic plainness ", and harks back to the sensuous incantation of the earlier sonnets. Its oddity at first approach is greater than in any previous work, yet familiarity brings out the " tool-smooth " and " bleak " precision of the imagery and the astonishing orchestration of the " lettering ".[2]

The forty-three stresses in the printed text are all necessary to fix beyond doubt both the rhythm and the sense—without undue loss of time and patience. Here, again, we are at first disconcerted by metrical stresses on prepositions and other seemingly weak words ; but a closer scrutiny shows that this pointing is altogether right : for example, " self ín self " (line 6) anticipates the violence of " páshed " ; " ánd " (line 8) is a menacing climax ; " agáinst thoughts " (line 14) emphasizes the painful friction, and renders necessary the metrical stress on " ín ", though in the actual reading the weight is distributed thus : " in groans gríndd ". How subtle, too, is the repetition of the phrase " but these two " in line 13, so that the unstressed part of the first statement is stressed in the second !

From the year 1880 onwards, Hopkins became more and more engrossed with music ; hence it is not surprising that his subsequent experiments in poetic form were coloured by musical modes.

He had a tendency to try his hand twice at every distinctive verse form he struck out, though usually the second effort shows some definite modification. There are, for instance, two curtal

[1] *Letters*, vol. i. p. 246.
[2] See Volume II, chapters iii. and vi. of the present work.

sonnets ; and the sheer bulk and something like the detailed, exegetic manner of *Sibyl's Leaves* is repeated, with marked differences, in *That Nature is a Heraclitean Fire* (No. 48). But before we look at this gargantuan offspring of the Petrarchan sonnet, we must examine the two extended sonnets written at Dromore in 1887.

In 1886 Hopkins is asking Bridges what a *coda* is.[1] Later he writes :

> " Next please tell me correctly how to make codas to sonnets ; with the most approved order of rhymes, and so on. And do not say that I know and that I can find for myself and that there is one in Milton (that one is not enough), . . . a sonnet is hot on the anvil and wants a coda. It is the only time I have felt forced to exceed the beaten bounds." [2]

The following obviously refers to *Tom's Garland* :

> " I wanted the coda for a sonnet which is in some sort ' nello stilo satirico o bernesco '. It has a kind of rollic at all events. The coda is an immense resource to have." [3]

Milton's unique caudated sonnet, *On the New Forcers of Conscience*, was of course imitated from the Italian, in which language the form was used only for joking or satirical matter. *Tom's Garland : upon the Unemployed*[4] (Type H) has just as serious a purpose as its Miltonic prototype. As we see elsewhere in his use of polysyllabic, split, and other quaint rhymes, Hopkins boldly took over some of the modes of lighter poetry and forced them to be serious (a healthy corrective to the dulness of serious modes in the hands of poetasters).

The caudated sonnet is admirably suited to invective. The two codas (each a trimeter and two pentameters closely linked by rhyme to each other and the sonnet proper) are like two Parthian shots : psychologically, the coda corresponds to that tendency of the indignant man to protract an argument in the hope of dealing a really crushing blow. Hopkins, too, has the excuse of indignation, which is as clamant in *his* last line as it is quietly scornful in Milton's.

[1] *Letters*, vol. i. p. 246.

[2] *Ibid.* p. 263. This letter is dated Nov. 2, 1887, yet *Tom's Garland* (MS. " A ") is dated Sept. '87. Hopkins, in looking back, must have antedated this sonnet. It is hardly likely that No. 48 is in question.

[3] *Letters*, vol. i. p. 266.

[4] *Poems*, No. 42.

Before completing *Tom's Garland*, Hopkins had already sent to Bridges *Harry Ploughman*,[1]

> " in which burden-lines (they might be recited by a chorus) are freely used : there is in this very heavily loaded sprung rhythm a call for their employment. The rhythm of this sonnet, which is altogether for recital, not for perusal (as by nature verse should be) is very highly studied." [2]

Although *Tom's Garland* is in " common rhythm, but with hurried feet ", Hopkins admits that there are

> " many resemblances to *Harry Ploughman*, a fault in me the sonneteer but not a fault that can be traced home to either of the sonnets. They were conceived at the same time." [3]

Harry Ploughman, however, is descriptive, not argumentative : " I want Harry Ploughman to be a vivid figure before the mind's eye ; if he is not that the sonnet fails ". In spite of the difficulties of syntax, the sonnet does not fail : for the present writer, it is one of this poet's outstanding successes.[4] The octave, with its rhythms and images drawn from the disciplined fighting forces (" shôuldér and shánk " ; " one crêw, fall tó ; Stand at stress ", etc.) is, as it should be, a poem in itself—the στάσις which prepares the audience for the κίνησις of the equally self-contained sestet. The five burden-lines echo the sense and words of their immediately preceding lines, and while they add a new virtue they do not nullify the advantages of the original sonnet-form. Like the caudated sonnet, *Harry Ploughman* (Type I) reveals possibilities of variation which later poets will be eager to develop.

The final outcome of all this experimentation was the magnificent *That Nature is a Herclitean Fire* (1888), which Hopkins inaccurately describes as " a sonnet with two codas ". Actually there are three codas with an extra burden-line at the end, making a total of twenty alexandrines, three trimeters and one dimeter. As with *Tom's Garland*, the first fourteen lines are rhymed like a regular sonnet of Miltonic structure. The description of the metre—" sprung rhythm with many outrides and hurried feet "—need not worry the plain reader, since all he has to do is observe the caesural pause, make sure of the

[1] *Poems*, No. 43. [2] *Letters*, vol. i. p. 263. Cf. vol. ii. p. 153.

[3] *Letters*, vol. i. p. 271.

[4] Hopkins himself depreciated the two Dromore sonnets ; yet he wrote both with conviction and enjoyment.

stressed syllables, and let his natural sense of rhythm do the rest. The reading of line 12, where no caesura is marked, is almost certainly

"Bóth are in an unfáthomable, | áll ís in an enórmous dárk"

and in the last line but two the stressing is:

"I am áll at ónce what Chríst is, | since hé wás what Í am, and . . ."

The codas are not mere excrescences: they are organic members of a well-proportioned poetic body. In conformity with its greater length, this "sonnet" has two distinct turns in the developing argument. The first is at the end of line 15, which concludes the section on *flux in external nature*; the second is in line 22, between the section on *flux in human nature* and the doctrinal resolution: "Enough! the Resurrection".[1]

To turn from this work (Type J) to the sonnets of desolation, written between *Carrion Comfort* and the poet's death, is to realize how persistently he kept his eye on the traditional mould. At certain times, when the mood of joy-in-creation was ousted by the mere desire to discharge a grief, he reverted to the regular sonnet in standard rhythm with occasional trisyllabic or hurried feet and a few counterpointed or sprung lines. The sonnet *To R. B.*,[2] for instance, falls between Types B_1 and C_1; but the greater severity and concentration of those that came like inspirations unbidden and against his will (e.g. "I wake and feel the fell of dark"—No. 45)[3] removes them into a class of their own, which we may call Type C_2.

These categories may seem arbitrary, or even pedantic; but they serve to show the extraordinary virtuosity and resourcefulness of the poet. His achievement was to have used, with mastery, ten different variations of the Italian sonnet-form, not to mention three minor modifications within two of the major types. If we except the three extended sonnets, Hopkins infringed only two of the ten indispensable rules laid down by Sharp: one relates to the use of the decasyllabic line and the other to obscurity. But perhaps neither rule had any sure foundations in poetic reality.

[1] See below, chap. v.

[2] No. 51. Cf. 69. No. 50, being Miltonic in structure but counterpointed, may be called Type A.

[3] Also Nos. 41, 44 and 47.

CHAPTER IV

DICTION AND SYNTAX *

ALTHOUGH Hopkins used, in his verse, many of the freer rhythms of prose, he did not hold the Wordsworthian view that the language of poetry should not differ from the language of prose. In an early essay called *Poetic Diction*,[1] he asks why, if the best prose and the best poetry use the same language, the writer should not prefer unfettered prose of the two. Verse alone does not add a beauty to thought, because prose thought (" bald prose and simple statement ") is actually made worse by metrical expression. It is plain, he adds, that verse both necessitates and engenders a difference in diction and in thought. The effect of verse on thought and expression he sums up in one word—concentration, by which he means not merely terseness, definiteness, emphasis, but rather *vividness of idea.*

This vividness of idea is achieved by various modes of Parallelism—from the duplicated statements of Hebrew poetry to the subtle similitudes of modern verse ; from the clearly marked " abrupt " formal modes to the transitional or " chromatic " modes which provide the intensity and *chiaroscuro* of great poetry. Moreover, this parallelism in verse-forms " tends to beget or passes into parallelism in thought."

Such parallelism in thought and syntax is one of the outstanding features of Hopkins's style. We have already seen how he used alliteration and assonance to bind together and unify related images, progressive phases of one main thought or emotion.[2] And if we examine the second half of a line like the following from *Sibyl's Leaves* :

> " Evening strains to be tíme's vást, | wómb-of-āll, hóme-
> of-āll, héarse-of-āll níght ",

we see how clearly interrelated are those three aspects of style —rhythm, diction and syntax. Without actually violating Aristotle's rule that " the diction should be conformable to the

* [*N.B.* In the present chapter the number in brackets after a quotation from a poem by Hopkins is the number of that poem in the Second Edition.]

[1] *Note-books*, p. 92, *et seqq.* [2] See also Volume II. chap. iii. of the present work.

rhythm", Hopkins uses here a diction which forces the rhythm out of its dactylo-trochaic norm, imposing upon it two long stressed monosyllables and three quantitative cretics; he thereby attains that greater emphasis of structure and expression which *poetic* thought demands.[1] He insisted on having those three compound epithets in that precise parallel form, without concession or compromise to suit a conventional rhythm and syntax.

Professor Gilbert Murray once said [2] that unless a poet used words of quite unmistakable scansion (e.g. *múlligatáwny* and *húllabalóo*) his line would be twisted away towards some familiar rhythm:

> "If you try in lyric to impose on the reader some rhythm that you think rare and beautiful and particularly expressive of some rare phase of feeling, you must prepare for disappointment."

To this theory and its facile products Hopkins's sprung and expressional rhythm offers a direct and successful challenge. The disadvantage of a slight uncertainty in scansion or of typographical disfigurement by stress-marks is more than compensated by a fuller exploitation of the English vocabulary, by a greater freedom for the "auditory imagination", the spontaneous poetic word, compound and word-group.

Hopkins's ideas and analogics frequently move forward in groups of twos and threes: "The gnarls of the nails, the niche of the lance" (4); "Her fond yellow hornlight wound to the west, | her wild hollow hoarlight hung to the height / Waste;" (32); "Cloud-puffball, torn tufts, tossed pillows flaunt forth," (48), etc. This parallelism in syntax and imagery is akin to a common feature of Welsh poetry which may have influenced Hopkins: this is *dyfalu*, the accumulation of images to illuminate one central idea.[3] Such profusion is seen in Vaughan's

[1] Putting this idea the other way round, Hopkins says: "An emphasis of structure stronger than the common construction of sentences gives, asks for an emphasis of expression stronger than that of common speech or writing, and that for an emphasis of thought stronger than that of common thought." (*Note-books*, p. 93.)

[2] *What English Poetry Can Still Learn from Greek.* (*Essays and Studies by Members of the English Association*, vol. iii., 1912.)

[3] E.g.—

"Fy mhwrs felfed, fy mherson,	"My velvet purse, my parson,
Fy nghoffr aur, fy nghyffur iôn,	My coffer of gold, lord of my substance
Fy ngheidwad hoff, fy mhroffwyd,	My dear preserver, my prophet,
Fy nghydymaith uniaith wyd."	My monoglot companion thou art."

(*Fy mhwrs, gormersi am hyn*,
attributed to Sion Cent.)

The Night (stanzas 5 and 6) and is found in Shakespeare ; in Hopkins it is everywhere the expression of enthusiasm or passion :

> " O look at all the firefolk sitting in the air !
> The bright boroughs, the circle-citadels there !
> . . . . . .
> Wind-beat whitebeam ! airy abeles set on a flare !
> Flake-doves sent floating forth at a farmyard scare !—" (8).

Another characteristic feature of Hopkins's diction is adumbrated in the early essay quoted above : why, he asks, if Wordsworth's principle is right, should the common habit of accenting the last syllable of past participles seem perpetually to add fresh beauty, and be used in verse but never in prose ? He then quotes Shakespeare's *Sonnet LII* :

> " So I am as the rich whose blessed key
> Can bring him to his sweet up-lockèd treasure."

This felicity he attributes to the fact that the structure forces us to appreciate each syllable ; " and we naturally dwell on all modifications affecting the general type which the ear preserves ".[1]

The last statement explains much that is unusual in Hopkins's handling of vocabulary and syntax. A slight deviation from the prose norm (as in that almost German compound, " up-lockèd ") forces us to dwell more intently upon the idea conveyed in it. Hopkins himself uses these lengthened participles with good effect : " Be shellèd, eyes " (3), " self ín self steepèd and páshed " (32—the first action is gentle, the second violent). But a more characteristic application of this principle is in his sudden but always calculated deviations from an essentially poetic diction to the prose or colloquial norm, or from a precedented to an unprecedented or ungrammatical arrangement of words. Both these devices (illustrated below) produce a salutary shock, a redoubled attentiveness in the reader. Yet this result would not have been achieved if Hopkins had not possessed, like Shakespeare, a genius for what has been called ' the magic of grammar ' —a sheer felicity in the terse arrangement of words, in dramatic concentration, which almost defies analysis :

> " My own heart let me more have pity on ; let
> Me live to my sad self hereafter kind,
> Charitable ; not live this tormented mind
> With this tormented mind tormenting yet." [2]

[1] *Note-books, loc. cit.* p. 94.

[2] *Poems*, No. 47. The second quatrain is no less remarkable.

As the inversion in the first line is spontaneous, almost colloquial, so the reiteration in the last two dramatizes the vicious circle of chagrin which begets more chagrin—the mind which continually preys on its own weakness.

Taken altogether, his lexical and syntactical neologisms, like his innovations in rhythm, produce an air of strangeness more marked than in any other English poet. Yet this " oddity " or " queerness ", as he himself called it, is not in itself an undesirable quality. Aristotle said that even the orator should give his phrase a " foreign " air, since all men are admirers of things out of the way ; and " in metrical composition the many things that produce this effect are very becoming ".[1] The main purpose of prose is to inform or persuade, and for this the natural unstudied manner is most appropriate : Hopkins's sermons, for instance, are simple, almost bald in style ; his letters are direct, vigorous, and relatively free from *ξένα*. But the aim of poetry being to move, to excite, the " foreign air " or strongly idiosyncratic flavour of his verse is a powerful emotive factor.

In his theoretical approach to words as symbols he draws, in his own interesting way, the now familiar distinction between *denotation* and *connotation*. The former he calls " definition, uttering " ; the latter " a prepossession of feeling or enthusiasm ", by which he seems to imply the emotion and attitude evoked by a word.[2] This emotive quality, the *soul* of the word, he again subdivides into *individual prepossession* and *historic prepossession* (i.e. its evolution in man collectively). The common failing of the Romantic school, in using words for their sound and vaguely poetical suggestiveness instead of for precise " uttering ", is condemned :

> " Some minds prefer that the prepossession they are to receive should be conveyed in the least organic, expressive, by the most suggestive way. By this means the prepossession and the definition, uttering, are distinguished and unwound, which is the less sane attitude." [3]

Hopkins therefore was a strict Classicist in his conception of words as tools rather than as pigments ; yet he did not ignore their connotative value. The strength of his diction (as, again, of Shakespeare's, of Donne's) lies in his power of preserving the organic unity of *definition* and *prepossession*, of writing poetry which

[1] *Rhetoric*, III. ii. 3. (Buckley's trans., Bohn, 1853, pp. 207–8.)
[2] *Note-books*, p. 95. [3] *Ibid.* p. 96.

is at once precise in statement and aglow with individual and universal feeling.

The ultimate test of an original poet is, perhaps, his skill in using what Coleridge called the *lingua communis*—that large body of words common to both prose and poetry. " I dearly love calling a spade a spade ", Hopkins wrote, and there is much plain, strong language in the poems. There is also refinement, delicacy, the aristocratic touch, and even a dash of preciocity, as when he calls a ship's screw a " whorl " (4) and a furrow a " sillion " (12). His vocabulary is, in fact, a personal thesaurus gathered from all sources, workaday and literary, local and cosmopolitan.

There is a phrase quoted in one of Patmore's letters—" native earth and real potato ",[1] in which Hopkins seems to indicate a predilection for homely indigenous words ; and if Patmore was a little amused at his friend's claiming for his style " the extreme of popular character ",[2] it was because Hopkins himself and scarcely realized the strangeness of his own Joseph's coat of popular and learned elements.

His vocabulary is so varied, colourful and figurative that the frequency of the homely, racy Old English or at least Teutonic word is not at once apparent. Yet a cross-section of his verse compared with one from an equal bulk of work by Milton, Wordsworth, Shelley, Keats, Arnold and Meredith shows that, he uses roughly five per cent. more words of Teutonic origin than do these other representative poets.[3] At times we see him deliberately and successfully seeking out the native word in contexts where, we are sure, most poets would have accepted a more obvious Latinate or Romance word : *never-eldering* (unaging—4) ; *inmate* (inhabitant—16) ; *no-man-fathomed* (unplumbed—41) ; *herds-long* (41 ; cf. " cries *count*less "—45) ; *rope-over* (muscular—43). Without resorting to freakish neologisms like William Barnes's suggested " pitches of suchness "

[1] *Further Letters*, p. 207. The " Potato Poet " there mentioned is probably either George Colman or the Rev. John Graham, whose poems in praise of the potato appeared in Croker's *Popular Songs of Ireland*, 1839. (Morley's Universal Library, No. 40, p. 49.)

[2] *Loc. cit.*

[3] The poems concerned, with their respective percentages of Teutonic words, are : (*a*) Hopkins : No. 16 (80%) ; No. 17, lines 1–18 (81%) ; No. 21 (72%) ; No. 43 (81%) ; No. 50 (82%) : (*b*) *On His Blindness* (76%) ; *Upon Westminster Bridge* (81·5%); *Ode to the West Wind*, lines 1–28 (71%) ; *On First Looking into Chapman's Homer* (76%) ; *Shakespeare* (70·5%) ; *Modern Love*, L (71%). Analysis : Hopkins, 79% ; Others 74%.

(for "degrees of comparison"),[1] Hopkins revived many obsolete native words, like *hallows* (8) and *housel* (23); and sometimes in a compound he will substitute a new native element for the more hackneyed one, as in *knee-nave* (43—knee-cap) and *song-fowl* (15), *stormfowl* (21). Fastidiously avoiding the trite archaisms which add nothing of value to the pages of Morris, Dixon and Doughty,—whilom, what time, eftsoon, etc.—he preferred to go straight to the founthead of native idiom, as many of his compounds show.

For example, *bone-house* (15), pejorative for "body", is the O.E. 'bānhūs' with a new "prepossession of feeling", while *bower of bone* (4) has the same anatomical flavour. The O.E. 'werewulf' seems almost to be included, by reference, in the total meaning of *manwolf* (42); and compounds like *hailropes, heavengravel* and *wolfsnow* (17) are redolent of the spirit of early Northumbrian sea-poetry. In *Yore-flood* (4) we are reminded of O.E. 'ȝēar-dagas', and *barebill* (25) is reminiscent of 'hildebil' or 'wīgbil'. Similarly *boldboys* (17), *mansex* (23), *manmarks* (48), *waterfearers* (58) and many more are all simple, primitive and essentially "popular" compounds.[2]

Richness, variety and a chromatic subtlety in the scale of meaning were more important to Hopkins than a semi-articulate purity; hence he adds:

> "It would be strange if τέχνη and τύχη together did not bring some fine results out of any lot of caleidoscopic elements; still to me a pure language seems a finer thing than a mixed one—*till the mixture becomes imperceptible.*" [3]

Hopkins, by avoiding as far as possible the later 'learned' borrowings from Latin (words of narrow or abstract reference and little poetic warmth) gave the older and more closely welded elements freer play. We see a perfect fusing in those hybrid compounds which show a touch of conscious artistry: *churls-grace* (43), *heaven-roysterers* (48), *gay-gangs* (48), *downdolphinry* (72).

[1] Commenting on Barnes's *English Speech-craft* (1878): "It makes one weep to think what English might have been; for in spite of all that Shakespeare and Milton have done with the compound, I cannot doubt that no beauty in a language can make up for want of purity. . . . Anglo-Saxon is a vastly superior thing to what we have now." (*Letters*, vol. i. p. 162.)

[2] Cf. the humble origin of words like 'tallboy', 'doughboy', and 'goldboy' (a working-class woman's name for the yellow discs used as dividend checks by a large Co-operative Society).

[3] *Letters*, vol. i. p. 166.

Despite the virtuosity, such words show a spontaneous glee, the liveliness of a living as opposed to a merely literary language.

In justifying the word *exploit* in No. 49, Hopkins says:

> "You will allow—would, I shd. think, urge on me—that where the ὄνομα κύριον has nothing flat or poor about it it is the best word to use in poetry as in prose, better I mean than its paraphrase." [1]

Hopkins honoured the current language by always using the blunt common word when truth demanded it, whether figuratively:

> "But you were a liar, O blue March day." (17),

or literally:

> "Is there any . . . catch or key to keep
> Back beauty . . . ?" (36).

"Back", he says, "is not pretty, but it gives that feeling of physical constraint which I want." [2]

Poetical language, he says elsewhere,[3] "should be current language heightened, to any degree heightened and unlike itself, but not an obsolete one." The degree, in his own work, is extreme but legitimate; and although he uses some obsolete words, the vital idiosyncrasy of the total style assimilates them with ease and profit. In *heightening* he rejected the frigid and pedantic periphrasis dear to the eighteenth century and elevated the commonplace by methods of his own:

> ". . . Here he feasts: lovely all is! No more: off with—
> down he dings
> His bleachèd both and woolwoven wear:
> Careless these in coloured wisp
> All lie tumbled-to;" (72).

This genial swimmer is first presented in a précis-by-omission of popular idiom: "Here he feasts his eyes. How lovely it all is! But no more gazing, etc." In the rest, both lettering and construction re-create the familiar; and the whole is a deft, individual heightening of current language, in which the dialectal or archaic "dings" does not intrude as it would in a conventional context.

[1] *Letters*, vol. i. p. 297. (Gk.=exact, literal word.) [2] *Poems*, p. 133.

[3] *Letters*, vol. i. p. 89: "I cut myself off from the use of *ere*, *o'er*, *wellnigh*, *what time*, *say not* . . . because, though dignified, they neither belong to nor ever cd. arise from, or be the elevation of, ordinary modern speech."

To find anything like the above among Hopkins's older contemporaries we must go to the work (mainly the prose) of Meredith—a writer who frequently displays the same spontaneous and puckish agility.[1]

To the important question of syntax we must return later; at present we have to complete our survey of the coinages, compounds, archaisms and provincialisms which make up Hopkins's eclectic but highly individual vocabulary.

Hopkins belonged to that relatively small class of poets (including Shakespeare, Keats and Meredith) who, not content with the language as they find it, tend in varying degrees to create their own medium of expression. He frequently uses nouns as verbs, and *vice versa*: "Let him *easter* in us" (4), "should *tongue* that time" (49), "the *achieve* of . . . the thing!" (12), "with *dare* and with downdolphinry" (72).[2] Sometimes he gives the current meaning a personal twist which makes for obscurity: "Let joy *size* At God knows when to God knows what" (47). Incidentally, these colloquial allusions to the Deity are not used with the usual nonchalance: they are imbued with the theological import of the sequel: "who's smile's not wrung, see you"; and here again "wrung" in the sense of "wrung out", "extorted", is a bold contraction.[3]

Every true metaphor, said Aristotle, is a *new* metaphor, and in this power of imaginative 'transference' Hopkins is a great master. Few poets can equal his gift of transforming and frequently exalting a common word by a surprisingly apt metaphorical application. His use of metaphor as pure image will be discussed in the next chapter, but here we may consider the strictly linguistic aspect of the subject.

Metaphor is often the process of doing exquisite violence to the language, and in Hopkins the wrench away from an accepted meaning is sometimes so drastic as to cause obscurity. In *The Deutschland*, the "sour scythe" of Death is said to "cringe"; this shows a reversion to the original meaning

[1] E.g. *One of Our Conquerors* (Chapman and Hall, 1892): "the noble forthroll of the notes" (p. 65); "the hurtled fair ones in sky" (i.e. clouds—p. 34); "Green ran the banks about" (a lake—p. 66); "the quick of thoughts" (p. 80). Also "the wind-whipped anywhither wave" (*Earth and Man*, 1883). Cf. below, p. 128.

[2] This licence is, of course, a frank reversion to Elizabethan practice: "How might she tongue me?" (*M. for M.* IV. iv. 28); "a sweet retire" (*Hen. V*, IV. iii. 86). See Abbott, §§ 290, 451.

[3] The meaning is: (*a*) "Be a little more casual, relax for health's sake"; and (*b*) "Be reconciled to having your pleasure whenever and however God wills it."

(O.E. ' crinċġan ', to bend, sink) and seems also to be reminiscent of Shakespeare's

> " Whip him, fellows,
> Till, like a boy, you see him *cringe* his face
> And whine aloud for mercy " (*Ant. and Cleo.*, III. xi. 99–101),

together with the allusion to Time's " bending sickle " in Sonnet CXVI. The word suggests, therefore, the swift descent of Death and the cowering, whining victim.[1]

There are other words to which the reader must bring a lively imagination and also a good etymological dictionary. Harry Ploughman's curls " wag or *crossbridle* " ; and as we are told next that they are " wind lifted, windlaced ", we know that *-bridle* is used here in the double sense of (*a*) ' rise ', as with pride, and (*b*) ' twist ', ' weave ', like the straps of a horse's bridle (cf. cognate ' braid ' < O.E. ' bregdan ' = twist, pull). Thus the word is elucidated, though obscurely, by its context. Similarly, in the phrase " flitches of fern " (33) the force of *flitches* derives not so much from the accepted meaning (slices, sides of bacon) as from the suggestive sound of the word (cf. switches, patches) and the influence of the preceding word, " heathpacks ". The resultant image of characteristic tufts of autumnal bracken may also be strengthened by the colour-association with smoked pig. Nevertheless, the curious reader will uneasily consult his dictionary, to find there that *flitch* (O.E. fliċċe ; cf. O.N. flikki, a patch) is related to *fleck* and probably also to *flake*. Thus the combined meanings—feathery flakes, long stems, and clumps may justify our taking *flitches* to be a portmanteau word from *flake*, *switch* and *patch*. This is supported by a line in the preceding stanza, in which the burn " Turns and *twindles* over the broth Of a pool ". *Twindles* is obviously a Carrollian compound of *twist*, *twiddle*, *spindle* and (as eddies do) *dwindle*.

There are many other words which, though immediately and powerfully suggestive, depend for their absolute precision upon meanings which must be thought out with some pains or sought out in the *New English Dictionary*: " This ruck and reel " (3),[2] the disturbing, dizzying turmoil and excitement of common life ; " Squander the hellrook ranks sally to molest him " ; (23),[3]

[1] Miss Edith Sitwell would probably find the word wonderfully onomatopoeic.

[2] Cf. the Scotch " a reel o' thunner " ; a lively dance.

[3] For " squander " in this sense, cf. Dryden in *Annus Mirabilis* (1666), stanza 67 :

> " They charge, recharge, and all along the sea
> They drive, and squander the huge Belgian fleet."

Drive off the blackguardly swindlers who would steal his money and his faith; "with ride[1] and jar"[2] (23), with the shock of a cavalry charge. Some of these words (*ruck*, *reel*, *-rook*, *jar*) have two or three relevant meanings which reinforce each other.

From such an intensely personal manipulation of meanings to frank coinages is but a short step. The coining of words by a poet like Hopkins is sometimes the expression of primitive consciousness and sensibility and sometimes of a learned sophistication. He shows a marked partiality for the epithet in -y; but in the mature poems he avoids the trite 'poetical' words like *dewy*, *starry* and invents others like "*barrowy* brawn" (43), "*palmy* snow-pinions" (=palm-like), "*twiny* boots" (72). The sensibility which sees candle light as "yellowy moisture" and a wood as "branchy, bunchy, bushy-bowered" (72) is akin to that of the child, who usually coins a -y epithet at need (e.g. 'chocolaty'). Most of these last adjectives are in common use, but the more colloquial were employed very sparingly by the decorous Victorian poets.

A good example of a bold, fresh and even boyish interpretation of sensory impressions is the phrase "rash smart sloggering brine" (4). The first two epithets throw an unusual emphasis upon the original meanings—speed and pain, while the third is an entirely new word made from the sporting term, 'slogger', a wild hitter. A coinage, however, is not justified unless its meaning, or the gist of it, is immediately apparent. Hopkins himself felt doubts about the phrase "*louchèd* low grass" (35), for he wrote to Dixon:

> "In the sonnet enclosed 'louchèd' is a coinage of mine and is to mean the same as *slouched, slouching*."[3]

The image (drooping, lolling blades in a tuft of field grass) is admirably precise when once the connexion with *slouch* is perceived; but not all readers would trust themselves on this point, especially in an age when the natural response to poetry has been largely stultified.

Beautifully lucid and apt for their particular purpose are a number of coinages arising from the poet's interest in individuation. In the *Journal*, Hopkins sometimes used the word "quains" (from "quaint") to describe the finely-wrought and characteristic

[1] Cf. Ainslie: "The rack and the ride o' the restless tide" (*Land of Burns*, 1822.)
[2] Cf. Spenser: "And yett his peace is but continual jarre!" (*F.Q.*, II. ii. st. 26).
[3] *Letters*, vol. ii. p. 109.

markings on natural phenomena—rocks, shells, clouds, etc.; so in No. 72, nature's artless art in marking, hewing and disposing boulders "along the loins of the hills" through which the river runs is tersely expressed in the phrase "chancequarrièd, *selfquainèd* rocks".[1] Other words compounded with *self* provide a further illustration of Hopkins's great debt to Shakespeare in the matter of diction. Shakespeare speaks of *self-affairs*, *self-breath*, *self-bounty*, etc., and dozens of analogous compounds are current to-day. Hopkins knew that the individual physical life in Man was valuable and tolerable only when leavened by "*Selfyeast* of spirit" (45). Self-interest or an obstinate individualism he renames *selfbent* (35); and in telling how "limber liquid youth" in the communicant Bugler (23)

"Hies headstrong to its wellbeing of a self-wise self-will",

the poet paradoxically enlists two derogatory words (*headstrong* and *self-will*) to point his approval of the boy's self-determined devotion.

Hopkins's love of distinctive form in all things inspired the regret, in *Binsey Poplars* (19), that ten or twelve strokes of the woodman's axe could "*unselve* The sweet especial rural scene". Another successful Shakespearian coinage is heard in No. 47:

"Soul, self; come, poor *Jackself*, I do advise
You, jaded, let be;"

The "Jack" of Shakespeare is a knave, a low-born, common fellow, as in the compounds *Jack-sauce* and *Jack-slave*; but in modern parlance "jack" signifies a person or thing that is useful, hard-working (or -worked), undistinguished but indispensable: —jack-tar, Jack of all trades, steeple-jack, jack-knife, jack-plane, roasting-jack. Hence *Jackself* represents Hopkins the faithful, conscientious drudge, the priest and professor who, after three years in Ireland, had "done God's will (in the main) and many many examination papers".[2] Two other compounds which express not so much the distinctive personality as the whole being in travail are the *selfwrung* and *selfstrung* of *Spelt from Sibyl's Leaves* (32).

One further example of this poet's eagerness to individualize both the experience and the medium of its expression occurs in *Henry Purcell* (21). The distinctive quality in the genius of

[1] For a visualization of this image, see the drawing of rocks "At the Baths of Rosenlaui" (*Note-books*, p. 106).

[2] *Letters*, vol. i. pp. 250–51.

Purcell is symbolized by the crescent-shaped markings on the quill-feathers of a sea-bird :

> " Have an eye to the *sakes* of him, quaint moonmarks, to
> his pelted plumage under
> Wings : "

" *Sake* ", he says,

> " is a word I find it convenient to use : I did not know when I did so that it is common in German, in the form *sach.* It is the *sake* of ' for the sake of ', *forsake*, *namesake*, *keepsake*. I mean by it the being a thing has outside itself, as a voice by its echo, a face by its reflection, a body by its shadow, a man by his name, fame, or memory, *and also* that in the thing by virtue of which especially it has this being abroad, and that is something distinctive, marked, specifically or individually speaking, as for a voice and echo clearness ; for a reflected image light, brightness ; for a shadow-casting body bulk ; for a man genius, great achievements, amiability, and so on." [1]

In present usage, the sense of *sake* is so vague and general that Hopkins was perhaps justified in using it as the matrix of a particular and private meaning. " For the sake of " usually means " for the love of " or " for the advantage of this esteemed person or thing " ; and *keepsake* means " something which keeps fresh the beloved mental image of . . ." If this mental image, comprising the *distinctive quality* and the *value* of the subject, is considered as the exterior being of that subject, we have a tangible distinction analogous to that which Hopkins makes between the actual " quaint moonmarks " and the sensible images (*sakes* or *phantasmata*) by which the whole individual thing is retained in the mind.[2] Again, the markings on the bird, being metaphorically assimilated to the distinctive qualities of the composer, are in effect both natural *namesakes* and natural *keepsakes* : through them we know and remember Purcell.

For most readers, perhaps, the poet's use of *sakes* is too abstract and subtle to be emotively valid. Certainly, the principle could never be " popular ", and it raises the question as to how far a poet's meaning should rely upon the external aid of notes. " *Sakes* ", he admitted, " is hazardous : about that

[1] *Letters*, vol. i. p. 83. In his next letter he adds : " That German word is *sache*, not *sach*, except in compounds."

[2] In his adaptation of *sake*, Hopkins may have been influenced, consciously or otherwise, by the Scotist principle of individuation with its concepts of *haecceitas* and *formalitates*. (See chap. i. pp. 22–23 and also De Wulf, *op. cit.* vol. ii. p. 72 *et seqq*.

point I was more bent on saying my say than on being understood in it" ; yet he was dismayed at finding that the whole poem ("one of my very best pieces") was unintelligible to Bridges.[1] He proposed, in 1887, to prefix short prose arguments to some of his pieces ; but in actual practice the explanations demanded of him by his friends were given grudgingly and with a certain disgust. His attitude was always : "My meaning surely *ought* to appear of itself". Epic, drama, ballad, and most forms should be at once intelligible ; but everything need not and cannot be :

> "Plainly if it is possible to express a subtle and recondite thought on a subtle and recondite subject in a subtle and recondite way and with great felicity and perfection, in the end, something must be sacrificed, with so trying a task, in the process, and this may be the being at once, nay perhaps even the being without explanation at all, intelligible."[2]

Another type of coinage in which Hopkins was both original and prolific is one which may be called the *compound by substitution.* One element in some familiar compound is replaced by another, just as a weaker acid is displaced by a stronger in the composition of a salt. In this way the strangeness and piquancy of the new word are tempered by an age-long familiarity, and the new word is enriched by tacit comparison or contrast with the old. The device has often been used by wits both naive and sophisticated, as in the plebeian 'screwmatics' (for 'rheumatics') and 'Holy Deadlock' as a plea for easier divorce. Used by Hopkins in serious poetry, the principle is similar to the horticulturalist's process of increasing and strengthening his varieties by grafting and cross-fertilization.

As a first excellent example we have *quickgold* (8), in which the tacit association with 'quicksilver' brings out the combined liquidity, solidity and brilliance of the stars. On the analogy of 'footmark', 'watermark' and 'hallmark' Hopkins coins *manmarks* (48) and *moonmarks* (21) ; and analogy rather than deliberate substitution probably accounts for "fresh youth fretted in a *bloomfall*" of No. 23 (contrasted, perhaps, with the maggoty 'windfall' of age). Similarly, his bold *lovescape* (4) to denote the wounds of Christ, though analogous to 'landscape', might have been formed directly from the back-formation, 'scape'. There can be little doubt, however, about *bluffhide* (43), for the

[1] *Letters*, vol. i. pp. 170–71. [2] *Ibid.* pp. 265–6.

ploughman's heavy square-toed boots remind us of a 'bluffhead' or headland [1] : *bluff-* is especially apt, as it suggests the character of Harry Ploughman. Hopkins's eye for detail must have found something highly symbolic in footwear, for in *Tom's Garland* (42) boots and their hobnails loom large. Tom's mate is his *fallow-bootfellow* (cf. 'bedfellow'), the 'fallow-' being added to denote 'yellow-clay-caked' and perhaps to *con*note the 'fallowing' or breaking up of land.

In *The Eurydice* we find conclusive proof that Hopkins was conscious, *ex post facto* at least, of this method of substitution. In the line "Death teeming in by her portholes," he had first written "mortholes" [2] (cf. Shakespeare's 'mort o' the deer' [3] and 'amort'); but here he wisely deferred to criticism : "About 'mortholes' I do wince a little . . ." [4] In the same poem, however, we have *forefalls* (cliffs dropping to the 'foreshore'—8); *duty-swerver'* (cf. Shakespeare's 'bed-swerver' [5]—54); *daredeaths* (from 'daredevils'—95); and in the last stanza *doomfire* is a very effective welding of the commonplace 'Doomsday' and 'hell-fire'. We may note in passing that Hopkins, like Spenser, was partial to native compounds with *fore-*; against the Elizabethan's *forelay*, *forelift*, *foretaught*, etc., we may set the Victorian's *forefending* (23), "*forethought* of" (i.e. "thinking about beforehand"—29), *forepangs* (41), "*forefoundering* seas" (53), *foredrawn* (predestinated—54), and, in his descriptive and theological vocabulary, the nouns *forepitch* (projection) and *forestall* (anticipation).[6]

Bridges points out, with obvious disapproval, the touch of Barnesian freakishness in Hopkins's description of God's smile which, at unforeseen times,

> "as skies
> *Betweenpie* mountains—lights a lovely mile." (47)

The use of *betweenpie* in the sense of 'intervariegates' can be justified, says Bridges, only by the existence of a verb 'to pie', which "seems to be forbidden by homophonic absurdities".[7] Actually there is a verb 'pie', meaning 'to mix type' (cf. 'printer's pie'); and the back-formation of a verb from the

[1] With this image, cf. in the same poem the "*crag*iron" of the ploughshare, which butts away the earth "as some bluff river headland its spray" (Browning).

[2] MS. "A". So "heavengravel" replaced *grimstones* (from 'brimstone'?) in MS. "B".

[3] *Winter's Tale*, I. ii. 119.

[4] *Letters*. vol. i. pp. 53-4.

[5] *Winter's Tale*, II. i. 92.

[6] *Note-books*, pp. 136 and 333.

[7] *Poems*, p. 117.

pseudo-participle 'pied' (from 'pie'='magpie') seemed so natural to Hopkins that in the *Journal* he speaks of the "white *pieings*" on a pigeon.[1] Moreover, the use of 'magpie' as a verb would not be unthinkable to a fellow-countryman of Shakespeare, and Hopkins may have deliberately substituted *between-* for *mag-* to produce just the idea he wanted. The two poet-critics who were the first to insist that Hopkins set down words in such a way that "*they had to be understood as he meant them to be, or understood not at all*" [2] have said also :

> "We must appreciate the accuracy of the term *Betweenpie*. Besides being again just the sort of homely kitchen language that the Jackself would use to describe how sky seems pressed between two mountains (almost as a smile is pressed between lips) it is also the neatest possible way of combining the patching effect of light . . . with the way this light is introduced between the mountains." [3]

The appreciation of such a word is largely a matter of individual sensibility and opinion ; but in most of the compounds we are discussing there is an *absolute* validity and beauty. The phrase "*treadmire* toil" (48) exploits all the unpleasant associations of 'treadmill' in a wider field of reference. In the line "from *groundlong* babyhood to hoary age" (69) not only are we reminded of 'groundling' (creeping plant and inferior spectator), 'endlong' (Spenser), 'flatlong' (Shakespeare), 'lifelong' and other traditional words ; the sprawling child impresses us with the main theme of the sonnet—that man is, physically, morally and intellectually, a lifelong groundling at a grotesque masque.

Hopkins tells Margaret that one day she will be unmoved "Though worlds of *wanwood leafmeal* lie" (31). In *wanwood* the meaning 'bloodless' is combined with the older meaning—'dark', 'black' ; and the bitterness of 'wormwood' lurks beneath. *Leafmeal* is an adverb made from 'piecemeal', and harks back to similar Shakespearian forms—*inch-meal* and *limb-meal* : *-meal* also implies the mealy fragments of dry rotting leaves.[4]

[1] *Note-books*, p. 176.

[2] Laura Riding and Robert Graves in *Survey of Modernist Poetry* (1927), p. 90. This statement, though usually true, has exceptions, as the present work shows *passim*.

[3] *Ibid.* p. 92.

[4] It is possible to make sense of this line by taking *-meal* as the word and not as a suffix, so that *wanwood* becomes an adjective ; but this reading weakens the force not only of "lie" (which calls for an adverb) but of the whole image. (Cf. *Tempest*, II. ii. 3 and *Cymb.* II. iv. 147.)

Somewhat puzzling at first, but equally successful, is the poet's manner of expressing anxiety for the young Bugler's future :

> " but may he not rankle and roam
> In *backwheels* though bound home ?—" (23)

This compound, following the implications of the boldly metaphorical " rankle " (fester, malinger, backslide, give constant pain), immediately suggests ' backways ', ' backwoods ', ' backwaters ' ; but *-wheels* brings in a relevant military touch, with the sense of turning aside, swinging right round and going back. And here again Hopkins may have remembered that Shakespeare used ' wheel ' in the sense of ' roam ', ' wander about '.[1]

A more popular vein and also a delicate fancy are shown in the " the *all-a-leaf* of the treetop " (64), where the substitution of *-leaf* gives a local habitation and a name to the general ideas in ' all alive ' and ' all alight '. Pregnant, too, is the same device in *To his Watch* (70) :

> " Mortal my mate, bearing my *rock-a-heart*
> Warm beat with cold beat company . . ."

There is first the contrast between the ' rock-a-by ' peace of the warm cradle (incubator of hopes) and the unrest of the poet's life, the cold ticking away of his precious minutes without fruition ; then there is a comparison between the sleep of the cradle and the final sleep of death : " but we were framed to fail and die ".

This principle of substitution sometimes appears in phrases, where a well-known idiom is suddenly transmuted by a slight change in one of its elements. Most subtle and effective is the change from ' world without end ' to *world without event* in the eulogy of St. Alphonsus (49), but every example is felicitous : *slips of soldiery* (23) from ' slip of a boy ' ; *ran revel* (30) from ' ran riot ' ; *rack or wrong* (35) from ' rack and ruin ' ; and in *hard at bay* (4) two trite phrases (' hard pressed ' and ' at bay ') are hammered into one. Such resourcefulness, at once so spontaneous and expert, is surely unique in the history of poetry.

Turning now to his more traditional hyphened compounds, we observe that no other English poet is proportionately so rich in these words, and none evinces a finer audacity in their making. Critics have said of Shakespeare that his apprehensions were

[1] E.g. " In an extravagant and wheeling stranger
Of here and everywhere." (*Othello*, I. i. 137.)
Cf. also *Troil. and Cress.*, V. vii. 2.

simultaneous, not consecutive; that he had "the instinctive passion for *a one word* to express *one act* of feeling".[1] The same is even more true of Hopkins, in whom Mr. Charles Williams notes "a passionate emotion which seems to try to utter all its words in one".[2]

On the subject of the compound Hopkins himself says:

> "English compounds do not seem real single words or properly unified till by some change in form or spelling or slur in pronunciation their construction is disguised. This seems in English a point craved for and insisted on, that words shall be single and specific marks for things, whether self-significant or not."[3]

Yet as he himself demonstrates, English rivals the flexible Greek in its suitability for the making of compounds; and if Hopkins seems at first, in his more daring asyntactic formations, to be striving against 'the genius of the language', it is because the full possibilities of English had not been so strenuously developed for over two hundred and fifty years.

In most of his hyphened noun-compounds, Hopkins was building on precedents from Shakespeare's *here-approach*, *self-and-vain-conceit*,[4] etc. to Browning's *leaf-and-twiggishness* (*Pacchiarotto*); but his virtuosity in this kind is unequalled. Because poetry must be vivid and concrete, he prefers the native strangeness of *womb-notbearing* (58) to the Romance 'barrenness' and 'sterility'; and other compounds, fortified by alliteration, present their idea with a sort of stark nakedness which at first shocks because it takes us right back to the primitive origins of poetic apprehension: *sea-romp* (waves 'mousing' with the drowned—4.17); "her *wild-worst*" (4.24); *May-mess* (8); *sinew-service* (43).[5] Many of these compounds, which range from two to five elements, are exquisite or dramatic 'miniature poems': "skies of *couple-colour*" (13); *earl-stars* (32); *ringlet-race* (54); *water-in-a-wallow* (17); *beauty-in-the-ghost* (36); *Miracle-in-Mary-of-flame* (4.34).

[1] Coleridge, *Anima Poetae*. [2] *Poems*, *Introduction*, p. xv.

[3] *Letters*, vol. i. p. 165. He continues: "It is noticeable how unmeaning out topographical names are or soon become, while those in Celtic languages are so transparent. . . . *Thimble* is singler than *thumbstall*, but it is a meaner word. . . . *Potato* is certainly one of the ugliest and most laughable words in the language and cannot well be used in verse, whereas *earthapple* is stately: *potato* has one virtue only, the being specific." He condemns Tyndal's *clangtint* for the German *Klangfarbe*; but he would probably have preferred *sidewalk* to *pavement*.

[4] See Abbott, § 430.

[5] Cf. also "móuthed to *flésh-búrst*" (4.8), where the stress on each syllable adds to the physical directness of the compound.

Hopkins's tendency in later years was to 'unify' his compounds as far as possible by dropping the hyphens, as in *self-disposal* (58), *goldnails* (61), *airworld, hawkmoth* (72), etc.; but his guide was always expediency: he would always retain the hyphen if a slight separation of the elements gave a clarity or vividness to the total image. In the curious *Amansstrength* of Harry Ploughman, however, he seems to have wanted a tight, compact word which would harmonize with the muscular tension of the whole figure ("hard as hurdle arms", "barrowy brawn", "as a beechbole firm").

His compound verbs, though rarer, are always forceful and essentially poetic: *fathers-forth* (13); *fire-featuring* (stars—32); *new-nestle* (56). Man "*day-labouring-out* life's age" (15) is probably intended to recall Milton's "Doth God exact day-labour, light denied?" (*On his Blindness*).

In his numerous compound epithets Hopkins, like Shakespeare, Keats and Tennyson, shows to an eminent degree what Ruskin has called "imagination penetrative". The compound epithet in English may be divided into two main types, (1) the poetical-descriptive, (2) the dramatic or rhetorical.[1] It is true that these epithets often degenerate into terse and metrically convenient prose statements without a trace of verbal magic: such are Hardy's "*tall-spired* town" (*Wessex Heights*) and "*brown-shawled* dame" (*Signs and Tokens*); but Hopkins never tolerated conventional flatness.

The first type derives, through Spenser and Milton, from the mythological and descriptive epithets of Homer (ῥοδοδάκτυλος Ἠώς, ἀργυρόπεζος)[2] and reaches its fine flower in the "*soft-conchèd* ear" and "*far-foamèd* sands"[3] of Keats. The second type, which may be almost prosaic when considered alone, but which takes poetic fire from its context, was much used by Shakespeare: "*to-and-fro-conflicting* wind and rain", "*haste-poste-haste* appearance", "*steep-down* gulfs".[4]

Hopkins uses all kinds, from the Keatsian "*silver-surfèd* cherry" (18) and "*lark-charmèd* . . . city" (which, as a description of "branchy" Oxford,[5] echoes Keats's oaks "*branch-charmèd* by the earnest stars")[6] to the Shakespearian "*black-about* air" (4.24)

[1] For certain suggestions and examples in this section I am indebted to Mr. Bernard Groom's excellent essay, *The Formation and Use of Compound Epithets in English Poetry from* 1579 (S.P.E. Tract No. XLIX. 1937).

[2] Cf. Spenser's "*rosy-fingered* morning" and Milton's "*tinsel-slippered* feet".

[3] *Psyche*, 4; *Hyperion*, ii. 172.

[4] *K.L.*, III. i. 2; *Oth.*, I. ii. 37; *Oth.*, V. ii. 280.

[5] *Poems*, No. 20.

[6] *Hyperion*, i. 74.

and such asyntactic phrase-words as *American-outward-bound* (4.12) and "*fault-not-found-with* good" (67). An unusually long compound like "*drop-of-blood-and-foam-dapple*/Bloom" (18) is a natural coupling of the Greek accumulation of epithets with the Keatsian dictum that poetry should surprise by a fine excess.

Two types of epithet used occasionally by Shakespeare but very rarely by later poets before Hopkins are the 'verb and object' (e.g. "*lack-lustre* eye")[1] and the 'bi-adjectival' (e.g. *wilful-opposite*).[2] Of the first type Hopkins has "*blear-all* black" and "*spendsavour* salt" in No. 26, "*wring-world* right foot" (40) and other equally vigorous examples. The 'bi-adjectival' epithet was revived by Carlyle (whose influence on Browning and Meredith, on Doughty and Hopkins too, should not be underestimated): in *The French Revolution* we find *angel-daemonic, giddy-swift, Brummellian-polite*[3]—epithets which are not 'poetic' but are sufficiently striking to make us wonder how other poets could have missed the possibilities so admirably realized by Hopkins. Milton, however, when speaking of the North Wind's "*cold-kind* embrace",[4] might well have suggested the "*kindcold* element" which breaks across the limbs of Hopkins's swimmer (72).

The epithet of three elements appeared sporadically from Herbert's "*Christ-side-piercing* spear"[5] to C. Rossetti's sensuous "*Bloom-down-cheeked* peaches".[6] In Browning also, among many others far less 'Hopkinsian', occurs the lovely *fawn-skin-dappled* (*A Pretty Woman*). But Hopkins, lyric poet *par excellence* of the sharp, flashing, condensed style, is the greatest adept in the use of these epithets of three or more elements: he could employ them more freely without strain or excess because they harmonize more completely with his whole manner. In "*dappled-with-damson* west" (4.5) and *brown-as-dawning-skinned* (17) he is following the lead of earlier poets; but in the dramatic sentence-epithet "*the O-seal-that-so* feature" (38) and in many more like "*wimpled-water-dimpled, not-by-morning-matchèd* face" (36), "*feel-of-primrose* hand" (3), "*hearse-of-all* night" (32), "*very-violet-sweet* . . . stallion" (14),[7] and *tatter-tassel-tangled* (64) he is showing that

[1] *As You Like It,* II. vii. 21.
[2] *King John,* V. ii. 124. See also III. iii. 43; IV. i. 67, 76.
[3] See Groom, *op. cit.* p. 313.
[4] *On the Death of a Fair Infant.*
[5] *Prayer* (I).
[6] *Goblin Market,* line 9.
[7] For a criticism and defence of this compound, see below, chap. v. pp. 190-1

originality which, as a condition of poetic genius, makes each poet " like a species in nature ". These long epithets, though a source of frigidity in prose, are (as Aristotle said) proper and sonorous in the mouth of the " Dithyrambic poet ".[1]

In exploring the possibilities of the compound epithet, Hopkins left very little to be discovered by later poets; but something of the peculiar energy imparted by these words in his own poetry could have been learned from Browning and Meredith. The older poet, an indomitable experimenter, used arbitrary formations with marked success, as in " *green-flesh* melons "[2] and " *many-tinkling* fleece "[3]; and in Browning's description of the cypress (*De Gustibus—*) Hopkins might have studied the effect of accumulation :

> " By the many hundred years *red-rusted,*
> Rough *iron-spiked,* ripe *fruit-o'er-crusted,*"

In Meredith, Hopkins would have appreciated the vivacity and heartiness of " long tail of *stern-ajerk* empty barges ", " bank of blueish *smack-o'-cheek* red ",[4] and the more delicate poetry of " *white-lightning* limbs "[5] or " *lost-to-light* ghosts ".[6]

To Mr. Groom's claim that Tennyson was " the greatest Victorian master of the compound epithet " we demur : in range and vigour Tennyson must yield to Hopkins. Tennyson's peculiar *forte,* the exquisite, exact observation of " *high-elbow'd* grigs "[7] and " *tiny-trumpeting* gnat ",[8] Hopkins does not try to rival; but he combines observation and poetic suggestiveness with a skill not inferior to Tennyson's in " *moth-soft* Milky Way " (4.26), " *frailest-flixed* snowflake " (37), " *crush-silk* poppies " (64), " *tool-smooth* bleak light " (32) and many other compounds.

We detect in Hopkins's use of the compound epithet an interesting development. In his youthful poems he was satisfied with echoes of Spenser and Keats—*satin-purfled* and *rosy-budded* (77); in his middle period he showed what has been rightly called " a creative handling of syntax " in the construction of compounds of every known and perhaps of every conceivable type; but in his latest period he tended to drop the compound

[1] *Rhetoric,* III. iii. For examples of the " frigid " use, see *The Rejected Addresses,* XVI. " Theatrical Alarm-Bell ", by the Editor of the M.P.

[2] *De Gustibus—*

[3] *Love Among the Ruins,* IX. Cf. Thomson's " many-twinkling leaves " (Spring, 158) and Aeschylus's ἀνήριθμον γέλασμα (*P.V.*, 90).

[4] *One of Our Conquerors* (1892), pp. 6 and 31. [5] *With the Huntress.*

[6] *Demeter and Persephone.* [7] *The Brook,* 54. [8] *Elaine,* 138.

of more than two elements, and often (as following Greek and Welsh poetry) to stress the singleness of the word by discarding the hyphen. To give, however, an adequate idea of the variety and beauty of Hopkins's epithets we must attempt a somewhat elaborate classification based as nearly as possible on grammatical form (see Appendix C, p. 286).

Turning now to other stylistic "graces", we find as much refreshing originality in his handling of archaic and dialect words as in his compounds and coinages. In a letter already quoted he says that "passing freaks and graces" are allowable in poetry so long as the basic contemporaneity of the language is not destroyed.[1] Himself a severe critic of the "blight" of archaism in other Victorian writers,[2] he justifies his own occasional use of such words when he says: "Some little flavours, but much spoils".[3] The old words he revives are mostly from Shakespeare and other Elizabethans, but he did not borrow so freely and casually as to fall beneath his own stricture:

> "The example of Shakspere (by a 'corrupt following', for it is an absurd fallacy—like a child having to repeat the substance of something it has been told and saying *you* and *I*, whereas it should say *I* where he said *you* and so on) has done ever so much harm by his very genius, for poets reproduce the diction which in him was modern and in them is obsolete."[4]

The words he retrieves can be justified on structural and other poetic grounds, and he almost invariably imbues them with new life, a fresh figurative import.

His adoption of an old or 'outlandish' word was often influenced, in part, by his extensive use of alliteration and assonance. Considerations of "lettering"[5] (i.e. alliteration, etc.) helped him to light on the appropriate archaism in "Heart, you *round* me right" . . . "reckon but, *reck* but" (32); "each *tucked* string tells" (34); "so fagged, so *fashed*" (36), and in many similar groups. The archaic word, to justify itself, should perceptibly fill a gap in the current language; it should supply a need in the verse, even if that need is only structural. In Hopkins there is usually a lexical gain as well.

[1] *Letters*, vol. i. p. 89. [2] See Volume II. chap. iv. of the present work.
[3] *Letters*, vol. i. p. 218. [4] *Ibid.* p. 218.
[5] In Volume II. we shall attempt a more exhaustive historical treatment of this important aspect of Hopkins's poetry.

The vigour and universality achieved by a skilful mingling of past and present elements are seen in the passionate climax of No. 48 :

> " This Jack, joke, poor potsherd, | patch, matchwood, immortal diamond,"

The obsolete *patch* (a paltry fellow, fool) and the archaic *Jack* and *potsherd* rub consonantal shoulders with common, everyday words ; the former, moreover, have meanings and " prepossessions " which are as modern as those of the latter [1] ; so that in the heat of declamation a uniformity of " historic prepossession " is subconsciously felt.

A few of Hopkins's archaic and obsolete words are of pre-Elizabethan provenance : in this same poem there is *stark*, which in Chaucer kept its original meaning—' strong ', and here means ' firm ', ' persistent ' ; there is also *chevy*, ' ride in chase ' (cf. *Chevy Chase*)—a word which, strengthened by tacit association with the modern form, ' chivy ' (chase about, harass) describes admirably the movement of light, wind-blown clouds :

> " flaunt forth, then chevy on an air-
> built thoroughfare : "

Less familiar, and far less successful, is the " *rudred*/Bud shelling, etc." in *The Woodlark* (64) : this word (M.E. ' rudd-redd ', rosy-cheeked ; O.E. ' rudu ', ruddiness) is utterly eclipsed by the lurid compounds which precede it—" blood-gush ", " Flame-rash ".

Hopkins avoided those obsolete words which Doughty and others affected with a Spenserian passion for ' atmosphere ' and ' genuine antique '—*mote* (vb.), *wonne*, *swink*, etc. ; but he used a few archaic words and meanings which were probably derived from Spenser : *reave*, ' take away ', ' strip ' (22, 35) [2] ; *fume*, ' pass away like smoke ' (24) [3] ; *nursle*, ' rear ', ' foster ' (21) [4] ; *gear*, ' dress ' (36) [5] ; *stead*, ' help ', ' avail ' (54).[6] The

[1] For modern meanings of *Jack* see above, p. 119 ; *patch* is the makeshift repair, second-best expedient, fallen Man ; *potsherd* is Biblical.

[2] *F.Q.*, II. viii. 15.

[3] With the theme of Hopkins's poem, cf. Spenser's

> " Even such is all their vaunted vanitie,
> Nought else but smoke, and fumeth soone away."
> (*Colin Clout*, l. 720.)

[4] Cf. Shakespeare's ' nousle ', to nourish delicately (*Per.*, I. iv. 42. Spenser's spelling is ' noursle ' (*F.Q.*, V. i. 6).

[5] *F.Q.*, II. iv. 26.

[6] *Ibid.*, II. ix. 9.

older meanings of *rash* (quick, urgent—4.19 ; 11 ; 58) [1] are found in both Spenser and Shakespeare.

Among words drawn, presumably, from the pages of Shakespeare some are obsolete forms like *thorough* (17) and *brinded* (brindled—13) ; some are current words used with the peculiar Elizabethan force : " I *can* no more " (40 ; cf. *Ant. and Cleo.* IV. xiii. 59) ; " but *let be*, let be : " (17.103 ; cf. *Ham.* V. ii. 238). Others are pure archaism : *round*, ' whisper ' (32), " *mealed*-with-yellow sallows " (' mingled-', plus the figurative sense of ' sprinkled '—8) ; while a few, since they were used only once by Shakespeare himself, throw some light on Hopkins's readings : *mammock*, ' tear in fragments ' (42 ; cf. *Coriol.*, I. iii. 71) ; *shive*-lights, ' strips of light ' (48 ; ' slice ' ; cf. *Tit. And.* II. i. 87) ; *fanged*, ' seized ', ' held ' (65 ; cf. *Tim. of Ath.* IV. iii. 23—though Hopkins may have intended a verb from ' fang ', tooth). Two others, *fettle* and *heft*, are still current in dialect, so that we cannot be at all sure of the poet's source.

It is instructive to examine, in some detail, the manner in which an original, true poet can use, without echo or imitation, the diction of a great predecessor. Juliet is told to " *fettle* (prepare) " her " fine joints 'gainst Thursday next " [2] ; and Hopkins makes the boisterous young blacksmith (father, as it were, of the dying " child, Felix ") :

> " . . . *fettle* for the great grey drayhorse his bright and battering sandal ! " (29)

Again, *rivelled* (wrinkled) [3] is a word Hopkins might have come across in Wyatt, Marston, Middleton, or some other minor Elizabethan ; it is probable, however, that he remembered Shakespeare's sole instance in *Troilus and Cressida* :

> " incurable bone-ache and the rivelled fee-simple of the tetter." (V. i. 26).

The back-formation, ' rivel ', is rare ; but Hopkins uses it with fine two-edged effect in *The Eurydice* :

> " But his eye no cliff, no coast or
> Mark makes in the *rivelling* snowstorm." (ll. 67–8.)

The wide invisible air is shrunken into a visible corrugation, puckered by the driving wind into successive gusts of thick

[1] *F.Q.*, II. x. 7 (" rash decay ") and *Troil. and Cress.*, IV. ii. 63 (" My matter is so rash "). See above, p. 94 (" rash-fresh ").

[2] *Rom. and Jul.*, III. v. 154.

[3] M.E. ' riueled ', O.E. ' rifelede '.

snowflakes, which at the same time force the shipwrecked Sydney Fletcher to screw up his face in a painful effort to see.

If we had not known that Hopkins was a priest, profoundly interested in the moral progress of all men, we might have discovered the fact in his ameliorative handling of certain Elizabethan words—*fetch* (n.), *heft*, *pash*, *latch* (vb.). Shakespeare's " fetch ", the trick or somewhat mean artifice recommended by Polonius to Reynaldo,[1] is raised by Hopkins into an exalted expedient : the nun in *The Deutschland* (4.19) :

> ". . . sees one thing, one ;
> Has one *fetch* in her : she rears herself to divine
> Ears,"

Another rare word freely adapted is *heft* (54). It is used only once in Shakespeare : Leonato says that a person who had unwittingly swallowed a spider in his wine would, on being told, crack his sides " with violent hefts ".[2] To this noun from ' heave ' (cf. weave, weft) Hopkins gives the meaning of striving up, effort to rise, ambition (with a suggestion of pride) :

> " Creatures all *heft*, hope, hazard, interest." [3]

In the same poem is the line already quoted in the ' Scotist ' section of Chapter I :

> " Man lives that *list*, that leaning in the will "

To give the line any depth, the common meaning of *list*, repeated in the following word, must be fortified by the original and transitional meanings — ' pleasure ', ' inclination ', as in " I find it still when I have list to sleep " (*Oth.* II. i. 104) and inversely in ' listless '.

Similar elevation and doubling of meaning give an unusual richness (and pathos) to that image of Christ's godhead " low-*latched* in leaf-light housel " (23), which at first sight means " dwelling humbly in a thin wafer as behind the latched door of a cottage ". It can mean this, and the disguised pun in " housel " is not untoward ; but Hopkins had in mind the stronger Shakespearian meaning of *latch*—' to catch, lay hold of ' [4] ; so

[1] *Ham.*, II. i. 38.
[2] *Wint. Tale*, II. i. 44.
[3] Cf. " tender-hefted nature " (*K. Lear*, II. iv. 174), and also the dialect meaning—' to lift, push '.
[4] O.E. ' læĉĉan ' ; cf. *Macbeth*, IV. iii. 193–5 :

> " But I have words
> That would be howl'd out to the desert air
> Where hearing should not *latch* them."

that apart from the simile in " leaf-light " the whole line can be taken *literally* : " God, in condescending humility, allows Himself to be held, imprisoned in the Host." Godhead is made accessible ; but the faithful must lay hold of it, as an opportunity is ' seized '.

A minor symptom, perhaps, of the general decline in linguistic and imaginative vigour was the disuse of that expressive Elizabethan word—*pash* (beat, batter). Vulgar language still has ' bash ' ; but when Hopkins, in *Sibyl's Leaves* (32), wished to describe analogically the merging of numerous small individual actions into the two amorphous masses, Right and Wrong, no word but the obsolete *pashed*, with its suggestive sound and correct " prepossession ", would serve his purpose.[1]

Finally, Hopkins imitates the free Elizabethan practice in certain adverbs. In "*force* I must be brief" (41) he is paring down to the quick Shakespeare's ' of force ' or ' force perforce ' ; in *by meanwhiles* (30), *betweenwhiles* (57) and *betweens* (79) he is boldly extending the use of the old Germanic adverbial ' -s ' (cf. ' nowadays '). In forms like *onewhere* (43), *what while* (better, for this poet's purpose, than the overworked ' what time '—36) and *all while* (25) we see Hopkins rearranging the "caleidoscopic elements" of language to produce an individual idiom.

This idiom must have proved a stumbling-block to many readers of that eccentric last line of *The Bugler's First Communion* (23). Having uttered, on behalf of the boy, pleas which would " brandle [2] adamantine heaven " if disregarded, Hopkins adds :

> " Forward-like, but however, and like favourable heaven
> heard these."

This seems to mean : " Presumptuous of me, and perhaps my fears are premature ; but however, that is just how I feel about this lad. And belike (or ' like enough ') heaven turned a favourable ear to my pleas." *Forward-like* is an adjective used with adverbial force ; a native equivalent of ' presumptuous ' (or ' premature '), its meaning is based partly on *praesumo*, ' picture to oneself beforehand ', and partly on such a colloquial

[1] Other Shakespearian words used by Hopkins are : *cog* (deceive—36), *coil* (turmoil—40), *dear* (vb., hold dear—39), *dearer* (adv., more seriously—46), *poised* (weighed, considered—27), *seared* (blighted—7), *scanted* (skimped— 15), *Spare* ! (forbear—36) *word* (vb., represent—4.29).

[2] ' shake ' (obsolete) ; it was usually intransitive.

form as 'impudent like'. The second *like* may be a deliberate shortening of the archaic 'very like'.[1]

As in his more numerous archaisms, Hopkins adopted a few dialect words of peculiar force or appropriateness whenever the subject-matter allowed of such "graces". From Scots he takes the expressive *fashed*, troubled (36); and in that delightful lyric, *Inversnaid*, the conventional *burn* and *braes* are accompanied by two subtle touches of local colour—the "wind-puff *bonnet* of fawn-froth" and the "bead*bonny* ash". Two other Scots words are *mell*, mix (56), the sound of which gives the liquid quality of the dappled May sky; and *throughther*, a syncope of 'through' and 'other' which dramatically epitomizes the dominant image in *Spelt from Sibyl's Leaves*. In the same poem, *Disremembering* is an Irishism, aptly enlisted as a mental and phonal image corresponding to the physical image, *dismembering*.

His three years' sojourn in Lancashire gave him two local words which are appropriately set to poems directly inspired by Northcountry places—the "*degged* (sprinkled) with dew" of *Inversnaid* and "the leavès *throng*" of *Ribblesdale* ("I mean 'throng' for an adjective as we use it here in Lancashire").[2] There are, however, two other words (both borrowed from the North-east) which are introduced boldly and successfully into poems of aesthetic and theological import. That Yorkshire and Brontë word, *wuthering*, honours and is honoured by its metaphorical application in *Henry Purcell*[3]; and the *sillion* down which "sheer plod" makes the plough shine in *The Windhover* has a fitness beyond the needs of rhyme: its meaning ('a strip of ploughed land' or just 'furrow') links it up naturally with the strong native words—*sheer*, *plod*, *plough*, *shine*, while its French origin relates it to those other French words which are derived from medieval courts and chivalry—*minion*, *dauphin*, *falcon*, *chevalier*. These together with the 'rich rhyme', *million* and *vermilion*, contribute to the total impression of splendour produced by the perfect characteristic activity of kestrel and humble plodder alike.

[1] *However* may also have the force of Shakespeare's:

> "If lost, why then a grievous labour won:
> *However*, but a folly bought with wit," (*Two Gent.*, I. i. 34–5.)

[2] *Letters*, vol. ii. p. 109.

[3] *Ibid.*, vol. i. p. 83: "*Wuthering* is a Northcountry word for the noise and rush of wind: hence Emily Brontë's *Wuthering Heights*."

In his resourceful exploitation of all the diverse elements in the richly composite English vocabulary, Hopkins is one of the very few poets who can be considered in the same category as Shakespeare. Without being pedantic or unwarrantably obscure, he could use (in Johnson's phrase) " words to which we are nearly strangers " and yet not distract our attention from the object.[1] His coinages, archaisms and dialect words always repay that mental search or even studious research which he often demands as the price of his meaning : indeed, " it is all a purchase, all is a prize ".

Hopkins held, with Coleridge, that in verse the words, the media, must have a particular beauty and ought to attract our notice ; but he is always careful to subordinate the parts to the whole, to preserve the essential unity of the poem. If any individual word is to be " dwelt upon ", it is because its attractive quality has a particular significance in the total effect or message. This special stressing is often artfully contrived by grammatical arrangement.

Hopkins's linguistic idiosyncrasy is perhaps most strongly marked in his syntax. Bridges praised him for his " period-building " [2] ; but it seemed to Bridges that he carried " emphatic condensation " to such extreme limits as often to oust clarity and euphony.[3] The same critic had written, many years earlier :

> " Poems so far removed as his came to be from the ordinary simplicity of grammar and metre, had they no other drawback, could never be popular ; but they will interest poets ; and they may perhaps prove welcome to the critic, for they have this plain fault, that, aiming at an unattainable perfection of language (as if *words—each with its twofold value in sense and sound—could be arranged like so many separate gems to compose a whole expression of thought, in which the force of grammar and the beauty of rhythm absolutely correspond*), they not only sacrifice simplicity, but very often, among verses of the rarest beauty, show a neglect of those canons of taste which seem common to all poetry." [4]

In defining a " plain fault ", Bridges here enunciates (in the words we have italicized) both the aim and the specific achievement of Hopkins. Certainly, recent criticism has gone far

[1] Few readers would know, off-hand, the precise meaning of " *random* grim forge " in *Felix Randal* ; yet a dictionary reveals at once the aptness of *random* to describe the rough masonry of the smithy.

[2] *Letters*, vol. i. p. 82. [3] *Poems of G. M. H.*, p. 99.

[4] *Robert Bridges and Contemporary Poets* (ed. A. H. Miles, 1906), p. 182.

towards establishing the fact that Hopkins attained his desired "perfection of language" much more often than he neglected real and universal canons of taste.

Hopkins's methods of treating grammar are broadly revealed in three types of syntax: (1) popular or colloquial; (2) conventional poetical; (3) learned, sophisticated, or stylized. Of conventional *prose* syntax (as found extensively in Wordsworth, Browning and most modern poets) there is scarcely a trace in the mature poems: we seldom get far before we meet some distinctive and essentially poetic turn of phrase. Again, there is very little conventional 'poetical' syntax which is not touched with some peculiarity of punctuation or rhythm which removes it from the ruck of traditional verse. He sometimes uses a form of inversion reminiscent of Gray; in the elegiac quatrains of No. 54 we find:

> "And are they thus? The fine, the fingering beams
> Their young delightful hour do feature down . . ."
> (Stanza 3.)

On this subject he says:

> "As you say, I do avoid inversions, because they weaken and because they destroy the earnestness or in-earnestness of the utterance. Nevertheless in prose I use them more than other people, because there they have great advantages of another sort.[1] Now these advantages they should have in verse too, but they must not seem to be due to the verse:"[2]

He criticizes Bridges for the conventional inversion of

> "'Tis joy the falling of her fold to view",

but does not see how it should be mended.[3] Moreover, his criteria, earnestness and inevitability, are of doubtful application: on both grounds some critics would condemn his own line:

> "and why must
> Disappointment all I endeavour end?" (50)

Certainly it would be hard to prove that this inversion was in no way "due to the verse", in spite of the fact that there is a kind of dramatic fitness in placing "end" where it is.

[1] E.g.—"Dine out we seldom do"; "Meant to write I have every day for long." (*Letters*, vol. i. pp. 55 and 135.)

[2] *Letters*, vol. i. p. 89. [3] Bridges removed the inversion; see *Letters, loc. cit.*

Usually, however, the inversions and other transpositions in Hopkins are of three other types: when they are not frankly colloquial, they are either free adaptations of Classical syntax or else entirely new locutions designed to express (though sometimes with a disconcertingly foreign air) the exact shade and quality of the poet's thought.

In common speech we frequently say, "Going down the road, are you?" instead of "Are you going down the road?". Such inversions convey the natural order and emphasis of ideas as they rise in the mind. The same dramatic fitness justifies the syntax of a passage already quoted for its rhythm:

> "Ah, touched in your bower of bone
> Are you? turned for an exquisite smart
> Have you? . . ." [1]

This is pathos: but a note of brutality is expressed in the very clumsiness of

> "What stroke has Caradoc's right arm dealt? what done?
> *Head of a rebel*
> *Struck off it has;*" [2]

Hopkins's use of colloquial forms might almost have been a practical response to Abbott's praise of Shakespearian to the detriment of Victorian English:

> "The spoken English so far predominated over the grammatical English that it materially influenced the rhythm of the verse, the construction of the sentence, and even sometimes the spelling of words. . . . Lastly, the use of some few still remaining inflections . . . the lingering *sense* of many other inflections that had passed away leaving behind something of the old versatility and audacity in the arrangement of the sentence, the stern subordination of grammar to terseness and clearness, and the consequent directness and naturalness of expression, all conspire to give a liveliness and wakefulness to Shakespearian English which are wanting in the grammatical monotony of the present day." [3]

With Shakespeare's many colloquial abbreviations we may compare Hopkins's "whose smile / 's not wrung" (47) and "'s cheek crimsons" (43). More remarkable is that unique *sense* of imaginary inflections to be found in Hopkins's asyntactic

[1] *The Wreck of the Deutschland*, stanza 18. See above, chap. ii. p. 48.
[2] No. 58, l. 26.
[3] *Op. cit.*, *Introduction*, p. 16.

constructions. With reference to the " difficulties of syntax " in *Harry Ploughman*, he even desiderates new inflections :

> " I do myself think, I may say, that it would be an immense advance in notation (so to call it) in writing as the record of speech, to distinguish the subject, verb, object, and in general to express the construction to the eye ; as is done already partly in punctuation by everybody, partly in capitals by the Germans, more fully in accentuation by the Hebrews. And I daresay it will come." [1]

Yet he feared (fortunately) that a private notation would seem " a confession of unintelligibility ".

" Naturalness of expression " was not always the first aim of either Shakespeare or Hopkins ; but " wakefulness " is an admirable word to describe a quality which these two poets share almost exclusively—an amazing adroitness in exploiting and adapting all the tried expedients of language.

Hopkins is often as direct and natural as a vivacious companion on a walk : " Harry bends, look " (43) ; " And the riot of a rout / Of, *it must be*, boys from the town / Bathing : " (72). We shall see later how this ' interjected absolute ' corresponds to the device in Welsh poetry called *tor ymadrodd.*[2] Incidentally, the colloquial separation of a preposition from its object is a trick which the more decorous and timid poets would never have tolerated. Exclamations are common, but the emotion is usually sincere and infectious :

> " Eh, how all rung !
> Young dog, he did give tongue ! " (30)

" Ah well, God rest him all road ever he offended ! " (29)

Here the happy provincialism, ' all road ', is a little obscured by the characteristic abbreviation of ' however ' to ' ever '.[3]

Once or twice the colloquialism is exaggerated ; the following, for instance, is vitiated by irrelevant associations of the playing field :

> " O well wept, mother have lost son ;
> Wept, wife ; wept, sweetheart would be one : " (17)

[1] *Letters*, vol. i. p. 265. [2] See Volume II. chap. iii. of the present work.

[3] Hopkins uses ' all road ' in a letter referring to Bridges's poem *O my vague desires* : " It is ' all road ' very remarkable " (*Letters*, vol. i. p. 117). The meaning seems to be ' all the way ', ' in every respect '. In the poem, however, " all road ever " may perhaps be taken as a conjunctive phrase meaning ' in whatever respects, to whatever degree '.

and this, from the same poem, is gushing, old-maidish :

> " And he boards her in Oh ! such joy
> He has lost count what came next, poor boy.—"

" O well wept " can, indeed, be justified on the analogy of Shakespeare's " O ! well begg'd ! " (*Coriolanus*, I. ix. 87) [1] ; but a tendency to sentimentalism which the poet usually kept well in check is fully exhibited in such rare expressions as " This very very day " (23) and " I ám so very, O, só very glád " (64—fragment).

In his best work, there is no sharp dividing line between popular and learned (or archaic) syntactic modes : the two are merged inextricably in the first line of *Henry Purcell* :

> " Have fair fallen, O fair, fair have fallen, so dear
> To me, so arch-especial a spirit. . . ."

" *Have* ", says Hopkins, " is the sing, imperative (or optative if you like) of the past, a thing possible and actual both in logic and grammar, but naturally a rare one ".[2] *Have done* ! is the only common form of this perfect imperative ; but the poet was justified in extending the principle to give a new individual turn to the Shakespearian optative :

> " *Fair fall* the bones that took the pains for me "
> (*King John*, I. i. 78.)

The same thought, which played a great part in Hopkins's own mind and action, is more clearly expressed in the last stanza but one of *The Loss of the Eurydice* :

> " And the prayer thou hearst me making
> Have, at the awful overtaking,
> Heard ; have heard and granted
> Grace that day grace was wanted."

Another manifestation of the spontaneous, conversational style where it borders on self-conscious rhetoric is the figure aposiopesis, which we have already illustrated from *The Deutschland* (stanza 28). It is used very convincingly in *The Handsome Heart* (No. 27) :

> " —Only . . . O on that path you pace
> Run all your race, O brace sterner that strain ! "

[1] See note by Bridges, *Poems of G. M. H.*, p. 108, line 105.
[2] See *Poems*, p. 108, No. 21.

Good speech is usually terse ; and in proportion as poetry contains the best words in the best order, it tends to cast out the otiose, to wear away " surplusage ", often by means of drastic ellipsis. In Hopkins this device, like others, is carried to extreme lengths ; but although it occasions some initial awkwardness or difficulty, the gain in power and pregnancy is usually decisive. If we consider the opening of No. 38 (condemned by one critic as " no white-hot welding of form and content, but only a painful stuttering ")[1] we see that the ellipsis is not merely desirable but *essential* to the poet's precise meaning :

> " To what serves mortal beauty | —dangerous ; does set dancing blood—the O-seal-that-so | feature, flung prouder form
> Than Purcell tune lets tread to ? "

This celibate poet cannot see a beautiful woman dancing without a sudden qualm and self-warning : " Beware ! This physical beauty *is* so fascinating, *does* so distract the mind from higher spiritual values ". The spasmodic utterance has an emotional and dramatic fitness, while the thought has a universal application. As the same critic says of the opening stanzas of *The Deutschland*, which he has studied with more care, " The poet had leapt at his thought directly, irresistibly, and allowed the form of his expression to be dictated by an emotional rather than a logical sequence."[2]

Everyone except the prose writer begrudges the formality of the relative pronoun. The omission of the third person objective relative is the rule in conversation (' The man I saw '); the omission of the third person nominative, as in

> " I have a brother is condemned to die "
> (*Meas. for Meas.*, II. ii. 33),

has not been widely approved ; but Hopkins once again took his stand by Shakespeare :

> " Deals out that being indoors each one dwells " (34).[3]

When, however, this ellipsis invades the second person, a disconcerting crudeness or even ambiguity arises : " mother have lost son " ; " O Hero savest " (17) ; " Squander the hell-rook ranks sally to molest him ; " (23). When this last example is

[1] David Daiches in *New Literary Values* (1936), p. 35.
[2] Daiches, *op. cit.* p. 27.
[3] Cf. above, chap. ii. p. 49.

read aloud (as Hopkins always wished to be read), the verb "sally" either takes the devastating sense of an imperative co-ordinate with "Squander", or else becomes a noun, object of the first verb, in the still dubious line: "Squander the hell-rook rank's sally to molest him". It is worth noting, however, that Hopkins was guilty of no other comparable solecism.[1]

Abbott remarked that the Elizabethan poets objected to scarcely any ellipsis, provided the deficiency could be easily supplied from the context.[2] Both Shakespeare and Browning can, at times, be elliptically elusive; and Meredith was criticized on the same grounds. In Hopkins, the pruning down can be more ruthless and is often more subtle, more strictly integral to the whole pattern of sound and thought—the expressional rhythm. Speaking of a sestet by Mallarmé, Mr. Aldous Huxley uses words which would apply equally well to the more concrete poetry of Hopkins:

> "It is a grammatical apocalypse. A whole world of ideas is miraculously concentrated by means of syntax into what is almost a point."[3]

Ellipsis contributes largely to the "syntactical magic" of the following passages, both of which approach the condition of music:

> "I cast for comfort I can no more get
> By groping round my comfortless, than blind
> Eyes in their dark can day or thirst can find
> Thirst's all-in-all in all a world of wet." (47)

> "Only what word
> Wisest my heart breeds dark heaven's baffling ban
> Bars or hell's spell thwarts. This to hoard unheard,
> Heard unheeded, leaves me a lonely began." (44)

—that is, "a lonely one who only began".[4]

A more drastic paring away reduces a considerable sentence to only three or four key words, as in No. 54: "Your feast of;" ("Your feast of physical beauty, as for instance . . ."); "Worst will the best." ("The worst will always prey upon, vitiate, the best."). Of these laconic utterances, the former leaves, perhaps,

[1] See *Poems*, pp. 97–8, for Bridges's just stricture. [2] *Op. cit.* § 382.

[3] Comment on "O si chère de loin et proche et blanche, si . . ." in his anthology, *Texts and Pretexts*. Mallarmé's peculiar symbolism and obscurity are usually remote from anything in Hopkins.

[4] With "began" as a noun-equivalent, cf. "also-ran".

too much room for personal conjecture, whereas the latter is clearly elucidated by its following context. Equally bold and gnomic, though perhaps more obscure, is a half-line in that promising fragment *To his Watch* (70) :

> " The telling time our task is ; time's some part,
> Not all, but we were framed to fail and die—
> *One spell and well that one.* There, ah thereby
> Is comfort's carol of all or woe's worst smart."

Hopkins held that the meaning of a difficult but authentic passage in poetry should, eventually, " explode ". The above explodes quite soon enough for one of the poet's persuasion : " We have *one spell* on this earth, *and* we must use *well that one* ". Thus death promises Heaven (" comfort's carol ") to the good, and Hell (" woe's worst smart ") to the wicked.

Our last example shows how two subordinate clauses can be given, by ellipsis, the concentrated force of a single pregnant word. The Handsome Heart, he says,

> " To its own fine function, wild and self-instressed,
> Falls light as ten years long taught how to and why." (27)

The logico-poetic significance is clear at once ; the exact grammatical structure is not so obvious, but seems to be : " *Falls* as *light as* it would fall if, for *ten years* (*long*), it had been *taught how to and why* ".

In later chapters of the present work we shall show how the grammatical structure of Greek and Latin poetry suggested to Hopkins an ' esemplastic ' [1] syntax which would combine greater freedom with a more compelling unity, concentration, and distinctiveness or " inscape " ; how in Welsh poetry, too, syntactic dislocation or interruption could impart vigour and dramatic immediacy. There Syntax will be treated historically in conjunction with Rhythm, because in Hopkins the various elements of style are more strictly integrated than in most other poets.[2] To match his sprung or expressional rhythm, he adopted a kind of sprung or expressional syntax—an arbitrary system in which words (like stresses), instead of falling into their conventional positions, are placed where they are required to express the shape and movement of individual thought.

[1] " Moulding into one "—a word coined by Coleridge for the Imagination, the " esemplastic power ".

[2] Volume II. chaps. ii. and iii. of the present work.

That Hopkins could deliberately mould his syntax to suit his conception of rhythm is proved by his own comment on a curious construction in *Peace* (22):

> "I'll not play hypocrite
> To own my heart:"

"To own" seems at first to be a qualifying infinitive, and the sense: "I'll not deceive myself with a spurious peace of mind". But in a letter to Bridges, Hopkins says: "*Own my heart* is merely *my own heart* transposed for rhythm's sake and then *tamquam exquisitius*, as Hermann would say".[1] A similar transposition (cf. Shakespeare's "Good my lord") is seen in "Mortal my mate" (70), which shows a nice distribution of emphasis without ambiguity. But the conscious effort of reading "To own my heart" as a syntactic anagram of what Hopkins really intended is distasteful: the pull of the natural verbal sense of "To own" is too strong to allow of a genuine 'Empsonian' pleasure in the ambiguity.

What we have called 'sprung' syntax is better seen in the 'syncopation' of extreme ellipsis, in the arbitrary placing together of emphatic words normally kept apart by weaker particles and connectives, as in

> "Whether at once, as once at a crásh Pául," (4.10)

> ". . . since (seems) I kissed the rod," (40);

in the deliberately patterned inversion of

> "Me, were I pleading, plead nor do I:" (44)

> "God's most deep decree
> Bitter would have me taste: my taste was me;" (45)

in the abrupt apposition and parenthesis of

> ". . . huddle in a main, a chief
> Woe, world-sorrow . . ." (41)

> ". . . that treads through, prickproof, thick
> Thousands of thorns, thoughts) swings though." (42)

in the broken logic and sudden recovery of

> "With, along them, cragiron under and cold furls—
> With-a-fountain's shining-shot furls." (43)

[1] *Letters*, vol. i. p. 196.

Many of Hopkins's bolder transpositions are based on Elizabethan practice, but without slavish imitation. Abbott says [1]: " We now dislike using such transpositions as

" ' A thousand men *that* fishes gnawed *upon* '."
(*Rich. III*, I. iv. 25) ;

yet Hopkins frequently " maroons " the preposition : " Than Purcell tune lets tread to ? " (38) ; and more flagrantly in

" What life half lifts the latch of,
What hell stalks towards the snatch of,
Your offering, with despatch, of ! " (24)

To secure a special emphasis Shakespeare wrote :

" and, supportable
To make the dear loss, have I means much weaker
Than you may call to comfort you," (*Temp.*, V. i. 146).

This principle is invoked and extended in the combined exclamation and statement and question of

" Those lovely lads once, wet-fresh | windfalls of war's storm,
How then should Gregory, a father, have gleanèd else from swarmèd Rome ? " (38)

To take the measure of Hopkins's skill in these matters, it is essential to realize how much of simple fervour and poetic subtlety has been gained by breaking up the normal word-order, viz.—" How else then should Gregory, a father, once have gleaned from swarmed Rome those lovely lads, wet-fresh windfalls, etc. ? " [2] The emphatic position of " else ", near the end, should be noted. The whole construction, though difficult at first, acquires a permanent strength from familiarity.

The transposition of adverbs and adjectives produces some highly characteristic cadences :

" Of the outward sentence low *lays him*, listed to a heresy, *here*." (21)

(This placing of a qualifying phrase between the objective pronoun and an emphatic completion of the verb is slightly varied in " I do advise / You, jaded, let be ; " (47) ; " that

[1] *Op. cit.* § 424.
[2] The force of " then " is, of course, temporal rather than illative : in the poem it refers to " once ".

hews mountain and continent, / Earth, all, out ;" (49), and elsewhere.) The Shakespearian reversal of adjective and article (" but *poor* a *thousand crowns* " [1]) is reproduced with good effect in " *wide* the *world's weal* " (42) and " I wear- / y of *idle* a *being but by where wars are rife* " (44). In *The Deutschland* occurs the line—

" And frightful a nightfall folded rueful a day." (Stanza 15.)

This not only suggests the more intense " *So* frightful a nightfall " but also enables *rueful* to operate both ways, as adverb and adjective. A similar reinforcement by position allows " Wisest ", in No. 44, to modify three words simultaneously—*word*, *heart*, and *breeds*. But it was Classical rather than Elizabethan influence that produced the sundering of adjective and noun in

" *Fresh*, till doomfire burn all,
Prayer shall fetch pity eternal." (17).

In Hopkins (as often in Greek or German) we sometimes find a qualifying phrase or clause standing immediately *before*, instead of after, the noun :

" the *rolling level underneath him steady* air," (12) ;

" are you that liar
And, *cast by conscience out*, *spendsavour* salt ? " (26) ;

" of *day and night delivering*
Water," (58, p. 79.)

It is a nice point (and one, perhaps, which allows of no general agreement) as to how far such constructions are ' contrary to the genius of the language '. Given that a living language is a fluid, developing organism, ever susceptible to new influences, and that the language of a true poet is to be judged by its *effect* and not by its good behaviour, we hold that the above examples are both legitimate and successful. In the two pre-eminently experimental poems (Nos. 42 and 43), we have no difficulty in accepting *cragiron under and cold* as joint epithets to describe the *furls* of wet earth turned over by the ploughshare (43) ; yet we cannot be entirely reconciled to such a grammatical contortion as

" (*feel*
That ne'er need hunger, Tom ; " (42)

[1] *As You Like It*, I. i. 2.

The purpose of this was, apparently, to set off the 'sprung' syntax against the regular metre, thus—

> "That né'er need húnger, Tóm ; Tôm séldom síck,"

The strange constructions in *Harry Ploughman* are justified by the result achieved : the syntax produces a sense of dramatic movement, the muscular responses excited in the poet. So too in the middle of *Tom's Garland* the syntax imitates the spontaneous, inchoate synthesis of a 'stream of consciousness'. As the poet himself says :

> "Here comes a violent but effective hyperbaton or suspension, in which the action of the mind mimics that of the labourer—surveys his lot, low but free from care ;"

The long parenthesis is terminated by a sudden movement :

> "then by a sudden strong act he throws it over the shoulder or tosses it away as a light matter."

Presumably his "low lot" is here symbolically associated with something he actually does throw over his shoulder—a coat or a bag.

In reading these two poems we are sometimes disturbed, not so much by the actual eccentricities of style as by the principle involved : despite our interest and pleasure, we hesitate to approve a method which, if carried a step further, would lead to the disintegration of language, the total failure of language to fulfil its prime function—to communicate. Finding it necessary to explain *Tom's Garland* even to Bridges, Hopkins added, with good sense : "I must go no further on this road". "No *further*", be it noted ; for he was by no means convinced that his syntactic complexities were illegitimate or unsuccessful : "Yet declaimed, the strange constructions would be dramatic and effective" . . . "it is a very pregnant sonnet".[1] Some readers have already expressed their agreement ; others will surely do so, though probably their number will always be limited.

That uncompromising epithet-phrase in *Tom's Garland* is paralleled by a perhaps more dissonant transposition in *The Lantern out of Doors* (10) :

> "Death or distance soon consumes them : *wind*
> What most I may *eye* after, be in at the end
> I cannot, and out of sight is out of mind."

[1] *Poems*, pp. 114–15.

The expression 'to wind eye after' a person receding through a crowd is perfectly precise; and a realistic touch is given by the *interruption*—" what most I may". The logical connexion of this clause with " them "—the men who pass out of sight—is a little obscure, but the poet is thinking of the " Rich beams " of the symbolic lantern, distinctive beauty " in mould or mind " or " what not else makes rare ".[1] It is interesting to place beside the above passage those lines in *Cymbeline* from which Hopkins probably borrowed the visual image :

> " Thou shouldst have made him
> As little as a crow, or less, ere left
> To after-eye him." [2]

The addition of " wind " re-creates the image; but Hopkins was not thinking of euphony when he reversed the positions of *after* and *eye*.

These occasional roughnesses, however, should not blind us to the general salutary effect of this poet's determination to break through conventional habits of feeling, thought and expression. Even his oddest trisyllabic, linked and " rove over " rhymes were partly expedients for preventing both the rhythm and the syntax from dropping too easily into familiar modes and cadences. The unusual rhymes of *The Bugler's First Communion* (23) have been condemned by readers who have overlooked the Why in their carping scrutiny of the How. In the first stanza, for instance, the familiar, parenthetical, almost chatty style is appropriately matched by a rhyme which, though *potentially* phonetic, is actually no more than an echo of the usual correspondences :

> " A bugler boy from barrack (it is over the hill
> There)—boy bugler, born, he tells me, of *Irish*
> Mother to an English *sire* (*he*
> *Sh*ares their best gifts surely, fall how things will),"

As we shall find later in the Welsh *cynghanedd*,[3] the aspirate in " he " is not counted in the rhyme-group; [4] and it is, of course,

[1] Hopkins says : " ' winding the eyes ' is queer only if looked at from the wrong point of view : . . . I mean that the eye winds/ only in the sense that its focus or point of sight winds and that coincides with a point of the object and winds with that. For the object, a lantern passing further and further away and bearing now east now west of one right line, is truly and properly described as winding." (*Letters*, vol. i. p. 66.)

[2] I. iii. 16.

[3] The elaborate system of rules governing metre and alliteration in Welsh classical poetry. The profound influence on Hopkins will be treated in Volume II. chap. iii.

[4] Cf. the perfectly satisfying rhymes : *beach her*, *feature* ; *suit* ! *he*, *beauty* (17, ll. 49 and 77).

frequently dropped in rapid speech. (So here the parenthesis " he / Shares . . ." comes in quickly as the generous thought strikes the speaker.) Moreover, the -sh in " English " makes the following pause and linked rhyme almost a phonal necessity.

Hopkins made matters difficult for himself (*and* his apologists) by always insisting, in his letters, on exact rhymes.[1] Hence some critics have assumed that he intended such an absurd reading as

> ". . . of *Irish*
> Mother to an English *sire 'e sh-*
> ares their best gifts surely . . ."

—where the pronunciation is equivalent to " sireish " ; or in *The Eurydice* (stanza 6) :

> " But what black Boreas *wreckt 'r 'e c-*
> ame equipped, deadly electric,"

Bridges, for instance, says :

> " His false ear-rhymes ask to have their slight but indispensable differences obliterated in the reading, and thus they expose their defect, which is of a disagreeable and vulgar or even comic quality." (*Poems*, p. 99.)

In actual fact, the group " *wrecked her ? he* /Came . . .", though it should be pronounced fairly quickly as befits the subject, is not to be judged as an ordinary rhyme : it is a new ' analytic ' or ' slow-motion ' rhyme, in which the Welsh *cynghanedd* and the vocalic correspondences of English rhyme are blended. Musically, it ' gives out ' detached elements which are rapidly synthetized in the rhyme-word, " electric "—an imitative effect. To a reader used to *cynghanedd* the device is neither outrageous nor unpleasing. In defending, quite reasonably, a similar rhyme Hopkins speaks of adjusting pronunciation so as to satisfy the ear ; [2] and if the reader prefers to retard the movement and obscure the rhyme-intention nothing really vital will be lost.

Had Hopkins put the above points to himself and to Bridges as clearly as he must have felt them intuitively, he might have been less willing to regret a few of his rhymes (" grubs in amber "),

[1] E.g.—" I can't abide bad rhymes and when they are spelt alike I hate them more ". (*Letters*, vol. i. p. 35.) All his own " bad " rhymes are spelt differently : *Bremen, women* (4.12) ; *portholes, mortals* (17, ll. 39–40).

[2] See *Letters*, vol. i. pp. 180–81.

and Bridges might have spared us a gratuitous passage in his *Notes*. For when the latter calls the rhyme *boon he on*, *Communion* " hideous " he is not defending an absolute canon of taste but is merely expressing a conservative opinion. Likewise, to have a " suspicion " that the poet thought the rhyme ingenious is not criticism. Trisyllabic rhymes of all types have usually been employed only in light jocular verse (like that of W. S. Gilbert and Mr. Noel Coward) ; and rhyme-convention, like sonnet-legislation, dies hard. Although Hood's *Bridge of Sighs* has some weak stanzas and has worn a little threadbare, it is still a serious and dignified poem ; there is nothing flippant in its trisyllabic rhymes (*slips of hers*, *lips of hers*, etc.). Hopkins's " hideous " rhyme belongs quite naturally to his " rove over " rhythm, and if it *is* one of the " grubs ", it at least belongs to the " amber " of a freshly-turned phrasing : " after a boon he on / My late being there begged of me ".

We may grant that Hopkins's rhymes were sometimes not as phonetically exact as he believed them to be ; but in an age like the present, when all shades of half-rhyme and assonance are even more popular than rhyme itself, the loss (if any) should appear negligible in the light of his indubitable originality and resourcefulness in this as in other forms of Parallelism.[1]

We cannot end this chapter better than by pointing out more of those syntactical devices by which chromatic parallelism and " a condition of music " are so effectively achieved.

That important structural characteristic of Hopkins's style, the asyndetic series of parallel statements,[2] is sometimes varied by the simple and primitive device of incantatory repetition, as in *Binsey Poplars* (10) :

" Rural scene, a rural scene,
Sweet especial rural scene."

The repetition of " beginning " at the end of *The Leaden Echo* (36) is frankly but not blatantly onomatopoeic, and the tolling of another ghostly bell is heard in the repetition of " fonder " and " yonder " at the triumphant close of *The Golden Echo*. This is

[1] Bridges complains of a " distressing " lack of correspondence between *burn all, eternal* (17) ; *handsome, and some* (29) : yet in his own *Eros and Psyche* we find Pyth*ian, man* ; *well,* or*acle* (both pairs in *April*, 10) ; *hers*, court*iers*, worship*pers* (*ibid.* 2) ; *grant*, suppl*iant* (*October*, 22), etc. etc. These rhymes may be " old-fashioned " and " conventional ", but *qua* rhyme they are not a whit better than the more original rhymes of Hopkins. Such trivial ' kettle and pot ' objections were unworthy of Bridges.

[2] See above, p. 110.

not the mechanical and slightly embarrassing reiteration of Poe's *The Bells*; it is the cunningly patterned climax of what has justly been called the most marvellous piece of sheer word-music in the language.

More often Hopkins uses phrasal or clausal repetition with variation and development:

(a) *simple assonantal*—

> "Thirst's all-in-all in all a world of wet." (47)
>
> "Flower of beauty, fleece of beauty, too too apt to, ah! to fleet," (36)

or (b) *fugal and climactic*:

> "The grey lawns cold, where gold, where quickgold lies."
>
> . . . .
>
> "I walk, I lift up, I lift up heart, eyes," (8)
>
> "Nine months she then, nay years, nine years she long" (51)

This last example shows another feature of Hopkins's semantic rhythm: the phrase "nay years" produces the effect of a change of key, and so also does the punning rhyme at the transition from the *Leaden* to the *Golden Echo*:

> ". . . despair, despair.
>
> Spare!
> There is one . . ."

Similarly, he is fond of placing in the very middle of the line a parenthetical word which makes a kind of resolved caesura and acts as a fulcrum or pivot to the movement of the verse:

> "Look at the stars! *look*, look up at the skies!" (8)
>
> "Do what you may do, *what*, do what you may," (36)
>
> "The times are winter, *watch*, a world undone:" (60)

The pivot-word may be mere expletive; there is a suggestion of sheer bravura; yet the whole line ripples with energy.

The variety of musical expression in Hopkins both invites and rewards a careful study. But Mr. Middleton Murry's opinion that Hopkins's aim was *la musique avant toute chose* is a damaging exaggeration. This view should be corrected by the poet's own comment on *The Eurydice* :

> " When . . . I opened and read some lines, reading, as one commonly reads whether prose or verse, with the eyes, so to say, only, it struck me aghast with a kind of raw nakedness and unmitigated violence I was unprepared for : but take breath and read it with the ears, as I always wish to be read, and my verse becomes all right." [1]

Once the shock of initiation is over, the music and the violence prove to be Pater's " *ex forti dulcedo* ".[2]

[1] *Letters*, vol. i. p. 79.

[2] See above, chap. i. p. 8.

CHAPTER V

THEMES AND IMAGERY

INEVITABLY much has already been said about Hopkins's imagery in the foregoing account of his diction. But there is a type of image, indeed an aspect of the whole subject of imagery, which can properly be discussed only in relation to those objects and experiences which are the prime *motifs* of the poetry. As a poet's chosen themes are determined by his experience, so his imagery—the symbolic language of his peculiar imagination—is given its orientation partly by that experience and those themes and partly by the familiar work of earlier poets who have been stirred by the same emotions.

Imagery is, for most poets, the chief expedient for raising the emotive potential of language. Individual as Hopkins's imagery always is in its final synthesis of intellectual and sensory elements, those elements themselves are frequently common to poets as diverse as the Psalmist and Caroline Bowles. Hopkins was primarily a religious poet, and Christian poets of all times have shown a marked unanimity in the moral and mystical significance they have attached to such objects as the stars, fire, rain, lightning, the plough, the soldier and the rod of chastisement.

As regards themes, a certain affinity with a poet stylistically so different as Cowper is revealed in the fact that both men were moved to successful poetic utterance by the sudden foundering of a naval vessel, by the felling of a row of poplars, by a portrait, and by a religious ' desolation '. The experience behind Cowper's *The Castaway* was probably similar in kind to that embodied in Hopkins's much more individual and powerful poem, " I wake and feel the fell of dark ". Nothing, however, could be more unlike the simple impersonal dignity of *The Loss of the Royal George* than the passionate garrulous realism of *The Loss of the Eurydice* (1878) or more unlike the formal anapaests and sententious close of *The Poplar Field* than the beautifully varied rhythm and sustained lyrical feeling of *Binsey Poplars* (1879). Yet the sensibility common to both sprang from a likeness in temperament and character : each man was a " stricken deer ",[1]

[1] Cowper's recurrent insanity was matched in Hopkins by a nervous prostration and depression which frequently resembled madness. See *Letters*, vol. i. pp. 216, 222, and *passim*.

celibate, in love with piety, nature, England, friendship, and the simple virtues. Hopkins's poetry is richer in texture and imagery because he was a poet of greater passion, a genius of more complex personality.

Before we proceed to trace similar affinities with Wordsworth and others, it is as well to note the main recurrent themes of Hopkins's poetry of God, Man, and Nature. *The Wreck of the Deutschland* stands like a great overture at the beginning of his mature work, rich in themes which are taken up, developed and varied, sometimes more than once, in the subsequent poems. The fragment No. 73, for instance, sums up in the language of simple devotion at least four of the main *motifs* in the great ode.[1]

The " finger of God " theme is heard again in the second poem of shipwreck :

> " The Eurydice—it concerned thee, O Lord : "—[2]

and also in *Carrion Comfort* (1885), though here it is a " lion limb " that is laid against the poet in his Jacob-like struggle with " the hero ". In this sonnet, too, recurs the paradox of God's " lightning and love ".[3] God scourges him so that his chaff might fly, his grain lie " sheer and clear ", and the knowledge that he is being so purged fills him with joy. It is this exaltation accompanying the pain that gives the experience the quality of mysticism—of that first stage in the Mystic Way called the Purgative Life.[4]

Implicit throughout *The Deutschland* is another theological concept—the ' salvific Will of God ' operating against man's stubborn malice.[5] It is introduced again in the sestet of *The Lantern out of Doors* (1877) by means of a neat paronomasia— ". . . out of *mind* " . . . " Christ *minds* " ; and later it reappears at the prophetic close of *The Eurydice*.[6] In *Andromeda* (1879) the operation of the salvific Will through Christ and His Church is embodied in a symbolic interpretation of a classical myth.[7]

Only a man passionately conscious of personal sin could have conceived the tragic symbolism of *The Wreck of the Deutschland*. The earnest priest's desire to see all men not only free from sin

[1] Cf. stanzas 2, 3, and 4 with *The Deutschland*, stanzas 1 and 5, 2 and 3, 9 respectively.

[2] Stanza 1.

[3] *The Deutschland*, stanzas 9, 10, 32, 33. Cf. No. 16, l. 14.

[4] For an examination of Hopkins's claims to be called a ' mystic ' or ' mystical poet ', see below, chap. vi. p. 226.

[5] Stanzas 2, 8, 9, 10, 33, and 34.

[6] Lines 103–4 and 117–20.

[7] See below, p. 185.

but actively praising God is set forth in *The Candle Indoors* (1879),[1] where the analogy used is as homely as that of the child's hymn :

> " Jesus bids us shine
> With a pure, clear light,
> Like a little candle
> Burning in the night."

With the sestet comes the note of self-criticism : " Look to yourself first. Begin by mending your own fading fire." A different treatment of the same subject is found in the fragmentary No. 60. Here the image of the guttering candle is exchanged for "dragons" of sin ; but the same Scotist insistence on the autonomy of the will comes out strongly in the last line :

> " Your will is law in that small commonweal . . ."

The nature-image in the opening lines—the wasting, withering of the visible world at a winter nightfall to symbolize man's growing moral and spiritual " distress "—looks like a first sketch for the more powerful expression of this theme in *Spelt from Sibyl's Leaves* (1881). The *dragon* image is here retained but successfully transmuted into the " dragonish " beak-leaved boughs which pattern the bleak sky like the damascened blade of a sword.

Fire and *light* in their various manifestations are frequently employed by Hopkins as symbols of the divine vital principle in all creatures, as their vital activity and their ultimate spiritual goal. Fire indicates the vital activity of God in the lightning of His purgative and salvific Will, or in the Pentecostal flame of His grace and inspiration.[2] From the embryo " Miracle-in-Mary-of-flame ", the Saviour becomes " a dayspring to the dimness of us ".[3] The stars are the street lamps of Heaven ; they " overbend us " and beckon us to follow the example of the saints ;[4] the Milky Way once guided pilgrims to the shrine of the Virgin at Walsingham.[5] Stars are again the symbol of the divine moral order[6] and of the divine sanction of kingship.[7] A lantern swinging along the night speaks of that distinctive beauty of mould or mind which momentarily brightens our pervading atmosphere of ugliness and commonplace.[8] The

[1] This sonnet is " . . . a companion to the Lantern (No. 10), not at first meant to be though, but it fell in." (*Letters*, vol. i. p. 84.)

[2] *The Deutschland*, stanzas 2, 3, and 10.

[3] *Ibid.* 34, 35.

[4] *Ibid.* stanza 5, and *The Starlight Night* (No. 8).

[5] *The Eurydice*, 102.

[6] *The Bugler's First Communion*, stanza 5.

[7] *Tom's Garland*, l. 11.

[8] *The Lantern out of Doors.*

live and lancing blowpipe flame typifies the first conception of "immortal song" in the poet's mind [1]; and fire is the visible sign of vital activity when it breaks from the poised and wheeling windhover, or when "kingfishers catch fire" and "dragonflies draw flame".[2]

The image of the "fading fire" gives great poignancy to the close of *The Windhover* (1877); but here the suggestion is rather of a vital *passivity*—total submission to God's Will. Both this poem and its objective counterpart, *In Honour of St. Alphonsus Rodriguez* (1888) restate another leading theme of the 'overture'—the beauty of Sacrifice.[3] On this subject Hopkins hoped to write a theological essay,[4] but he seems to have exhausted his inspiration in the short *Morning Midday and Evening Sacrifice* (1879), *The Golden Echo* (1882) and the fragment on the martyrdom of *Margaret Clitheroe* (date uncertain)—to say nothing of his own sometimes too assiduous application to duty. For the constant sacrifice of self for others, without the reward of seeing some appreciable diminution in the world's sin and misery, brought inevitably a bitter disappointment and weariness, the "jading and jar of the cart" as he calls it in *The Deutschland*.[5]

Only once did the poet's dejection produce a work of the most downright Swiftean cynicism. In No. 69 (1889) Hopkins (like Wordsworth) sees grandeur in natural forces and (like Milton) sublimity in the fall of the rebel angels; but the story of that little drudge, Everyman, is by comparison unheroic, even contemptible:

"What bass is *our* viol for tragic tones?"

All men, no matter what their rank, are at bottom the same. Physically and spiritually they live hand-to-mouth. Even the priest, who denies himself to keep alive precariously the flame of the spirit, sees life as the grotesquery mirrored in smooth spoons and realizes how relatively tame and fussy are his moods of desperation and desolation.[6]

[1] No. 51.
[2] No. 34.
[3] *The Deutschland*, stanzas 16, 22, 23.
[4] *Letters*, vol. ii. p. 102.
[5] Of his life as a parish priest in Liverpool he said: "And the drunkards go on drinking, the filthy, as the Scripture says, are filthy still: human nature is so inveterate. Would that I had seen the last of it." (*Letters*, vol. i. p. 110.)
[6] The meaning is elucidated by the first draft in MS. "H":

"In spoons have seen my masque played and how tame
My tempest and my spitfire freaks how fussy."

This is not the smiling, aloof cynicism of La Rochefoucauld but the bitter, self-implicated cynicism of Hamlet—the cry of the disappointed idealist. The poem expresses, as Bridges said, a passing mood; yet a similar disgust appears at the end of No. 41, and in giving way to such depressions Hopkins was falling short of his own ideals as a Jesuit priest.[1]

Nevertheless, against all this despair the poet's supreme religious consolations were first stated in *The Deutschland* and later reaffirmed, sometimes in separate poems: e.g., the comfort of the Resurrection,[2] of Divine Grace,[3] of the Host,[4] of God's Immutability,[5] of the Virgin and other saints,[6] of the blessing of Patience.[7] Moreover, the poet in him always found consolation in the mystical instress of natural beauty,[8] in the comeliness and strength of the human body,[9] and fostered a growing sympathy with the courage and sufferings of "dear and dogged man".[10]

His love of May-skies, stars, clouds, dawn and sunset is (in spite of its specifically Christian implications) akin to that of the great Romantic poets. His nature-imagery often combines the sensuousness and 'rift-loading' of Keats with the restless energy of Shelley:

> "Down in dim woods the diamond delves, the elves'-eyes!
> The grey lawns cold, where gold, where quickgold lies!"
> (*The Starlight Night.*)

But altogether, he stands in a much closer relationship to Wordsworth, both in his choice of subjects and in his consistently metaphysical apprehension of natural phenomena. This affinity is shown in his passionate admiration of the great *Immortality Ode*,[11] and is not seriously disturbed by the playfully satiric triolet about "The child is father of the man".[12] (If there is a serious motive behind this poem it is that Hopkins, as a Catholic, did not consider "natural piety" as sufficient: the child has much more to learn from the father than the father from the child.) More practically the kinship with Wordsworth is revealed in their common, though different, expression of those moral and super-rational values discussed in Chapter I,[13] and also in their intimate contact with the ordinary child and man.

[1] Cf. the review by Hugh Kelly in *Studies*, June 1936.
[2] Nos. 15, 36, 48
[3] Nos. 27, 38.
[4] Nos. 23, 89.
[5] No. 13.
[6] Nos. 18, 37, 49, 58.
[7] Nos. 22, 46.
[8] Nos. 8, 14.
[9] Nos. 17 (ll. 73–84), 29, 38, 43.
[10] Nos. 29, 35.
[11] See *Letters*, vol. ii. pp. 147–8.
[12] No. 68.
[13] See above, p. 21.

This direct and realistic interest in human character and human relations places both poets apart from the doctrinaire Shelley and Swinburne, the 'enchanted' Keats and Tennyson, and indeed from almost all the other nineteenth-century poets, including that hearty psychologist, Browning. Like Crabbe, Blake, and Elliott, Hopkins was discontented with the working lot of the common man, but the terms of his satire were general, not particular, and his strongest complaint was against the religious order of his time :

> " Day and night I deplore
> My people and born own nation,
> Fast foundering own generation." [1]

In many poems he shows a deep concern for the spiritual welfare of the young [2] and for the ultimate conversion of " rare dear Britain ".[3]

A poem suggested by Wordsworth and carried out, as Hopkins admits, in his manner, is *Brothers* (1880). Wordsworth's poem of the same title dissipates its pathos in verbosity. Hopkins, by concentrating quite as much feeling in the lively narration of one brief episode, proved that " pathos has a point as precise as jest has ".[4] As an expression of the pathos of decrepitude, Wordsworth's *Simon Lee* would be greatly improved by the omission of two or three painfully naive stanzas. In *Felix Randal* (1880), Hopkins treats the same subject with a surer discrimination between sentiment and sentimentality. The strong but not exaggerated feeling in line 11 is quickly relieved by what is almost a note of triumph, culminating in the bold proleptic metaphor of the " bright and battering sandal ".

The disgust felt by Hopkins at the materialism and exploitation of labour in the Victorian industrial world was first expressed in the " Communist " letter of 1871 [5]; and the same disgust, caught up in a mood of devotion, touched two of his sonnets with the noble indignation of Wordsworth's " The world is too much with us ", *London*, 1802, etc. *God's Grandeur* (1877) exposes the squalor which accompanies material progress, the loss of vital sensation which results from the overlaying of nature with artificial amenities : " nor can foot feel, being shod ". The " dearest freshness deep down things " is symbolized first by the

[1] No. 17, ll. 86–8.
[2] Nos. 9, 17, 23, 54.
[3] Nos. 4, 17.
[4] *Letters*, vol. i. p. 86.
[5] *Letters*, vol. i. pp. 27–8 : " Horrible to say, in a manner I am a Communist ".

broad glares like sheet lightning given off by shaken goldfoil, and then by the iridescence of oil that " gathers to a greatness " as it is crushed from the seed.[1] In another sonnet (No. 11) the sea and a singing lark (manifestations, respectively, of the eternal power and beauty of nature) serve the same symbolic purpose :

> " How these two shame this shallow and frail town !
> How ring right out our sordid turbid time,
> Being pure ! "

As Wordsworth preferred the ancient Greek supernaturalism to none at all, so Hopkins looks back to the " cheer and charm of earth's past prime ", and even farther to " earth's sweet being in the beginning, /In Eden garden " (*Spring*) ; and to describe the apparent decadence of man he borrows an idea from Parmenides (with also, perhaps, a glance at Darwin) :

> " Our make and making break, are breaking down
> To man's last dust, drain fast towards *man's first slime.*" [2]

In those five poems in which he voices care and " dear concern " for the spiritual welfare of the young, the poet is like a prospector who has found a trickle of oil which will, if rightly worked, gather to a greatness.[3] In *The Sea and the Skylark*, *Ribblesdale*, and *The Valley of the Elwy*, the freshness, the evidences of God's grandeur are discerned only in the inferior creation—in the still beautiful setting of man's struggle to conquer everything but his own sinfulness.

Having grieved at what man has made of man, Hopkins turns, in *Duns Scotus's Oxford* (1879), to deplore what man has made of bricks and mortar :

> " Thou hast a base and brickish skirt there, sours
> That neighbour-nature thy grey beauty is grounded
> Best in ; "

There is an obscure irony in the antithesis of debased architecture and the beautiful colleges of the age of Scotus—the scholastic philosopher who upheld the dignity of man.

Hopkins seems to sum up the social decadence by pointing to that phenomenon which constitutes one of our own most urgent problems—the Unemployed.[4] *Tom's Garland* (1887) is

[1] *Letters*, vol. i. pp. 168–9.
[2] See *Note-books*, p. 102 : " Men, he thought, had sprung from slime ".
[3] Nos. 9, 23, 27, 30, 54.
[4] *Poems*, p. 114, No. 42 (note).

virtually a condemnation of that order of society which permits a large number of able-bodied men to remain outside the hierarchy of social usefulness. If we change the order of this sonnet and its counterpart, *Harry Ploughman* (a "direct picture of a ploughman without afterthought")[1] we have the obverse and reverse of the working man—his physical activity and his social significance. Yet the tone of Hopkins's appraisal of the workless is that of an aristocratic, slightly irritated conservatism, which seems to us unduly harsh. Using the ancient analogy between the state and the human body, he takes the garland of gold round the king's head (symbol of the sun and stars) to stand for the Divine Right of lawful administration, and the garland of steel hobnails on the navvy's boots as the insignia of the industrious, contented working classes (the "mighty foot" of the state); but the economic outcasts are treated collectively with a scorn which leaves out of account the victims of a bad system:

> "gold go garlanded
> With, perilous, O nó; nor yet plod safe shod sound".

There is an objective truth in his division of the unemployed into two main types:

> "This, by Despair, bred Hangdog dull; by Rage
> Manwolf, worse;"

but to stigmatize them all as "packs" which "infest the age" is to create in the reader uneasy doubts as to where the poet's sympathies really lie. Between 1871 and 1888 he seems to have changed his ground, for in the letter which explains this poem he speaks of "fools of Radical Levellers", and adds:

> "And this state of things, I say, is the origin of Loafers, Tramps, Corner-boys, Roughs, Socialists and other pests of society."[2]

Like Wordsworth, Hopkins relinquished the revolutionary for the constitutional, traditional view of social problems; and the same love of the enduring features in man's life gave to both an interest in the topographical poem.

Only two of Hopkins's lesser poems are purely topographical: *Penmaen Pool* (1876) was written in holiday mood, sparkles with a playful fancy, and is altogether a charming thing of its kind. *Inversnaid* (1881) has grace, vigour, a tang that Burns would have liked; but here, as in *Binsey Poplars*, the "especial scene" is

[1] *Poems*, p. 116. [2] *Ibid.* p. 115.

but the local habitation of a cherished idea—the need for preserving wild nature :

> " O let them be left, wildness and wet ;
> Long live the weeds and the wilderness yet." [1]

The motive underlying *The Valley of the Elwy* (1877) and its companion poem, *Ribblesdale* (1882) is, as we have said, essentially a religious one. In the Elwy sonnet, the smell of a friendly house is a " cordial air " which, like a bird's mothering wing, makes a natural hood all over the kindly family ; and this smell, we are told, is the symbol of what the wild beauty of Wales *should* be to the Welsh but is NOT.[2] The idea is " very far fetched " (a term of approbation with Hopkins), and the poet did not realize how he was confusing the reader by leaving him to infer that these good people were natives of the Elwy valley, whereas actually they were " the Watsons of Shooters Hill ".

Ribblesdale was inspired by a Pauline text [3] and a Wordsworthian feeling for what Hopkins calls the " pathos of nature ". The external world is man's fellow creature ; but in its act of being, the " sweet landscape " is relatively perfect, whereas man, the " eye, tongue or heart else " of Earth, does not correspond. Man is, indeed, the heir of God (as St. Paul says), but a perverted heir—

> " To his own selfbent so bound, so tied to his turn
> To thriftless reave both our rich round world bare
> And none reck of world after . . ."

Whatever of Earth's beauty survives man's depredations makes a strong tongueless plea to God to deliver His creature from " the bondage of corruption ".[4] In the slums, coalpits and slag heaps of industrial England Hopkins saw the whole terrestrial creation still groaning and travailing in pain ; and by a justifiable ' pathetic fallacy ', Earth too

> " Wears brows of such care, care and dear concern."

[1] " I have something, if I cd. only seize it, on the decline of wild nature, beginning somehow like this—

> ' O where is it, the wilderness,
> The wildness of the wilderness ? . . .' "

(*Letters*, vol. i. p. 73.)

[2] *Letters*, vol. i. p. 76. Cf. the same thought in the poet's attempt at a Welsh *cywydd* (see Volume II. chap. iii. of the present work).

[3] In MSS. ' A ' and ' D ' Hopkins quotes *Romans* viii. 19, 20, " cum praecc. et seqq."

[4] See *Letters*, vol. i. pp. 90, 110, 299.

The poetry of Hopkins is *par excellence* the poetry of death and resurrection, of mutability and recovery, of desolation and consolation. The problem of suffering; the decay of human beauty, moral and physical; the frustration of noble hopes and aspirations—by all these he is moved, now to musical lament, now to denunciation of the sin which provokes God's wrath, and at times to complaint and protest against the inscrutability of the Divine Purpose.

Poignant regret before the fact of decay and mortality is expressed with a Housman-like terseness and pathetic point in *Spring and Fall* (1880), a title in which "Spring" suggests Eden (cf. No. 9) and "Fall" suggests the penalty of Adam:

> "It is the blight man was born for,
> It is Margaret you mourn for."[1]

But whereas in Housman and Hardy, for all the dogged stoicism, there is always the leaden echo of final extinction, in Hopkins one hears continually, between the bouts of pain and grief, the golden echo of immortality.

This article of Christian faith is embodied in one of his greatest poems, *That Nature is a Heraclitean Fire and of the Comfort of the Resurrection* (1888). Hopkins claimed that in this poem a great deal of early Greek philosophical thought had been "distilled"; but as he himself remarked, the liquor of the distillation does not taste very Greek.[2] There is, indeed, nothing in the poem which cannot be interpreted satisfactorily in the light of Christian doctrine and natural observation. In a brief paraphrase, its meaning is as follows:

> "Everything in nature is in a perpetual state of flux: air, earth, and water make a constant cycle of integration and disintegration—a motion which creates the dynamic beauty of the visible world. In fact, the inexhaustible energy of being and becoming throughout all creation is like a huge self-fuelling, non-consumed bonfire. And even man, the most clearly individuated being, higher and apart from all others on earth—he too dies and is quickly forgotten, swallowed up in the general flux. This thought fills us with horror, until we remember that through Christ's promise the disintegration of the physical body is (or should be) the immediate beginning of a richer life for the immortal spirit. Strong in this faith, we take heart, we exult, etc."

Nevertheless, early Greek philosophy undoubtedly acted as the catalyser in the chemical fusion of all the scattered images

[1] As there was no *real* Margaret (*Letters*, vol. i. p. 109), the nature symbol in this poem might have been suggested by *Isaiah*, lxiv. 6: "and we all do fade as the leaf; and our iniquities, like the wind, have taken us away".

[2] See *Poems*, p. 118 (note).

and impressions which make up the nature-symbol in this remarkable work. Further confirmation of this is found in a comment by Hopkins on Dixon's poem called *Life and Death*:

> "These very subtle and original speculations . . . as they follow out natural suggestions only and take no account of the supernatural have a quite heathen air; they remind one something of Empedocles and the early Ionian and Eleatic philosophy." [1]

The early Greek thought "distilled" into the imagery of *The Heraclitean Fire* is mainly the hylozoist philosophy of the Ionian school. To Thales the basic element was water; to Anaximenes it was air; to Heraclitus [2] it was fire. Speaking of Heraclitus, M. Jacques Maritain says:

> "In his view, all things are differentiations produced by discord or strife (πόλεμος πατὴρ πάντων) of a single mobile principle which he conceives in the form of fire, a fire ethereal, living, and divine." [3]

Transformation took place in two directions, upwards and downwards: earth, water, fire—fire, water, earth. This balance was preserved, and thus the apparent permanence of things was maintained. Heraclitus did not distinguish between the spiritual and the material; the universal law of *change* was the law of man's life also: "man is kindled and put out like a light in the night". As the poem says:

> "But quench her bonniest, dearest | to her, her clearest-
> selvèd spark
> Man, how fast his firedint, his mark on mind is gone!"

For a single corporeal substance, Empedocles substituted four specifically different elements—earth, water, air, fire; and Hopkins, while retaining *fire* as the essence of life, adapted the three other elements as symbols of the Heraclitean flux in nature. Air and water give us the "Cloud-puffball, etc." of the opening lines. Clouds turn to rain, so that water and earth give us "pool and rut"—the mud which is parched, peeled, squeezed and then dust-blown by the boisterous wind; moreover the principle of change through strife is clearly suggested in the words "ropes, wrestles, beats earth bare". The obliteration of man's footprints in the mud affords a natural transition to the more vital symbol—the fourth element, fire. In the general flux, the mental image of the dead man fades from the mind of the living as surely as

[1] *Letters*, vol. ii. p. 61. [2] In the prime of his age about 500 B.C.
[3] *An Introduction to Philosophy* (1930), p. 52.

the diversely active, adventurous body ("world's wildfire") is reduced, as in cremation, to a handful of "ash".

Hopkins was also deeply interested in the "Great Parmenides of Elea" (*b.* 540).[1] This thinker, contrary to Heraclitus, held that change, motion, and all the diversity of things are but an illusory appearance: for him there existed only 'being' (τὸ ἐόν), the immutable, eternal one. Hopkins's view of these two concepts would certainly be close to that of the modern Catholic philosopher, Maritain, who says:

> "Thus Parmenides, reaching the opposite pole to Heraclitus, fixed, as he did, once for all one of the extreme limits of speculation and error, and proved that every philosophy of pure being, for the very reason that it denies that kind of non-being which Aristotle termed *potentiality* and which necessarily belongs to everything created, is obliged to absorb all being in absolute being, and leads therefore to monism or pantheism no less inevitably than the philosophy of pure becoming."[2]

It is likely that in the *Heraclitean Fire* Hopkins, as preacher-philosopher-poet,[3] wished to pay some homage, however 'private' and obscure, to these early Greek thinkers; at the same time he would show that the purest "distillation" of their separately inadequate theories is to be found in the Christian ontology, which accepts the facts of 'flux' and 'being' without becoming enslaved to either. When Hopkins, translating Parmenides, said "Being draws-home to Being", he felt the difference between Absolute and contingent being, as he did when he wrote

> "Thee, God, I come from, to thee go,
> All day long I like fountain flow
> From thy hand out, swayed about
> Mote-like in thy mighty glow."[4]

—or when, describing the resurrection of the dead, he cried:

> "I am all at once what Christ is, since he was what I am . . ."

[1] See *Note-books*, pp. 98–102.

[2] *Ibid.* p. 62. Hopkins's reading of Parmenides was to a certain degree subjective: "His great text . . . is that Being is and Not-being is not—which perhaps one can say, a little over-defining his meaning, means that all things are upheld by instress and are meaningless without it. An undetermined Pantheist idealism runs through the fragments which makes it hard to translate them satisfactorily in a subjective or in a wholly outward sense. His feeling for instress, for the flush and foredrawn, and for inscape /is most striking and from this one can understand Plato's reverence for him as the great father of Realism . . ." (*loc. cit.* p. 98). Cf. Maritain, *op. cit.* p. 61.

[3] "I am going to preach to-morrow and put plainly to a Highland congregation . . . what I am putting not at all so plainly in a sonnet . . ." (*Poems*, p. 117).

[4] No. 73.

The fact that air, water and earth, as used in the poem, are not strictly physical differentiations of fire at all, indicates that the prime motives and materials of the imagery were not philosophical but sensory ; and we can trace the growth of the poet's nature-images from natural observation to imaginative interpretation. Like Coleridge and Tennyson, Hopkins used his *Journal* to fix images in the first heat of delighted perception, and it is instructive to see how the sense-impressions incorporated in the poem had been casually garnered over a period of from fourteen to eighteen years. Five of the *Journal* entries given below belong to the period 1869–71 ; the other two are dated '73 and '74 :

Note-books—	*The poem—*
p. 136— " herds of towering *pillow clouds*, one great stack in particular over Pendle was knoppled all over in fine *snowy tufts* . . ." p. 140— " *bright* woolpacks that pelt before a gale in a clear sky are *in the tuft*." p. 181— " tall *tossed clouds* . . ." p. 144— " slanted *flashing travellers*, all in flight, *stepping one behind the other*, their edges *tossed with bright ravelling* . . ." p. 145— " clouds *in march* behind Pendle . . . *marching across the sky in regular rank* . . ."	"*Cloud*-puff ball, torn *tufts*, *tossed pillows* flaunt forth, then chevy on an air- built *thoroughfare* : heaven-roysterers, in gay-gangs, they throng ; they *glitter in marches*."
p. 190— " young *elm*leaves *lash* and lip the sprays." p. 124— " The hangers of smaller but barky branches . . . look like *ship-tackle*."	" Down roughcast, down *dazzling* whitewash, wherever an *elm* arches, Shivelights and *shadow-tackle* in long *lashes* lace, lance, and pair."

The repetition in the jottings of words like *tufts*, *tossed*, and *march* shows that these images must have been present in the poet's mind whenever he saw certain cloudscapes. One doubts whether they ever became ' unconscious ' : Hopkins must have toyed with them continually in the hope of one day being able to organize them in a poem. Until that was done they would remain an obsession.

Cloudscapes and treescapes (or the *inscape* and *instress* of clouds and trees) always excited in Hopkins that sensibility which is close to religious emotion. The resultant vision was often quasi-mystical, and it might have been pantheistic had not his God been transcendent as well as immanent. The earlier *Hurrahing in Harvest* (1877) was " the outcome of half an hour of extreme enthusiasm as I walked home one day from fishing in the Elwy " [1] ; yet its cloud-images had been maturing in his sub-conscious mind for six years :

Note-books (1871)—

p. 145— " A simple *behaviour* of p. 143— *silky* lingering *clouds* . . ." p. 144— " the clouds *meal white* . . ." p. 143— " Later /*moulding*, which brought rain."	" what lovely *behaviour* Of *silk*-sack *clouds* ! has wilder, wilful-wavier *Meal*-drift *moulded* ever and melted across skies ? "

It would be absurd to suppose that Hopkins was here using the note-book and tweezer method of composition, picking out pretty ideas and arranging them in a convenient pattern. He seems to have preferred the advice of Coleridge to the alleged practice of Tennyson :

> " A poet ought not to pick nature's pocket : let him borrow, and so borrow as to repay by the very act of borrowing. Examine nature accurately, but write from recollection, and trust more to your imagination than to your memory." [2]

[1] *Poems*, p. 107.

[2] *Specimens of Table Talk* (1835), vol. i. p. 208. Cf. Prof. Livingstone Lowes' *The Road to Xanadu* for an account of Coleridge's own practice.

We know that Hopkins did not, as a rule, copy his observations directly into his *Journal* ; they were set down roughly on loose sheets and entered up with due care sometimes months afterwards. This rewriting fixed the image and made it immediately available to the right creative impulse. He was so possessed by his images of cloud, tree and water that they fell out, under the stress of poetic inspiration, in considerably better form and order than at their inception. How admirably, for instance, does he combine the " pillow clouds " seen in 1869 with the " tossed clouds " observed in 1873 to form the gleefully boyish " tossed pillows " ; and then replace the conventionally poetical " snowy " by the daringly prosaic " whitewash " !

In 1869 again he described the *nymphaea scutifolia* lying on the water as having " leaves *dimpled* in the middle and beautifully *wimpled* at the edge " (p. 125). Just thirteen years later, in *The Golden Echo*, the not-by-morning-matchèd face of youth is said to be " *wimpled-water-dimpled* ". And an equally successful shifting of the verbal image on to another object is found elsewhere, as when the " *bright pieces* of evening light " [1] which beautified Netley Abbey in 1871 suggested the " *piece-bright* paling " of stars which shuts home Christ the Spouse (No. 8—1877).

Many of these early jottings throw light on the *meaning* of some of the more original or ambiguous images in the poems. In a note of 1869, Hopkins speaks of " opposite *bays* of the sky " [2] ; and the same architectural metaphor is repeated in each of the two poems of shipwreck :

> " Yet did the dark side of the bay of thy blessing
> Not vault them . . . ? " (*The Deutschland*, 12.7.)

> " Bright sun lanced fire in the heavenly bay."
> (*The Eurydice*, 22.)

The latter, Hopkins explains, means that " a bright sun was darting fire from the bay of heaven " [3] ; but the whole line is beautiful even when misunderstood. Most readers, too, must have puzzled over the " fond yellow *hornlight* " that is wound to the west in the evening picture of *Spelt from Sibyl's Leaves*. The metaphor was anticipated in 1870 by a simile which described the Northern Lights as " like the crown of *horny rays* the sun

[1] *Note-books*, p. 154. [2] *Note-books*, p. 125. [3] *Letters*, vol. ii. p. 33.

makes behind a cloud" (p. 134). *Horn* [1] suggests also the *colour* of the rays, as we see by a later note:

> "Bright sunset: all the sky hung with tall tossed clouds . . . westward lamping with tipsy bufflight, the colour of yellow roses" (p. 181.)

The effect of light playing on the hair of a man's arm is perfectly rendered in *Harry Ploughman*:

> "Hard as hurdle arms, with a *broth* of goldish *flue*
> Breathed round;"

Here "broth" is used in the sense of 'a thick brew' (cf. the brewing of fog in *A Christmas Carol*). We get a further clarification in a note on dream-images,[2] in which Hopkins speaks of the "*brothy* motes" made by the shut eyelids in the ordinary use of the function of sight. Simultaneously, the hair on Harry's arm recalled sub-consciously an impression of 1868:

> "a slender race of fine *flue* cloud inscaped in continuous eyebrow curves hitched on the Weisshorn peak . . ." [3]

Hopkins himself speaks of images as being "stalled by the mind" (p. 127), and few poets have revealed the process so completely and admirably. Like "the spectra made by bright things looked hard at", the high lights of his poetry are the after-images caused by an assiduous scrutiny of ordinary sense-data. The ashtrees observed against the bright pieces of evening light on that visit to Netley Abbey might well have provided all the details for such a striking and original image as

> "Only the beak-leaved boughs dragonish | damask the tool-smooth bleak light; black,
> Ever so black on it." [4]

Generally speaking, his verbal delineations of trees, clouds and water reveal the artist whose hand has lovingly traced their shapes with a careful Pre-Raphaelite pencil.

As a poet of the roll and tumble of water—"wild, rash and reeling water" [5]—Hopkins is unsurpassed. Yet the exquisite studio-work of the poems could not have been achieved without the varied field-work of the *Journal*. The following parallels

[1] Cf. *Note-books*, p. 5 (1863), where there is a long note on *Horn*.
[2] *Note-books*, pp. 126–7.
[3] *Ibid.* p. 110.
[4] *Spelt from Sibyl's Leaves.*
[5] *Poems*, p. 79.

show the process of condensation and refining which produced the vigorous sea-pictures of *The Wreck of the Deutschland* :

Note-books—	*The Poem—*
p. 135— " the water swung with a great down and up again . . . the sight was the *burly water-backs* which *heave after heave* kept tumbling up from the broken foam."	"Through the *cobbled foam-fleece* what could he do With the *burl* of the fountains of air, *buck* and flood of the wave ? " (Stanza 16.)
p. 180— " Painted white *cobbled foam* tumbling over the rocks and *combed away* off their backs again."	" And it crowds and it *combs* to the fall." (Stanza 4.)
p. 181— " *flinty* waves. . . . In an enclosure of rocks the peaks of the water *romped* and wandered . . ."	" The sea *flint*-flake . . ." (Stanza 13.) ". . . rolled /With the *sea-romp* over the wreck." (Stanza 17.)

Turning from the availability of his experience in the field of external nature to the availability of those numerous impressions derived from a long preoccupation with religion and religious poetry, we find that a fair proportion of his imagery is a rediscovering or reforging of familiar symbols and analogies. Flagrant verbal echoes, which he called an evil, a disease of education,[1] he always strove to avoid ; and his immunity from this weakness was almost complete. Yet his originality often belongs rather to the fresh handling of his thought-material than to anything new in the material itself.

Much of his imagery is taken directly from the Bible. Unlike Christina Rossetti and others, however, he does not lift the image almost verbatim from its context [2] ; he invariably gives it a personal twist, as in the following :

" Your spouse *not laboured-at nor spun.*" (No. 3)

" *Are you beam-blind, yet to a fault*
In a neighbour deft-handed ? are you that liar
And, cast by conscience out, *spendsavour salt* ? " (No. 26)

[1] *Letters*, vol. i. p. 206.

[2] With Hopkins's idiosyncratic treatment of Corinthians I. ii. 9 (see above, chap. ii. p. 67) cf. Christina Rossetti's *Advent* :

" Eye hath not seen, ear hath not heard, etc."

Sometimes his free handling of an apothegm is like an elaborate musical 'variation on a theme':

> "The hoary head is a crown of glory, if it be found in the way of righteousness." (*Proverbs* xvi. 31.)

> "The vault and scope and schooling
> And mastery of the mind,
> In silk-ash kept from cooling,
> And ripest under rind . . .
> Your offering, with despatch, of!" (No. 24)

The purport of the whole stanza is:

> "As flakes of silky ash round wood embers conceal a core of heat, so grey hairs should signify the honours of age—knowledge, experience, skill, wisdom. But the ageing man is in a perilous plight, unless all these attainments are offered up (and quickly) in the service of God." [1]

Occasionally his Biblical image is one which had been borrowed by many of the lesser religious poets of three centuries. The familiar concept of God's chastening rod (*Ezekiel* xx. 37) appears three times in Hopkins and once in the expression "I kiss the rod". The same token of submission had been used by Francis Quarles (a true poet) and by the versifiers Caroline Bowles and Eliza Cook. The passage in Caroline Bowles has basically the same thought as that given out with much more poetic force in *Carrion Comfort* (ll. 10–11):

> "The very rod
> If we but kiss it, as the stroke descendeth
> Distilleth balm to allay the inflicted smart." [2]

Many of Hopkins's images seem, indeed, to be reminiscent of his early reading; otherwise the following parallels are remarkable coincidences:

(1) "These hairs of age are messengers
Which bid me fast, repent, and pray;" (Lord Vaux.)

"... these most mournful messengers, still messengers,
sad and stealing messengers of grey?" (*The Golden Echo.*)

(2) "The God of hosts in slender host doth dwell."
(R. Southwell [3]: *The Blessed Sacrament.*)

"Low-latched in leaf-light housel his too huge godhead."
(*The Bugler's First Communion.*)

[1] *Letters*, vol. i. p. 98.

[2] *Abjuration: Poetical Works of Caroline Bowles* (1867), p. 290.

[3] The Jesuit martyr (*d.* 1595): as Hopkins says: "a minor poet, but still a poet". (*Letters*, vol. ii. p. 94.)

Even a hymn of the poet's Anglican days had left its mark :

" He shall come down like showers
Upon the fruitful earth . . ." (J. Montgomery.)

" A released shower let flash to the shire, not a lightning of fire hard-hurled." (*The Deutschland*, stanza 34.)

Other ' reminiscent images ' show with what close attention he had read the religious poets of the seventeenth century. That image, in *The Deutschland*, of the soul hunted by God (to be given, later, its fullest expression in Francis Thompson's *The Hound of Heaven*) was anticipated in George Herbert's *Temptation* (stanza 1) but more remarkably in a poem by Francis Quarles :

" O whither shall I fly ; what path untrod
Shall I seek out to 'scape *the flaming rod*
Of my offended, of my angry God ? "[1]

It is difficult to resist the inference that stanza 3 of *The Deutschland* is an unconscious but more intense and dramatic refashioning of Quarles's last two stanzas :

" If not to thee, where—whither—should I go ?

Then work thy will. If passion bid me flee,
My reason shall obey ; my wings shall be
Stretched out no further than from thee to thee."[2]

[1] Cf. Hopkins's " lightning and lashed rod " (stanza 2).

[2] *Emblems* (edn. of 1833), Book III. No. 12. Quarles gives the source of his own ideas in the prose sequel : " *S. August. in Psalm xxxiii.* Whither fly I ? to what place can I safely fly ? . . . Wheresoever, O Lord, I go I find thee . . . what way have I, but to fly from thee to thee . . ." There is some evidence, based on ' association of ideas ', that Hopkins had read the selection from Quarles in vol. xxi. of *The Sacred Classics* (ed. Cattermole and Stebbing, 1835), pp. 191–7. The above poem stands third, and the very next opens with a comparison between man's life and an hour-glass ; so also does the next stanza of *The Deutschland* (No. 4). Later, Quarles calls life

" the flourishing array
Of the proud *meadow,* which to-day
Wears her *green plush,* and is to-morrow hay."

The *meadow* appears in stanza 11 of *The Deutschland*, while " plushy sward " symbolizes mundane enjoyment in *The Habit of Perfection*. Again, at the end of the first poem quoted, Quarles makes *trash* rhyme with *flash* as Hopkins does in *The Heraclitean Fire,* and the second poem begins :

" So, now the soul's sublimed : her sour desires
Are recalcined in heaven's well-temper'd fires : "

A further parallel is between the opening lines of Hopkins's *The Caged Skylark* and *Emblems,* Book V. No. 10 :

" My soul is like a bird, my flesh the cage
Wherein she wears her weary pilgrimage
Of hours."

Quarles was a sincere and graceful poet; but as a personality George Herbert was stronger and more closely akin to Hopkins. In one of his shorter poems, *The Storm*, we find a concise statement of the central ethical theme of Hopkins's two poems of shipwreck:

> " tempestuous times
> Amaze poor mortals and *object their crimes*.
> . . . .
> Poets have wronged poor storms: such days are best,
> They purge the air without; *within, the breast*."

In Herbert, as in Hopkins, the great paradoxes of religion are stated with a poignant, personal urgency—God's anger and love, the sour-and-sweet of faith, the creature's alternate wrestling with his Creator and meekly accepting His Will:

> " Ah, my dear angry Lord,
> Since Thou dost love, yet strike,
> Cast down, yet help afford;
>
> And all my sour-sweet days
> I will lament, and love." (*Bitter-Sweet.*)

The image, in *The Deutschland*, of the sloe which flushes the man with its " sour or sweet " might have been suggested by the above or by

> " Be to me rather sharp and tart . . .
> Such sharpness shows the sweetest friend . . ." (*Paradise.*)

Calm and gentle as Herbert's muse is when compared with that of Hopkins, yet he too was "full of rebellion " and must have endured similar chastisement:

> " After so many deaths I live and write . . .
> It cannot be
> That I am he
> On whom Thy tempests fell all night." (*The Flower.*)

So Hopkins complains " And I that die these deaths . . ." (No. 69), and in *Carrion Comfort* objectifies his midnight desolations as " turns of tempest ". Again, when he says that Tom Navvy treads prickproof through " thousands of thorns, thoughts " he is remembering his Herbert: " I found that some had stuffed the bed with thoughts, /I would say thorns " (*Love Unknown*).

A good example of the combined working of memory and imagination appears in the doctrinal sestet of *The Starlight Night.*

Against this poem in MS. " A " (p. 91), Bridges quoted the following passage from Herbert's *The Church Porch* :

> " Raise thy head ;
> Take stars for money,—stars not to be told
> By any art, yet to be purchasèd." [1]

The similarity in thought is obvious ; but the words used by Hopkins : " Ah well ! it is all a *purchase*, all is a *prize* " (line 8) seem to be drawn from his ' unconscious ' reservoir of Shakespearian impressions :

> " A beauty-waned and distressed widow . . .
> Made *prize* and *purchase* of his wanton eye." [2]

(This elevation of words from a profane context to a " sacred matter " is in keeping with the poet's technical habit—his elevation of ' tumbling metre ', colloquial syntax, the pun, the *double entendre*, trisyllabic and run-on rhymes.) The final association of the stars with " Christ and his mother and all his hallows" is a fresh variation of an image dating from the " saints in light " of Colossians i. 12 and the concept of Civitas Dei : Giles Fletcher compared the saints in heaven to stars [3] ; and according to Milton

> " Attired with stars, we shall for ever sit
> Triumphing over Death." [4]

It is significant, however, that Hopkins uses rustic and homely analogies—the harvest-home and the palings round a simple dwelling.

If Hopkins knew the poetry of Edward, Lord Herbert of Cherbury [5] (brother of George), he might have taken from one poem, *To His Watch, When He Could Not Sleep*, the first hint for his own incomplete sonnet, *To his Watch.* Both poets make the obvious comparison between the action of the timepiece and the wearing away of man's life ; but whereas Herbert's theme is simply the inexorable march of time, Hopkins stresses the moral—that life is an unrepeated, stern probation. A point of resemblance is that both poets speak of time as a part of eternity, Hopkins with literal bluntness :

> " The telling time our task is ; time's some part
> Not all,"—

[1] Stanza 29.
[2] *Richard III*, Act III. vii. 174–6.
[3] *Christ's Victorie*, iv. 23.
[4] *On Time.*
[5] Not mentioned in the *Letters* and *Note-books*. The *Poems*, edited by Churton Collins, appeared in 1881.

Herbert in a final quatrain which is almost Hopkinsian in manner :

> " through you we bide
>
> The doom of Fate, whose unrecall'd decree
> You date, bring, execute ; making what's new
> (Ill and good) old ; for as we die in you,
> You die in Time, Time in Eternity."

A more likely original, perhaps, is the passage in which Quarles uses the same analogy between the mechanism of the watch and the morally responsible human being :

> " Look not, my watch, being once repair'd, to stand
> Expecting motion from thy Maker's hand.
> He's wound thee up, and cleansed thy clogs with blood :
> If now thy wheels stand still, thou art not good."

This " Epigram " follows a longer poem in which Quarles compares his soul to a clock whose wheels " want vigour to fulfil / Her twelve-hours task " [1] and in his fragment Hopkins too hints at the drudgery of the daily round.

Some images which are, or seem to be, reminiscent take us back to Chaucer, Spenser and Shakespeare. In *The Hous of Fame* (II, 283), Chaucer says that a stone thrown into water will make anon " A litel *roundel* as a cercle ". With exquisite craftsmanship, Hopkins polished and reset this idea as

> " Why, *raindrop-roundels* looped together
> That lace the face of Penmaen Pool." (No. 5)

Even more obviously derived is that " lantern out of doors ", which interests our eyes as the bearer moves

> " With, all down darkness wide, his wading light." (No. 10.)

The ethical aspect of the symbol, couched in similar words, had been Spenser's :

> " Vertue gives her selfe light, *through darkenesse for to wade*." [2]

Lastly, an interesting line of development in the sardonic legal

[1] *Emblems*, IV. 8.

[2] *Faerie Queen*, I. i. 12. Spenser's " wade " is probably pure archaism (O.E. wadan, ' to walk ').

image as applied to death may be traced from Shakespeare through Hopkins to Francis Thompson :

> " Shall worms, inheritors of this excess,
> Eat up thy charge ? " (Sonnet CXLVI.)[1]

> " Flesh fade, and mortal trash
> Fall to the *residuary* worm ; " (*Heraclitean Fire.*)

Thompson, with no less wit, shifts the image from probate to conveyancing :

> " And yet is he successive unto nothing
> But patrimony of a little mold
> And *entail* of four planks." (*An Anthem of Earth.*)

The above examples and parallels go to show that a large proportion of the images in even the highest poetry are at bottom illustrations of the great commonplaces, the fundamentals of human experience. Hopkins's treatment of these ideas, even when he echoes another poet's verbal image, is exactly equivalent to Shakespeare's handling of his many literary sources : borrowing without plagiarism, he transmutes baser metals or stamps good gold with his own individual superscription.

In an illuminating study, Dr. Tillyard has shown how poetry can be *direct* or *oblique*.[2] A poem may be entirely figurative in method and yet permit of only one reasonable interpretation : on the other hand, it may be either literal or figurative in its general terms and yet allow of two interpretations—one simple and obvious, the other parabolic and perhaps only partially realized by the poet himself at the time of composition. Something like this obliquity was observed by Hopkins in the lyric passages of Greek tragedy (" perhaps not so much in Euripides as in the others ") : he found there " two strains of thought running together and like counterpointed "—the *overthought*, which everybody sees and which might be paraphrased, and the *underthought*,

> " conveyed chiefly in the choice of metaphors etc. used, and often only half realized by the poet himself, not necessarily having any connection with the subject in hand but usually having a connection and suggested by some circumstance of the scene or of the story." [3]

[1] The only sonnet of wholly religious import.
[2] *Poetry, Direct and Oblique* (1934).
[3] *Further Letters*, pp. 105–6. He quotes Aesch., *Suppl.*, 4 f. etc.

Such an *underthought*—a distinct undercurrent of allusiveness to the great story of Job—can be found in *King Lear*; and a similar *underthought*, harking back to Job and to Shakespeare himself, is traceable in some of the greater poems of Hopkins. Lear says of Goneril:

> "thou art a boil
> A plague-sore, an embossed carbuncle
> In my corrupted blood." [1]

Job's story is one of trial through suffering, while Lear's is one of purgation; but the stature and bearing of the sufferers give them a similar universal significance. The storm in *King Lear* may be considered as much a symbol of divine intervention and judgment as the rain, snow, thunder, lightning and whirlwind which precede the Voice of God in *Job* (Chapters 36–7).

In Hopkins, these storm-phenomena are used with both direct and oblique effect. The imagery of *Job* is refashioned in the "whirlwind-swivellèd snow". the "hailropes" and the "black Boreas" of *The Deutschland* and *The Eurydice*. Total submission to God, like that of Job, is sternly enjoined for all men:

> "But to Christ, lord of thunder,
> Crouch;" [2]

Even if, in *The Deutschland*, such images as the *flower* that is cut down, "dayspring", and "*Orion* of light" could not with certainty be called subliminal reference to *Job*, there would be no mistaking the following significant paraphrase:

> "Who shut up the sea with doors? . . . and said, Hitherto shalt thou come, but no further: and here shall thy proud waves be stayed." (*Job*, xxxviii. 8–11.)

> "I admire thee, master of the tides,
> Of the Yore-flood, of the year's fall:
> The recurb and the recovery of the gulf's sides,
> *The girth of it and the wharf of it and the wall*;" [3]

An *underthought* derived from *Job* and from the highly charged world of Shakespearian tragedy helps to give poignancy and universality to Hopkins's intensely personal later sonnets. That he had been deeply impressed by the power of the heath-scenes in *King Lear* is suggested by the opening of one four-lined fragment:

> "Strike, churl; hurl, cheerless wind, then;" [4]

[1] II. iv. 226–8. [2] *Eurydice*, 109–10. [3] Stanza 32. [4] No. 71.

But just as great representative characters like Job, Jeremiah, Hamlet and Lear seem to endure and epitomize in their little world of man a whole macrocosm of suffering, so these sonnets of Hopkins (numbered 40, 41, 44, 45, 46, 47, 50, 51 and 69) are welded by the evocative quality of their imagery into a great disjointed soliloquy, the utterance of a protagonist comparable in tragic significance to those mentioned above. These sonnets are cries " like dead letters " from man to God, cries which

> " huddle in a main, a chief
> Woe, world-sorrow ; on an age-old anvil wince and sing—" [1]

This latter image is the tragic echo of that eager plea made ten years earlier :

> " With an anvil-ding
> And with fire in him forge thy will." [2]

The man who desired to be hammered into shape now complains that he is being hammered *out* of shape, destroyed by the weight of the blows. And as the tempest in Lear's mind was caused by *filial* ingratitude, so this priest's turns of tempest were partly induced by what he (after Jeremiah) virtually describes as *divine* ingratitude :

> " Wert thou my enemy, O thou my friend,
> How wouldst thou worse, I wonder, than thou dost,
> Defeat, thwart me ? " [3]

In Hopkins's " winter world ", as in the tragic worlds of Lear, Hamlet and Macbeth, all is cheerless, dark and deadly because it is the antithesis of his imagined spring world of productiveness and righteous self-fulfilment :

> " See, banks and brakes
> Now, leavèd how thick ! lacèd they are again
> With fretty chervil . . ." [3]

Like Hamlet, he is worried about the definition and performance of his heaven-appointed duty. It is the lot of both men " to seem the stranger ", partly through intellectual idiosyncrasy, partly through religious or moral persuasion. Even the rare cynical mood of No. 69 may be matched not only by Hamlet but also by certain utterances of Lear and Macbeth.[4]

[1] No. 41. [2] *The Deutschland,* stanza 10.

[3] No. 50. The first four lines paraphrase, freely, *Jeremiah*, xii. 1.

[4] ". . . unaccommodated man is no more but such a poor, bare, forked anima as thou art " (*King Lear,* III. iv. 109–11). Cf. also *Macbeth,* V. v. 19–28.

Several times, in the *Letters*, Hopkins speaks of his own " blackguardly nature " ; and his abnormal sense of personal imperfection was comparable, in its effects, to the stricken conscience of a Macbeth. As Macbeth murdered sleep, so Hopkins suffered night-terrors for what seemed, to his scrupulous mind, commensurate crimes. We can never read the first line of No. 45—

" I wake and feel the *fell of dark*, not day "—

without associating this hairy beast of darkness with another memorable phrase—the " fell of hair " [1] which would rouse and stir at a dismal treatise and at the phantoms of guilt.

Small wonder if Hopkins, like Lear, felt the approach of madness. Lear, sublime even in his failure to reach the stability of Job, cries out : " You heavens, give me patience, patience I need ! " and again : " No, I will be the pattern of all patience." [2] Similarly Hopkins, in No. 46, tries to win Patience (" hard thing ! "), though *his* method is a rational assessment of the costs and gains : patience, in one apt image, is the natural heart's ivy masking the ruins of " wrecked past purpose " ; in another it is a bee, filling its crisp combs.

If we compare, *mutatis mutandis*, the struggles of both men against adverse circumstance and inherent weakness, we see how both had " to do without, take tosses, and obey " (*ibid.*) ; and in the old king's distraction it was the Fool who, with his wry jests, tried to give his master that sense of proportion which would save him from the worst results of his own actions. The parallel here has already been drawn by Professor Abbott : " In a mood that recalls the Fool in *Lear* ", he says, Hopkins, in No. 47, begs a truce to the self-torment of the preceding sonnets.[3] " Prithee, nuncle, be contented " [4] . . . " come, poor Jackself " : in the latter, the potential humorist slaps the potential saint on the back and with a wry smile bids him call off thoughts and leave comfort root-room.

But the most striking expression of this *underthought* or disguised reference is in the sestet of the sonnet which speaks of " world-sorrow "—No. 41. In an early encounter with God, Hopkins, looking *upwards*, had been overawed by His majesty, trodden " hard down by the horror of height ".[5] Now, after his encounter with the world, and bruised by God's buffeting,

[1] *Macbeth*, V. v. 11. Cf. I .iii. 135 : " Whose horrid image doth unfix my hair . . ."
[2] II. iv. 274 and III. ii. 37.
[3] *Letters*, vol. i. p. xxxix.
[4] *King Lear*, III. iv. 113.
[5] *The Deutschland*, stanza 2.

thwarting hand, he must look *downwards* into a bottomless pit of evil, doubt and despair :

> " O the mind, mind has mountains ; cliffs of fall
> Frightful, sheer, no-man-fathomed. Hold them cheap
> May who ne'er hung there."

Obsessed with the thought of human vice, the deranged Lear cries :

> " There's hell, there's darkness, there is the sulphurous pit " ; [1]

but a more significant association of height and danger begins when Gloucester says to Edgar :

> " There is a cliff whose high and bending head
> Looks fearfully in the confined deep ; " [2]

and the amazing visual efficacy of Edgar's description of the vertiginous height as seen from the brink is among the unforgettable things in all poetry.[3] So Keats testified, when he spoke of himself as " one who gathers samphire, dreadful trade ! " [4] The spiritual counterpart of such a precarious occupation is easily imagined : it is the tension between the upward pull of high principles and aims and the downward pull of physical and moral weakness—the flesh and the Devil. The life-line attaching man to God cuts across the horizontal of his daily needs, and at the point of contact (and greatest tension) he must gather his " samphire ", perform his pre-ordained task. With Keats it was to glean his brain, to express himself through poetry ; with Hopkins it was the more complex task of self-expression in art and self-effacement in his vocation. Hopkins ' translates ' the precipice into the supernatural order by adding the epithet " no-man-fathomed " ; and the words " hung there " suggest the daring climber who, his life-line broken, is left clinging to the sheer cliff-face with no help from above and certain destruction below.

It is noteworthy that Lear also, in his entirely different character and circumstances, is torn between self-expression and self-effacement—the egoism of kingship and the humility imposed first by his delegation of power and later by an insight quickened in suffering. It is this suffering which seems to provide the *underthought* of the last two lines of Hopkins's sestet—a sub- or un-conscious reference to the storm, the wretched half-clad

[1] IV. vi. 131.
[2] IV. i. 74–5.
[3] IV. vi. 12–25.
[4] *Letters* (ed. M. B. Forman), vol. i. p. 30.

condition of the three outcasts, the hovel on the heath. Kent exclaims, " Alack ! bare-headed !

> Gracious my lord, hard by here is a hovel ;
> Some friendship will it lend you 'gainst the tempest ; "

and Lear replied :

> ". . . Where is this straw, my fellow ?
> The art of our necessities is strange
> That can make vile things precious. Come, your hovel."

Four times, however, must Kent say, " Good my lord, enter " before the king complies :

> " In, boy ; go first. You houseless poverty,—
> Nay, get thee in. I'll pray, and then I'll sleep." [1]

In this powerful scene, almost every detail is of symbolic import. Such vicarious experience is as natural a source of reference for a later poet as the facts of his own life. Thus with a sudden change of metaphor (indicating a temporary failure to endure the trial of patience and faith) Hopkins shows the strange art of his own necessities :

> " Nor does our small
> Durance deal with that steep or deep. Here ! creep
> Wretch, under a comfort serves in a whirlwind : all
> Life death does end and each day dies with sleep."

The last line, in which the poet falls back upon the most elemental physical consolations for his loss of spiritual health, anticipates the equally desolate conclusions of Nos. 45 and 69. And an indirect but authentic explanation of the " cliffs of fall " image comes from another Jesuit, Father Martin D'Arcy. Speaking of ' desolation ', separation from God, the difficulty of maintaining the religious life, he says :

> ". . . and were it not for some ineradicable, intellectual certainty which persists against all the appearances, we should be tempted to abandon this religious life as make-believe . . . and if daringly we take our life in our hands and throw ourselves out of our pen to find our heart's desire, we meet ' cliffs of fall, frightful, sheer, no-man-fathomed.' " [2]

[1] III. ii.

[2] *Mirage and Truth* (1935), p. 199. Another interesting comment on this sonnet s by Mr. Aldous Huxley : " Never, I think, has the just man's complaint against the universe been put more forcibly, worded more tersely and fiercely . . . God's answer is to be found in that most moving, most magnificent and profoundest poem of antiquity, the book of Job." (*Texts and Pretexts*, p. 67.)

The difficult poise and dangerous tension of this sonnet looks back to *The Windhover* which, although composed eight or nine years earlier, is typical of the poet's attitude to his central problem whenever his mood was one of ' consolation '. The complex images and subtle ambiguities of this great poem are indeed best approached retrospectively from the standpoint of the later sonnets.

The Windhover is yet another of those poems which make a profound appeal long before their full significance is grasped. The whole octave may be read with little difficulty as a vigorous and colourful piece of nature-poetry, a description of the kestrel in action. The rich imagery drawn from French chivalry, the manège, and the graceful art of skating elevates the bird into a universal type of beautiful characteristic activity. The technical term " rung upon the rein " compares the sweeping curves of the bird's flight to the circle described by a horse at the end of the trainer's long rein.

One phrase, in line 7 of the octave, has provoked some speculation among critics :

" *My heart in hiding*
Stirred for a bird,—"

The sonnet carries the unique dedication *To Christ our Lord*, so that even a reader who knew not Hopkins could have no doubt about the religious and specifically Christian connotation of " heart " in this passage. The poet's emotions—sympathy, admiration, love—were ever aroused by all natural or " mortal " beauty, but principally by the supreme pattern of " immortal " beauty—the character of Christ. For this ideal, the poet had renounced worldly ambition, the fullest life of the senses ; hence his heart was " in hiding " with Christ, wholly dedicated to His love, praise and service.[1]

" My heart in hiding " is the first giving out of the essential moral theme of the poem. The whole poem, it must be

[1] The phrase " in hiding " might have been suggested by his own translation (undated) of St. Thomas's *Adoro te* (*Poems*, No. 89), in which *latens deitas* becomes " Godhead here *in hiding* ". Crashaw had rendered this " my hidden life ", and even in *The Windhover* the deeper implication may be : " Christ in my heart, loving me as I love this bird, loves this bird too." We must discount Mr. W. Empson's view that " in hiding " implies that the more dangerous life is the windhover's (*Seven Types of Ambiguity*, p. 255), and also Dr. I. A. Richards's opinion that " in hiding " means, exclusively, " from the life of the senses, from the life of imagination and emotional risk, from speculation . . . hiding in the routine of meditation, in doctrine, etc. . . ." (*The Dial*, Chicago, Sept. 19, 1926.)

remembered, is addressed not to the bird, or to the reader, or to the poet himself, but primarily and deliberately to Christ. Certain critics, by slurring over this fact, have made the admittedly difficult sestet seem unwarrantably vague, ambiguous and pathological : neglecting the meaning as determined by the poet's *will*, they have exhausted their ingenuity in probing the arcana of his unconscious mind, attributing to him in the process motives which he himself would have rejected as incompatible with his purpose, beliefs and vocation. Such probings have their value, but only when assessed in relation to the poet's conscious purpose. The truth is that in the sestet Hopkins holds up to a passionate but critical judgment two conflicting sets of values, one represented by the " kingdom of daylight's dauphin "—the windhover, the other by the Kingdom of Heaven's " chevalier "—Christ. As the psychological critics have shown,[1] and as the poet himself was aware, the sonnet embodies a spiritual conflict. The poet's decision is, moreover, cathartic : he finds relief in his reconciliation of opposite, discordant tendencies in the active personality and the consciously controlled character.

The reconciliation is between the claims of this life and the claims of the next [2] ; between the value and the danger of " mortal beauty " [3] ; between the desire for freedom of expression—the natural function " wild and self-instressed "—and the will to suffer, to subject oneself to the ascetic rule, to dedicate all one's powers to Christ's employment. The resolution of the conflict depends upon recognition of the fact that " mastery " and " achieve " in those mental and physical acts which excite the admiration of onlookers (activities of personality) may be sublimated—assimilated by the character and revealed with greater merit in the supreme act of sacrifice, which is derived from, due to, and rewarded by, Christ.

So the sestet begins :

> " Brute beauty and valour and act, oh, air, pride, plume here
> Buckle ! "

The verb is imperative, making the whole a plea to Christ. The adverb " here ", though ambiguous, means primarily " in this

[1] Dr. Richards and Mr. Empson, *locis cit.* The views of these two critics have been widely adopted and quoted, e.g. by Elsie Elizabeth Phare in *The Poetry of Gerard Manley Hopkins* (1933), pp. 133–8.

[2] Cf. " I am a eunuch—but it is for the kingdom of heaven's sake." (*Letters*, vol. i. p. 270.)

[3] Cf. *Poems*, No. 38.

world, this life ; in *my* particular being even as it happened in *Your* being when You became Man ". The wild beauty and instinctive self-discipline of the kestrel are symbols of the controlled beauty given " back to God " and the military self-discipline of the Ignatian ideal. As the bird co-ordinates all its faculties in graceful flight and dangerous swoop, so the poet asks Christ's help in buckling or enclosing within the belt of the Jesuit rule all his own rich faculties.[1] The likeness between the bird and the partially repressed personality of the poet is obvious, so that the mind is capable of holding, in one act of comprehension, another relevant meaning of " buckle "—to bend, crumple up under weight or strain.

External evidence that Hopkins had this idea in mind is to be found in a letter and a sermon :

> " Christ our Lord . . . was doomed to succeed by failure ; his plans were baffled, his hopes dashed, and his work was done by being broken off undone." [2]

Having dwelt upon traditional accounts of Christ's physical beauty, he concludes :

> " In his Passion all this strength was spent, this lissomness crippled, this beauty wrecked, this majesty beaten down." [3]

And there is another striking piece of evidence in one of Shakespeare's plays.[4] For Hopkins, then, the example of Christ's life linked together three relevant and complementary meanings of " Buckle ! "—buckle within (discipline), buckle to (labour), buckle under (sacrifice). Moreover, the story, implicit throughout the *Letters*,[5] of the poet's own ' imitation of Christ ', is epitomized in the sestet of this sonnet.

[1] Cf. Shakespeare's use of " buckle " in

> " He cannot buckle his distempered cause
> Within the belt of rule." (*Macbeth*, V. ii. 15–16.)

[2] *Letters*, vol. ii. pp. 137–8.

[3] *Note-books*, pp. 262–3.

[4] *II Henry IV*. I. i. 140–42 :

> " And as the wretch, whose fever-weaken'd joints,
> Like strengthless hinges *buckle under life*,
> Impatient of his fit, *breaks* like a *fire*
> Out of his keeper's arms. . . ."

Hopkins, too, in the same line as *Buckle* ! uses *fire* and *breaks*. It is also significant that in the next scene of the play Falstaff says : " He that *buckles* him *in* my belt cannot live in less." (*Oxford Shakespeare*, line 160.)

[5] See especially *Letters*, vol. i. p. 175.

The rest of the tercet states the immediate outcome of this discipline which entails suffering and sacrifice :

> ". . . AND the fire that breaks from thee then a billion
> Times told lovelier, more dangerous, O my chevalier ! "

In a direct or straightforward reading, all this could be addressed to the kestrel, the " chevalier " of the air ; but if, as we have decided, the stress is on " my ", it is certainly intended for the listening Christ, the perfect example of *spiritual* activity as the bird is a perfect example of *physical* activity. By the same token, the glamour of " chevalier " is reflected back on to the poet himself, who resembles, in opposite ways, both the bird and the Master. By an act of will, the poet has turned from the ruthless freedom and joy of the kestrel to the compassionate servitude of Christ (" O ḿy chevalier ! "). Hopkins himself, when free to act, was the curvetting and caracoling knight-errant of poetry ; but the King he chose to serve was He who once rode, slowly and humbly, upon an ass. The mental transition from " chevalier " to *chivalry*, and thence to *soldier of Christ* (the Jesuit priest) makes the next symbol of humble, useful toil—the plough [1]—both natural and moving. The sequence [2] is : " The windhover flashes a trail of beauty across the morning sky ; but the beauty in action, the inspiration, the glory of Christ (and in a lesser degree of the plodding, inhibited poet-priest) is far, far lovelier. The taut, swooping windhover is the terror of the air ; but the disciplined life of the spirit is much more dangerous, because it is menaced by, and must itself attack and overcome, a far greater foe—the powers of evil." And " no wonder ! " the poet cries, in his certainty and somewhat pained ardour—

> " No wonder of it : sheer plod makes plough down sillion
> Shine . . ."

The price, however, must be paid. How unlike the swoop of a hawk is the following symbol of ' a man of sorrows ', the jaded drudge, the gradual cooling off of youthful vigour and zeal—" blue-bleak embers " ! It is a martyrdom, but the consolation is there too :

> ". . . and blue-bleak embers, ah my dear,
> Fall, gall themselves, and gash gold-vermilion."

[1] Cf. the same image as used by Donne (quoted above, chap. i. p. 10.

[2] Of the changes of colour and image in the sestet Dr. Richards says, finely : " A prose indication of these fixes them in greater independence and sharper opposition than they possess in the rapid co-presentation of the poem." (*Loc. cit.*)

As Mr. Empson points out, these images suggest the Crucifixion, the martyr's blood and the crown of gold. As at the end of the *Heraclitean Fire*, the collapse in defeat, agony and death is a reward, a sudden change as from ash to immortal diamond. The words " ah my dear ", borrowed from Herbert,[1] have a double significance : they express sympathy with Christ for his anguish and martyrdom [2] and at the same time a tender reproach that He should give His devout but frail servant such a heavy cross to bear.[3]

That two verbs in the last line of *The Windhover* should be repeated at the beginning of *In Honour of St. Alphonsus Rodriguez* (1888) shows that this sonnet is meant to exemplify, in the life of a particular saint, the moral generalization of the earlier poem. Honour " flashed off exploit " links the particular activity of the falcon to that of the martyr, while " *gashed* flesh or *galled* shield " indicate the visible and trumpeted heroism of the Christian martyrs whose names are household words. This Alfonso, however, earned his canonization by the sheer plod of having " for 40 years acted as hall porter to the College of Palma in Majorca " and of having overcome his desolations with exquisite fortitude. Like that of Hopkins, his " war " was all " within ", and in paying him this worthy homage the poet reveals the deep significance of his own stern trials. Hopkins, being a man of genius, had probably more appetencies to repress, more pains to endure—" For disappointment and humiliations embitter the heart and make an aching in the very bones ".[4] As he says in *Patience* :

> " We hear our hearts grate on themselves : it kills
> To bruise them dearer. Yet the rebellious w
> Of us we do bid God bend to him even so."

Throughout Hopkins's numerous ' military images ' runs the idea of the Church Militant. This vocational view of Christ and the Christian as ' soldier ' is developed most completely

[1] See his *Love* :

> " I, the unkind, ungrateful ? Ah, my dear,
> I cannot look on Thee."

[2] ". . . but that God should be crucified fascinates—with the interest of awe, of pity, of shame, of every harrowing feeling." (*Letters*, vol. i. p. 188.)

[3] Hopkins called *The Windhover* the best thing he ever wrote (*Letters*, vol. i. p. 85). He also said that Christ was " the only just literary critic " (*Letters*, vol. ii. p. 8). Hence the dedication precludes any conscious expression of dissatisfaction or peevish rebelliousness in the poem.

[4] *Letters*, vol. ii. p. 9.

in No. 39. In the two sonnets just examined, the leading *motif* was the superiority of *inward*, personal values to *outward* appearances ; in *The Soldier*, on the contrary, the average member of the regular fighting forces presents a sad contrast between the dignity and worth of his profession and the relative baseness of his character (" frail clay, nay but foul clay."). Yet seeing a redcoat or tar we bless him because the " heart " (our generous idealism) esteems the artist according to his art, sets the same value on the soldier as on soldiering, and takes the scarlet coat as the symbol of blood poured out for others. This tacit reference to " Greater love hath no man than this, etc." makes a natural transition to the perfect co-ordination of labour and love in the chivalry of " Christ our King " :

> " He knows war, served this soldiering through ;
> He of all can reeve a rope best."

By " this soldiering " Hopkins means the " spirit of war " in which every good man resists the powers of evil. The next line implies that Christ, the sum of all perfections, is always in spirit with the man who is earnestly doing his duty. Leaning from heaven, the King applauds the " Christ-done-deed " because, being " all that man can do ", it is equivalent in merit to the supreme sacrifice of " God-made-flesh ".[1]

" Were I come o'er again ", Christ says in the last line, " it should be this ", and this text sums up the allegorical symbolism of *Andromeda* (1879), the only mature poem in which Hopkins employed, for his own purposes, a complete episode from Greek mythology. " Time's Andromeda " we take to be the Bride of Christ, the Roman Catholic Church, and " this rock rude " to be St. Peter who, though revered by Catholics as the first Bishop of Rome, was nevertheless, in relation to his Master, imperfect. The association of St. Peter and the Rock had been used in *The Deutschland* to describe the combination of steadfastness, fear, and high example in the tall nun :

> " The Simon Peter of a soul ! to the blast
> Tarpeian fast, but a blown beacon of light." [2]

Unequalled in her beauty and her affliction, the Church has been " attempted and pursued / By many blows and banes "

[1] This sonnet will never please the thoroughgoing pacifist. But Hopkins was not a pacifist, but a patriotic Englishman, as witness his recruiting song, *Poems*, No. 59.

[2] Stanza 29.

—by persecution, heresy and schism ; and in the nineteenth century it was being threatened by " a wilder beast from West " which probably means rationalism, Darwinism, the new paganism of Whitman, and all similar forces which to Hopkins would be " against faith and morals ".[1] Perseus, then, stands for Christ the Bridegroom, who delays His coming, tests the patience of His Church, yet all the while

" hangs
His thoughts on her, forsaken that she seems,"

until at last, like a thief in the night, he alights " disarming "—

" With Gorgon's gear and barebill, thongs and fangs."—

that is, with evidences of Death and Hell conquered, but also with the sword and scourge of retributory justice. We should note the significant ambiguity of " disarming " : the Redeemer's coming will allay fears, deprive Evil of its power, and bring final peace.

The one other poem in which Hopkins attempts a sustained allegory is the unfinished *Epithalamion* (1888). Skilfully pieced together by Bridges from the chaotic fragments of the poet's pencilled MS., this delightful summer idyll can be so completely enjoyed as " poetry of earth " that the sudden exegetic turn, by which Hopkins hoped to elevate the subject to the intended doctrinal plane, strikes the reader as extraneous and unconvincing:

" What is . . . the delightful dene ?
Wedlock. What is water ? Spousal love . . ."

These symbols are at least adequate ; but when the trees, flowers and ferns became " Father, mother, brothers, etc." the poet himself must have felt that in consecrating the matter he had lost the dream.

He is more successful when, instead of employing a comprehensive ' dark ' symbol to be elucidated in due course, he gives out one basic analogy and elaborates it in a series of far-fetched but emotionally apt images. In the earlier devotional poem, *The May Magnificat* (1878), the attribution to the Virgin Mary of a poet's eye for the beauties of Spring seems artificial until the sympathy between " Nature's motherhood " and

[1] See the *Letters*, *passim*, for Hopkins's adverse opinion of such men as Goethe, Hugo, Swinburne and Whitman. For his attitude to Darwinism, see *Letters*, vol. i. pp. 172, 289–90.

Mary's motherhood is neatly summed up in a double-edged word :

"Their magnifying of each its kind
With delight calls to mind
How she did in her stored
Magnify the Lord."

Hopkins calls the Blessed Virgin "mighty mother", the very term that George Meredith applied to that austere, indeterminate deity—Earth. How intimate and tender the anthropomorphism of Hopkins's faith can be is brought out by setting his later and greater poem, *The Blessed Virgin Compared with the Air We Breathe* (1883), by the side of any one of Meredith's.[1] To Hopkins, Earth was but a foster-nurse ; man, made in God's image, should have a spiritual Mother who is higher, not lower, in the scale of being. In reading *The Blessed Virgin*, we feel that if dogma had not provided an intermediary between absolute Godhead and common humanity, the poet's intensely human sympathies would have led him to create one as a private symbol. In Shelley's metaphysic, matter is a "screen" or "vest" interposed between the spirit of man and the burning limbs of his divinity—the Spirit of Nature.[2] Similarly, Hopkins, sustaining admirably his parallel between the spiritual functions of the Mother of Divine Grace and the physical properties of "world-mothering air", works up to this climax :

"Through her we may see him
Made sweeter, not made dim,
And her hand leaves his light
Sifted to suit our sight."

Mary's immaculate humanity is the screen through which the powerful radiation of God shines with a tempered glow. In like manner the atmosphere mitigates the sunbeam ;

"Whereas did air not make
This bath of blue and slake
His fire, the sun would shake,
A blear and blinding ball
With blackness bound, and all
The thick stars round him roll
Flashing like flecks of coal . . ."

[1] E.g. *Earth and Man, Earth's Secret, Ode to the Spirit of Earth in Autumn,* etc. Cf. also the pantheism of Swinburne's *Hertha.*

[2] *Prometheus Unbound* Act II. Scene v. "Life of Life !"

Such "bare glory" was the wrath, vengeance and destruction attributed to "god of old". It was the advent of Christ and the Holy Family that made meekness and love the prime aspirations of the religious in the Western world. Hopkins took the realistic view that man's apprehension of God is mainly emotional; hence man, a mere child in relation to such mysteries, must attain to the Infinite Father through the tender spiritual motherhood of Mary :

> "Be thou then, O thou dear
> Mother, my atmosphere . . .
> Fronting my froward eye
> With sweet and scarless sky ;"

To apply the term 'conceit' to the basic analogy and to most of the incidental images in this poem is to abuse criticism, unless by the implied 'far-fetchedness' we mean (as Hopkins did) a quality which delights and illuminates as much as it surprises. To one who denies God the poem must, we suppose, seem nugatory. To a Catholic its imagery should require no justification. And many others will see in Mary the symbolic representation of a universal truth—the value of the highest moral perfection as a stepping-stone to the Deity.

In its fusion of Catholic theology and private speculation, in the tenderness of its devotion and the easy flow of its interrelated images, this poem is nearer to the style and spirit of Crashaw than any other poem by Hopkins.[1] He admitted that it was "partly a compromise with popular taste", and regretted that "the highest subjects are not those on which it is easy to reach one's highest" [2]; yet Patmore liked this poem best [3]—probably because Hopkins, without ceasing to be himself, follows up the witty delicacy of Marvell—

> "Laying, like air's fine flood,
> The deathdance in his blood ;"

with the fine abandon of Crashaw—

> "And makes, O marvellous !
> New Nazareths in us,
> Where she shall yet conceive
> Him, morning, noon, and eve . . ."

[1] Cf. the *Hymn to St. Teresa* and *The Flaming Heart.*

[2] *Letters,* vol. i. p. 179.

[3] *Further Letters,* p. 205.

Of that type of ingeniously intellectual imagery so frequent in the seventeenth century 'Metaphysicals' there is a fair proportion in Hopkins. All his poetry is metaphysical in the sense that it embodies the inherited metaphysic of the Roman Catholic Church presented in the 'subtle evolution' of original ideas and individual perceptions. But for some readers, the doctrinal or theological elements on the one hand and the strictly metaphysical elements on the other—the passionate thinking of the individual, in detachment, about his own being and experience—do not always coalesce.[1] Yet Hopkins's theological tenets had become so much a part of his being that the combination of elements does seem, to those who share his beliefs, as organic as it is in Donne. The result, however, is different: in Donne there is more wit, paradox, ratiocination; in Hopkins the intellectual resourcefulness admits a larger proportion of vivid description, sensuousness, and suggestion—all legacies, no doubt, from the Romantic school. Nevertheless, in the delicacy, ingenuity, and almost fantastic wit of many of his images, Hopkins continues the tradition of Donne, Herbert, Crashaw, Vaughan, and Marvell.

The 'metaphysical' manner shows itself in unexpected comparisons between the natural object and the artificial, the organic and the mechanical, the ideal and the commonplace. If Johnson could ask, "Who but Donne would have thought that a good man is a telescope?"[2] others to-day may wonder whether anyone but Hopkins would have compared a good man to a well (No. 4.4), a nun faced with death to an electric bell (*ibid.* 31) a singing lark to a winch (No. 11), a lungful of air to a meal (No. 37.12), and a Protestant to a crocodile (No. 86). Yet in their contexts all these 'conceits', except the last, are well worth their carriage. The "fawning crocodiles" that "wound their winch of wicked smiles" around the condemned Margaret Clitheroe are, perhaps, most eligible of all Hopkins's images for a place in that museum of literary curiosities which holds Crashaw's "Two walking baths, etc."[3] But in his finished poems Hopkins never indulged in the wiredrawn analogies of

[1] For example, Professor Abbott complains that in *The Heraclitean Fire* "the Resurrection" jumps out of the pattern (*Letters*, vol. i. p. xxxvii). Yet to anyone who feels as Hopkins did about the flux, personality, the Fall and the Atonement, "the Resurrection" will seem, as it seemed to the poet, necessary to *complete* the pattern—of philosophy and of the poem. Cf. the similar adverse criticism by Mr. B de Selincourt (above, chap. i. p. 19.)

[2] Life of Cowley.

[3] *The Weeper.*

Donne or the " enormous and disgusting hyperboles " of Cowley. From Crashaw, indeed, he may have borrowed one inspired conceit. In the *Hymn to Saint Teresa*, Crashaw says :

> " The virgin-births with which thy sovereign Spouse
> Made fruitful thy fair soul."

By this he means the sons of her vows, the souls saved by her prayers. Hopkins is reminded of the Virgin Birth by the nun's cry of *Christ, come quickly* (No. 4.24) ; but this, he adds, was " heart-throe, birth of a brain ".

Another ' metaphysical ' characteristic in Hopkins is the possession of a searching, microscopic eye and an abnormally developed tactile sense, the resulting image being a figurative interpretation of precisely observed phenomena. There is a revelation in the bare reminder that air " girdles each eyelash ", whether the similitude of " mercy " and " Mary " so mantling the guilty globe is, to us, significant or not.[1] Exquisite, too, is that terse comparison between the action of light in photographic portraiture and the shaping fingers of an artist : " The fine, the *fingering* beams . . ."[2] Again, speaking of the new relation of man's spirit to his body after the resurrection, Hopkins says :

> " *meadow-down is not distressed*
> *For a rainbow footing it* nor he for his bónes rísen."[3]

The very precariousness of this analogy expresses the ontological precariousness of the subject, the ineffability of the supernatural.

The boldness of a conceit, combined with that deeper imaginative insight into nature which can be traced back to Marvell and Vaughan, informs the following images, primary and secondary :

> " And the azurous hung hills are his world-wielding shoulder
> Majestic—as a stallion stalwart, very-violet-sweet ! "[4]

Here we are made to feel the strength and gentle beauty of Christ's character permeating the world of His creation. We are reminded of Pater's principle—*ex forti dulcedo*.

[1] *The Blessed Virgin*, ll. 2–3.
[2] *On the Portrait of Two Beautiful Young People*, stanza 3.
[3] *The Caged Skylark*.
[4] For an answer to Bridges's adverse criticism of the " stallion stalwart, very-violet-sweet " image (*Poems*, p. 96), see *Survey of Modernist Poetry* by Laura Riding and Robert Graves (1927), p. 93.

This reconciliation of two seemingly opposed qualities (the animal-like roughness and strength of mountains and their ethereal quality under soft light) [1] is paralleled not only by the association of the windhover with Christ and his poet-priest but also by other striking images. In *The Deutschland*, the " gospel proffer . . . Christ's gift " is compared to one of those silvery rills which streak the sides of Welsh mountains after rain. The soul, steadied by its faith, is

> " *roped* with, always, all the way down from the tall
> Fells . . . a vein
> Of the gospel proffer . . ." (Stanza 4.)

The participle " roped ", while truthfully describing the appearance of the down-flowing rill, suggests also the power that draws *upwards*, as water is raised from a well (see line 5—" as a water in a well ") or as a climber is rescued from " cliffs of fall " (cf. No. 41).[2] The association with *rope*, therefore, suggests a force which simultaneously binds and releases, like Divine Grace.

Again, in stanza 6, there is a pregnant ambiguity when Hopkins speaks of the revelation of the Divine principle through phenomena and events—the instress of " stars and storms " :

> " But it rides time *like riding a river* ".

The phrase " riding a river " can be read, satisfactorily, in three different ways. One reading, " like crossing a river on horseback ", would imply that as the Incarnation cut clean across time and history (the flowing river), so the revelation " dates from day / Of his going in Galilee ".[3] Another meaning of *ride* is ' to ride at anchor ', float, be borne up ; so that " rides time " would mean that although time bears everything else away, this principle remains. Lastly, *ride* may signify move, be carried on : " But this principle is carried along on the current of time, is present and potent in all periods of history "—a reading which is supported by a line in the next stanza :

> " Though felt before, though in high flood yet ".

Whichever reading was intended by the poet or was uppermost in his mind, they all (especially the last two) grow to one point.

[1] See Riding and Graves, *loc. cit.*
[2] Cf. Dr. F. R. Leavis in *New Bearings in English Poetry* (1932), pp. 179–80.
[3] Suggested to me by Father J. O'Donohoe, S.J., of Manresa House, Roehampton.

Once or twice an image is definitely sullied by an apparently unconscious ambiguity or vagueness. When Hopkins salutes a bridegroom with

"God with honour *hang your head*,"[1]

the garland or other decoration is obscured by the strong suggestion of 'shame'. The same defiance of idiom caused what Bridges describes as "the wrongness" of

"With *a rope's end round the man*, handy and brave—"[2]

but here the reader has been prepared for the correct signification by the two preceding lines. Obscurity is shot with a strange suggestiveness when the cuckoo's ballad is said to rebound "Off *trundled* timber" (No. 66)[3]; and when, in *Margaret Clitheroe*, the spirit of hell is "to her virtue *clinching*-blind". This compound suggests the eyes of a bigot fast shut; but when we unmask a pun on the name Clinch (the judge who condemned Margaret) the sense gains a clarity which is of dubious value.

To complete our survey of the range and variety of Hopkins's imagery we must pass from his Metaphysical or Caroline predilections to his more modern, Romantic strain. Half-way stand the playful 'baroque' images of *Penmaen Pool* ("hoar messmate hobs and nobs with him"; "ale like goldy foam / That frocks an oar"). A change from the learned to the naive poet appears in "Thrush's eggs are *little low heavens*" (No. 9), and the "horseback brown" and "candy-coloured" mountain streams belong to the same order of infantine responses.[4] A fresh, primitive sensibility, with its corresponding impulsiveness of expression, gives us the combined homeliness and synaesthesia of the following:

"and thrush
Through the echoing timber does so *rinse and wring*
The ear, it *strikes like lightnings* to hear him sing;"[5]

Tactile and visual impressions objectify the aural. The tense flashing, ablutionary quality of the bird's song, with its alternate gushes of clear and constricted sound, is perfectly rendered. By the same visualization of sound, the lark's passionate trilling, like twine unwinding from a tight reel, makes

"crisps of curl off wild winch whirl." (No. 11)

[1] *At the Wedding March* (No. 28). [2] *The Deutschland*, stanza 16.

[3] This seems to be a transferred epithet: it is the sound that is trundled from tree to tree. [4] Nos. 33 and 72. [5] No. 9.

Hopkins's imagery is Romantic only in the freshness of its perceptions, its first-hand treatment of natural phenomena. Nature, for him, had no magic casements opening on to nebulous, fascinating, but otherwise unprofitable faery lands. Beauty, for him, was never a narcotic, but was always a powerful stimulus to his social and numinous emotions. To him a wild bird was not, as to Keats and Shelley, a symbol of escape into sweet oblivion or an airy void : it is a stinging reminder of his own hard vocation (*The Windhover*), of the flesh which lusteth against the spirit (*The Caged Skylark*), of the drab failure of material civilization (*The Sea and the Skylark*), of the sterility of his own moral and aesthetic nature (No. 50) ; or it is the symbol of Peace which brings no idle pleasance but " work to do " (No. 22), of the bright, healthy realities, the sheer ecstacy of living (*Spring*, *The Valley of the Elwy*, *The Woodlark*), of the pied, inscaped and individuated beauty of all God's creatures (*Pied Beauty*, *Henry Purcell*). The homing pigeon occurs twice, each time with a high moral significance (No. 4.3 ; No. 27). Likewise, trees gave colour and a rich laciness to the frieze of life ; yet with Hopkins as with so many ' mystical ' poets, they were a " milk to the mind " because their boughs break in the sky, tabour on it, grope towards heaven (*On the Portrait, etc.*, stanza 8 ; *Ash-boughs*). He showed a boyish enthusiasm for the bright, hidden or elusive things—the glowing ' conker ', stippled trout, birds' eggs ; and a feminine love of spring flowers and soft fabrics—primrose, bluebell, violet, crush-silk poppies, velvety wind and plushy sward. But all these, with the plush-capped sloe and the ripe peach that yields at a touch, are symbols not only of God's grandeur, of His infinite productiveness for man's delight, but also of that sensual gratification or lower spiritual pleasure which must be held in ' detachment ', given back to God in the interests of the *higher* spiritual good.

In his tactile and gustatory images, Hopkins is as sensuous as Keats, but more direct and forthright. Keats would not have said, " I am . . . heartburn . . . : my taste was me ". The sloe-image in *The Deutschland* [1] may, however, owe something to that memorable image of taste in the *Ode to Melancholy* ; for the same sense of contiguous pain and beauty, of inseparable joy and sorrow, informs both poems. " What can it be, this glee ? " Hopkins asks of his own tears ; and Keats's Melancholy is seen by none save him whose strenuous tongue " Can burst

[1] Stanza 8.

Joy's grape against his palate fine ". In spirit and form, however, the two images illustrate an important difference between Hopkins's imagery and that of most other poets : Keats's image is *contemplative* ; Hopkins's image is *dramatic*, informed with all the glow and movement of a living act. Crashaw, describing the Incarnation, had said that Christ left His Father's Court and came

" Lightly as a lambent flame " [1] ;

but for Hopkins the painter of this descent of the Holy Ghost must be Michelangelo or El Greco, not Raphael :

> " The heaven-flung, heart-fleshed, maiden-furled
> Miracle-in-Mary-of-flame."

It is this dramatic motile imagery which is so characteristic of Hopkins, and which assimilates him, as we have already remarked, to no other poet so much as to Shelley—the dynamic, Heraclitean Shelley of *The West Wind*, *The Cloud*, and " Worlds on worlds are rolling ever ". Not that Shelley presents thought and action with such dramatic immediacy or with such violent effects as Hopkins does, but he too found a special beauty in growth, change, and movement.

Keats's conception of Beauty is usually embodied in images of relaxation, sleep, or statuesque immobility.[2] To Hopkins, earthly beauty, though exquisite in its static aspects, is always more arresting and significant when it is flashed off exploit, motion, development : once inscape has been discovered, he says, motion multiplies it.[3] Beauty is often a progression of inscapes ; and in a journal note on the behaviour of an opening flag flower, Hopkins seems to desire that God-like faculty which would enable him to see the whole progression at once :

> " A beautiful instance of inscape sided on the slide, that is /progressive sidings of one inscape . . . and of course if the whole ' behaviour ' were gathered up and so stalled it would have a beauty of all the higher degree." [4]

In the image from *The Deutschland* quoted above, the poet seems to be trying to gather up and stall the whole ' behaviour ' of

[1] *To the Countess of Denbigh : Against Irresolution and Delay in Matters of Religion*, l. 70.

[2] E.g. the various personifications of Autumn in the *Ode* ; the ' motion instantaneously arrested ' of the *Ode to a Grecian Urn* ; Joy with hand ever at his lips (*Ode to Melancholy*) ; the quiet " rosy sanctuary " of the *Ode to Psyche*, etc.

[3] *Note-books*, p. 133.

[4] *Note-books*, p. 148. Cf. the withering Horned Violet, which " ran through beautiful inscapes " (p. 149).

Christ at the time of His physical conception in the Virgin Mary.

As Christ incarnate was " heaven-flung ", so Christ crucified was " our *passion-plungèd* giant ". Hopkins's faith in the ultimate identification of Christ with perfect beauty and ideal activity seems to have occasioned in the poet, and also in nature, an inspired restlessness or impetuosity—a gust to hurl or be hurled, as if God were participating with his creatures in some jubilant cosmic sports or circus. In *Spring*, the blue sky is " all in a rush /With richness ", as though the clouds, like the racing lambs, must also " have fair their fling ". Ears of ripe corn are hurled by the wind " this side, that side ",[1] while our nuptial swimmer, diving greedily into the waters of spousal love, is also hurled (symbolically, perhaps) through the regions of earth, air, and water.[2] Something like the timber " trundled " by the cuckoo's note is the illusory movement observed in the poplars of Binsey, which

> " Quelled or quenched in leaves the *leaping* sun ".[3]

Even the blood of the murdered Winefred is active, for it " swings and dances " on Caradoc's blade.[4]

Keats, in his last sonnet, admired the steadfastness of one bright star. Hopkins, however, saw a host of stars, first as static " fire-folk " and " circle-citadels ", then as dynamic creatures —white pigeons fluttering from the dovecote, and

> " *Wind*-beat whitebeam, airy abeles set on a *flare*." [5]

Such an association of *wind* and *fire* is recurrent in this poet's work (" white-fiery and whirlwind-swivellèd snow ", " a blown beacon ",[6] " lanced fire . . . black Boreas " [7]), and is probably due to Biblical influence—the whirlwind and fire of Ezekiel (I. iv.), the rushing wind and tongues of flame in the Pentecostal visitation (*Acts*, II. ii.–iii.).

Hopkins belongs to the class of English poets, headed by Shakespeare, who are remarkable for the rich flow of their imagery. One type of cumulative imagery elaborated, after Shakespeare, by Donne is the logically developed series or ' subtle evolution ' of related images which grow ever more ' conceited '

[1] *The Golden Echo.* [2] *Epithalamion.*

[3] No. 19. Cf. the " burst of summertime " in *Cheery Beggar.*

[4] *St. Winefred's Well*, p. 76. [5] *The Starlight Night.*

[6] *The Deutschland*, 13 and 29.

[7] *The Eurydice*, stanza 6. Cf. also *The Windhover*, lines 7 and 10 ; the *Heraclitean Fire*, lines 5 and 9.

and of dubious application. This type was not cultivated by Hopkins. He preferred that other Shakespearian method—a rapid succession of independent images which are related only by some inner necessity and by their admirable fitness and relevancy. The quick-fire of his figurative ideas admits no stately epic similes, like those of Milton or Arnold, and no romantically elaborated pictures like those in Shelley's *To a Skylark*.

In its prime intention and general method, Hopkins's total complex of style is Classical rather than Romantic. His poems are most completely unified and satisfying, his imagery is most subtle and dynamic, when he is handling some deeply felt ethical or human theme. Yet even when such a motive is lacking, he can still give us, in a descriptive piece called *Moonrise*,[1] images which are both precise and idiosyncratic :

> " I awoke in the Midsummer not to call night, | in the white and the walk of the morning :
> The moon, dwindled and thinned to the fringe | of a finger-nail held to the candle,
> Or paring of paradisaical fruit, | lovely in waning but lustreless,
> Stepped from the stool, drew back from the barrow, | of dark Maenefa the mountain ;
> A cusp still clasped him, a fluke yet fanged him, | entangled him, not quit utterly . . ."

This, in the year 1915, would have passed for an Imagist poem. The Imagist ideal of rendering particulars exactly in hard, clear terms is not in itself adequate for exploring the deepest recesses of the spirit ; but Hopkins was one with those poets in striving to put *meaning* before mere suggestion and sound.[2] He surpasses them, and most other modern poets, in sound and suggestion ; and though at times the approach is difficult, the hard core of meaning is always there for the seeking.

In order to give a unified and concise cogency to the above exposition of Hopkins's poetic method and the principles underlying his choice of themes and images, we have been obliged to restrict quotation and jump quickly from one poem to another. Hence only a few poems, like *Andromeda*, the *Heraclitean Fire*, and *The Windhover*, have been treated adequately as self-contained

[1] *Poems*, No. 65.

[2] Their *credo* appeared in the *Imagist Anthology* (ed. Amy Lowell) of 1915. See also T. E. Hulme's *Speculations*.

works of art. To compensate for this apparent deficiency in our examination of the mature poems, we shall include, in our second volume,[1] a further chapter of appreciations. In this a number of the more important poems, which have so far been drawn upon only for incidental illustrations, will be scrutinized and assessed more thoroughly in their proper chronological and biographical setting.

[1] Chapter v.

CHAPTER VI

CRITICS AND REVIEWERS

> "*Survey the* whole, *nor seek slight faults to find*
> *Where nature moves, and rapture warms the mind.*"
> (Pope's *Essay on Criticism.*)

THE soundness of the above precept (so frequently honoured in the breach) has seldom been so richly and curiously demonstrated as in the case of Gerard Manley Hopkins. The following dossier of the proceedings in which this poet stands his trial before the bar of posterity is furthermore an illustration of the profound truth of two other axioms enunciated by Pope:

> "Great Wits sometimes may gloriously offend
> And rise to faults true Critics dare not mend."

> "A perfect Judge will read each work of Wit
> With the same spirit that its author writ."

The spirit in which the poet writ is itself not exempt from judgment; but a fair approach to this question is hardly possible until justice has been done to the aims and achievement of the poet *according to his own lights*. The aberrations which result from a disregard of this natural order stand out egregiously against the more judicious opinions recorded in the following pages.

This chapter is also a summary of the efforts of Hopkins's admirers to foster the 'taste' which the poet sought to create and by which he wanted to be judged—a purpose in which these reviewers and critics have, on the whole, nobly succeeded. Partly because many of the early reviewers were not true critics, and partly because a new *species* in poetry is naturally difficult to assess, the first edition of the *Poems* (1918) took twelve years to exhaust; so that Bridges's qualms about their reception were, from the publisher's point of view, justified. Nevertheless, in critical acuity many of the Press notices of the first edition can rarely have been surpassed in the annals of journalism, and they deserve to be made accessible to the general reader. Writing to Hopkins, in 1884, about "the Gallery Gods—i.e. the common run of ' Nineteenth Century ', ' Fortnightly ' and such critics ", Patmore said :

> " I feel *absolutely* sure that you would never conciliate *them*." [1]

The attempt was not made until the " Gallery Gods " had been schooled (by Whitman, Bridges, Meredith, and Doughty) [2] into a tolerance and receptivity which gave their natural intelligence free play.

Sir Henry Newbolt once said that in studying poets we should note whether they have been irradiated by public favour or thrust back upon themselves by neglect.[3] We may add that public approval to a poet is like a term of office to a radical politician : it tends to impose discipline and restraint. Without his due meed of praise, the poet of genius may develop a compensatory narcissism which invests idiosyncrasy with an exaggerated significance. That was always a danger with Hopkins. He was more self-sufficient than most artists :

> " There is a point with me in matters of any size when I must absolutely have encouragement as much as crops rain ; afterwards I am independent." [4]

These words were in acknowledgment of Bridges's approval of the *St. Winefred* fragments, and full credit must be accorded to him for his share in drawing out and preserving the work of a poet who might otherwise have languished into silence and total obscurity.

When, in 1877, the literary correspondence with Bridges had properly commenced, Hopkins began to feel the benefit of a friendly yet candid criticism—a stimulus which tended to evoke, and a measure of praise which partially rewarded, his highest efforts. We say " partially " after due consideration ; for Bridges's inability to appreciate *The Wreck of the Deutschland*, and his blunt refusal even to read it again,[5] made it difficult for Hopkins to embark on another long poem (e.g. the " great ode on Edmund Campion ") [6] with any strong hopes of success. Bridges was sincere ; his discernment was well in advance of his time ; his championship of his friend was on one occasion even truculent [7] ; but the fact remains that he could not tender

[1] *Further Letters*, p. 206. [2] See chap. vii.
[3] Preface to his critical anthology, *New Paths on Helicon*, 1928.
[4] *Letters*, vol. i. pp. 218–9. [5] *Ibid.* p. 46.
[6] *Ibid.* pp. 135, 147, 150, 227 ; vol. ii. p. 76.
[7] In a letter to Hall Caine ; see *Letters*, vol. i. p. 129.

that perfect combination of sympathy and critical understanding which an unpublished poet, working under severe vocational and physical disabilities, really needed. The extent of Hopkins's virtual isolation and how much, as a creative artist, he lost thereby may be gauged if we compare two remarks made to Bridges: the first, of 1878, was anent *The Deutschland*:

> "I do not write for the public. You are my public and I hope to convert you."[1]

The second was of 1888, by which time his public included Dixon and Patmore:

> "what I want . . . to be more intelligible, smoother, and less singular, is an audience."[2]

Against those writers (and there are too many) who have denied to Bridges any real understanding and appreciation of his friend's poetry, we may quote Hopkins's own words:

> "It gave me of course great comfort to read your words of praise."[3]

Writing to Hopkins six years later, Patmore says:

> "Bridges . . . spoke with the sincerest admiration and *love* of your poetry."[4]

Moreover, Bridges confessed to Dixon that no poetry ever carried him out of himself so completely as that of Hopkins—surely the most remarkable compliment ever paid to an unpublished poet.[5] On the other hand, Bridges frequently gave Hopkins long jobations about eccentricity, affectation, etc., and was constantly reminding him of what he called essential "canons of taste". These strictures, sent direct to the working poet, were of real value; in a large measure they account for the fact that after *Tom's Garland*, a veritable *impasse*, Hopkins could so mellow and stabilize his style as to produce the last two "Miltonic" sonnets. The only censure which in all fairness may be passed on Bridges concerns personal opinions too confidently paraded as universal canons of taste in critiques published after Hopkins's death.

The shortcomings and reservations of Bridges's appreciation were partly compensated by the whole-hearted praise, tinged with adulation, which Dixon so often expressed. He too had felt

[1] *Letters*, vol. i. p. 46. [2] *Ibid.* p. 291. [3] *Ibid.* p. 52.
[4] *Further Letters*, p. 208. [5] *Letters*, vol. ii. p. 100.

Hopkins's power " of carrying one out of oneself with healing ".[1] Like so many readers in the last ten years, Dixon hailed his poems with " delight, astonishment and admiration " ; pronouncing them the most extraordinary he had ever read and " amazingly original ", he declared at once that they ought to be published.[2]

Such a response might be attributed to gratitude and friendly bias, had it not been supported by a remarkable and by now canonical piece of critical divination :

> " I can understand that your present position, seclusion and exercises would give to your writings a rare charm— . . . something that I cannot describe, but know to myself by the inadequate word *terrible pathos*—something of what you call temper in poetry : a right temper which goes to the point of the terrible ; the terrible crystal. Milton is the only one else who has anything like it : & he has it in a totally different way : he has it through indignation, through injured majesty, which is an inferior thing in fact." [3]

The comparison with Milton is just. Before Hopkins, Milton gave poetry a moral tone and denounced profane writers as " libidinous and ignorant poetasters ". In Milton too there is a pathos which ascends to the universal through the particular —for instance, in *Lycidas*, *Samson Agonistes*, *On His Blindness* and other sonnets.

Pursuing with somewhat less clarity the same comparison, Dixon writes :

> " With all possible differences of originality on both sides, [your verses] have the quality which Taine has marked in Milton : & which is more to be noted in his minor pieces than the great ones, of admiration—I forget Taine's expression, but it means admiration (or in you other emotions also) which reaches its fulness and completeness in giving the exact aspect of the thing it takes : so that a peculiar contentation is felt." [4]

The passage in Taine to which Dixon seems to refer is one in which the French critic is enumerating Milton's masters—the

[1] *Letters*, vol. ii. p. 32. [2] *Ibid.* pp. 26–7.

[3] *Ibid.* p. 80. As a later quotation shows, Dixon had been reading Taine on Milton. It is not irrelevant to cite the following, on Milton's prose : " Bold expressions, exaggeration of style, cause us to hear the vibrating voice of the suffering man, indignant and determined ". (*History of English Literature*, 1872, vol. i. p. 429) ; also : " he is drunk with justice and vengeance " (p. 431).

[4] *Letters*, vol. ii. p. 100.

whole splendid English Renaissance and all the Classical and Italian sources whence it had sprung. Milton, says Taine,

> "found the trick of rich colouring, their magnificent sentiment of living nature, their inexhaustible admiration of forms and colours."[1]

Taine says nothing about "giving the exact aspect of the thing"; indeed, if this phrase means anything, it indicates a quality which from Macaulay to T. S. Eliot has often been denied to Milton.[2] Taine himself says rightly that Milton's composite style "does not catch the lively first glow of sensation"—which is exactly what Shakespeare's style does, and Hopkins's no less. Milton wrote "not by impulse, at the mere contact with things, but like a man of letters"[3]; whereas Hopkins, in Dixon's own words, is unmatched

> "in the power of forcibly and delicately giving the essence of things in nature."[4]

Professor Abbott is perhaps unfair and misleading when he says that Dixon was an admirer rather than a critic of Hopkins. In the Popean acts of surveying the Whole before seeking slight faults to find, and of judging with the same spirit that his author writ, he was a more astute critic than Bridges. He saw at once what posterity is slowly discovering, namely, that in poems so highly individuated as *The Loss of the Eurydice* (which "no one could read without the deepest and most ennobling emotion"),[4] *The Windhover*, *The Sea and the Skylark*, *Duns Scotus's Oxford*, etc., a certain boldness and novelty of style is inseparable from the total perfection. For us to-day there is no extravagance in his "deep and intense admiration"[5]: it is the due of genius when rightly employed.

The stimulus provided by such words was sorely needed. "To my joy", Hopkins replies, "I came upon what you had written . . . I thank you very much for your comforting praises."[6] After Hopkins had refused to be drawn into publication, Dixon urged him to go on writing poetry:

> "Surely one vocation cannot destroy another: and such a Society as yours will not remain ignorant that you have such gifts as have seldom been given by God to man."[7]

[1] *Loc. cit.* p. 433.
[2] See Macaulay's *Essay* and Eliot's *A Note on the Verse of John Milton.*
[3] *Loc. cit.* p. 433. [4] *Letters*, vol. ii. p. 32. [5] *Ibid.* p. 33.
[6] *Ibid.* pp. 33 and 36. [7] *Ibid.* p. 90.

Hopkins knew that the business of his Society was not the encouragement of dilatory poets; but Dixon's words probably had some effect in increasing Hopkins's production after 1881.

Unlike so many later critics who have been caught on the barbed wire of what they call Hopkins's harsh, crabbed, wanton and violent style, Dixon quickly and easily penetrated to the essence—"the rareness, the sweetness that is in all".[1]

The third of Hopkins's poet-friends, Coventry Patmore, was typical of that class of critics who feel the underlying power of Hopkins's poetry, and even sense the beauty, but reject the style on *a priori* grounds. Before reading the poems, Patmore confesses that he is "the worst *off-hand* critic of really new work that I know".[2] Nevertheless, he continues, once his mind is made up his judgment may rank with the best of the "gallery-Gods":

> "for it is founded on the severe and instinctive principles which I believe I owe mainly to my Father's having taught me from my early boyhood a contempt for what is meretricious and a love for all the best models within my reach."[2]

Hopkins himself had declared that "the examples of the great masters are the soul of education"; but to anyone who has read Dr. I. A. Richards on 'Critical Preconceptions and Presuppositions' or the abuse of traditional standards,[3] Patmore's next letter will not be surprising:

> "I have read your poems—most of them several times—and find my first impression confirmed with each reading. It seems to me that the thought and feeling of these poems, if expressed without any obscuring novelty of mode, are such as often to require the whole attention to apprehend and digest them; and are therefore of a kind to appeal only to the few. But to the already sufficiently arduous character of such poetry you seem to have added the difficulty of following *several* entirely novel and simultaneous experiments in versification and construction, together with an altogether unprecedented system of alliteration and compound words;—any one of which novelties would be startling and productive of distraction from the poetic matter to be expressed."[4]

Patmore's reading (he had retained the poems only a fortnight) did not reach the stage in which he should have perceived that

[1] *Letters*, vol. ii. p. 110. [2] *Further Letters*, p. 204.
[3] See *Practical Criticism*, chap. viii.
[4] March 20, 1884 (*Further Letters*, pp. 204–5).

these novelties of style could be integral and not merely extraneous to the matter expressed. Sub-conscious preoccupation with "the best models" and the "meretricious" would normally account for such a failure.

> "System and learned theory are manifest in all these experiments; but they seem to me to be *too* manifest."

Ars est celare artem is, of course, the assumption at the root of this finding. A second assumption is explicitly stated:

> "'Thoughts that *involuntary* move harmonious numbers' is, I suppose, the best definition of poetry that ever was spoken."

Hopkins's reply is unfortunately lost, but the gist of it may be gathered from a letter sent by Patmore to Bridges:

> "To me his poetry has the effect of veins of pure gold imbedded in masses of impracticable quartz. He assures me that his 'thoughts involuntary moved' in such numbers, and that he did not write them from preconceived theories. I cannot understand it. His genius is, however, unmistakable, and is lovely and unique in its effects whenever he approximates to the ordinary rules of composition."[1]

Such an approximation he found in *The Blessed Virgin Compared to the Air We Breathe* and a few other pieces, and it was conceded that the novelties here might in time become "additional delights"; but, he adds,

> "I do not think that I could ever become sufficiently accustomed to your favourite Poem, *The Wreck of the Deutschland*, to reconcile me to its strangeness."[1]

Patmore is the perfect gentleman-poet, condescending to criticism as to something outside his proper field; modest, diffident, admitting the partiality and limitation of his own tastes and saying that Bridges's appreciation of Hopkins is a fact that he cannot "get over":

> "and I deliberately recognize in the author of 'Prometheus' a sounder and more delicate taste than my own."[2]

Professor Abbott thinks that Patmore's "deafness" is the more remarkable because he, like Hopkins, was both curious and learned in prosody.[3] It is often noticed, however, that a deep interest in prosody is actually the cause of critical intolerance,

[1] *Loc. cit.* [2] *Ibid.* p. 206. [3] *Further Letters*, p. xxix.

of a strange insensibility to the finer spirit of any poetry which does not conform to a preconceived prosodic standard. George Saintsbury could not grasp the significance of Hopkins's "new rhythm"[1]; Bridges himself called *The Deutschland* "presumptuous jugglery"; and T. S. Omond, the author of *English Metrists*, must round off a lifetime of valuable prosodic research by declaring, in a brief paragraph, that Hopkins's poems are at once repugnant and negligible.[2]

Mr. Omond rightly regarded Patmore's Essay on *English Metrical Law* (1857) as inaugurating the "new prosody"—the system, fully elaborated by Lanier, which makes *time* and not accent or stress the essential basis of rhythm. But although Hopkins had said that "stress is the life of sprung rhythm", he had nowhere in practice or theory absolutely denied the time-element; on the contrary, as we have seen in our studies

[1] Hopkins thought Saintsbury "a good critic" (*Letters*, vol. i. p. 129); but the latter was not at his best in his two pronouncements on Hopkins. The first was in *A History of English Prosody*, edn. of 1923, vol. iii. Bk. xi. chap. ii. p. 391: "Hopkins's ideas on prosody . . . belonged to the anti-foot (sic) and pro-stress division. But even if it were not for old things and days, it would be unfair to criticize lines like

'I want the one rapture of an inspiration'

—which you can, of course, scan, but where 'one' seems to be thrust in out of pure mischief—or many others. He never published any; and it is quite clear that all were experiments."

The second is a mere footnote in the 1932 edition of the *Camb. Hist. of Eng. Lit.*, vol. xiii. chap. vi. pp. 210–11: "He developed partially acute, but not generally sound, notions on metre; and though, quite recently, broken-backed rhythms like his have been often attempted, the results have scarcely been delightful. In his own case, though the process of appreciation is most like the proverbial reconstruction of a fossil beast from a few odd bones, it shows that they belonged to a poet."

[2] *English Metrists* (1921), *Postscript*, p. 263. It is only fair to Mr. Omond to quote his text in full: "Readers who enjoy fantastic new would-be developments of metre will study these poems and their author's teaching about 'Sprung Rhythm' and other mysteries, and will find ample material in the one poem entitled 'The Wreck of the *Deutschland*'; others, neither intolerant of nor unhopeful for new experiments, will turn from them with repugnance. The Editor's introduction and notes are, as always, clear and helpful . . . and not infrequently registering dissent from his eccentricities, especially in rhyming. The double rhymes in 'The Loss of the Eurydice' are simply atrocious, and curiously enough the Editor has singled out for special censure one of the least offensive of these. I cannot believe that these poems deserve or will receive attention from even the most determined seeker after novelties."

In criticizing the metric of Bridges, Mr. Omond says: "Divorced from time, stress in English has never proved a sufficient basis of metre. . . . Even in the master's beautiful 'London Snow' I for one miss temporal fabric. Critics are slow to appreciate new departures; my judgement may be biassed. But poets, also, sometimes depart in wrong directions. I cannot believe that, even in the hands of a singer like Mr. Bridges, verse which lacks the foundation common to all verse can be more than tuneful prose." (*Ibid.* p. 217.)

of *The Deutschland*, *The Windhover*, etc., isochronous intervals are in fact the mental or ideal basis of his rhythm: he did however hold, with Patmore, that the equality of metrical intervals is "no more than general or approximate". This stipulation of approximate values is as necessary to a just prosodic criticism of Patmore's own irregular odes as of Hopkins's *Echoes*. Indeed, in many of Hopkins's poems, as in Bridges's *London Snow*,[1] the temporal fabric is almost regular.

To T. S. Omond, the chief modern representative of the 'philosophic' school of prosodists, the temporal fabric of verse looms so large that it sometimes obscures the eternal values of poetry. George Saintsbury, the leading historian of English verse-forms, the champion of equivalence and of "the blessed trisyllabic swing and swell", once exclaimed:

> "In English, by the grace of God and the Muses, the poetry makes the rules, not the rules the poetry."

Yet he did not recognize the supreme justification of his dictum in the work of Hopkins. Coventry Patmore, though an acute theorist, had written so many thousands of smooth octosyllabics that not even the sinewy fluctuant Odes could obliterate the groove and prevent the canalization of his later views and responses.[2] Beside these critics, Robert Bridges stands out as a poet-metrist of commendable tolerance and versatility, and

[1] It is amazing that Mr. Omond should be unable to apply the principle of equivalence and to establish the isochronism of this poem. The following quantitative and accentual scansion, which represents a personal reading, is at least adequate to show the remarkable temporal equality of the first six lines:

"When men were all asleep the snow came flying, =18
In large white flakes falling on the city brown, =18
Stealthily and perpetually settling and loosely lying, =20
Hushing the latest traffic of the drowsy town; =18
Deadening, muffling, stifling its murmurs failing; =18
Lazily and incessantly floating down and down:" =18½

(A long syllable =2; a short =1; two rapid shorts =1½; a rest, marked by 𝄾, =1. The syllable -ing is counted long.)

[2] "I suppose it comes of my all along having followed a single line of my own." (*Further Letters*, p. 204.)

would seem to have been the fittest man of his time for the difficult task of giving Hopkins to the world. He had, however, certain limitations and prejudices which debarred his work from achieving final perfection.

Four years after Hopkins's death, Bridges persuaded A. H. Miles to admit Hopkins into the last volume of *Poets and Poetry of the XIXth. Century* (Second Edition, 1893). The selected pieces (seven poems and a fragment) [1] included none of the greater and more difficult works ; and though much may be said for giving the public an inferior uncorrected version of *The Starlight Night*,[2] together with *Spring* and *Inversnaid*, rather than *The Windhover*, *The Echoes*, and *The Heraclitean Fire*, it may also be argued that the greater power and originality of the latter would have made a deeper impression and evoked a wider curiosity, despite the inevitable protests and misunderstandings. In his brief Memoir, Bridges does quote the octaves of two of the later sonnets and calls them examples of the poet's best style ; [3] and he boldly asserts that if Hopkins's poems were collected into one volume " they would appear as a unique effort in English literature." If he hoped thereby to attract some enterprising publisher, his next statement was as sure a deterrent as it seems to us an unwarranted exaggeration :

> " Most of his poems are religious, and marked with Catholic theology, and almost all are injured by a natural eccentricity, a love of subtlety and uncommonness . . ."

The suggestion of disfigurement in " marked with " is confirmed by the proximity of " injured " ; and throughout the Memoir there is nothing to counteract the impression that the poems chosen by Bridges are the best, the only ones, indeed, which are tolerably free from Catholic theology and eccentricity.

The *Poems of Gerard Manley Hopkins*, edited with notes by Bridges, eventually appeared in 1918. This has been called (by Professor Abbott and others) " a masterpiece of editing ", and we must certainly acknowledge the care and discrimination with which Bridges, after collating the various manuscripts, has arranged and presented the poems. His patience and skill in

[1] These are, in the numbering of *Poems* : 77 (thirty-five selected lines), 3, 8, 9, 26 31, 33, 51. Miles's last volume (1906) is entitled : *Robert Bridges and Contemporary Poets* ; from this edition we quote.

[2] See Bridges's note to the poem in *Poems*, p. 105 ; also p. 94, paragraph 3. The version in Miles has " quivering citadels ", " Ah well ! it is a purchase and a prize ", and other infelicities.

[3] Nos. 44 and 50.

deciphering and imposing order on the chaotic lines of the widely admired *Epithalamion* can be appreciated only by those who have themselves examined the autograph.[1]

The *Editor's Notes*, however, with their critical introduction, do not everywhere display thoroughness, understanding, and discretion. The actual glosses on the text are for the most part excellent ; the information supplied is usually adequate and is aptly illustrated by brief excerpts from the poet's letters. We make an important exception, however, of the one poem which, by its nature, length and difficulty, demanded the most detailed and sympathetic annotation—*The Wreck of the Deutschland.* For this task Bridges was by temperament and predilection unfitted [2] ; though where he could not reveal or explain he at least refrained from attacking. Nevertheless, the inadequate editing of this great poem prevented almost a generation of readers from approaching it in the right spirit of confidence and understanding.

The schematized critical observations which were intended to serve as a guide to the poet's style have provoked many dissentient voices, and have revived in an acute form the old problem *de gustibus.* For example, Bridges begins his section on *Mannerism* as follows :

> " If these poems were to be arraigned for errors of what may be called taste, they might be convicted of occasional affectation in metaphor . . . or of some perversion of human feeling, as for instance, the nostrils' relish of incense ' along the sanctuary side ', or ' the Holy Ghost with warm breast and with ah ! bright wings ' . . ."

These are described as " mostly efforts to *force* emotion into theological or sectarian channels " ; but is it not more than possible, nay, most likely, that Hopkins's emotion was spontaneous

[1] The order of the stanzas in the unfinished *On a Piece of Music* (No. 67), as printed in the Second Edition of 1930, is not that of the poet's autograph. In the First Edition, Bridges printed only the first line, directing the reader thence to two pages of facsimile, in autograph, and included in the volume. In a closely reasoned, and to our mind convincing, article in *The Month* (Feb., 1936), Fr. Geoffrey Bliss argues that although the poem's logical intention could be gathered by reading the stanzas closely and repeatedly in *any* order, the arrangement in the Second Edition is not the best possible. He finally gives his own arrangement, which is much more satisfactory. Again, the nine sections of another fragment, *The Woodlark* (No. 64), are printed by Bridges in the same order as that of the autograph. Fr. Bliss, in a later article (*The Month,* June 1936), gives this charming piece of nature-music its most advantageous form. (For both versions, see Appendix D.)

[2] Cf. Hopkins in *Letters*, vol. i. pp. 50–1 : " The Deutschland on her first run worked very much and unsettled you, thickening and clouding your mind with vulgar mud-bottom and common sewage ", etc.

and sincere? Bridges's comment reveals a curious lack of understanding, a mistrust, against which Hopkins himself vigorously protested.[1] To examine the above objections, the last, an unfairly distorted version of the closing lines of *God's Grandeur*,[2] seems to us groundless. What is amiss—the Biblical incarnation of the Spirit as a dove, or the tellurian magnitude of the bird, or the interjected "ah!"? Again, the objection to the nostrils' relish of incense in *The Habit of Perfection* [3] is anti-Catholic sentiment rather than literary criticism. For centuries and for millions of people, incense has been a symbol of purification, of devotion to a transcendent ideal. It is used so in the poem, where the underlying meaning is: "I must renounce what I have enjoyed—the sensual gratifications of the worldly life; but how much sweeter is that spiritual perfection, which I now seek!" To take this "relish" as a mere olfactory whim is like criticizing Keats for preferring, in the *Nightingale*, French wine to Scotch whisky.[4]

Bridges also speaks of "the exaggerated Marianism of some pieces" without indicating any legitimate norm and without specific reference.[5] We may doubt whether the reader of Hopkins's poetry is in any way helped by being told that the Editor, personally, does not hold with the Catholic's theological conception of the Virgin Mary. Such an opinion, if fully substantiated by a critical examination of *The May Magnificat* and *The Blessed Virgin*, would make an interesting essay or chapter; but it would still be out of place between the covers of Hopkins's *Poems*.[6]

Bridges's last example of 'perverted feeling' is what he calls "the naked encounter of sensualism and asceticism which hurts *The Golden Echo*". But this view proceeds from a palpable and

[1] Speaking of the Corpus Christi rite, he says: "It is long since such things had any significance for you. But what is strange and unpleasant is that you sometimes speak as if they had in reality none for me . . ." (*Ibid.* p. 148.)

[2] "Because the Holy Ghost over the bent
World broods with warm breast and with ah! bright wings."

[3] "Nostrils, your careless breath that spend
Upon the stir and keep of pride,
What relish shall the censers send
Along the sanctuary side!" (Stanza 5.)

[4] Stanza 2, "O for a draught of vintage!" etc.

[5] The only poems implicated are Nos. 18 and 37.

[6] We realize that this opinion is not incontrovertible. It is our view, however, that in his first comprehensive utterance the poet should have the rostrum to himself. If he speaks a difficult language, his first editor should be a sympathetic interpreter, not a heckler. This is a hard word; but on a large number of critics the comments of Bridges, however well intentioned, have certainly produced the effect of heckling.

even gross misunderstanding. As Mr. W. J. Turner has pointed out, this " naked ençounter " is the essential element of the poem : it is the whole dramatic *motif*, that conflict of interests which gives the work its peculiar realism and power.[1] The polyphony of metaphysical, theological, and rhythmic elements in the greater poems of Hopkins was a new thing the great significance of which Bridges had not grasped.

It was of course only right that Bridges should warn Hopkins's readers of the main difficulties they would encounter, and this he did in his *Preface to Notes*. It is a pity, however, as the trend of later criticism has shown, that he did not present the facts more objectively. There is something amiss when we hear Bridges telling readers that they must " have courage to face " these many blemishes, extravagances, errors of taste, etc., and " must in some measure condone them " before they can discover the great beauties,—while at the same time younger poets of the calibre of Robert Graves,[2] Herbert Read,[3] W. J. Turner,[4] Edith Sitwell,[5] and C. Day Lewis [6] are quietly telling the same readers to ignore the Editor and trust in Hopkins and in their own instinctive reactions.

" Faults of style " (" the rude shocks of his purely artistic wantonness ") are briefly set out under the headings *Oddity*, *Obscurity*, *Omission of Relative Pronoun*, *Identical Forms*, *Homophones*, and *Rhymes*. As these features have already been dealt with in earlier chapters, we merely add that many of the charges relating to these " definite faults " must be pronounced ' not proven '. Bridges quotes Hopkins's confession of 1879 : " No doubt my poetry errs on the side of oddness " ; but he does not quote the plea for *The Deutschland*, uttered eight months earlier, which holds for many of us a more significant truth :

> " Besides you would have got more weathered to the style and its features—*not really odd*." [7]

In the opinion of Bridges,

> " these blemishes in the poet's style are of such quality and magnitude as to deny him a hearing from those who love a continuous literary decorum and are grown to be intolerant of its absence."

[1] *The Nineteenth Century*, February 1931.
[2] *Loc. cit.*
[3] *Form in Modern Poetry* (1932), pp. 47–8.
[4] *Loc. cit.*
[5] *Aspects of Modern Poetry* (1934), p. 51 *et seqq.*
[6] *A Hope for Poetry* (1934), chap. ii.
[7] *Letters*, vol. i. p. 50. Cf. *ibid.* p. 79 : " Moreover the oddness may make them repulsive at first . . ." (April 22, 1879).

Then the diction :

> " His adjectives not only at first reading but also at the tenth or twentieth, distract the mind altogether from their meaning by their strangeness. *Silk-sack clouds*, *azurous hung hills*, *majestic as a stallion stalwart*, *very-violet-sweet*, *mild night's blear-all black* and the like are traps for the attention, not aids to visualization."

Patmore would have sympathized. But at this day we can only wonder how a person that found " silk-sack clouds " difficult to understand ever came to be a reviewer of poetry.

Finally he thinks that Bridges has been too optimistic in believing that the public will like this poetry. The beauties are " scattered "—

> " and they are never far from extravagant ugliness. A perfect line is exceedingly rare ; and a poem which is good as a whole, even in spite of faults, is hard to discover."

The best this reviewer can hope for is that a few poets will discover, absorb and render again the little which Hopkins had to offer to English verse : they will perhaps " extract the gold from the quartz and put it into circulation ". He thus falls heavily between the stools of Bridges and Patmore.

The *Oxford Magazine* [1] was also Patmorean. Hopkins's work lacks " the inevitable quality of real poetry ". Having tried *Harry Ploughman*, this critic turns with relief to Masefield's sketch of the ploughman at the end of *The Everlasting Mercy*. He quotes the first stanza of *The Deutschland*, then adds :

> " But how quickly is that beauty obscured by the violence and confusion of the stanzas which follow ! "

The sequel to this is hardly believable, but it really is there :

> " But whatever be our final judgment of the poems, Bridges is the perfect devoted editor ! Bouquets all go to him. Bridges is trying to breathe life into that which cannot live save by its own vitality, by the virtue of some more direct vision and more complete expression than it was given to Gerard Hopkins to attain."

Few editors can ever have been invested with such an odour of sanctity ; as another reviewer [2] says :

> " Few volumes so slight have received so close and so pious care."

[1] May 23, 1919. [2] *The Methodist Recorder*, May 27, 1919.

A saner view of Hopkins's worth and the Editor's humble function had already been expressed by Bridges himself in the last two lines of his dedicatory sonnet :

> " Go forth : amidst our chaffinch flock display
> Thy plumage of far wonder and heavenward flight ! "

A whole chorus of presumably not indolent reviewers shook their heads over this " slight volume " and raised the same discouraging cry :

> " Hopkins is one of the most unpopular poets and destined always to be." [1]

> " He must remain a poet's poet." [2]

> " The subject matter is too prevailingly theological to gain a wide reading . . . a strange talent, but the poems will claim few readers." [3]

This pessimism, illegitimate offspring of Bridges's pious care, casts a gloom even over the long-delayed second edition of 1930 :

> " His worst faults are so bad that they will forever disable him from popularity." [4]

Yet by 1937 the second edition was in its fifth impression and (in commercial jargon) selling well.

" Donne ", said Ben Jonson, " for not being understood, will perish." In the long run, that prophecy has not been fulfilled ; but if Donne had been introduced to the public for the first time in 1770, with a critical preface and notes by Dr. Johnson, that edition also would have been pronounced " final ", and the public response would have borne the same inverse ratio to the poet's true stature as in the case of Hopkins.

Somewhat Johnsonian in tone is the following from a thirteen-line notice in *The Spectator* [5] :

> " The poems themselves, despite occasional flashes of the illuminating fire, are on the whole disappointing ; they are too often needlessly obscure, harsh and perverse. The metrical effects which Mr. Hopkins studied with such assiduity do not seem to be worth the pains bestowed on them."

[1] *Chicago Post*, May 30, 1924.
[2] Mr. Middleton Murry in *The Athenaeum*, June 6, 1919. (See also below, p. 216
[3] *The Dial*, May 17, 1919. [4] *The Tablet*, December 6, 1930.
[5] May 10, 1919.

Again, the very nadir of insensibility! But many of these early readers betray the bewilderment and unconscious confusion of an honest mind brought suddenly up against a strange phenomenon:

> "Hopkins had an exquisitely refined literary sense, but it permitted him to lapse into nearly every literary fault. He was a cultivated scholar, but this did not stay him from fantastic misuse of the English language." [1]

There is a sense, of course, in which every innovation in language is a misuse, just as there is a sense in which every development in literature is a breach of decorum.

As a moment's relief from so much disparagement, we turn to a critique which candidly resolves the last critic's dilemma. A sudden clearing of the fog of prejudice gives historic significance to the following:

> "It is the whole book that prepares one for the individual poems, making the extravagances seem *not* extravagances in the wild yet ordered world of that book."

After quoting the last part of *The Heraclitean Fire*, this critic continues:

> "There you have examples of his faults wilfully displayed: but to us at least, in the climax of that poem, they seem no longer faults. . . . It could not be said in better words." [2]

Such criticism strikes hard at the authority of the Editor's *Preface to Notes*.

The metrical innovations were not always received as contemptuously as in *The Spectator*, for instance:

> "In magical phrase, in easy movement, in the downright simplicity of effect, he can be, and more often than not is, a master. As a metrist he has no equal in English."

But how is one to reconcile these superlatives with the following protests from the same pen?—

> "*The Wreck of the Deutschland* is his tangled worst, a veritable *chasse-cousin*. . . . Life is too short for *Spelt from Sibyl's Leaves*." [3]

[1] *Studies*, June 1919.
[2] *Times Lit. Supplnt.*, Jan. 9, 1919. See also below, pp. 216, 219, 220, 223 and 226.
[3] *The Ave Maria*, April 1919.

On the question of metre and rhythm, however, the reviewers as a body were all at loggerheads :

> " Amid much that is uncouth there is such success in new movements as only the Laureate himself has paralleled." [1]

> " What use are the stress marks ? . . . On the other hand, we *should* be glad of some help towards making rhythmical such a stanza as ' The Eurydice, it concerned thee, O Lord ', etc." [2]

While one reviewer treats rhythm as a detachable accessory of poetry and complains that he cannot identify a single " hanger " [3] (and it is a serious defect in Bridges's editing that he gives no help in this matter), another more astutely considers form in relation to total effect :

> " Hopkins was exploring not merely the instrument of verse, but the undiscovered regions of his own, and the universal, soul." [4]

The Tablet finds that Hopkins's prosody is simply a matter of " commonsense stress scansion " ; the poet does not leave the unstressed syllables to take care of themselves :

> " Rather he marshals them with most meticulous and sensitive art to endow his line with emphasis, or speed, or hesitation, or airiness, or clamour." [5]

Without being aware of it, this critic had noted the effect of Hopkins's strict attention to quantity and time, and had understood immediately the principle of expressional rhythm.

Fortunately, he was not the only one. In an extraordinarily sensitive and prophetic critique, the reviewer in *Poetry*, Mr. Edward Sapir, said :

> " There is no blind groping in this irregular movement. It is nicely adjusted to the constantly shifting speed of the verse. Hopkins's effects, with a few exceptions, are in the highest degree successful. Read with the ear, his verse flows with an entirely new vigour and lightness, while the stanzaic form gives it a powerful compactness and drive. It is doubtful if the freest verse of our day is more sensitive in its rhythmic pulsations than the sprung verse of Hopkins." [6]

Mr. Middleton Murry, in his *Athenaeum* essay,[7] expressed an unusual point of view. He reduces the whole of Hopkins's

[1] *Glasgow Herald*, Jan. 2, 1919.
[2] *Studies*, June 1919.
[3] See above, chap. iii. p. 95.
[4] *Times Lit. Supplnt.*, *cit.*
[5] April 5, 1919
[6] Sept. 1921.
[7] Later reprinted in *Aspects of Literature*.

poetic creed to one phrase of Verlaine's : " la musique avant toute chose ". Selecting, as the most concise expression of Hopkins's artistic intention, a line from the last sonnet :

"The roll, the rise, the carol, the creation,"

Mr. Murry claims that

> " a technical progression onwards from the *Skylark* of Shelley is the main line of Hopkins's poetical evolution. . . . Musical elaboration is the chief characteristic of his work."

This finding, though an exaggeration of essential truth, effectually disposes of those critics who seemed to think that Hopkins was merely anticipating the percussive and syncopated cacophanies of the modern jazz band. He admits that there is compression—

> " but not beyond immediate comprehension ; music, but a music of overtones ; rhythm, but a rhythm which explicates meaning and makes it more intense." [1]

That, if we substitute " *ap*prehension " for " *com*prehension ", is a discovery from which there can be no turning back. When, however, he refers to *The Golden Echo*, he first calls it " the strangest but most successful of the poems " and then proceeds to give himself (and almost every other critic) the lie :

> " Yet is not the music too obvious ? Is it not always on the point of degenerating into a jingle ? "

Mr. Sturge Moore thought otherwise : he wanted a much more facile jingle and rewrote the opening of *The Leaden Echo* as follows :

" How to keep beauty ? is there any way ?
Is there nowhere any means to have it stay ?
Will no bow or brooch or braid
Brace or lace
Latch or catch
Or key to lock the door lend aid . . . ? " [2]

A more general attitude was expressed by *Everyman* :

> " *Binsey Poplars* and *The Echoes* are his most unblemished poems. The latter has an Elizabethan loveliness with the added weight of modern thought." [3]

[1] Contrast *The Oxford Magazine, cit.* : " These poems are almost all immediately incomprehensible, and in some cases strike the ear with a discordant defiance of verbal beauty actively unpleasant."

[2] *The Criterion*, July 1930 ; already quoted by Dr. Leavis in *New Bearings*, p. 173.

[3] See above, p. 212.

Mr. Murry could dwell on Hopkins's mere music because he, unlike most readers, was not troubled by the communication of thought, which, he says,

> " was seldom the dominant impulse of his creative moment, and it is curious how simple his thought often proves to be when the obscurity of his language has been penetrated."

That is misleading half-truth. Hopkins's dominant impulse was always to embody serious thought in perfect poetic form. Moreover, " simple " as applied to thought carries a suggestion of triteness which in this context is altogether inappropriate. Mr. Edward Sapir, fully aware of the importance of Hopkins's matter, adopted also the right attitude towards his manner :

> " We must beware of exaggerating the external difficulties ; they yield with unexpected ease to the modicum of goodwill that Hopkins has a right to expect of us." [1]

Most of the Catholic reviewers thought the same ; thus *The Tablet* :

> " Obscurity is there but is usually only verbal and yields to a little patient thought." [2]

Mr. Murry, again, was among those who found fault with Hopkins's texture :

> " A coarse and clumsy assonance seldom spread its snare in vain. Exquisite openings are involved in disaster."

Examples of such disaster are *Peace* and *The Windhover* :

> " ' stirred for a bird ' was an added excellence to the poet's ear ; to our sense it is a serious blemish."

Hopkins, then, must have appeared a mass of blemishes ; yet still Mr. Murry found him musical. However the anomaly be explained, Hopkins would have been more acceptable had he been less like himself and the Welsh poets and more like Shelley or Wordsworth. On this note the chorus swells somewhat derisively :

> " Alliterations, assonances and jingles would have delighted the late lamented Max Nordau." [3]

> " A sort of breathless hunt after assonant monosyllables is one of this poet's amusements." [4]

[1] *Poetry, cit.* [2] April 5, 1919.
[3] *The New Statesman, cit.* Max Nordau wrote that once-famous onslaught against *fin de siècle* decadence—*Degeneration*, 1892. [4] *Studies, cit.*

Even the *Times Literary Supplement* lapsed for a moment into the language of the Gentiles ; having said finely that in this poet words become independent, as if they were whole sentences, and " bang in one after another ", the writer adds :

> " His worst trick is that of passing from one word to another, like the Jewish admirer of Mr. Jaggers in *Great Expectations*,[1] merely because they are alike in sound. This at its worst produces the effect almost of idiocy, of speech without sense and prolonged merely by echoes . . . a bad habit, like stuttering, except that he did not strive against it."

Yet this is the critic who decided that the extravagances were *not* extravagances when viewed in relation to the whole book.[2]

The second of these reviewers quoted *Sibyl's Leaves* as an " awful example ". Undeniably this poem has the greatest initial oddity—a strangeness due to the comparative plainness or meanness of undifferentiated prose texture in most earlier poetry. Not until the powerful cumulative rhythm and the passionate meaning have been mastered is it possible to appreciate the skill with which assonance and verbal echo have been made to intensify the emotion and expression.

Not all the early critics were disconcerted by these phonal devices. Where some saw evidence of labour others found every sign of a healthy spontaneity :

> " What comes so readily must have a deep natural basis, and in the artist's hands becomes capable of far elaboration. . . . It is a fine spirit that dwells behind the arabesque wrought tapestries of these poems." [3]

> " One marvels at his mastery not merely of the Anglo-Saxon form, but of the spirit behind the form ; and one feels that it must be an innate rather than an acquired mastery."

The Deutschland is favourably compared with Francis Thompson's *A Judgment in Heaven.* Thompson is a conscious technician, whereas Hopkins

> " is lisping the syllables of a native, if at times hardly intelligible, rapture." [4]

[1] Chap. xx.
[2] See above, p. 215.
[3] *The Tablet*, April 5, 1919.
[4] *Chicago Post*, *cit.*

The incidental labour, the difficulty of the style (which Hopkins himself admitted) [1] is thus acutely defined :

> " I can think of Gerard Hopkins under no other figure than that of ' the flagellant of song '. I feel . . . as if every word had been born in anguish and had awoken with a cry. . . . His sonnets, with their amazing intricacies, are the result of the toils and tortures of a giant." [2]

> " For Hopkins poetry meant difficulty ; he wrote it to say more than could be said otherwise ; it was for him a packing of words with sense, both emotional and intellectual. The defect of the newest English poetry is that it says too little. . . . Hopkins begins where most other poets leave off, not out of affectation but because he wishes to go further." [3]

The intimate connexion between spirit and form had obviously not escaped the most perspicacious critics. As the *Chicago Post* put it :

> " Hopkins exhibits, more than any other poet with whom I am acquainted, the perfected mating of rapture and technical virtuosity—freedom achieved in restraint." [4]

Incidentally, the same writer, and at least one other, recognized the important fact underlying Chapter III. of the present work, namely, that Hopkins excelled in the sonnet, had found freedom in it and had enlarged its possibilities.[5]

Perhaps the most interesting summary statement on the whole question of style is another which anticipates the trend of our own critical researches :

> " As to oddity, new things are apt to seem odd at first, and this poetry . . . is new in this, *that it attempts to do continuously what other poets have been content to achieve by rare moments*, and in virtue of what must generally seem to the poet a kind of miraculous luck—I mean the entire ' wedding of the term to its import ', not only by way of the term's notation and connotation in meaning, but also by way of its very sound and cadence." [6]

Referring to Bridges's remark of 1893, that Hopkins met defeat

[1] *Letters*, vol. i. p. 136.
[2] *The New Witness*, Jan. 24, 1919.
[3] *Times Lit. Supplnt.*, *cit.*
[4] See above. The author of this excellent review was Mr. Samuel Putnam.
[5] *Poetry*, *cit.* Mr. Putnam adds that Hopkins's sonnets are the best since Rossetti.
[6] *The Tablet*, April 5, 1919.

in attempting " an unattainable perfection of language ", the same reviewer says :

> " A breach in the walls of the impossible has been made. . . . But the newness is not a break with established canons, but rather a new degree of fidelity to their precepts, a new faith in the possibility of such close adherence."

Naturally the question of style evoked certain affinities and comparisons. " For pure ecstasy, *The Starlight Night* is to be compared only with Shakespeare's 'Hark, hark, the lark'.[1] Miss L. I. Guiney, in one of the most graceful appreciations, was the first to relate Hopkins to Donne [2] ; while another reviewer declared him to be like Crashaw

> " in his extravagance and the manner in which he redeems it by good faith."

There were the inevitable comparisons with Browning and Doughty, in which Hopkins was found to be more crabbed and obscure than the former and more eccentric than the latter. Mr. Peter McBrien, of *The Irish Rosary*,[3] was apparently the only reviewer who thoroughly relished *Tom's Garland* (quoted in full). He admired this poetry " laden with a wealth of concrete but intensely significant pictures ", and continues :

> " Readers will be struck with the close resemblance of this poem to Meredith's prose when the novelist is at what might be called psychological picture-work."
>
> " Hopkins's poetry daringly condenses into verse the ascetic fire of the finest parts of Meredith's *Egoist* and *Diana of the Crossways*."

Certain phraseological parallels between parts of *The Egoist* and some of Hopkins's poems might almost be taken as presumptive evidence that Hopkins had actually read that novel (published in 1879).[4]

[1] *Chicago Post*, *cit.* [2] *The Month*, March 1919. [3] June 1919.

[4] With that stippled, staccato picture of girlhood in line 15 of *The Golden Echo* (1882) cf. Meredith's picture of Clara : " curls, half-curls, root-curls, vine-ringlets, wedding-rings, fledgeling feathers, tufts of down, blown wisps—waved or fell, . . . loose and downward . . . long round locks of gold . . ." (Constable, 1918 ; pp. 85–6). An expression in *Andromeda* (Aug. 12, 1879), " her Perseus ", is used to convey the same idea of welcome deliverance in *The Egoist* (p. 101). Coincidentally " hearth's fire' appears in *The Deutschland* (st. 35), and " hearth-fire " in the novel (p. 133). It is just possible, however, that the central image of *Epithalamion* (1888) was suggested by the following : " Clara bathed in mirth. A boy in a summer stream shows not heartier refreshment of his whole being ". (*The Egoist*, p. 174.) It may be doubted whether Hopkins, having read Meredith, could have refrained from mentioning him. Yet can we believe that he had not read Donne and Crashaw, about whom he is equally silent ?

In considering the following criticism, we have to remember that the " rhetoric of poetry " desiderated by Hopkins was not conventional rhetoric :

> " He works his words hard and accomplishes much with them because he is no rhetorician. He eschews the merely fine sounding or poetical word. As with Flaubert, his aim is the precise adjustment of word to meaning." [1]

When compared with two dynamic Whitmanesque poets of more recent times, Hopkins easily holds his own :

> " For long-breathed, impetuous rhythms, wind-like and sea-like, such verse has nothing to learn from the best of Carl Sandburg." [2]

" Long-breathed " is an apt epithet for those sustained, pulsing rhythms which we have called " cumulative " ; but Hopkins's rhythms are too carefully timed and controlled to be styled " impetuous " in the sense that the freer rhythms of Whitman, Sandburg, and D. H. Lawrence merit the description. The same critic would compare Hopkins with Lawrence but for the former's

> " far greater sensitiveness to the music of words, to the rhythms of ever changing speeds of syllables."

Turning from style and rhythm to what Hopkins himself would have considered a far weightier matter, we are to-day struck with the sympathetic insight which enabled many of these early critics to penetrate beneath the poetry to the man, to the lofty religious aspiration and heroic character :

> " It must be supposed that nothing less than intolerable virtue would be tolerable to this strong and courageous soul. . . . He must have possessed the virtues of the soldier and the saint." [3]

Another gathered that Hopkins was contemptuous of the idle day-dreams of Romantic poetry : he was a " natural Platonist ", discovering God through the beauty of the physical universe :

> " Mysticism meant for him an intensification, not a denial, of life." [4]

[1] *The Tablet, cit.*

[2] *Poetry, cit.* Sandburg (*b.* 1878) has written *Chicago Poems* (1916), *Cornhuskers* (1918), *Smoke and Steel* (1920), etc.

[3] *The New Witness, cit.*

[4] *The Westminster Gazette*, March 7, 1919.

Mr. Sapir was dissatisfied with the way Bridges had presented Hopkins, both as man and poet :

> " Neither mannerisms of diction and style nor prosody define the essential Hopkins. The real Hopkins is a passionate soul unendingly in conflict. The consuming mysticism, the intense religious faith are unreconciled with a basic sensuality that leaves the poet no peace." [1]

The exaggeration in such words as " unendingly ", " consuming ", and " unreconciled " is palpable and regrettable, and must be linked up with the fact that Mr. Sapir was probably the first critic to assess Hopkins by Freudian standards :

> " A Freudian psychologist might call him an imperfectly sex-sublimated mystic. Girlish tenderness is masked by ruggedness."

According to Patmore, this union of the masculine and feminine natures is found only in the highest beings, in the spiritually consummated *homo*, who is himself " a marriage." [2]

The measure of the response which this poetry could *immediately* evoke, even in a critic who showed no particular sign of Roman Catholic sympathies, may be gauged from the following :

> " The whole book thrills with spirit, a spirit that does not disdain sense but heightens it. . . . There is beauty everywhere without luxury, the beauty which seems to come of painful intense watching, the utter disinterested delight of one who sees another world, not through, but in this one. It is as if he heard everywhere a music too difficult, because too beautiful, for our ears, and noted down what he could catch of it ; authentic fragments that we trust even when they bewilder us." [3]

The word " trust " suggests the angle from which Bridges's critical comments may be justly arraigned. The evidence provided above makes it abundantly clear that Bridges did not give readers of poetry credit for sufficient imaginative perspicacity to divine the poet's intention, sense his vision as in a glass darkly, even before the novelties of mode had been fully understood. Such perspicacity was not lacking ; but being

[1] *Poetry, cit.*

[2] See " The Bow Set in the Cloud " in *Religio Poetae* (1898), pp. 54–5.

[3] *Times Lit. Supplnt., cit.*

in most people a delicate and shy thing, it was in many readers partially or wholly stultified by the Editor's equivocal attitude.

Educationists know that if you keep on telling a pupil that he is a dull fellow he will probably act on the assumption that you are right ; but if you rashly include in your disparagement certain active intelligences, you will quickly find rebels—as Bridges did among his reviewers :

> " In the face of this agonising poem [" My own heart let me have more pity on "—No. 47] one can only marvel at the Poet Laureate's imperturbable exegesis of the word ' betweenpie '. . . . From our best friends deliver us, O Lord ! " [1]

In one Catholic paper an article entitled *Improper Editing* betrays a note of rancour :

> " Thirty years after the poet's death Dr. Bridges graciously permits us to inspect (for a fee of 12/6) the work of a greater thinker than himself." [2]

Fourteen years later the tone is still harsh :

> " His first critic, Robert Bridges, recognized Hopkins as a fine poet and proved his admiration by keeping his poems in cold storage for thirty years." [3]

It would be invidious to pursue the matter further ; and certainly there will always be critics who, like the Catholic Miss Guiney, will commend Bridges for having gradually paved the way for " this powerfully original, idiosyncratic genius, headstrong, disturbing, best come at by degrees." [4]

The progress made in Hopkins criticism between 1919 and 1931 is fairly indicated by the following from a review of the Second Edition :

> " The oddities and obscurities of the style—all thoroughly examined by Dr. Bridges in the Notes—are part of the fascination ; without them, indeed, Hopkins would not be Hopkins." [5]

[1] *Poetry, cit.* ' betweenpie ' is also defended by Riding and Graves in *Survey of Modernist Poetry*, p. 92. (See above, chap. iv. p. 122.)

[2] *The Universe*, March 14, 1919.

[3] G. W. Stonier in *Gog Magog and other Critical Essays* (1933), p. 43.

[4] *Improper Editing—A Counter-Blast*, *The Universe*, March 21, 1919.

[5] *Liverpool Post*, January 7, 1931.

The extreme of Dixonian acceptance is explained by Mr. W. J. Turner, whose position as a poet gives value to his personal confession :

> " I have to admit that I can rarely see any faults in the poetry I like, while the poetry I dislike seems to me to be just one huge mistake from beginning to end. Either a man is a master or he is not. If he is a master, then all his infringements of rules and precedents are part of his idiosyncratic expression, and cannot be criticized except from the *a priori* standpoint that the whole effect of his poetry is bad. But if he is recognized as a master this is absurd." [1]

Although this seems to reduce criticism to a blunt " I know what I like ", the attitude has a basis in psychological truth. The act of appreciating a poem implies an exalted mood of *acceptance*. Although certain details looked at microscopically may seem odd or otherwise displeasing, they do not jar in the total symphony of impressions : they are like strings which do not vibrate at all or discordant tones which are effectively drowned in the prevailing harmony. When the discordant features do obtrude too persistently, the poem fails to achieve its emotive purpose, and the reader reacts as Mr. Desmond MacCarthy did, quite recently, to Hopkins :

> " Coventry Patmore's opinion of Hopkins's poetry (' Veins of pure gold imbedded in masses of impracticable quartz ') seems to me the right one." [2]

The future, we believe, will find more gold and less quartz ; and we have already found that the quartz is not impracticable.

We turn now from the ephemeral to the more permanent and influential (though not necessarily more astute or significant) works of criticism—the essays and studies which have appeared in book form.

The Second Edition of 1930 was introduced by a suggestive and gracefully written critique from the pen of another poet —Mr. Charles Williams. Reversing the method of Bridges, Mr. Williams tells the reader much more about Hopkins's beauties and positive qualities than about his faults. He prepares the uninitiated for the " breathless ascent ", the intellectual

[1] *The Nineteenth Century*, February, 1931.
[2] *The Sunday Times*, May 22, 1938 (Review of *Further Correspondence*).

man-handling they will suffer at their first contact with the powerful new mind ; and his concise exposition of the chief stylistic innovations is an incentive to appreciation, not a deterrent. Yet even this critic almost nullifies his good work by one ill-considered sentence on his last page :

> " His poetic tricks, his mannerisms, his explorations in the technique of verse, are not in the earlier poems and are disappearing from the later." [1]

If Mr. Williams had attained to the last felicity of reading these poems with the same spirit that their master-author writ, he would not have used the objectionable word " tricks " ; but the sheer inaccuracy of his last statement is extraordinary. Are there no explorations of verse-technique in *That Nature is a Heraclitean Fire* and in *Epithalamion,*[2] both of 1888 and among the most admired of his works ? The critic almost suggests that he prefers the immature pre-*Deutschland* poems to the rich harvest of 1877–85, to say nothing of the " dragon " itself. It is also implied that Hopkins's sprung and counterpointed rhythms were the aberrations of a genius not yet under control—a curious anomaly.

In the course of his suggestive comparison between Hopkins and Milton, Mr. Williams says that the former, like Francis Thompson, was only " on the verge of mystical vision ; neither actually seems to express it." [3] According to that extreme definition of mysticism which makes it the experience of an absolute spiritual union with God, neither these two nor any other English poet is a mystic. The broader definition implicit in the *Oxford Book of English Mystical Verse* (" intimations of a consciousness wider and deeper than the normal ") embraces a self-styled atheist like Shelley, oriental and occidental pantheists, together with devotional poets who worship what Shelley calls (in his ' mystical ' poem [4]) the " poisonous names " on which his youth was fed. In the Oxford anthology Swinburne celebrates Hertha and " the one God, Pan " throughout eighteen and a half pages ; Hopkins, to sing of Christ and the Virgin Mother, is accorded less than six.[5]

[1] *Poems of G. M. H.*, p. xvi.

[2] " Most surprising and delightful of all, perhaps, is the fragment *Epithalamion.*" (*Times Lit. Supplnt., cit.*)

[3] *Poems of G. M. H.*,. p. xiv. [4] *Hymn to Intellectual Beauty* (edn. of 1932, p. 128).

[5] He is represented by *Poems,* Nos. 3, 7, and 37.

Christian mysticism implies a *scala perfectionis*, a progress upwards to a permanent calm 'possession' of God, the stages being: (1) the Purgative Life, (2) the Illuminative Life, (3) the Unitive Life. Hopkins certainly never reached the last stage, though there are definite evidences in his prose and poetry that he knew the first and had glimpses of the second. The late Evelyn Underhill (an authority recognized by many) has said:

> "When we pass to the mystical poets, we find that nearly all their best efforts are due to their extraordinary genius for indirect, suggestive imagery . . . artistic, sidelong representations of the mystic's direct apprehension of the Infinite on, so to speak, its cosmic and impersonal side."

Having quoted, in illustration, from Vaughan, Blake, Whitman, Thompson, and St. John of the Cross, she adds:

> "Sometimes the two aspects, personal and impersonal, are woven together by the poet: and then it is that we come nearest to an understanding of the full experience he is trying to express. A remarkable example of this occurs in Gerard Hopkins, perhaps the greatest mystical poet of the Victorian era." [1]

She quotes in illustration stanzas 1 and 5 of *The Deutschland*; she might have given with equal cogency stanzas 2 and 3.

Plotinus, whose mystical Platonic doctrine was caught up into the body of Christian thought by St. Augustine and St. Bonaventure (both acknowledged mystics), speaks of virtue as the pre-requisite for a higher approach to God, and of the tendency of theocentric thought to strive upwards till it rests in "the Good"—

> "for only he [has failed] that has failed of only this, for whose winning he should renounce kingdoms and command over earth and sky, if only, *spurning the world of sense from beneath his feet, and straining to this*, he may see." [2]

How similar are the accents of Hopkins !—

> "The heart rears wings bold and bolder
> And hurls for him, O half hurls earth for him off under
> his feet." [3]

Since however, as Mr. Williams suggests, the sense of division and pain, of summons and effort, is more common in Hopkins's

[1] *The Essentials of Mysticism* (1920), pp. 70–2.
[2] *Enneads*, I. vi. 7 (Mackenna, vol. i. pp. 85–7).
[3] *Hurrahing in Harvest*, No. 14.

poetry than the sense of fulfilment and beatific vision, he must be termed at best an imperfect mystic. For the highest virtue he always strove, and his most earnest desire was *vacare Deo*; but between the wish and the end were interposed all the toils and worries of his profession and, as the *Letters* show, all the allurements and ambitions of art and scholarship. His was indeed a divided soul.[1]

Simultaneously with the Second Edition appeared the sympathetic *Life of Gerard Manley Hopkins* by G. F. Lahey, S.J. The biography, brief but admirably presented, satisfied a long-felt need for more knowledge of this unique personality; and the facts of his life illuminated for most critics some of the darker passages in the poems, revealed the poet's spiritual orientation, and so paved the way for a deeper understanding of his creative activities.

Father Lahey's criticism, though in many ways inadequate, is the rationale of the Dixonian attitude of almost complete acceptance.[2] This acceptance was in large measure due to Lahey's first-hand knowledge of an earnest Jesuit's problems, desolations, and aspirations; but it was also due to a sensibility which was a creative reflex of the sensibility which fashioned the poetry. His aim was not to make a profound and complete analysis and evaluation of Hopkins's poetic achievement, but to remove the main difficulties and impart his own enthusiasm.

It must be objected, however, that there is a certain indiscretion in dividing the main critical section into two chapters called respectively *The Craftsman* and *The Artist*. Admittedly the first treats of prosody and other formal aspects of the poems, while the second deals more directly with aesthetic values; but the average reader, mindful of Bridges's animadversions, would be likely to draw the conclusion that in Hopkins the " craftsman " and the " artist " were separate or at least dissociable entities. The dichotomy fosters the idea, put forward by Patmore and

[1] See *Letters*, vol. i. p. 135 *et seqq*. It is significant that the opportunity afforded by his ten month's Tertianship was not utilized for the writing of his " dithyrambic ode " on Fr. Edmund Campion, S.J.—a congenial subject.

[2] He follows Bridges in his treatment of the rhymes in *The Eurydice*, and on two points evinces the same misunderstanding of Hopkins's intentions. Contrary to the poet's *Preface*, Fr. Lahey explains the term " rove over " as a mere adjunct of linked or running rhymes (" sire-he-shares " should be read quickly to harmonize with its counterpart " Irish "); whereas actually " rove over " implies a principle of scansion, and Hopkins nowhere insists that natural expression should be distorted to produce what would be a ludicrous cacophony. (See above, chap. iv. pp. 147–8.)

denied by Hopkins, that the poet worked too consciously to learned theory, and tends to suggest that the turning of a page from " The Craftsman " to " The Artist " indicates a *progression* from technical virtuosity to the more authentic moods and modes of inspiration. It is of course usual and legitimate to speak of a poet's ' craftsmanship ' ; but a craftsman in verse who is not at the same time, and for the same reasons, an *artist*, is certainly no true poet. In the case of Hopkins, it is impossible to make a real distinction between the ' craft ' of sprung rhythm and the ' art ' of expressional rhythm ; between the ' craft ' which distorts grammar and the ' art ' which turns that distortion to good effect.

The conclusion to the chapter on " The Craftsman ", however, in which the critic speaks of that " preliminary ascesis " which poetry of such specialized significance demands, is a pointed challenge to the sticklers for ease and decorum in poetic style :

> " It is this which has resulted in that strange anomaly existent in all the fine arts, of a genius who commands respect and enthusiasm from those who possess an ' ascetic ' aestheticism ; but who receives neglect or even abuse from those who will not, or cannot, ' plough the rock until it bear ! ' "

The most interesting body of frankly agnostic opinion emanates from the criticism and personal influence of the Cambridge psychologist, Dr. I. A. Richards. His article in *The Dial* (Chicago) of September 19, 1926, was one of the first critiques to honour certain poems with a searching analysis. Disparaging the poet's Christianity as pointedly as he scoffs at the entire race of prosodists, Dr. Richards is attracted to Hopkins mainly because of the latter's powerful and original manipulation of language as a " tool ". The subtle obliquities of *The Windhover* fascinate and tease the critic until he has, as he thinks, mastered all their implications. On the other hand, Hopkins's prosodic theories are dismissed as mere excuses to justify complete rhythmical freedom.

This erroneous view was partly corrected by a fellow-psychologist, Mr. C. K. Ogden, whose informative article in *Psyche* (1936) has already been mentioned.[1] He is to be congratulated for securing a first picking of the periodical reviews, though he quotes them solely in connexion with rhythm. Mr G. M. Young's " formidable indictment " of Hopkins as rhythmist is given in

[1] See above, chap. ii. p. 44 ; also below, Appendix B.

full and refuted with a pretty wit and obvious relish. According to Mr. Young,[1] Hopkins's theories of metre

> " are as demonstrably wrong as those of any speculator who has ever led a multitude into the wilderness to perish . . . the root of his error lay in an ignorance of the subject so profound that it was not aware that there was anything to know."

Furthermore, the influence of Hopkins

> " has been as pernicious as it has been potent, and unless the rising generation has enough poetic learning to see where it is taking them, and enough poetic vigour to throw it off, I am afraid the next and last *Oxford Book of Verse* will bear as its sub-title, ' Or, the End of an Old Song ' ".[2]

That is worth reading even though we must disagree, emphatically, with this critic's major premise. The second statement points to what was, in 1936, a very real danger.

Mr. Ogden, as soon as he turns from the rhythm to the meaning of one of the poems, shows no less than Dr. Richards a somewhat complacent inability (or refusal) to appreciate Hopkins's earnest religious nature and serious ethical purpose. In its moral import, *The Soldier* (No. 39) has an obvious simplicity and a latent depth, both of which Mr. Ogden distrusts, partly on legitimate grounds of belief, but partly because Hopkins's attitude to the professional soldier and sailor has much in common with that of Tennyson, Kipling, Housman, Newbolt, and Chesterton. But although he underestimates the ' common touch ' in

[1] *Forty Years of Verse, The London Mercury*, December 1936.

[2] A similar attitude of outraged superiority towards both Hopkins and Bridges as prosodists has been expressed more recently by Mr. D. S. MacColl in his article *Patmore and Hopkins : Sense and Nonsense in English Prosody* (*London Mercury*, July 1938). Unfortunately for his argument, he shows clearly that he has made no patient attempt to understand Hopkins's theories. We are told, for instance, that Hopkins had an altogether imperfect ear, because certain lines in *Henry Purcell* and *Felix Randal* have " seven stresses instead of six ". This simply means that the critic has ignored the outrides (see above, chap. iii. pp. 101–2). Again, to prove the " absurdity " of Hopkins's theory of Counterpoint in verse, MacColl misquotes and distorts the example from Milton in *Note-books*, p. 241 :

> " Hóme tó his möther's hóuse priváte retürned
> Could anything be more perverse than the stresses on *to* and *-ate* ? " (p. 223)

But Hopkins *did not intend these syllables to be stressed* in reading. (See Volume II. chap. ii. of the present work.)

Even a sympathetic critic, like Mr. R. L. Mégroz, can misunderstand so badly as to give (contrary to the poet's perspicuous note) *three* stresses to every line in *The Eurydice* (*Modern English Poetry*, 1933, pp. 235–7).

Hopkins's sentiment and symbol, Mr. Ogden clearly perceives the popular character of his rhythm and diction. Alliteration, he says, reinforces the repetitive technique so blatantly that we seem to hear the voice of the sergeant-major :

> " YUSS—WHÓly dewy ÁWLa, SÉEin guvva SÓUL dear,
> BLÉSS im? BĹESS
> Our-r (roll of kettledrums) RÉDcoats, OÚR tars, BÓTH etc.
>
> The march past of the souls dear is distinctly Victorian—with pigeon-chested, drum-and-fife *élan*, thin shanks (red piping on navy blue) metronomic, and a cane or two twirling in unison with the perspirational acrobatics of the Big Drum, which gives us the six-beat line to *wár thére expréss*. (Hált ! Order árms ! Stánn a tése !) "[1]

The humour of this cavalierly-subjective comment should not blind us to the fact that it distorts the picture. The critic suggests that Hopkins was launching a private purgative or recruiting campaign ; but he does not add that the recruiting was all on behalf of Christ rather than Caesar. As rhythm, he finds the sonnet unique ; but he entirely agrees with Miss E. E. Phare's objection that

> " in *The Soldier* the homeliness of speech seems to me overdone. Hopkins writes with a bluff vigour which is not native to him and which is not effective in counteracting the sentimentality of the poem."[2]

Apart from the first sixteen words (the frankly Victorian expression of a sentiment which, never extinct, becomes normal in war-time) the sonnet is no more sentimental than the Parables. Moreover, the charge of overdone homeliness is exaggeration : to be precise, there are *three* touches of homely style—the Shakespearian " seeing of " (where the *of* is introduced for the sake of euphony), the colloquial " tars ", and the abrupt " Here it is " for " This is the reason " (line 3). And is it not too paradoxical to maintain that the kind of vigour found in *The Soldier* (be it " bluff " or otherwise) is " not native " to the author of the *Letters*, *The Deutschland*, *The Eurydice*, *Carrion Comfort*, *Harry Ploughman*, and a dozen other poems ?

In the Preface to her essay, Miss Phare acknowledges help and encouragement received from Dr. Richards ; and beneath

[1] *Psyche* (1936), p. 38.
[2] *The Poetry of Gerard Manley Hopkins* (Cambridge University Press, 1933), p. 119.

the impatience of her attitude towards the poet's deeper religious motives and beliefs, we seem to detect the influence of her mentor.[1]

The Deutschland, for instance, is said to show "lack of balance, shallowness, febrility"; it is vitiated by "a craving for violent sensational effects"; "there is something in it which strikes one as artificial in the bad sense."[2] Only a strong 'metaphysical' antagonism to the doctrines of Christianity or a strange inability to perceive, feel, and understand could account for such extreme generalizations. How different are the findings of Dr. F. R. Leavis[3] and André Bremond, S.J.,[4] who penetrate with ease to the deep personal and universal significance of the symbolism, and at the same time appreciate the essential beauty and relevance of rhythm and texture; of Miss Edith Sitwell,[5] who testifies to the enormous power of the imagery, and analyses the subtle tones and overtones of the musical pattern with the sensitive ear and mind of a creative artist; of an Australian critic, D. P. McGuire, who calls it one of the greatest of the poems, and says that "from the first lines we are conscious of the intensity, the austerity, the grandeur of Hopkins's vision."[6] In the course of her critique, Miss Phare does make some suggestive and laudatory comments on the poem; but her criticism as a whole reveals a distrust (which she herself calls "typically English") of poetry that deals with "intimate religious experience".[7] This attitude causes her to accuse the poet over and over again of simulating emotions that he does not feel:

> "I think it is that in places at any rate the poet has tried to make himself believe that his feelings on the subject under consideration were more intense than was actually the case, at any rate at the moment of writing."[8]

[1] Dr. Richards has always inculcated a contempt for religious beliefs. These "bundles of invested emotional capital" account for the fact that Hopkins is "intellectually too stiff" (*The Dial*, *cit.*). Again we read: "For it is no accident that Science and Religion conflict. They are different principles upon which impulses may be organized . . ." (*Principles of Literary Criticism*, xxxiv.); and also:

> "Countless pseudo-statements, about God, . . . about the soul, its rank and destiny . . . have suddenly become, for sincere, honest and informal minds, impossible to believe." (*Science and Poetry*, p. 60.)

[2] *Op. cit.* pp. 17, 70, 108.

[3] *New Bearings in English Poetry* (1932), chap. v.

[4] *Art and Inspiration in Hopkins* (*New Verse*, No. 14; April 1935).

[5] *Aspects of Modern Poetry* (1934), chap. ii.

[6] *The Poetry of Gerard Manley Hopkins* (1934; English Association, Adelaide Branch, Pamphlet No. 2), pp. 14–15.

[7] *Op. cit.* p. 106.

[8] Pp. 108–9.

Miss Phare seems to have forgotten Wordsworth's definition of lyric poetry as " emotion recollected in tranquillity."

After *The Deutschland*, No. 26 is denounced as affected, " guindé " :

> " There is affectation in the very title, *The Handsome Heart: at a Gracious Answer*. The poet is, I think, far less deeply touched by the incident than he takes himself to be." [1]

We are bound to suspect the critic of imperfect understanding, for the perfectly natural metaphorical shift from an earthly to a heavenly gift—" Of heaven what boon to buy you, boy "—is condemned as " forced playfulness ". This passage seems to us as jocular as the *Catechism*, but no more so.

Complete failure to understand the emotions and ideals of a good Catholic priest vitiates Miss Phare's criticism of two other intensely sacerdotal poems, *The Bugler's First Communion* and *Felix Randal*.[2] The former is charged with forced and sham " heartiness " (cf. the " bluff vigour " of No. 39) ; but to recount in detail her adverse comments on such expressions as " Low-latched in leaf-light housel " and " slips of soldiery " would be merely to repeat that what is felicitous to one reader is not necessarily so to another. Miss Phare shows, like Patmore, a disarming diffidence when she says :

> " Destructive criticism of this kind is not very valuable " ; (p. 50)

she is sure of one thing only—that the poem fails.

Unfortunately, the decision just quoted was not final, for the destruction begins all over again on *Felix Randal*—" though a much better poem " :

> " The loose, almost uncontrolled rhythm and the exaggerated phraseology [3] . . . alike suggest that the poet is abandoning himself to an unchecked emotionalism over which the intellect exercises no censorship " (p. 52).

Miss Phare is seldom so tautologistic as in that sentence ; but if

[1] P. 115. Cf. *Letters*, vol. i. pp. 92 and 95. [2] Pp. 48–53.

[3] Here are quoted the last two lines :

" When thou at the random grim forge, powerful amidst peers,
Didst fettle for the great grey drayhorse his bright and battering sandal."

These lines embody the grand apotheosis—the permanent spiritual value of physical beauty and useful work well done. (They also happened to be the first lines to convince the present writer that Hopkins was a great master of language.)

sheer repetition could convince us we should reject the poem not merely as bad art but as a piece of revolting hypocrisy :

> " There is a suggestion too that by force of will he is working himself up to a pitch of grief for Felix Randal which normally he would not reach . . . encouraging his emotions to take more sway over him than they would normally . . . trying to work himself up into a frenzy of compassion " (pp. 52–53).

This veritable frenzy of denunciation is followed by another spasm of diffidence :

> " *Felix Randal* fails, though it is difficult to say why, and the rather peevish fault-finding in which I have been indulging does not make it clear why it should be so." [1]

This, we submit, is not the voice of authoritative criticism. Against it we may set a more sympathetic opinion :

> " Aussi n'a-t-il rien écrit de plus parfait que les deux pièces sur les expériences et les consolations de sa vie apostolique : la *Première Communion du petit Clairon* et la mort de Félix Randal." [2]

Full appreciation of *The Bugler* does, perhaps, require some special sympathy with the Christian sacrament of Holy Eucharist or Communion ; but *Felix Randal* (" plus austère . . . plus parfaitement beau ") should strike home by reason of its purely human qualities.

In the same essay a disservice is done the poet by some gross distortions of his meaning. Speaking of *Morning Midday and Evening Sacrifice* and *The Echoes*,[3] Miss Phare says :

> " In these two poems Hopkins seems to conceive of the sacrifice of youth to Christ as involving actual immolation, spoliation of physical beauty . . ."

The rest of the passage is mere flippancy. It should hardly be necessary to explain that Hopkins did not expect all men and women to become dedicated priests and nuns ; the more universal application of his austere injunctions is that human beauty, both physical and mental, should always be subservient and tributary

[1] Miss Phare adds : " It seems that the motion of accepting or rejecting a poem comes from the very quick of the will." Cf. Dr. Richards, quoted above, chap. i. p. 31, note (1).

[2] André Bremond in *La Poésie Naïve et Savante de Gerard Hopkins* (*Etudes*. October 5, 1934), pp. 43–4.

[3] *Op. cit.* pp. 121–2.

to the full Christian life : one's life should not be organized as a selfish exploitation of these attractive gifts. It is all the more strange that Miss Phare should associate Hopkins dubiously with fanatical asceticism and Pagan concupiscence (cf. Bridges : " the naked encounter of sensualism and asceticism "), since she admires *To What Serves Mortal Beauty* [1] and writes about it with keen discernment.

Again, to speak of Hopkins's " pantheistic poems " is to accuse him of a heresy which he must almost rise from the grave to repudiate. How utterly perverse, too, is the comparison between the " pantheisms " of Wordsworth and Hopkins, in which the latter is said to be

> " all the time struggling and straining to arrive at the assurance of the divine presence which he longs for." [2]

It is true that Wordsworth's pantheistic feeling of oneness with all Nature is persistent and " passive ", whereas Hopkins must greet his transcendent but at the same time immanent God only on days when he is specially favoured—days on which reason and divine grace co-operate. Yet when the vision does come to Hopkins, it is surely as swift and spontaneous as that of Wordsworth ; and in its ultimate poetic expression it is usually more direct, concrete, vigorous and convincing—e.g. " I kiss my hand /To the stars, etc." ; " And hurls for him, O half hurls earth for him off, etc."

In dealing with the religious aspects of Hopkins's poetry, Miss Phare wrote under the extreme disadvantage of not having read the collected *Letters*, some of the revelations in which must have forced her to modify her views. But now, having frankly reviewed the score of excruciating pages in her study, we must gratefully acknowledge the urbanity and competence of the rest. Miss Phare's most important contributions to the understanding of Hopkins are her comments *passim* on his imagery ; her comparisons between Hopkins and related poets such as Wordsworth and T. S. Eliot ; and especially her excellent critiques on certain poems which she likes well enough to examine without peevishness, namely, *The Blessed Virgin*, *Spring and Fall*, and *On a Portrait of Two Beautiful Young People*. Her discussion of *The Windhover*,

[1] ". . . a very delicately balanced piece of work ", in which the poet explains how we should behave " in face of that beauty of person which an illiberal asceticism might consider nothing more than a snare " (p. 119).

[2] P. 44.

in which she supplements the inhibition-seeking of Dr. Richards and the subtle but overworked ambiguity-hunting of Mr. William Empson [1] with an interpretation of her own, still just misses the poet's real intention and meaning. It is significant that *Spring and Fall*, which is free from doctrinal elements explicitly stated, is a great favourite with the critical 'school' of Dr. Richards.[2]

Towards the end of her essay, Miss Phare makes a significant observation :

> "I sometimes suspect that we are many of us so certain that becoming a Jesuit must involve some unnatural and undesirable deformation or repression that we are prepared to see oddities in a Jesuit where there are none." [3]

This fact accounts for much warped criticism of Hopkins, and to the opinions we have already examined we must add those of Mr. Herbert Read, a poet and critic whose enthusiasm for Hopkins has in many ways done much to clear away thickets of prejudice and misunderstanding which would otherwise have debarred Hopkins from a sympathetic hearing.

In an essay of 1933,[4] Mr. Read divided the poems into three groups :—(1) poems which are the direct expression of religious beliefs ; (2) those which have no direct or causal relation to any such beliefs at all ; and (3) those which are not so much the expression of belief in any strict sense but more precisely of doubt.

Among the poems considered to have no causal relation to beliefs are *The Windhover*, *The Echoes*, and *The Caged Skylark* ; in these poems and many others "the poetic force comes from a vital awareness of the objective beauty of the world." But

[1] Mr. Empson examines the poem in chap. vii of his book, *Seven Types of Ambiguity* (Chatto and Windus, 1930), under the seventh type of ambiguity. This type occurs "when the two meanings of the word, the two values of the ambiguity, are the two opposite meanings defined by the context, so that the total effect is to show a fundamental division in the writer's mind" (p. 244). . . . "Opposites, again, are an important element in the Freudian analysis of dreams. . . . Now a Freudian opposite at least marks dissatisfaction. . . . Thus in the first three lines of the sestet we have a clear case of the Freudian use of opposites . . ." (p. 284 *et seqq.*). These presumably agnostic critics cannot believe that such a poet could wish, primarily and absolutely, to be a good servant of Christ.

[2] See *Seven Types of Ambiguity*, p. 187 *et seqq.*, and *Practical Criticism*, pp. 81–4, 89–90, for some appreciative critiques.

[3] P. 141.

[4] *New Verse*, No. 1, January 1933. See also Mr. Read's essay on Hopkins in *Twentieth Century Critical Essays* (Oxford World's Classics), 1935, p. 355 *et seqq.*

the distinction is not absolute; it involves, indeed, a serious aberration. Undoubtedly the objective beauty of the physical world is *a* prime motive in all three poems, but the higher "supernatural beauty" of Christian belief is no less basic, causal and formative: it is the ontological substrate or soil in which the seed, the immediate physical stimulus, takes root and grows. *The Leaden Echo* is, designedly, almost pagan; but *The Golden Echo*, into which it is deliberately merged, is patently Christian. Again, where would all the beautiful obliquity of *The Windhover* be without its powerful and subtle implication of the Christian ideal of Sacrifice? What is the essential meaning of *The Caged Skylark* if it be not the contrast between soul and body in physical durance and the "uncumbered" state of man's spirit "when found at best"—that is, after the resurrection of the body? Yet Mr. Read finds no asceticism in *The Windhover*, and actually suggests that the dedication "To Christ our Lord" is a patent deception, added by the poet as a sop to his conscience.

From this position it was only a short step to the palpable error of Mr. Read's third category—poems which are the expression of doubt. Admittedly, some of the "terrible sonnets" might seem, at first, to be the expression of "faith tense but not firm", faith "held in opposition to his obstinate reasonings"; but the information supplied by the *Letters* makes it clear that a man of Hopkins's calibre would have resigned his priesthood had he experienced any real doubt. The poet's own affirmations of unwavering fidelity seem to have converted Mr. Read, for in a letter to the present writer, he magnanimously says:

> "In so far as I have, in my essay on Hopkins, implied that there was an open conflict between the poetic impulse and the theological faith in Hopkins, I confess I was wrong." [1]

Mr. Read's original view was largely determined by his psychological tenet that poetic creativity is the result of a conflict between sensibility and belief. But psychological critics of Hopkins have been too prone to slight or ignore the evidence of his co-religionists—men of integrity and experience like the late Rev. Joseph Keating,[2] the Rev. G. F. Lahey, the Rev. Martin D'Arcy,[3] and the Rev. André Bremond. The judgment of these

[1] This letter is dated September 18, 1935.
[2] See *The Month* for July, August, and September 1909.
[3] See his essay on Hopkins in *Great Catholics* (1938).

learned Jesuits has been adequately summed up in the words of the French critic :

> " Le miracle poétique est, ici, que l'art est à la fois suprême et spontané, que l'émotion du tourment sacré y parle toute pure."

The Rev. André Bremond discovers in Hopkins's poetry " une haute valeur spirituelle ". Similarly Mr. Bernard Kelly treats the poems almost as a handbook of devotion : he recommends that his Catholic readers, before making a serious study of *The Wreck of the Deutschland*, should meditate for one week on the Passion of Our Lord.[1]

Before we turn to Bremond's main thesis, there is one other living poet and critic whose brief Patmorean pronouncements on Hopkins call for examination. Mr. T. S. Eliot, whose Anglo-Catholicism would preclude him from any marked philosophical antipathy, had been looking round for the perfect orthodox and traditional poet ; but Hopkins, he says, does not satisfy the conditions. On the technical side,

> " his innovations certainly were good, but like the mind of their author, they operate within a narrow range, and are easily imitated though not adaptable for many purposes ; furthermore they sometimes strike me as lacking in inevitability—that is to say, they sometimes come near to being purely verbal, in that a whole poem will give us more of the same thing, an accumulation, rather than a real development of thought and feeling." [2]

Most of the external features of Hopkins's style can be almost as easily imitated as those of Mr. Eliot ; but this fact need not affect our estimate of either poet any more than *The Splendid Shilling* affects the status of Milton. That Hopkins's range, in subject-matter, was relatively narrow must perhaps be allowed —though the philosophical implications of his poetry are wider and deeper than would appear to any but the assiduous, probing reader ; [3] it does not follow, however, that his technical innovations could operate only within the same restricted field, or that Hopkins himself could not have adapted them, had he wished to do so, for many more equally worthy purposes. Some indication as to what can be done with his rhythmical innovations has already been given by Bridges, Mr. Eliot himself, and by a

[1] *The Mind and Poetry of Gerard Manley Hopkins* (Pepler and Sewell, 1935). Another excellent study is by Mr. Daniel Sargent (*Four Independents*, 1935).

[2] *After Strange Gods* (1934), p. 47.

[3] To this question we shall return in our second volume.

number of younger poets of to-day. Their attempts at assimilation, together with others far less successful, will be examined in the next chapter.

The charge of lacking inevitability is one which is likely to be heard with decreasing frequency as the understanding and appreciation of Hopkins becomes more and more academic and traditional. For the very reason that we think highly of Mr. Eliot's own poetry, the above charge comes strangely from his pen, since his own most original poems do not at first overwhelm us with the quality of inevitability, and have even been condemned, by Mr. Herbert Palmer [1] and others, as pedantic, laboured, and precious.

The same argument may be applied to his last stricture. It implies no peevish retaliation, no belittlement of Mr. Eliot's achievement, when we reply that " accumulation " rather than " development " of thought and feeling is more noticeably a characteristic of his own poems than of Hopkins's—and this in spite of the latter's fondness for an Hebraic parallelism. Free association and the eschewing of a logically linked progression of ideas is a method which lends itself to accumulation and repetition, even without the help of Miss Gertrude Stein. Let any impartial critic read the *Rhapsody on a Windy Night*, *Gerontion*, *The Waste Land*, and *Ash Wednesday*, and then turn to Hopkins's *The Windhover*, *Spelt from Sibyl's Leaves*, *Carrion Comfort*, *The Wreck of the Deutschland*—but why enumerate? Almost any one of Hopkins's poems will show a more *palpable* development of thought and feeling than those of Mr. Eliot, which are mainly an accumulation of powerful and skilfully juxtaposed images—" " thoughts of a dry brain in a dry season ", images of futility and fear, or reiterated strivings to reconcile the sensual man and the ascetic in the balanced religious life. We do not deny a necessary development of thought and mood in Mr. Eliot's poems ; we do say, however, that many of his images are so ' private ' and his transitions so abrupt, that if these poems depended for their effect upon " development ", they would produce an adequate response in very few readers.

Again, when Mr. Eliot says that Hopkins's technical innovations came near to being purely verbal, we are reminded of Dr. Leavis's criticism of part of *The Waste Land* :

> " The link between the hooded figure of the road to Emmaus and the ' hooded hordes swarming ' is not much more than verbal."

[1] See Mr. Palmer's *Cinder Thursday* and *Post-Victorian Poetry*.

—though as the same critic deemed it necessary to point out, there is an " essential association " between most of the seemingly disparate images in the whole poem.[1] Nevertheless, a main characteristic of Mr. Eliot is that " he is both vague and definite at once ", whereas Hopkins (in spite of surface obscurity) is almost always definite. This definition is conducive to *development*, as Mr. Eliot's deliberate vagueness is best served by the method of *accumulation*.

Furthermore, we learn with surprise that Hopkins, the author of so many poems of ecstasy and pain, of aspiration and despair, of mystical vision and passionate familiar colloquy with God, is no more than a ' devotional ' poet : he is not a *religious* poet in the more important sense in which Baudelaire and Villon were religious poets—not even in the sense in which Mr. James Joyce's work is " penetrated with Christian feeling." That, no doubt, is a paradox which Mr. Eliot could, if he chose, brilliantly expound ; but without that convincing exposition it remains a capricious view of Hopkins which most critics will reject.

It is true that Hopkins was not qualified to plumb, subjectively, the lowest depths of human degradation. His sense of the perversity of man is as strong as Baudelaire's, his cries *de profundis* are as poignant—indeed, they are more poignant ; but the spiritual issues in his poetry develop their full intensity not in *ténèbres qui puent* [2] or *miasmes morbides* [3] (though these are powerfully suggested, as in Nos. 45 and 69) but rather in

" Le feu clair qui remplit les espaces limpides." [3]

—that is, in expressing the divine beauty and the divine truth which Villon and Baudelaire often glimpsed but did not inveterately pursue. In *Élévation*, Baudelaire indicated an empyrean of religious poetry which Hopkins was to explore more thoroughly: happy the man, says Baudelaire, whose thoughts, like larks,

" Vers les cieux le matin prennent un libre essor,
Qui plane sur la vie, et comprend sans effort
Le langage des fleurs et des choses muettes ! "

This Hopkins did ; for as the Rev. André Bremond says : " Tout lui est mot ou syllabe d'un verbe divin créé." [4]

[1] *New Bearings in English Poetry*, p. 101. Dr. Leavis significantly concludes by saying that the organization of *The Waste Land* " may, by analogy, be called musical. It exhibits no progression . . . the thunder brings no rain to revive the Waste Land, and the poem ends where it began." The word " progression " is inapt ; Dr. Leavis means " development ".

[2] *Les Fleurs du Mal : Préface.* [3] *Ibid., Elévation.* [4] *Loc. cit.* p. 37.

On the moral plane, moreover, Hopkins sees as clearly as Baudelaire the equivocal nature of Beauty ; but whereas the former says : " De Satan ou de Dieu, qu'importe ? ",[1] the latter insists that the " dangerous " aspect of Beauty must be envisaged, like the Gorgon, in the polished Athene-shield of ethical wisdom ; for Hopkins, Beauty must be as good in its ultimate effects as in its immediate appeal. To us it seems unnecessary to ask which of these two attitudes is the more *religious*.

Our faith in Mr. Eliot's position is not increased when we are told that Hopkins should be compared " with the minor poet nearest contemporary to him : George Meredith ".[2] So Hopkins, humble apostle of Jesus Christ, resembles Meredith, chief hierophant of the ' philosophy of Earth ', because " they have the same technical tricks ". Mr. Eliot allows that Hopkins has the dignity of the Church behind him, and is consequently in closer contact with reality, whereas Meredith,

> " beyond a few acute and pertly expressed observations of human nature has only a rather cheap and shallow philosophy of life."

This curt dismissal of Meredith's achievement as a poet will alienate many critics who would otherwise have supported the alleged ' minority ' in Hopkins ; but the technical link with Hopkins is too tenuous to justify Mr. Eliot's comparison, and the question of Hopkins's status must be postponed to the last chapter of our second volume.

It is impossible, within the limits of this chapter, to review all the attempts that have been made to qualify and curtail Hopkins's undeniable success—as, for instance, Mr. F. W. Bateson's self-contradictory statements concerning this " massive concrete poetry " in his book dealing with the developing tradition of the English language.[3] We have quoted enough, however, to show the main trends of opinion ; and if any absolute and

[1] *Hymne à la Beauté*. [2] *Op. cit.* p. 48.

[3] *English Poetry and the English Language* (1934), pp. 117–18. E.g.—" Hopkins's abortive revolt against the Pre-Raphaelite tradition goes back to the year 1876 . . . Hopkins was too early. The language had not increased sufficiently in precision by then for the massive concrete poetry of Hopkins to be possible at all without very special precautions. The clumsy, and, as one feels now, unnecessary concentration of his style was in fact necessary in 1876. Without the restriction it imposed, the tendencies of the language would have carried him away into the vagueness and diffuseness that he was in revolt against."

Hopkins's linguistic experiments, it seems, are to be blamed and commended in the same breath.

reliable critical truth emerges from our conspectus it is that which is contained in the Rev. André Bremond's main thesis :

> " Si l'art de Hopkins fait la difficulté plus grande que de raison, c'est chez lui, nous le verrons, surtout l'excès de probité artistique. Les ressources de l'art le plus savant sont au service de la poésie la plus sincère, la plus spontanée, la plus naïve."

" Naïve ", we must observe, because his taste had been " purifié par le sacrifice " : the controlling intellect is always at hand to give the inspired form its final shape :

> " L'art savant est créateur de l'œuvre entière ; il ne se borne pas à donner un vêtement convenable à une pensée toute faite."

The artistic form, together with the thought, is the poetry itself : one cannot separate them. In this essential connexion between thought and form, Hopkins surpasses Patmore : in Hopkins, " tout est pensée, les mots, les sons et la diversité très savante du rhythme." In rendering " l'idée des choses ", the exact *inscape* of an object,

> " il faut observer d'une observation *poétique* divinatrice, mais aussi patiente, aussi soumise à l'objet que celle du savant."

Up to this point, Bremond's definition would fit any metaphysical poet ; but he now particularizes :

> " Ajutons que cet intellect dominateur et cette sensibilité extrême qui tendent à fusionner dans la simplicité d'une forme renouvelée, sont pénétrés chez Hopkins d'une intense ferveur chrétienne, que toute pièce est sans effort ordonnée à Dieu, que tout vers, au moins chaque strophe, donne un son de louange ou de prière." [1]

Praise or prayer : how different is this interpretation of the poems from that which finds in them a lugubrious record of inhibition, doubt, perversion and misery !

The most recent contribution to the world's knowledge and understanding of this much misunderstood poet is, fortunately, one of the most worthy. Dr. Pick's book [2] is thoroughly sound on those matters in which Miss E. E. Phare's study (1933) was frequently unsound and misleading. The sub-title, " Priest and Poet ", is justly chosen ; but the emphasis is mainly on the Priest, and the bias is deliberately religious and philosophical. The

[1] *Op. cit.* pp. 24, 36, 37, 38.

[2] *Gerard Manley Hopkins, Priest and Poet*, by John Pick (Oxford University Press, 1942).

author deals competently with the doctrinal and professional background of the poet's work ; he utilizes to the full, and with admirable judgment, the direct evidence provided in Hopkins's note-books, letters, sermons, and the unfinished commentary on *The Spiritual Exercises*. So marked, indeed, is the bias towards an *apologia*—an explanation and justification of Hopkins's theological tenets and philosophical implications ; so eager is Dr. Pick to defend the Jesuit priest's way of life, his professional Superiors and even the Society of Jesus itself against those critics who have cast doubts on their integrity and wisdom, that the very poems themselves may seem to be drawn on rather for their documentary evidence than for their intrinsic literary qualities.

This bias, as we have said, is not regrettable : it is distinctly salutary. It will go far towards neutralizing the serious misrepresentations and perverse estimates of many agnostic or non-Catholic critics : for instance, both the Editor of the *Poems* and the Editor of the *Letters* are on several occasions justly rebuked and corrected.

Nevertheless, our final impression is that the monograph is incomplete or lacking in balance. We are allowed to follow the developing *motifs* and attitudes of the devout priest, the man alternately inspired and self-tormented ; we are shown the fine flower of his emotion and thought in the mature poems ; but we are not admitted to those subtle processes by which all the multifarious materials of poetry (linguistic and prosodic as well as ideological) are converted into the finished masterpiece. As a literary study Dr. Pick's book is inadequate, having indeed far less to say on this aspect of Hopkins's work than Father Lahey's much earlier monograph.

The peculiar value of the later book lies in the precision and emphasis with which the author expounds Hopkins's sacramental view of nature, " the One ablaze in the many " ; above all in his able exposition of the continuous and pervasive influence of *The Spiritual Exercises* and, in a secondary degree, of works like *The Imitation of Christ*. In dealing with the Scotist influence, Dr. Pick acknowledges the investigations of one predecessor [1] ; but he leaves the reader with only a vague idea of the actual style and substance of the Schoolman's metaphysic—the syllogistic matter which seems at first to be so little amenable to poetic treatment.

[1] The present writer (p. 36). It is a pity, however, that Dr. Pick either did not know or did not appreciate the pioneer work of Mr. Christopher Devlin, S.J., in *New Verse*, No. 14.

The term " Sprung Rhythm " is not to be found in the Index ; there is no mention of those potent influences, Shakespeare and Milton ; yet the references to Asceticism and *The Spiritual Exercises* are scattered over fourteen and forty-one pages respectively. But to compensate for this onesidedness, Dr. Pick shows how the Christian view of nature—as interpreted theologically by Scotus and Aquinas, mystically by St. Augustine and St. Francis, and in a poetically concrete manner by Father Hopkins—places man's love of God and man's love of God's creatures in their true relationship and perspective ; how thereby these Christian thinkers discredit the vagueness of pantheism on the one hand and the pagan perversion called 'nature-worship' on the other. To have done so much, and to have shown conclusively the positive beauty of Hopkins's striving to live and write like a veritable *alter Christus*, is surely to have earned our sincere gratitude.

CHAPTER VII

HOPKINS AND MODERN POETRY

THE appreciative *Times* reviewer of the Second Edition of Hopkins's poems made the following bold pronouncement :

> " It would hardly be an exaggeration to say that Hopkins was the most original of the poets of the nineteenth century."

Tennyson, Browning, Arnold and Swinburne were all truly individual, but none of them broke down so violently as Hopkins the old rhythmic forms. These others (together with the two Rossettis and Francis Thompson) were all inventive and each added something new to English poetry—

> " but no poet writing to-day feels that he can learn technical secrets from these poets, whereas Hopkins is full of strange powers (and an unexhausted technical prowess) which he feels he must assimilate and possess." [1]

Whether at this critic's suggestion or from natural impulse, many poets, since 1930, have with varying degrees of success taken cuttings from the Hopkins tree and sought to establish them in their own poetic gardens.

The fact that most of these imitations have proved singularly unsuccessful was indicated, in 1934, by Miss Edith Sitwell [2] ; having considered some of them she declared that Hopkins should never be regarded as a model, " since he worked his own discoveries to the uttermost point ; there is no room for advancement, for development, along his lines."

While agreeing that Hopkins pushed his style and rhythm to their limits, not all critics and poets will subscribe to Miss Sitwell's sweeping denial of a possible beneficent influence : subtle reflections and judicious variations of Hopkins's peculiar beauties may at any time enhance the work of some truly individual maker. Without attempting to pass judgment, we quote, in illustration, from a volume of poems published only the other day :

> " O look how the loops and balloons of bloom
> Bobbing on long strings from the finger-ends
> And knuckles of the lurching cherry-tree
> Heap and hug, elbow and part, this wild day . . .

[1] *Lit. Supplnt.*, Dec. 25, 1930. [2] *Aspects of Modern Poetry*, p. 52.

> And hovering effortlessly the rooks
> Hang on the wind's effrontery as if
> On hooks, then loose their hold and slide away
> Like sleet sidewards down the warm swimming sweep
> Of wind." [1]

We discern here both direct suggestions of Hopkins and also the influence of some individual younger poets—Mr. Cecil Day Lewis and Mr. Stephen Spender, for each of whom (and especially the former) the lure of Hopkins has proved irresistible. But before we can define the precise nature and scope of Hopkins's influence on modern poetry, and even while we are doing so, it will be necessary to take into account certain other dead poets, with whose marks on modern poetry those of Hopkins might otherwise be confused.

Professor Barker Fairley and others have recently given Hopkins a nineteenth-century peer: Charles Montagu Doughty (*b.* 1843), though he published no poetry before 1900, had been planning it as early as the eighteen sixties, and like Hopkins himself had been in revolt against the sweetness and monotony of what was in many ways a dying if not already dead tradition. It is the opinion of these critics that the so-called Georgian poets of the present century merely confirmed the death and burial of a pale derivative Romanticism, so that in the last ten years new channels of expression have been sought by our younger poets " on lines suggested by Doughty and Hopkins ".

This view is not based upon a comprehensive survey of the facts. It ignores the potent and progressive influence of Browning and Whitman; it slurs over the merit and traditional development of the 'Georgian' poets; to say nothing of the powerful shock and stimulus provided by Ezra Pound, T. S. Eliot, and James Joyce.

The influence of Browning on twentieth-century poets has been adequately demonstrated by Mr. A. Allen Brockington. [2] Browning not only left his unmistakable mark on Doughty, Hopkins and Bridges, but also gave impetus and orientation to poets so diverse as G. K. Chesterton, Walter de la Mare, W. W. Gibson, John Masefield, and W. H. Auden; by this we mean that certain qualities developed by these poets were bold innovations in Browning.

[1] " Stormy Day " in *Awake! and other Poems*, by W. R. Rodgers (Secker and Warburg, 1941).

[2] In *Browning and the XXth. Century*, 1932.

As the late Sir Henry Newbolt pointed out, Browning's technique was important because he had forced a new diction into the old metres, and thereby brought the everyday moods within the scope of poetry.[1] Moreover, Chesterton's shrewd remarks on Browning's obscurity are in a large measure applicable also to the obscurity of Mr. T. S. Eliot: Browning, he says, is not obscure, as he is not grotesque, for the reason that he has such new things to say. He is both these things primarily

> "because he likes to express himself in a particular manner. The manner is as natural to him as a man's physical voice, *and it is abrupt, sketchy, allusive, and full of gaps*." [2]

Mr. Pound, Mr. Eliot, and other modernists are far more allusive than Browning, and this largely accounts for their more frequent obscurity. They also cultivate obscurity, like the French Symbolist poets, because they prefer the emotive suggestion, the evocative hint, to direct statement. Yet Mr. Eliot certainly has some new things to say and some unusual mental states to describe, and the subtle obscurity which appears in these passages derives rather from Donne and Meredith than from Browning or Hopkins. Nor can we leave out of account the influence of Blake; for although the esoteric mythology of the *Prophetic Books* has found few direct imitators, the dark symbolism and bold imagery of the *Songs of Experience* have undoubtedly helped to engender some of the best poetry of W. B. Yeats, Mr. Eliot, Mr. Day Lewis, Mr. Charles Madge and others.

For the first traces of Hopkins's undeniable influence on modern poetry we must go back to the 'Georgians'. Sir John Squire has shown that these 'Georgians' did not form a homogeneous school.[3] They were extremely varied, and were united only by a common admiration for the oldest of their number, Dr. Bridges. Apart from the simple and sweet lyric note in the work of Bridges, and the delicate intellectual ingenuity of his sonnets, the main technical influence on the younger men derived from the modified sprung rhythm of *London Snow*, *The Passer-By*, etc. Not only in the rhythm of these poems, but in the diction also, we can find the impress of Hopkins, who himself pointed out to his friend a number of unconscious echoes from his own verse. Moreover, he correctly attributed these echoes to the intense and peculiar urgency of sprung rhythm in its first

[1] *New Paths on Helicon* (Nelson), "Conclusion", p. 207.

[2] *Robert Browning* (1903), p. 156. [3] *Essays on Poetry* (1923), "Robert Bridges".

complete manifestation—*The Wreck of the Deutschland.*[1] Hopkins claimed (as we have claimed for his own poetry) that the freer rhythm had helped his friend's snow-piece "by making it more original in diction". It is significant, therefore, that when Sir John Squire was explaining the change brought about by Bridges in the rhythms of certain twentieth-century poets, he should quote, as prototype, a line from *London Snow*:

> "Stéalthily and perpétually séttling and lóosely lýing."

This profusion of unstressed syllables confidently marshalled into metrical step by the heavy accents, was recognized as a desirable emancipation from the overworked syllabic metres. W. B. Yeats had felt the same need for innovation, for in 1922 he wrote: "I had begun to loosen rhythm as an escape from rhetoric"[2]—by which he meant, of course, conventional diction. The result of his loosening was the movement of his famous lyric, *The Lake Isle of Innisfree*, though the rhythm of this poem, like that of Mr. John Masefield's *Cargoes*, *Sea-Fever*, etc., was rather a development from Meredith's *Love in a Valley*, with its tendency towards sing-song, than from the more masculine and muscular sprung rhythm. Genuine sprung rhythm did not, in fact, appear; but we can safely trace the influence of Bridges in the free resolutions and metrical inversions of Mr. Walter de la Mare's *The Listeners* (1912):

> "'Ís there ánybody thére?' said the Tráveller,
> Knócking on the móonlit dóor;"

of Mr. Laurence Binyon's popular ode *For the Fallen* and (as poetry) much finer piece, *The Airman*:

> "Nów at lást vóyaging | a fábulòus domínion
> Surpassing all the measures of his kind,
> Hé, a frée ríder | of the úndulàting sílences,
> Has in himself begotten a new mind;
> Máde hìm a compánion | of the wínds of Héaven, trávelling
> Unpaven streets of cloudy golden snows. . ."[3]

[1] *Letters*, vol. i. pp. 111–12, 121–2. Hopkins quotes:

> "Or peering up from under the white-mossed wonder,
> 'O look at the trees!' they cried, 'O look at the trees!'"
> (*London Snow*, ll. 23–4)

and compares the lines with *The Deutschland*, st. 5, l.6:

> "Since, tho' he is under the world's splendour and wonder",

and the first line of *The Starlight Night*.

[2] *The Trembling of the Veil* (*Autobiographies*, edn. of 1926, p. 190).

[3] Quoted by Newbolt in *New Paths on Helicon* (1928), vol. i. p. 24.

This is neither pure stress-rhythm nor pure syllabic metre, as we see by the regular second, fourth and sixth lines. There is also a clumsy disregard of syllabic quantity in line 19 : " Chárioting with béats of fíre | the fíery-*beating* héart of mán ".

Mr. de la Mare ventures on extended paeonic feet :

> " Fell échoing through the shádowiness of the stíll hóuse " ;

while Mr. Binyon makes good use of the monosyllabic foot and pause :

> " Móte in the hóllow vást, ‸ drówned amid the vívid líght."

Yet the preceding line, with its " counted " rhythm, is a flat negation of sprung rhythm : " A dáring, à defíance, à desíre ! "

Mr. Sacheverell Sitwell, in *Canons of Giant Art* and other poems, has produced a less ambiguous type of irregular blank verse. The authors of *A Survey of Modernist Poetry*, when quoting the following lines, suggest the influence of modern music " in the readiness with which the monotony of the metrical pattern is varied " :

> " The húge flóor of ócean, ‸ únfoamed, ‸ shíning . . .
> Have néver shóne, ‸ gólden, ‸ in its wáke befóre ".[1]

Such lines can be found in the work of Donne and Cowley, and it was probably from the same early seventeenth-century source that Mr. Eliot derived the delicately expressive rhythms of his important poem *The Waste Land* (1922). Many of his lines *could* be read as sprung rhythm ; but the uncertainty of the scansion places the poem rather in the category of freely varied syllabic verse.

Bridges did not demonstrate fully the power of sprung rhythm for imitative and deeper expressional purposes ; but once Hopkins had become widely known, there emerged, sporadically, a form of sprung rhythm which was a definite strengthening of that attempted by Bridges. Here is the opening of Mr. Stephen Spender's *The Express* :

> " Áfter the fi̋rst ‸ pőwerful ‸ pla̋in manife̋sto,
> The bláck ‸ státement of pístons, withóut more fúss
> But glíding líke a quéen she léaves the státion."[2]

That is excellent imitative rhythm, and shows the influence of Hopkins and Bridges merged with all that is best in the most

[1] *Op. cit.* pp. 168–9.
[2] *Poems* (1933).

recent poetry—its keen awareness of the contemporary scene, its adept use of metaphors drawn from the language of current prose.

In 1928, speaking of the direct influence of Bridges, Sir Henry Newbolt said :

> " Such poems as *London Snow*, *On a Dead Child* and *A Passer-By* were not only of striking beauty : those who were ready for the lesson saw at once their significance for the poet. Here was the peculiarly English principle of stress turned to account as the formative principle of verse . . . regularized and made into the law itself." [1]

The total ignorance or omission of Hopkins by a writer of such standing is remarkable. Again, when we remember how Bridges was put to school by Hopkins in the *Letters*, it is strange to read this :

> " But it was the analysis of stress-prosody . . . which first suggested to the poets of the time I am reviewing a possible way of dealing with the all-important question of a fresh and sincere diction. When Bridges said, as he often said in those days, to the friends with whom he talked poetry, ' What we must do is to get out of the old ruts ', he was not advocating the mere abandonment of old metres, as instruments dulled by familiar use : he was proposing to resharpen the cutting edge of poetical diction."

Newbolt fixed 1902 as the year in which " there was growing up somewhat rapidly a special intolerance of ' poetical diction ' " ; [2] but Hopkins had felt and expressed a strong disapproval nearly thirty years before.

Between the publication of Bridges's *Shorter Poems* (1890) and Hopkins's *Poems* in 1918, a fresh departure from the old standard metres was introduced, mainly by the Imagists—F. S. Flint and Mr. Ezra Pound. *Vers libre* or ' free verse ' was a natural development from the unmeasured verse of Whitman, Matthew Arnold,[3] and W. E. Henley [4] ; for the Imagists, it seemed the best means of producing new rhythms to express new moods.[5] Nominally free from all syllabic constraint, ' free verse ' consists of spare, taut, subtly controlled speech-rhythms ; at less than its best it is typographically disguised prose.

[1] *New Paths on Helicon* (Nelson), p. 211. [2] *Loc. cit.* pp. 210, 212.

[3] *The Strayed Reveller*. [4] E.g. *Poems* (1900), Nos. xi. and xxii.

[5] See *Some Imagist Poets* (1915) ; also Mr. Pound's *Umbra*, F. S. Flint's *In the Net of the Stars*, and Ford Madox Hueffer's *Collected Poems*.

Mr. Herbert Read, himself one of the best exponents of 'free verse', has identified this medium with sprung rhythm: the latter, he says,

> "is the rhythm of all genuine *vers libre* or free verse which has arisen since Hopkins's time." [1]

Elsewhere he declares that sprung rhythm, being the most ancient and widely used form of verse, and the most natural to an Englishman, is bound to replace the "Italianate" syllabic measures:

> ". . . before another generation has passed I doubt if any other measure but sprung rhythm will be in use." [2]

It is true that the rhythm of 'free verse', like sprung rhythm, is progressively forged from within (not imposed from without) and allows of free variation from monosyllabic to paeonic feet, the natural see-saw of rising, falling, and rocking movements:

"Emérging at mídnight (rocking)
to cóol my áching éyes with the síght of stárs (rising)
I héar the níghtingále (rising)
thróbbing in the thícket by my gárden gáte (falling)

and I thínk (rising)
A póet in the óld dáys would have máde a sóng (mixed)
of your sóng and the stárlit níght (mixed)
the scént of wállflowers clínging to the gróund. (mixed)

But nów it is dífferent: (rocking)
you síng but wé are sílent (mixed)
our héarts too sádly pátient (mixed)
áll these yéars. (mixed)

Form and rhythm are both expressional. The alternate long and short lines suggest the pulse of the bird's song; the clearly defined stanzaic pattern gives point to the shortened lines of stanza 3, which, like their mixed or uncertain rhythm, express the sad perturbation, the regret and resignation of the poet's

[1] *English Critical Essays* (Twentieth Century), "The Poetry of Gerard Manley Hopkins", p. 366.

[2] Review of Hopkins's *Letters* (vols. i. and ii.) in *The Criterion*, April 1935.

mood, In the concluding stanza, the long lines are restored—with significant alteration of position :

> " Sing ón ! The níght is cóol.
> Mórning and the wórld will be lít
> with whítebeam cándles shíning and Ó the fraíl
> and ténder dáring spléndour of wíld chérrytrees." [1]

Here the more fluent rising and falling rhythms indicate the more traditional response to natural beauty, while the diction is heightened by touches of Hopkinsian richness—" whitebeam ", " cherrytrees ", assonance and internal rhyme.

Altogether it is strong, spare poetry ; but still there are important differences between this kind of ' free verse ' and sprung rhythm as Hopkins used it. Save in two poems (Nos. 36 and 72), Hopkins's rhythm is, despite the nominal disclaimer, authentic *metre* : the lines are measured ' in time ', though the measure is often unusually elastic.[2] His handling of rhythm is also more strictly architectonic : the sonnet-form, however boldly varied, imposed beneficial limitations. Excellent as ' free verse ' can be, we have met nothing in Pound, Eliot, Read, or D. H. Lawrence to match the powerful, tense cumulative rhythm of *Spelt from Sibyl's Leaves*, or the climactic timing of the much freer *Echoes*. Briefly, in the mere rhythm of stress, slack and pause, Hopkins is closer to the music of the greatest traditional verse.

The tendency of ' free verse ' and plain sprung rhythm alike to drop into the looseness of prose had to be counteracted or compensated by internal and end rhyme, assonance, alliteration, ' sprung ' syntax and other aids to concentration, emphasis, and distinctive form. It was the lack of rhetorical and textural stiffening which seemed to Hopkins a weakness in Bridges's poems in sprung rhythm. He would have felt the same lack in the loose alexandrines of *The Testament of Beauty* and in most of the ' free verse ' written since his time.

The *vers libriste* who comes nearest to the Hopkinsian *élan*, in the boldness and parallelism of his diction as well as in rhythm,

[1] *Day's Affirmation*, from *Poems*, 1914–1934. For an explanation of the mark used to show the distributed stress in " your song ", " you sing ", etc., see Hopkins's use of the mark in the version of *To What Serves Mortal Beauty* printed in *Letters*, vol. ii. p. 129 ; also above, chap. iii.

[2] Cf. *Poems*, Author' Preface, p. 4 : " In Sprung Rhythm, as in logaoedic rhythm generally, the feet are assumed to be equally long or strong and their seeming inequality is made up by pause or stressing ". It is essential to keep this statement in mind.

is D. H. Lawrence. Actually, his rhythm points to Whitman rather than Hopkins; but the almost Shakespearian vigour and largesse of his diction shows itself in compounds and phrases like "sword-blade-born", "flower-sumptuous-blooded", "fleece of night" (cf. Hopkins's "fell of dark"). His incidental phrasing is often magnificent, but most of his verse is nearer to prose than anything in Hopkins. His free rhythms are, in the words of an otherwise admiring critic,[1] too frequently "careless, unpolished". It is only in short passages that one finds something like a balanced synthesis of rare poetic qualities, and even then the emotion is not subjected to the same intellectual control as in Hopkins:

> "Oh but the water loves me and folds me
> Plays with me sways me lifts me and sinks me, murmurs:
> Oh marvellous stuff!
> No longer shadow!—and it holds me
> Close, and it rolls me enfolds me, touches me, as if never
> it could touch me enough."

Formally, this harks back to the 'dithyrambic' sequences and doxologies of medieval Latin; [2] but in sensibility it is more crudely primitive than the nature-song of Hopkins. Lawrence's rhythms, instead of making the full stride from Whitman to Hopkins, frequently compromise with a looser if more intellectually resourceful 'Swinburnese':

> "Iron, dawn-hearted
> Ever-beating dawn-heart, enveloped in iron against the
> exile, against the ages . . ."

Thus the *élan vital* in the almond breaks

> "Into blossom, into pride, into honey-triumph, into most
> exquisite splendour." [3]

Since the name of Hopkins is frequently linked with those of Whitman and Lawrence whenever "major influences" in modern poetry are discussed, it is necessary to underline essential differences. To the Jesuit, the extravagant egoistic sensuality of so much of Lawrence's work would have seemed as far below

[1] Miss Dilys Powell, from whose chapter on Lawrence in *Descent from Parnassus* the above examples, as representing his best work, have been deliberately chosen.

[2] E.g. the doxology by Pierre de Corbeil, quoted in Volume II. chap. ii. of the present work.

[3] Miss Powell adds: "To the end of this magnificent poem the themes balance and interweave . . . it is the contrapuntal method in poetry" (pp. 36–6).

civilized moral standards as his technique was lacking in the astringent qualities of the highest art. A common preference for direct and vigorous speech-rhythms, an occasional similarity in diction and in the use of a kind of Hebraic parallelism—even that sharp perception of natural phenomena which distinguishes both poets from most others of our time, should not obscure the fact that in their respective attitudes towards the spirit of man and the spirit of art these two geniuses were poles asunder.

It is usually held that besides the three names mentioned above the main formative influences in modern poetry are Mr. Ezra Pound, Mr. T. S. Eliot, "late Yeats", and Wilfred Owen.[1] This is true of that group of younger poets, clustered around Mr. W. H. Auden, which used to be called the "advance guard"—partly because of their entirely new lean, cerebral, and sometimes pretentiously obscure style, and partly because many of them have shown marked Communistic sympathies. There is, however, a considerable body of recent poetry which forms an unbroken line with that of the Georgians, and which shows no perceptible traces of Hopkins, Doughty, Eliot, or of any other powerful and apparently disruptive influence: we may instance Mr. W. J. Turner, Lady Dorothy Wellesley, Miss V. Sackville-West, Mr. Edmund Blunden—all still young in inspiration; and the best work of the much younger Mr. Roy Campbell is a triumph of traditional beauty both in form and imagery.[2]

On the young poets of the 'advanced' school—poets who are acutely aware of the contemporary scene and of the world's out-of-joint condition—the influence of Hopkins is never so fundamental and pervasive as that of Mr. Ezra Pound and Mr. T. S. Eliot. Not even the great poet of *Byzantium* [3] had proved so decisive for Auden, Day Lewis, Spender, Bottrall and MacNeice as the poets of *Alfred Prufrock* (1914), *Hugh Selwyn Mauberley* (1920), and *The Waste Land* (1922); both masters have, indeed, joined forces with Hopkins in teaching their successors to find the significant symbol, an "objective correlative", and to base their rhythms not on conventional prosody but on the "auditory imagination". In the matter of form and rhythm, Mr. Eliot has generously acknowledged his indebtedness to Mr. Pound

[1] Wilfred Owen's *Poems* were published in 1931.

[2] See *The Flaming Terrapin* (1926), *Adamastor* (1929), *Georgiad* (1931), *Flowering Reeds* (1933), etc. There is also the poetry of Robert Nichols, L. A. G. Strong, Andrew Young, etc.

[3] See *The Tower* (1928), *The Winding Stair* (1933).

—*il miglior fabbro*. In an article called *Isolated Superiority* (*The Dial*, January 1928), Mr. Eliot says:

> "A man who devises new rhythms is a man who extends and refines our sensibility. . . . I cannot think of any one writing verse of our generation and the next, whose verse (if any good) has not been improved by the study of Pound's."

The compliment to Mr. Pound's rhythmical subtlety is justified, in spite of the injustice of condemning a number of poets who have taken their pitchers to older springs.

As a polyglot student of many ancient and medieval schools of poetry, Mr. Pound (whose first poetry appeared in 1909) [1] was probably given a fresh orientation by the same prototypes as those which helped to shape the rhythms of Hopkins, namely, Greek choral and lyric poetry and Old English alliterative verse. His desire to rejuvenate English rhythms with some of the qualities of the Greek is manifest in the sapphics of *Apparuit*,[2] with its subtle rove-over lines:

> "Golden rose the house, in the portal I saw
> thee, a marvel, carven in subtle stuff, a
> portent. Life died down in the lamp and flickered,
> caught at the wonder . . .
>
> Swift at courage thou in the shell of gold, cast-
> ing a-loose the cloak of the body, camest
> straight then shone thine oriel and the stunned light
> faded about thee . . ."

According to W. B. Yeats, that hauntingly beautiful poem *The Return* [3] seems to be the work of "a brilliant improvisator translating at sight from an unknown Greek masterpiece"; the poet gives the impression that he "has not got all the wine into the bowl".[4] This characteristic withholding of part of the poem, says Yeats, is probably the source of that lack of form and consequent obscurity which is the main defect of the school of Auden. With Hopkins it was otherwise: in *his* bowl, however tart or strong the wine, there was seldom a drop missing.

Mr. Pound's translations from the Chinese, says Yeats again, "created the manner followed with more learning but with less subtlety of rhythm by Arthur Waley" [5]; so that although the

[1] With *Personae* and *Exultations*.

[2] First published in *Ripostes* (1912).

[3] From *Ripostes* (1912).

[4] *The Oxford Book of Modern Verse*, Introduction, pp. xxv–xxvi. For an account of the influence of Greek poetry on Hopkins, see Volume II. chap. ii. of the present work.

[5] *Ibid.* p. xl.

publication of Hopkins's *Poems* in 1918 made sprung verse the fashion, and turned the eyes of poets from Bridges to the more original master, some impetus to the new mode must have been given by Mr. Pound before that date and by Mr. Waley's widely admired translations from 1919 onwards.[1] In *The Temple*, Mr. Waley varied the five-stress line thus :

> " When the wind came, jewels chimed and sang
> Softly, softly like music of Paradise.
> White pearls like frozen dewdrops hanging ;
> Dark rubies spilt like clots of blood . . ." [2]

Another rhythmical innovation, or rather revival, in modern poetry is the copying of Old English alliterative verse. Mr. Pound's free translation of *The Seafarer* [3] seems to have set the fashion, although sporadic renderings in the original metre, like Tennyson's *Brunanburh* and William Morris's *Beowulf*, had for some years thrown down a weak challenge to syllabic verse. The old measure has always had its champions (Guest, Marsh, Lanier, etc.) ; and it was J. W. Mackail who said that the native metre " has retained an affinity to the structure of the language which has made it tend to reappear when the dominant metrical forms were exhausted from over-use ".[4] In 1914, an academic critic suggested that a closer scrutiny should be made of the exact relations of modern to Old English poetry in respect of measure and alliteration.[5] Mr. Pound's *Seafarer* reads like a practical comment : its pattern and sprung rhythm are usually accurate and strong :

> " Bitter breast-cares have I abided,
> Known on my keel many a care's hold,
> And dire sea-surge, and there I oft spent
> Narrow nightwatch nigh the ship's head . . ."

though at times, when alliterative stress and speech-accent conflict, the rhythm is ambiguous :

> " List how I, care-wretched, on ice-cold sea . . ."

In more recent poetry, there are examples of alliterative sprung rhythm which are derived directly from Old English

[1] *A Hundred and Seventy Chinese Poems* (1919).

[2] *The Temple and Other Poems* (1923), p. 106.

[3] First published in *Ripostes* (1912).

[4] *Life of William Morris*, vol. i. p. 284.

[5] A. Blyth Webster in *Translation from Old English* (*Essays and Studies*, English Association, vol. v. pp. 167–8).

rather than from Hopkins. Mr. Auden, for instance, catches the very spirit and cadence of *The Wanderer* :

> " There head falls forward, fatigued at evening,
> And dreams of home,
> Waving from window, spread of welcome . . ."

The whole poem, *Chorus from a Play*,[1] shows a subtle blending of a kind of Greek logaœdic rhythm and the Old English stress-metre.

In our second volume we shall trace a rhythmical resemblance between the longer lines of the *Later Genesis* and the sprung alexandrines of Hopkins's *Heraclitean Fire.*[2] At present we may compare two lines of Pound's *Seafarer* with one of the most important measures struck out in recent times—the "loose alexandrines" of *The Testament of Beauty* (1929) by Robert Bridges :

> 'For thís there's no móod-lofty mán | óver éarth's mídst,
> Not thóugh he be gíven his góod | but will háve in his
> yóuth gréed ; " (*The Seafarer*, ll. 39–40.)

These lines are most conveniently read as accentual alexandrines, like many in Bridges :

> " Fróm the térrifýing júngle of his háunted chíldhood
> where the preȟistóric hórror stíll lúrketh untámed,
> mán by slow stéps withdréw, and fróm supplý of néed
> féll to pursúit of pléasure, untíll his lúxury
> supplánting brútality invénted a néw sháme . . ."[3]

Bridges claimed that his alexandrines were based " on the secure rock of Milton's prosody ".[4] This is true ; for although the metre allows of great variety and the employment of the whole range of the modern English vocabulary, it has in fact a *syllabic* basis : the normal line has twelve or thirteen syllables, and the scansion entails elision and half-stresses (that is, the giving of metrical stress to light or slack syllables). The many irregularities are due to a free use of inverted feet and equivalence, the latter being often extended to include the monosyllabic feet and paeons of sprung rhythm, e.g.—

" Tréspassing sómewhat háply ón náture's allótments . . ." (p. 82)

' that oúr háppiest espóusals are náture's frée gíft." (p. 89)

[1] *Poems* (Second Edition), p. 43. [2] Chapter iii. [3] III. ll. 40–4.

[4] See *Robert Bridges and The Testament of Beauty*, by Oliver Elton (English Association Pamphlet, No. 83, 1932, p. 3).

Though in many ways the logical outcome of his study of Milton and of his experiments in quantitative hexameters, these " loose alexandrines " of Bridges owe most to the sprung alexandrines of Hopkins's *St. Winefred's Well.* Hopkins, too, sometimes stressed weak syllables ; but the essential differences are that Hopkins's stressing is more calculated, that his rhythm is more subtle and varied : though many of his lines are of twelve syllables, he sometimes admits eleven, fourteen, fifteen, and even sixteen :

> " I cán scour thee, fresh búrnish thee, sheáthe thee in thy
> dárk láir ; these dróps . . ." (p. 76).

Bridges wisely eschewed all those textural devices which would have fathered his rhythm too obviously on Hopkins. The " loose alexandrines " are in the tone of talk ; yet they are flexible enough to embrace narrative, speculation, satire, and lyricism. It might well be urged that for a long poem they constitute the finest measure that has yet been evolved.

One of the younger poets, Mr. Louis MacNeice, once criticized Hopkins for the alleged inconsistent practice of " tying his sprung rhythm to an arbitrary numerical frame ", so that every line must have, say, five stresses, under the " wrong assumption " that all five stresses are equal to each other and that any set of five stresses equals any other set of five stresses.[1] We believe with Hopkins, however, that for *most* poetic purposes even a theoretical pattern is better than none ; and the advantage of his method is that the reader does at least know how many stresses to look for. In the following extracts from a poem mainly in sprung alexandrines but admitting, apparently, five-stress lines, Mr. MacNeice is presumably showing us how sprung rhythm should be used :

> " Just as those who gaze get higher than those who climb
> A paradox unfolds on any who can tamper with time.
> Where bus encumbers upon bus and fills its slot
> Speed up the traffic in a quick motion film of thought
> Till bus succeeds bus so identically sliding through
> That you cannot catch the fraction of a chink between the two
> But they all go so fast, bus after bus, day after day,
> Year after year, that you cannot mark any headway
> But the whole stream of traffic seems to crawl
> Carrying its dead boulders down a glacier wall . . ." [2]

The whole poem is interesting, original, bright with a witty imagery ; but who save Mr. MacNeice would venture to scan the above lines ?

[1] In *A Comment, New Verse,* No. 14 (April 1935), p. 26.

[2] *New Verse,* No. 5 (October 1933), p. 6.

To many they will sound like doggerel, though a few stress marks might have brought out an appropriate imitative rhythm.

We proceed now to examine more closely the influence of Hopkins upon the diction, syntax, and texture of recent poetry, and incidentally to determine how far he shares this tutelage with Charles Montagu Doughty (*b.* 1843) and others.

Apart from Hopkins and Doughty, few poets of the last two hundred years have followed up hints given by Shakespeare and Milton in the matter of extreme syntactical licence. Moreover, most poets since Browning have shown an increasing respect for Wordsworth's theory of poetic diction (the brilliant efflorescence of latinate vocables in Francis Thompson being recognized as outside the main line of development). When, therefore, the year 1906 was (as Harold Monro said) " brought to its knees by the vast load " of Doughty's epic, *The Dawn in Britain*, the poem's archaism, unusual syntax and plethora of punctuation marks would at that time have made a universal appreciation impossible, even if the length and handling of the fable had been found entirely satisfactory. Doughty's poetry has been praised by such men as Edward Garnett, Lascelles Abercrombie, Edward Thomas, and Herbert Read ; though even to-day opinions about him are sharply divided.[1] But when, between 1925 and 1935, Hopkins had become widely known, and poets and critics had begun to assert the importance of subordinating grammatical punctilio to such qualities as concentration, precision, integrity of imagination, Doughty was again brought forward by his admirers, this time as a poetic twin of Hopkins :

> " Doughty and Hopkins, for those who know both, are as natural a pair to name together as Wordsworth and Coleridge. They are quite separate in so far as neither knew the other's verse, but they were nearly of an age and they shared the same revolt against a declining tradition long before that revolt became widespread. For though not a line of Doughty's appeared before 1900, he was planning his poetry in the eighteen sixties." [2]

Hopkins (continues Professor Barker Fairley) would have read Doughty with ecstasy, exclaiming :

> " This was the sort of thing I did myself. Here was an ally. Why didn't I know this man instead of that timid fellow, Bridges ! " [2]

[1] See, for instance, the article *Charles Doughty—a Corpse* in *New Verse*, No. 17, Oct.–Nov. 1935.

[2] *Selected Passages from ' The Dawn in Britain '*, arranged with an Introduction by Barker Fairley (1935), pp. xiv–xv.

Apart from the fact that Hopkins disliked what he knew of Doughty's prose,[1] such a contemptuous thought about his friend Bridges would never have found lodgment in his mind. Nevertheless, he might well have liked the " confused syntax " of the following description of Esla's decoy-flight from her weird sisters:

> " As guileful lapwing lures
> Feet of crude fowler, from her fledgeling's nest;
> So them she leads, so them misleads; as danced
> She merry round, (whose murderous meaning is;
> Seize on her tender limbs, and rend, and cast
> Them, to sea's running waves, from these dread brinks!)
> They hoary women, past now age and spent,
> By cranks and windles, from those perilous rocks;
> Aye crying, like to one wildered, were those wands . . .
> Nor fears death Esla: she would die, to save,
> Whom her soul loves. Have outstripped her light feet,
> Their cold lean joints." [2]

The movement of the verse, at first reading so clogged with commas and semi-colons, is intended to give a greater emphasis than usual to the individual word and phrase. Doughty, like Hopkins, felt that the conventional syntax tended to produce a facile, conventional rhythm and response; hence his ideas seem often to have been set down just as they occurred to him, without artificial rearrangement—as in the lengthy parenthesis; or with a certain psychological precision (" past now age ") and dramatic urgency (" Have outstripped . . ."). Very Hopkinsian are the " cranks and windles "; and so also is the last sentence, with its inversion which at first reads like a literal translation from a synthetic language.

Doughty's inversions, transpositions, and omissions (though often the cause of temporary obscurity) frequently give an extraordinary freshness and vividness to the language: the figurative meaning may be emphasized at the expense of the literal:

> " Seemed tempest-cloud, which from her neck, outblows,
> Her weed." [3]

The retarding punctuation leaves no scope for " the roll, the rise, the carol, the creation " as we hear them in Hopkins; but a similar handling of syntax, adapted to epic style, again and again causes the bare words to pass straight into poetry without the

[1] *Letters*, vol. i. pp. 283–4, 290. [2] *Selected Passages, etc.*, pp. 11–12.
[3] *The Dawn in Britain*, vol. i. p. 82. (*S.P.*, p. 2.)

usual intermediary assistance of a prose basis.[1] The following could hardly be bettered :

> " Cold cliffs, of that sea-deep,
> Are blue-ribbed ice ; whence oft strange lofty sounds
> Are heard, as lute-strings knapped, of the ice-god." [2]

Doughty has remade blank verse as Hopkins remade the sonnet —destroying the glaze of characterless fluency, infusing a new life. The surface ruggedness often conveys a delicate awareness ; the expression is raw and amorphous, like sensation itself :

> " She weens, she heard
> As moan ; or the wind was, mongst fallen crags ?
> And for that sudden fear, she would have fled.
> Like startled roe, yet listens ! " [3]

Much of Doughty's Spenserian archaism and viscous punctuation must have reminded many readers of Hopkins's remark that the poet's name rhymes with " gouty " ; but the truth about this punctuation has been aptly stated by a recent critic, who is fully aware of the affinity with Hopkins :

> " Doughty meant his poetry to be read aloud and his punctuation is rhetorical, that is, it rather indicates pauses to the voice, than points grammatical structure. Like Hopkins he needs to be read with the ear, not the eye, then many knots and seeming harshnesses resolve themselves. . . ." [4]

Certainly Hopkins's punctuation is mainly structural ; but many of the effects produced by Doughty are similar to those achieved by Hopkins in *The Deutschland*, *Harry Ploughman*, and *Tom's Garland*.

Doughty's syntax and idiom can be German : " So went forth view, what this were for a shore " [5] (*was für ein* . . .). Or like Hopkins he can use a kind of Greek syntax, striving (successfully, we think,) to accomplish what may be thought proper only to an inflected language :

> " But Cloten, from the row-lock, who washt forth
> Was, with his oar, whereto those bound him ; rides
> It embraced, all that day, the windy surges,
> (And he yet lives, by favour of some god !)
> And the next night." [6]

[1] Cf. Professor Fairley, *S.P.*, p. xvi. [2] Vol. ii. p. 131. [3] Vol. iii. p. 18.
[4] Anne Treneer in *Charles M. Doughty* (1935), p. 191. See also pp. 328–31.
[5] Vol. iii. p. 17. [6] Vol. iii. p. 16.

"Bewept, long-age, then, spouses of high gods,
Earth-world, beneath, forlorn, deformed, and drowned,
Was erst so fair. But sith their straitened mood
Began appease, singing the golden-haired
Belin, an heavenly melody, among the gods." [1]

In a passage which deserves to be quoted in full, Professor Fairley points out [2] a striking resemblance between Hopkins's description of the Windhover in flight and two excerpts from *The Dawn in Britain* :

" First there is the breaking of the word ' kingdom ' between two lines—technically, to accelerate the pace of a passage descriptive of a falcon flying—and, second, the un-English packing of the adjective in ' the rolling level underneath him steady air ' which seems to balloon the ocean of air on which the falcon rides. To match the first of these devices there is in Doughty the sailing of a magic ship across the deep . . . the word ' wing-sailed ' in Doughty being split like ' kingdom ' in Hopkins :

' Was heard, from waves, rebellowing to fast land,
A more than mortal shout, wind-spurned, the wing-
Sailed Red Mare, towards far sea-rim swiftly flies.' [3]

It is exactly the same device with the same accelerating purpose. And for the second—the crowded adjective phrase to express the brimming air under the falcon—Doughty has an even closer parallel ; he is describing a sea-god's chariot turning landwards to drown a legion and he requires a swelling flood of ocean as Hopkins of air. Even the word ' rolling ' is there to clinch the resemblance . . . :

' And follow (an infinite spume-sprinkling train ;)
The, on gólden axe-tree rolling, broad divine
Wheels, in wide salt sea-flood, of stormy god '." [4]

That interrupted utterance called in Welsh *tor ymadrodd* [5] and used frequently by Hopkins is common also in Doughty :

" (He óf some, *here*, cast timber, would knit float ;" [6]

" and seemed the Avalon maid,
Her, *prayer-spread virgin arms*, Christ's voice say, Fold
About My lambs . . ." [7]

[1] Vol. vi. p. 192.
[2] In an article entitled *Charles Doughty and Modern Poetry* (*London Mercury*, June 1935, pp. 128–37). We have slightly shortened the passages quoted.
[3] Vol. vi. p. 211.
[4] Vol. v. p. 170.
[5] See our second volume, chap. iii.
[6] Vol. iii. p. 20.
[7] Vol. vi. p. 116.

There are scores of other touches which remind us of Hopkins —a stress-mark to accommodate extra syllables (see above, 'golden'), an ellipsis, an isolated word, an image, a compound, a coinage :

> "Save that, *seems*, this hath face of some sea-moss,"[1]
>
> "But not *Hoarbeard*, all-witty Woden, *god* !"[2]
>
> "The *hoary girdled*, infinite, night of stars,"[3]
>
> "Beneath those *flocks and herds now of shire stars*,"[4]
>
> "And *ring-gold* seemed the hero's *ravelled* locks ;
> And like to *harvest shocks his side-long* beard,"[5]

Doughty maintains a broadly homogeneous individual style, and handles his characters and episodes with a power and pathos which justify those who consider him a great and neglected poet. He has his flatnesses, and never reaches the superb mastery of Hopkins's higher flights ; yet his fresh manipulation of words in the poetic sentence should prove as stimulating to later poets as that of Hopkins.[6] His use of that obsolete poetic diction which Hopkins so carefully avoided (*woeworth !*, *mote*, *uneath*, etc.) was justified, if ever it could be, by his subject ; but there is less to be said for hackneyed expressions like "heavenly eyne" and "blissful haven", which do not fuse with the more original parts and so produce a disturbing tone of pastiche.

Doughty sometimes reinforced his diction with borrowings from Welsh, Dutch, Danish, etc., and this reminds us of a comment made by Mr. Herbert Read :

> "Most of Hopkins's innovations are in the nature of new combinations of existing words, sometimes contracted similes, or metaphors, and in this respect his vocabulary has a surface similarity to that of James Joyce."[7]

This is true ; and there are two other 'modernist' writers (at present poised between notoriety and reputation as regards their handling of the language) who, though probably not influenced

[1] Vol. iii. p. 19. [2] Vol. i. p. 83. [3] Vol. iii. p. 23.
[4] Vol. vi. p. 135. [5] Vol. v. p. 102.
[6] Testimony to this is given by Mr. Hugh Macdiarmid in *At the Sign of the Thistle* (1934) and *Stony Limits* (verse ; 1934).
[7] *Op. cit.* p. 368.

by Hopkins, show enough " surface similarity " to be considered here : they are Miss Gertrude Stein and Mr. E. E. Cummings.

It is only in James Joyce's latest prose (*Finnegans Wake*, 1939) [1] that we find that amazing personal dialect which has some points of contact with the style of Hopkins. Following Vico, who contemplated a mental vocabulary which would provide an ideal synthesis of all existing languages, Joyce used a synthetic language to present a composite picture of human life *sub specie aeternitatis* : times, places, characters and words are all telescoped in this effort to achieve universality and concentration. As one critic says,

> " The universality of Joyce's theme dictates an intensive technique—a greater density of word texture. Meanings can no longer lie side by side. Into one word he crowds a whole family of them. A letter added or left out—the sound of a vowel or consonant modified and a host of associations is admitted within the Gates." [2]

Hence when Joyce speaks of " sfumastelliacinous hair ", we hear echoes of Latin and Italian in a concentrated tone-picture of spray, smoke, and stars.

Like Hopkins, but on a much larger scale, he employs puns, half-puns, Lewis Carroll portmanteau words and witty coinages in which one element of a familiar word is replaced by another :

> " Nuvoletta in her lightdress, spunn of sixteen shimmers." [3]

Joyce had arrived at almost the same conception of " texture " as Hopkins : he sometimes weaves his strange compounds into the same intricate and running harmonies of alliteration, assonance, and internal rhyme :

> " It may be that he reglimed ? presaw ? the fields of heat
> and yields of wheat where corngold Ysit ? shamed and shone." [4]

> " Beside the rivering waters of, hitherandthithering waters
> of. Night ! " [5]

[1] First published, serially, in *Transition*, as " Work in Progress ".

[2] Mr. Frank Budgen in " The *Work in Progress* of James Joyce and Old Norse Poetry ". (*Transition*, Summer, 1928 ; Paris.)

[3] Here, apparently, a girl of sixteen summers is described by the associations of *little cloud*, *light*, and *nightdress*. (Quoted by Miss Sitwell in *Aspects of Modern Poetry*, pp. 217–18.)

[4] *Work in Progress*, 4th instalment. (*Transition*, July 1927.)

[5] *Anna Livia Plurabelle*, Fragment of *Work in Progress* (1930), p. 32.

In this last excerpt, the punctuation is reminiscent of Doughty; but a word like "Ysit" is typical of a style which is continuously far more private and obscure than the most difficult passages in Hopkins. Though a far more sophisticated writer, Joyce resembles Hopkins in occasional sentences which are musical and comparatively lucid. In the following, "a thousand years of human destinies seem to be crowded into the silence and fury of a snowstorm on a river:

> 'Countlessness of livestories have netherfallen by this plage, flick as flowflakes, litters from aloft, like a waast wizard all of whirlworlds.'"[1]

It is a fascinating technique; and Hopkins would have envied him "flowflakes" and "whirlworlds".

To all save a few learned and imaginative philologists, the greater part of *Finnegans Wake* must remain an alluring enigma. But as it is difficult to believe that Joyce received no stimulus from Hopkins, so it is probable that a posterity which is familiar with the latter will find the transition from conventional prose to the mysteries of Joyce a little less exacting.

Another modernist upon whom academic critics hesitate to pronounce judgment is Mr. E. E. Cummings. He also is highly sophisticated, with a sophistication that is an uncommon mixture of *naïveté* and subtlety: he writes, indeed, in a manner Swift might have described if Gulliver had made a fifth journey to a people resembling the English-speaking coterie in Paris of the nineteen twenties. Mr. Cummings plays so many tricks with spelling that beside him Hopkins is decorum itself; yet in his own way Mr. Cummings was probably as sincere as Hopkins in his attempt to break with what he considered to be outmoded and effete habits of expression.[2] His odd typographical and orthographical devices are intended to convey the stream of sensation with unprecedented exactitude; but his preoccupation with mere technique often becomes morbid, and illustrates the result of going beyond the point at which Hopkins said: "It is plain I must go no further on this road." Had Hopkins continued on the lines of

[1] Mr. Frank Budgen, *loc. cit.*

[2] He has published: *Tulips and Chimneys* (1923); *XLI Poems* (1925); *&* (1925); *Is 5* (1926); *Poems* (London, 1937).

Sibyl's Leaves, *Tom's Garland*, and *Harry Ploughman*, he might have caught up with the following:

> " life hurl my
> yes, crumbles hand (ful released conarefetti) ev eryflitter,
>   inga. where
> mil (lions of aflickf) litter ing brightmillion ofS hurl;
>   edindodg : ing
> whom are Eyes shy-dodge is bright cruMbshandful
>   quick-hurl edinwho
> Is flittercrumbs, fluttercrimbs are floatfallin,g ; allwhere :
> a : crimflitterinish, is arefloatsis ingfallall ! mil, shy,
>   milbrightlions
> my (hurl flicker handful
> in) dodging are shybrigHteyes is crum bs(alll)if, ey, Es."

This, we are told,

> " is an attempt to represent, in the manner of the early futurists, the book of life torn into a million fragments as small as confetti, the bread of life crumbled nervously under the disorganizing influence of shy bright eyes, bright like the million stars." [1]

It has more affinity with Joyce and the paintings of Picasso than with the firm logic of ideas in Hopkins; yet here also is an extension of Doughty's private system of punctuation and above all of Hopkins's bold, independent manipulation of the elements of language. Beside such vivid compounds as *brightmillion*, *floatfalling*, and *shybright* we find tmesis and deliberate Spoonerisms: words, disintegrated as mere intellectual counters, are reconstructed on other planes, visual and aural. On the same theme, we may perhaps imagine a mundane Hopkins, tongue in cheek, parodying himself thus:

> Life hurl my . . . yes, bread crumbles ; like released
> Confetti are every a fluttering million (spare !)
> And littering whirled brightmillion crumbs of, there,
> Life, for whom eyes' shydodge is light increased.
> Handful quick-hurled in flittercrumbs is, ceased,
> Life's page in torn floatfalling fine allwhere
> White pieces : con- are flickering -fetti tear-
> ing shybright eyes, stars ; morsels from eyes' feast . . .

This movement towards the disintegration of conventional linguistic values has been termed, by Miss Laura Riding, *The*

[1] Poem quoted and thus paraphrased in *A Survey of Modernist Poetry* (Riding and Graves, 1927), pp. 288–9.

New Barbarism.[1] The high-priestess of the cult is Miss Gertrude Stein, who for over thirty years has been writing prose and verse the principal aim of which has been to divest words of their historical meanings and invest them with an hypnotic, repetitive rhythm—sometimes for the mere pleasure of an abstract design, a chaste tone-pattern ; sometimes to convey definite nostalgic emotions by a combination of verbal impressionism, onomatopœia, and free-association. The abnormal sensibility of Miss Edith Sitwell detects in Miss Stein's poems a world of meaning and " visual impressions so terrifyingly sharp that all our present surroundings are abolished " [2] ; for example :

> " Sweet sweet sweet sweet sweet tea
> Susie Asado,
> Sweet sweet sweet sweet sweet tea.
> Susie Asado.
> Susie Asado which is a told tray sure.
> A lean on the shoe this means slips slips hers . . ."

This beginning of Miss Stein's extremely esoteric description of an amiable, slipshod, canary-bright spinster may well be an impressionistic, non-representational offshoot of that feeling for the pure musical suggestion of words which Hopkins displayed in the last lines of *The Echoes* and *Binsey Poplars*, and again in *The Woodlark* :

> " With a sweet joy of a sweet joy,
> Sweet, of a sweet, of a sweet joy
> Of a sweet—a sweet—sweet—joy."

The obvious and important difference is that in Miss Stein's poem the canary-note is a symbol of the " canary-like brightness of disposition " in Susie, whereas in Hopkins it is simple onomatopœia.

As with Joyce, there is an occasional surface similarity between the sound of Hopkins's verse and the sound of Miss Stein's solipsist utterances ; as Mr. Alan Pryce-Jones has said :

> " It is queer, too, that Hopkins should have discovered the fertile trick on which Miss Gertrude Stein depends, of chance connexions of sense brought out of homophones, and sound relations." [3]

In Hopkins the " trick " is certainly fertile, and productive of indubitable poetry ; in Miss Stein, however, alliteration,

[1] In *Contemporaries and Snobs* (1928), Part II., " T. E. Hulme, The New Barbarism, and Gertrude Stein ".

[2] *Aspects of Modern Poetry*, p. 219 *et seqq.*

[3] *London Mercury*, May 1931, p. 52.

assonance and internal rhyme are usually " abstract ", intellectually sterile. When Hopkins speaks of

"Those goldnails and their gaylinks that hang along a lime,"

we are at once conscious of word-music and word-picture ; but in Miss Stein's verse there is either no pretence of logical sequence or else the juxtapositions are so private, the suggestion so precarious, that no worth-while synthesis is possible :

> " Drink pups drink pups lease a sash hold
> See it shine and a bobolink has pins. It shows a nail.
> What is a nail. A nail is unison.
> Sweet sweet sweet sweet sweet tea." [1]

Only a foreigner with no knowledge of English could confuse Hopkins's jingles with the distant barbaric tom-toms of Miss Stein's pure inane :

> " Put it there in there where they have it
> Put it there in there there and they halve it
> Put it there in there there and they have it
> Put it there in there there and they halve it." [2]

The almost hypnotic fascination of a repetitive thought-and-tone pattern (as in excited infantile speech) was first fully exploited by Hopkins :

> " When the thing we freely forfeit is kept with fonder a care,
> Fonder a care kept than we could have kept it, kept
> Far with fonder a care (and we, we should have lost it) finer, fonder
> A care kept.—Where kept ? Do but tell us where kept, where.—
> Yonder.—" [3]

In Miss Stein it lends a technical interest to a happy, persistent mania :

> " They do say look at it.
> To look at it. They will look at it. They will say look at it." [4]

The device is used again in the prose of Joyce, but it does not recover the dignity of true poetry until we come to Mr. T. S.

[1] See *Aspects of Mod. Poetry*, *loc. cit.*

[2] *Survey of Modernist Poetry*, p. 281. See the whole section, pp. 280–9.

[3] *The Golden Echo*, *Poems*, No. 36.

[4] From *Saints in Season* (*Survey of Modernist Poetry*, pp. 284–5. The authors add : " Miss Stein's persistence in her own continuousness is astonishing : this is how she wrote in 1926, and in 1906 ").

Eliot' *Ash-Wednesday* (1930), where it is musically eloquent of spiritual desolation and indecision, of striving again and again :

> " Because I do not hope to turn again
> Because I do not hope
> Because I do not hope to turn
> Desiring this man's gift and that man's scope . . ."

Mr. Eliot has certainly been influenced by Miss Stein (the general tone and trend of whose work he nevertheless deplores) ; [1] but a poet at once so individual, sensitive and eclectic could hardly fail to show some traces of Hopkins. His fondness for alliteration and internal rhyme had been revealed since *Prufrock* (1917) :

> " And time yet for a hundred indecisions
> And for a hundred visions and revisions
> Before the taking of a toast and tea."

It is, however, not until we come to a chorus in his pageant play *The Rock* (1934) that we meet a texture so familiar as

> " Moon light and star light, owl and moth light
> *Glow-worm glowlight on a grassblade.*" [2]

On the whole, Mr. Eliot has resisted the fascination of the Hopkinsian manner more successfully than many of his juniors ; yet the incantatory choruses of his greatest play, *Murder in the Cathedral* (1935), show a similar return to the spirit of the Greek choric measures, to the pulsing verses of the medieval Latin doxology, to the crowded affirmations and perfervid catalogues of Whitman. A free logaœdic or sprung rhythm is often knit (as sandy soil is knit by the roots of pine-trees) by internal rhyme, assonance and repetition :

> " The merchant, shy and cautious, tries to compile a little
> fortune,
> And the labourer bends to his piece of earth, earth-colour,
> his own colour . . ." [3]

> " Clear the air ! clean the sky ! wash the wind ! take the
> stone from the stone, take the skin from the arm,
> take the muscle from the bone, and wash them.
> Wash the stone, wash the bone, wash the brain,
> wash the soul, wash them wash them ! " [4]

Nowhere do we find that combination of the rich, strong, and exquisite that we have in Hopkins ; partly, perhaps, because

[1] See *Survey*, pp. 274–5.
[2] P. 84.
[3] Third Edition, p. 12.
[4] *Ibid.* p. 75. Cf. pp. 18 and 64.

Mr. Eliot has realized that the clotted, concentrated poetry of that unique master is not for protracted regalement and is certainly the most difficult and dangerous to emulate.

Another highly original 'modernist' poet, and one whose deep, understanding appreciation of Hopkins (based on natural affinity) might have led us to expect a more positive influence, is Miss Edith Sitwell. Most of her verse has been published since 1918, and from *Bucolic Comedies* (1923) onwards we find in her work an entirely individual blending of elements from Donne, Rimbaud, Christina Rossetti (of *Goblin Market*), Gertrude Stein,[1] and a little of Hopkins. Apart from her extraordinary sensuousness, which is scarcely to be matched by Keats or Francis Thompson, Miss Sitwell has elaborated, both as poet and critic, a theory of poetic texture which is something like a rationale of Hopkins's practice on lines suggested by Rimbaud's sonnet on the vowels. Her sensory impressions are, as she claims, genuinely primitive in their incidence ; but her fastidious culture and intensive self-training as a poet have coated much of her verse with a veneer of artificiality and preciosity which disguises its essential simplicity.

Miss Sitwell's examination of the texture of certain stanzas in *The Wreck of the Deutschland* and of " The furl of fresh-leaved dogrose down " [2] (a piece of almost pure 'Sitwell') shows clearly that she found in Hopkins [3] that instinctive felicity in modulating sound to image which she herself has achieved (and sometimes explained) in her own poetry. She does not imitate the rich consonancy or sprung rhythm of Hopkins, but she uses, in her own way, many of his devices : she calculates the effect on rhythm, and on speed, of *tone-colour*—of rhymes, assonances and dissonances at different places within the line. In illustration, we quote the beginning of *The Drum* :

" In his hall senatorial
Black and manorial
House where decoy-duck
Dust doth clack—
Clatter and quack
To a shadow black,— . . .

Said the musty Justice Mompesson
What is that dark stark beating drum . . ."

[1] " The poems in *Façade* are, for the most part, abstract patterns, difficult technical experiments." (*Selected ems*, p. 26.)

[2] *Poems*, No. 63.

[3] See her *Aspects of Modern Poetry*, pp. 56–66.

Her comment is characteristic :

> " The sharp and menacing rhythm of the first four lines is given by the fact that " black " in the second line is at the opposite side from " duck " and " clack " in the third and fourth, and this throws reversed shadows . . ."

And so the exegesis of *o*'s and *a*'s, *d*'s and *t*'s goes on to a considerable length.[1]

Rich as Miss Sitwell's poetry is in word-painting, in new and valuable experience, the effect of her work in bulk is diminished by a tendency to repetition and monotony.

Before passing on to consider the technique of those younger poets who, for a few years at least, threatened to inaugurate a haphazard and largely un-Catholic 'school of Hopkins', we must pause to examine a remarkable affinity and collateral influence from abroad—the German poet, Rainer Maria Rilke (1875–1926). For some years now Rilke's poetry has in this country been made a cult.[2] His peculiar poetic and pantheistic mysticism is a far cry from the orthodox Christian theology and quasi-mysticism of Hopkins. But Rilke's subtle imagination and rich verbal music, like the similar qualities in the English Jesuit, can be exceedingly fascinating even to those who cannot accept his fundamental beliefs about Life, Death, and the nature of God.

Rilke makes great use of alliteration, assonance, and internal rhyme ; yet his resemblance to Hopkins is not merely technical. He, too, has " an acute and strange visual sense, piercing down to the essence of the thing seen ".[3] As Hopkins projected himself into a Windhover and a Caged Skylark, so Rilke, for a different purpose, discovers a powerful personal symbol in a caged panther :

> " Ihm ist, als ob es tausend Stäbe gäbe
> und hinter tausend Stäben keine Welt."

How admirably is the passing of bar by bar before the panther's eyes suggested by the Hopkinsian " Stäbe gäbe " ! In the next

[1] *Selected Poems* (1936), p. 32.

[2] Recent translations are as follows : *The Duinese Elegies* (E. and V. Sackville-West) ; *Poems* (J. B. Leishman) ; *Requiem and other Poems* (J. B. Leishman) ; *The Duino Elegies* (Stephen Spender and J. B. Leishman) ; *Sonnets to Orpheus* (J. B. Lieshman) ; *Later Poems* (J. B. Leishman).

[3] Miss Sitwell on Hopkins (*loc. cit.*).

line, moreover, both tone-quality and picture recall a characteristic line in Hopkins :

> " Der weiche Gang geschmeidig starker Schritte . . ." [1]
> (velvety softness wedded to striding strength)

> " Or as a stallion stalwart, very-violet-sweet ! . . ." (No. 14)

Rilke's preoccupation with *texture* in the Hopkinsian sense (although no direct influence is traceable) appears in the following excerpts from *Sonette an Orpheus* (1923) :

> " Atmen, du unsichtbares Gedicht !
> Immerfort um das eigne
> Sein rein ausgetauschter Weltraum. Gegengewicht
> in dem ich mich rhythmisch ereigne." (Zweiter Teil, I)

> " Ĭst er ein Hiĕsiger ? Nein, aus beiden
> Reichen erwūchs seine weite Natūr.
> Kūndiger böge die Zweige der Weiden,
> wer die Wūrzeln der Weiden erfūhr." (Erster Teil, VI)

Beginning with the close vowels of " Ist " and " Hiesiger " (to signify, perhaps, the restricted life of the living), the quatrain opens out into a duet between the diphthong *ei* and the vowel *u* (the two realms, Life and Death ?), with the binding *obbligato* of the alliterative *w* (the continuity of the Orphean poet's consciousness in both realms ?).

Like Hopkins, again, Rilke can make one word grow significantly out of another :

> " Rühmen, das ists ! Ein zum Rühmen Bestellter,
> ging er hervor wie das *Erz* aus des Steins
> Schweigen. Sein *Herz*, o vergängliche Kelter
> eines den Menschen unendlichen Weins." (Erster Teil, VII)

Though never actually " sprung ", Rilke's later rhythms are at once nervous and fluid : in his deft *Hakenstil* the poetry flows like a molten mass. His semantic rhythm, moreover, is

[1] *Der Panther* (*Neue Gedichte*), quoted for its " tonal-qualities " by Jethro Bithell in *Modern German Literature*, 1880–1938 (1939), p. 219.

often, as with Hopkins, patterned forth in a bold repetition of significant words—a homophonic progression in which similarity of sound emphasizes the connexion between subtle variations of meaning :

> " Denn unter Wintern ist einer so endlos Winter,
> dasz, *über*winternd, dein Herz *über*haupt *über*steht." [1]

He again resembles Hopkins in his rapid flow of images, in his power of transforming the common word, and in his creative handling of syntax. As Mr. Jethro Bithell says, Rilke's

> " syntactical tricks serve him to veil the meaning in his last Duino and Muzot phase : phrases such as *nicht dass du Gottes ertrügest die Stimme* and *Manche, des Todes, entstand ruhig geordnete Regel* read like transliterated Latin." [2]

The current interest in Rilke has probably helped to confirm the more narrowly technical influence of Hopkins upon some of the younger poets we are now about to examine. Of these, not more than three or four can be said to be established. Their inclusion in this chapter is not a tacit admission of their absolute merit, but merely a collective symptom of the power of Hopkins's poetry to engage and stir so many active minds two generations after his death.

Mr. C. Day Lewis has tried to define the nature and scope of that influence. Hopkins, he says, produced an effect opposite to that of Wordsworth. By Hopkins, the language of poetry was removed as far as possible from ordinary language : it becomes incantation again. His prosody, on the other hand, has swung to the other extreme, for it is based on the rhythm of common speech. Mr. Lewis continues :

> " We find in post-war poetry a tendency to combine these two results, to use common speech rhythms together with a mixture of simplified, superficially unpoetical language and highly poetical incantatory language." [3]

Mr. Lewis should have made it clear that in Hopkins colloquial and incantatory language, speech rhythm and musical rhythm, are fused and blended rather than mixed (see, for instance, *Felix Randal*). The ' mixture ' derives more properly from Pound and Eliot ; and though capable of excellent results in the latter, it is responsible for some very frigid effects in the younger imitators.

[1] *Sonette an Orpheus*, Zweiter Teil, XIII. [2] *Op. cit.* p. 234.
[3] *A Hope for Poetry* (1934), p. 9.

Mr. R. E. Warner, addressing a wild goose, can juxtapose such lines as :

> " your unearthly song, your neck like thunder and lightning
> and your mysterious barbaric love.
>
> The publishers admitted that you were interesting
> but hardly to the taste of the general public . . ." [1]

" It is in his ordering of words," says the same critic, " that Hopkins is the technical forerunner of the post-war poets, the first ' modern ' poet . . ." [2] Because of his intellectual wrestling with language, Hopkins's influence coincides with that of Donne ; but Hopkins has also taught present-day poets a greater resourcefulness in word-making—in the compound, for instance :

> " O charged-to-the-full in secret slow-beating heart . . ." [3]
>
> " I smell men's quick-as-water-ripple skin." [4]
>
> " Those lake-long, wood-ash-grey, thought-clouded eyes . . .
> Bracken-brown, barley-gold
> Curved and curling masses of your brindled hair." [5]

Mr. Auden has been reminded more than once of the following " undigested fragment of Hopkins " embedded in his style :

> " Me, March, you do with your movements master and rock
> With wing-whirl, whale-wallow, silent budding of cell ; " [6]

Here Mr. Auden was echoing *Carrion Comfort* : " Thy wring-world right foot rock ". Like Bridges, moreover, he could not forget the *Deutschland* :

> " Ah, water
> Would gush, flush green these mountains and these valleys." [7]

—which recalls " Gush—flush the man " (stanza 8).

Mr. Ronald Bottrall is a poet of unquestionable talent, but he is peculiarly susceptible to influences. His form and diction

[1] *New Verse, No. 15* (June 1935), p. 13. [2] *A Hope for Poetry*, p. 63.
[3] W. H. Auden : *The Orators* (1932), " Journal of an Airman ".
[4] John Pudney : *Spanish Coast* (*The Listener*, October 1935).
[5] Jan Struther : " — M —" (*London Mercury*, May 1936).
[6] *New Country* (ed. Michael Roberts, 1933), p. 214. See also C. Day Lewis, *A Hope for Poetry*, p. 63. [7] *The Criterion*, July 1933.

owe most to Pound and Eliot; but in one poem, after the typically Poundian colloquialism of

> "We do not lack money for the Arts;
> A fifty-shilling tailor will have an option
> On them . . ."

he suddenly paraphrases Hopkins:

> "The soul has precipices, slippery footholds. Fearful
> To stand amid the whorlèd rocks and antres vast." [1]

Again, in *Festivals of Fire* [2] (a poem which imitates the method of *The Waste Land*), Mr. Bottrall abandons the frankly prosaic tone of his earlier verses for the more palpable poetic splendours of Hopkins:

> "Then how unlace, trace
> The flying blaze, maze of hither
> Thither, come go? Trumpet dazzles
> Raze the path to the castle gate . . ."

The images in Hopkins which seem to have made the deepest impression are those based on the bird of prey (*The Windhover*) and the boisterous wind. Mr. Randall Swingler, for instance, finds in the buzzard a symbol of escape, of release from a constricting world:

> "have also seen
> The buzzard, tall from the fenced northland,
> Veer on his tilting wing-span, sheer
> In airstream stalling:
> And welcomed wildness, a mountain mood
> Wave-rocking or wind-riving." [3]

This bird-image has also been used by Auden and Day Lewis, and seems to have been adopted as a Communistic *leit motif*—the group-symbol of revolutionary idealism. Mr. Lewis combines it with a pattern of internal cross-rhyming which, as he says, "can impart a subdued, sustained, melodic tone to verse, and enable the writer to use rhyme words which have grown stale as end-rhymes:

> "Now to be with you, elate, un*shared*
> My *kes*trel joy, O *hover*er in the wind
> *Over* the quarry furiously at *rest*
> *Chaired* on shoulders of shouting wind." [4]

[1] *Salute to them that know*, from *The Loosening and Other Poems* (1931).
[2] Published in 1934.
[3] *Before the Sea*, from *Difficult Morning* (1933).
[4] *Op. cit.* p. 72. See the opening of Mr. Lewis's *The Magnetic Mountain* (1933).

We may note in passing that Mr. Swingler has been influenced not only by Hopkins's rhythm, diction, and imagery, but also by his intense feeling for individuation :

> " Lord, O never let lose this habit
> Of expected strangeness, a kind
> Of alertness . . . to select
> The deep, the dangerous uniqueness down in things." [1]

The doubtful distinction of being the first declared disciple of Hopkins was earned by Mr. Monk Gibbon who, in 1932, published *Seventeen Sonnets*, with the following dedication :

> " To the Memory
> of
> GERARD MANLEY HOPKINS
>
> The influence of whose work
> will be seen in some if not all."

The influence is, indeed, pervasive ; and the skill with which Mr. Gibbon handles his borrowed instrument is adequately shown in the first sonnet :

> " THE POETRY OF GERARD MANLEY HOPKINS.
>
> Incomparable treasure, heart's blood spilt
> Out of heart's anguish, high heart, all-hoping heart,
> Child-innocent, clean heart, of guile or guilt,
> But heart storm-tried, fire-purged, heaven-chastened (chart
> Clear mapped but course sore-battered, when the worst
> Skies clashed, light flashed—God visioned, none the less
> God terrible—from that too great cloud stress
> Came rain, came words at last and falling fast.)
> And why ? To blossom beauty, seeding truth
> In stillness thirty years, the saturate earth
> Bounty for bounty yielding ; tempest ruth
> Vindicate (not despair that deals out dearth).
> No havoc out of all heart's havoc wrought
> But only heaven comfort, pilgrim sought."

Since most of the imitators are of the Marxist school, it is important to notice that Mr. Gibbon stresses the religious significance of the master's work. So also does the author of a nineteen-lined poem called " To Gerard Manley Hopkins " [2] :

> ". . . Manly thy ascesis of the athlete grinding sense
> On the whetstone of the blade-edge of the fleet foot agonist,
> manly
> The incense of thy prayer . . ."

[1] *Op. cit.* X. [2] By T. E. Casson (*Sunday Referee*, April 29, 1934).

The conclusion is plangently rhetorical :

> " Holy, Muse-enchanted, solitary from libidinous
> Dithyramb of the Bacchic god deafening Cithaeron,
> Saint, sage, singer, mystes, whom the angels of God
> environ ! "

Coming so pat from the mouths of other poets, the tense, taut style which had been wrung spontaneously from the exaltations and agonies of Hopkins strikes us as all amiss, at best as a kind of clever impersonation. Mr. Monk Gibbon, at times, catches the manner perfectly :

> " On life, on love, on honour, each what will
> Strings lyre, harps homage out, his chosen theme
> Urging to speech what little speech can spill,
> Building word-hold for else-were-wordless dream." [1]

Mr. R. P. Hewett tries objective description in the well-known accents—idiosyncrasy and little else : [2]

> " Here the green empty miles lie sweet ; branches random-fangled
> Netted, lac'd, trac'd, fretted, silent show through the blue
> Cold-rolled sky ; through black pack'd knuckled twigs a-tangled,
> All lies flat, misty, chequered with plump young bushes fresh and new."

Mr. Hewett's *Poems* were written between his sixteenth and twenty-first years. But the sharp effect of combined assonance and clotted consonants has proved irresistible to many young writers. Mr. Christopher Lee begins a frankly Hopkinsian sonnet thus :

> " Against the stack's rough edge the sky stirs, cracks
> lets oozelight ebb (no flood this) over space
> uncharitable ; sweeps comfort-shadow grace
> of hedgebed by, gleams dew's drip, berry's wax.
> Branches stand out, numb knee asserts, hurts, slacks
> and bends . . ." [3]

In this way the reader's mind " jolts on the juts of thought " to a conclusion which brings little compensative illumination.

A number of young poets have learnt to look with the eye of Hopkins at the inscape of trees in repose or in movement ; at the grace and mastery of a bird's flight ; at the beauty of muscular

[1] *Op. cit., Chacun son gout*, p. 15. [2] *Poems* (1936), p. 22. [3] *Poems* (1938), p. 25.

bodies in action. Mr. R. E. Warner executes a winsome variation on the bird-theme in a manner suggested by the opening lines of *The Heraclitean Fire* :

> " Leaves, summer's coinage spent, golden are all together whirled,
> sent spinning, dipping, slipping, shuffled by heavy-handed wind,
> shifted sideways, sifted, lifted, and in swarms made to fly
> spent sun-flies, gorgeous tatters, airdrift, pinions of trees." [1]

But when lapwings are described as " minions of the rush of air " the origin of both motive and style is too apparent.

The last line of *Felix Randal* seems to have provided the inspiration for Mr. T. H. White's sixteen-line poem—*A Dray Horse.*[2] The poet makes a valiant effort to achieve the Hopkinsian rhetoric of verse : he bangs a bass drum and shows a fine muscle, but in doing so he deafens the reader and strains himself :

> " Meek Hercules, passion of arched power bowed to titanic affection ;
> Docile though vanquishing, stout-limber in vastness, plunging and spurning thy road ;
> Taughten thy traces, triumph past me, take thy shattering direction
> Through misty Glasgow, dragging in a tremendous beer wagon thy cobble-thundering load.
>
> Thy wineskin of bright blood holds dim traits of trembling Diana,
> Of the blood hunter, the quelled virgin, surging to fast, to urging thighs ;
> Speaks of that ground-beater in her beauty, that trampler, turf-disdainer ;
> Poised, reined, heeled, hurled to an impetuous rise.
>
> Speaks of him also, the sprig of racecourses ; Satan, wild-eyed, wild-oat sower ;
> Of him, the nappy scion, the nerve-spun heritor of splenetic sires ;
> Him, the sinew-modelled, fancy-manèd, high-stepping pace goer ;
> The dandy tragedian, consumed by mental fires.
>
> But thou, nearer than these, art bodily perfection ;
> Dear horse, thou art certainly the most beautiful of things.
> Thou art fire-stamping Colossus : thou art thunder.
> Go, Hercules, beget thy stallion kings."

[1] *The Listener*, March 13, 1935. [2] *Ibid.*, July 12, 1933.

We may fitly conclude these examples of direct imitation with an excerpt from the poet-critic who has denied the existence of a 'school of Hopkins'. Mr. Cecil Day Lewis has given us, in the first movement of his "symphonic poem" *A Time to Dance*,[1] what appears to be the longest attempt at sustained 'Hopkins'. It is a spirited account of the pioneer flight from England to Australia of two lieutenants, Parer and M'Intosh, in "a craft of obsolete design, a condemned D. H. nine".

In form and rhythm the poem derives from two sources—Tennyson's *The Revenge* [2] and Hopkins's *The Wreck of the Deutschland*. Tennyson's swinging and cleverly varied logaœdics are suitably sprung and heightened by 'kennings', alliteration, pararhyme, and all the usual devices. The diction, which has more than a dash of Kipling-Masefield raciness, is richer for the metrical freedom:

> "Fog came, a wet blanket, a kill-joy, the primrose-of-
> morning's blight . . .
> Snaring the sky with treachery, sneering
> At hope's loss of height."

Occasionally, echoes of Hopkins are obtrusive:

> "what centuried strata of life
> Fuelled the fire that haled them to heaven, the power that
> held them
> Aloft? For their plane was a laugh
> A *patch*, brittle as *match*stick, a bubble, a lift for a ghost." [3]

Hopkins's syntactical and rhyming idiosyncrasies are reproduced:

> "flame streamed out behind
> A crimson scarf of, as life blood out of a wound . . .
>
> put her at the air, a
> Sorry hack . . .
> Said the mechanic Parer."

Lastly we turn to an even more important aspect of Hopkins's influence—the question as to how far he can be held responsible

[1] Published in 1935.

[2] ". . . the most remarkable technical achievement of Victorian poetry." (*A Hope for Poetry*, p. 11.) Presumably Mr. Lewis considers Hopkins a twentieth-century poet.

[3] Cf. *That Nature is a Heraclitean Fire* (No. 48): "patch, matchwood . . ."

for the persistent obscurity of so much modern verse. Mr. Day Lewis is not reassuring :

> " The search for methods for restoring freshness to words contributes to the obscurity of post-war poetry. Poets have gone back to old grammatical usages and have taken new grammatical licences. . . . Where Mr. Auden's earlier poems are obscure, it is due much more to an elliptical use of language than to any confusion of thought or a non-conductivity of the images. . . . Although Hopkins founded no school, his naif and successful experimentation with words entitles him to the position of inaugurator of this revolution in language." [1]

The statement is misleading. Granted that Hopkins has taught poets to utilize more completely the resources of the language, it is nevertheless unfair to associate his grammatical licences (which are usually integral to thought of admirable precision) with the wanton vagueness, the continuous and unexplosive obscurity of much of the verse of Mr. Auden, Mr. Charles Madge, and Mr. George Barker. In the most difficult passages of Hopkins, *some* meaning, some poetic light leaps from the page at once, and lends a fascination to our search for the whole import. But in much recent poetry the splendid obscurities of Hopkins are replaced by passages or entire poems in which a genuine intellectual quality is unsupported by sensuous feeling and imaginative glow—that transforming power without which language remains flat and prosaic.

For example, the following stanzas from Mr. Auden's early charade, *Paid on Both Sides*, are among the least obscure in the whole extremely immature work. A woman whose husband has been killed in a vendetta has just borne a child :

> " [. . . Back curtains draw. Joan with child and corpse.]
>
> J. Not from this life, not from this life is any
> To keep ; sleep, day and play would not help there
> Dangerous to new ghost ; new ghost learns from many
> Learns from old termers what death is, where.
>
> Who's jealous of his latest company
> From one day to the next final to us,
> A changed one ; would use sorrow to deny
> Sorrow, to replace death ; sorrow is sleeping thus.
>
> Unforgetting is not to-day's forgetting
> For yesterday, not bedrid scorning,
> But a new begetting
> An unforgiving morning." [2]

[1] *A Hope for Poetry*, p. 71. [2] *Poems* (Second Edition), p. 12.

This owes much to Hopkins, but not enough: Hopkins was more liberal with his "clews". We find ourselves asking: "What is 'this life'—the child's or human life?" . . . "'any' what?" . . . "Is 'to keep' active or passive in its relation to *any*?" and so on. The lines have a formal subtlety, and the intellectual conundrum can be solved with patience; but the light of certainty does not flood all parts, and the exercise is not poetically stimulating.

Mr. Charles Madge is another young poet who has been honoured by inclusion in *The Oxford Book of Modern Verse*; but he seems to have carried away from Hopkins the perverse notion that poetry can be strictly non-representational, 'abstract':

"*Apprehending.*

Master to me: fly turning clouds to walls
approaching steep to life if that is square.
The hold on me of the held-onto hand
shows where bones lie, and if I ever knew
the touched quick once, big now is here instead . . ."[1]

This kind of obscurity is common to-day; but its superficial connexion with Hopkins is entirely specious.

One important result of the many imitations of Hopkins has been to familiarize readers with the style of the master and so remove from his work that appearance of queerness and eccentricity which was for so long a barrier to complete appreciation. Certainly the verse of the younger writers is always more significant when there is nothing more of Hopkins in evidence than a taut compact style, a direct and resourceful diction, and a form of sprung rhythm which, while rarely approaching the mastery of the original, gives an additional range to the poetic instrument.

[1] *New Verse*, July 1933, p. 6. Cf. Miss Edith Sitwell's comment: "Here we have all Hopkins's difficulty and obscurity, but none of his strength, of his vitality, of his acute visual sense . . ." (*Op. cit.* p. 69.)

APPENDICES

APPENDIX A

(See Chapter II)

In the two hundred and eighty lines of *The Wreck of the Deutschland*, there are not more than fifty or sixty in which initial difficulties of stressing need arise ; in most of these lines doubt is dispelled as soon as the reader considers the alliterative, rhyming, and assonantal syllables in relation to the vital meaning. The syllables which we have in Chapter II. preferred to mark as half-stresses could, of course, be rationalized by means of the notation used by Hopkins himself in the MS. of *To what serves Mortal Beauty* (see Chapter III. p. 91). In this way the first four words of *The Deutschland* would be scanned, *and* read : " Thou mastering me God ! ". There is more than one way of reading Hopkins, as there is more than one way of playing a great sonata ; and we personally adopt the system of half-stresses because we prefer in every instance to give slightly more weight to the syllable bearing the rhythmical beat. In MS. " A ", stresses are marked in a few lines ; when these are quoted below they are indicated thus—(A). These stress-marks, though probably the author's own, may represent the reading of Bridges :

Stanza 8 :

Wíll, móuthed to flésh-búrst,[1]
Gúsh !—flúsh the mán, the béing with it, sóur or swéet,
Brím, ín a flash, fúll !

(Here the mark ⁀ indicates " hurried syllables ".)

Stanza 9 :

Be adóred among mén [1]
Gód, thrèe-númberèd fórm ;

. . . .

Beyónd sáying swéet, pàst télling of tóngue,

Stanza 10 :

Or as Áustin, a língering-óut swéet skíll, (A)

. . . .

Mástery, bút be adóred, bút be adóred Kíng. (A) [1]

Stanza 13 :

Wíry and whìte-fíery and whírlwind-swivellèd snów (A)

[1] In these lines the nether-loops are variants of ⁀ to indicate elision of adjacent vowels.

Stanza 19:

A máster, hér master and míne!

. . . . .

Has óne fétch in hér: she réars hersélf to divíne
Eárs . . .

Stanza 21:

Súrf, snów, ríver and eárth
Gnáshed . . .
Thou mártyr-máster: in thý síght . . .

Stanza 24:

Í was under a róof here, Í was at rést,

. . . . . .

The cróss to her she cálls Christ to her, . . .

Stanza 25:

Bréathe, àrch and oríginal Bréath . . .
Bréathe, bòdy of lóvely Déath.

. . . . .

They were élse-mínded then, áltogéther, the mén (A)
Wóke thee with a *we are perishing* in the wéather of Gennésaréth. (A and B)

Stanza 26:

Whát by yóur méasure is the héaven of desíre,

Stanza 28:

Ípse, the ónly one, Chríst, Kíng, Héad:

. . . . .

Dó, dèal, lórd it with líving and déad:

Stanza 30:

Wórd that héard and képt thee and úttered thee óutríght. (A)

Stanza 32:

Of the Yóre-flòod, of the yéar's fáll;

. . . . . .

The gírth of ít and the wharf of ít and the wáll;
Stánching, quénching ócean of a mótionable mínd;
Gróund of béing and gránite of ít: past áll
Grásp Gód, thróned behínd . . . (A)

Stanza 33:

With a mércy that outrídes . . .

Stanza 34:

The hèaven-flúng, hèart-fléshed, máiden-fúrled (A)
Míracle-in-Máry-of-fláme,

[The "*fl*ame" of the Holy Spirit is miraculously "*fl*ung", then "*fl*eshed" and "*f*urled" in the maiden, Mary.
This progression is brought out by the full stresses.]

. . . . . .

A released shówer let flásh to the shíre . . . (A and B)

Stanza 35 :

Dáme, at oúr dóor
Drówned, and among oúr shóals,
Remémber us in the róads, the heaven-háven of the Rewárd :
Our Kíng back, oh, upon Énglish sóuls !
Let him easter in us, be a dáyspring to the dímness of us, be a crímson-cresseted east,
More bríghtening her, ráre-dear Brítain, as his réign rólls,
Príde, rose, prínce, hero of us, hígh-priest,
Our heárts' charity's heárth's fíre, our thóughts' chivalry's thróng's Lórd.

All the full stresses in this canorous last stanza accord with those marked in MSS. " A " and " B ". Here as elsewhere, the half- or secondary-stresses, phrase-marks, loops, give the present writer's interpretation of the poet's total rhythmical intention.

APPENDIX B

(See Chapter III)

Additional Facts about Outrides

In his search for the real rhythmical intention underlying Hopkin's use of outrides, Mr. C. K. Ogden (in his *Psyche* Editorial, 1936) [1] brought to light some interesting facts. Counting altogether 104 outrides scattered through fifteen poems in MSS. " B " and " H " (*Poems*, Nos. 7, 12, 14, 15, 19, 20, 21, 23, 29, 40, 43, 53, 61, 62, 63), Mr. Ogden classifies them according to the type of foot in which they are found. If the short pause postulated after each outride be ignored, and the whole line be scanned as ordinary sprung rhythm, the outrides are merged into feet of from two to six syllables. Fifty-four outrides are immediately followed by some sort of punctuation ; seven more (making sixty-one) would be followed by some punctuation mark in normal English usage. In ninety-four of the total number, the constitution of the foot in which the outride occurs is sufficiently clear ; and if the feet are read smoothly, ' paeonic ' (´ × × ×) and ' dactylic ' feet predominate. The distribution is as follows :

Paeonic :	43.
Dactylic :	43.
Trochaic :	5.
´ × × × × :	2.
´ × × × × × :	1.
	94.

[1] Pp. 33–5.

Mr. Ogden finds ten doubtful cases when the constitution of the foot depends on the placing of a stress in another part of the line. Two of these have already been mentioned in Chapter III. (pp. 84, 99): first, the peculiar marking of two outrides in a paeonic foot ("It gáthers to a gréatness . . ."—No. 7); second, the line in No. 12 which we have decided to read:

"Tímes told lóvelier, more dángerous, O mý chevaliér!"

All but two of the remaining doubtful cases are lines in which the outride is immediately followed by two equally "stressy" syllables. These are best indicated by Hopkins's mark ⌐—¬, for, as he says, "though one has and the other has not the metrical stress, in the recitation-stress they are to be about equal".[1] Thus if we use the poet's mark, with a slightly thicker vertical stroke to indicate the 'ideal' or expected beat, we can safely dispense with Mr. Ogden's inquiry concerning the constitution of the whole foot when read smoothly; for the sole purpose of the outride is to produce a rhythmic effect *different* from that of the ordinary dactylic or paeonic foot: it is, as Hopkins plainly says, to produce a calculated break in the rhythmic flow—an effect similar to 'counterpoint':—

No. 15:

"Thís in drúdgery, dáy-labouring-oút life's áge."

"Bút uncúmbered: méadow-dówn is nót distréssed"

No. 20:

"Rúral rúral kéeping—fólk, flócks, and flówers."

No. 21:

"Have an éye to the sákes of him, quáint móonmarks . . ."

"Óff him, but méaning mótion fáns fresh our wíts with wónder."

No. 23:

"Fórward-líke, but hówever, and like favourable héaven heard thése."

(Stanza 12.)

(Unless the suffix "-like" is stressed, the outride will not come, as the poet says it must—and as it does in every other stanza—, "between the 3rd. and 4th. foot".[2] Transferring the stress from "-like" to "favourable" would make the outride irregularly forward-like; and this may have been the poet's intention. Furthermore, although a stress or accent on the first syllable of "however" is possible and heard, it is certainly unusual. The slight pause required, by definition, after "and" can perhaps be justified oratorically: it emphasizes the poet's apprehension.)

[1] *Letters*, vol. ii. p. 129. [2] *Poems*, p. 109; 23 (note).

No. 29 :

"How fár from thén fórethought of, all thy more boísterous yéars,"

No. 40 :

"But áh, but Ó thou térrible, why wouldst thou rúde on mé . . ."

APPENDIX C

(See Chapter IV)

Types of Compound Epithet in the Poetry of Hopkins

(1) The 'objective' compound : *widow-making* . . . seas (4.13) ; *world-wielding* shoulder (14).

(2) The 'instrumental' compound : *bell-swarmèd* . . . city (20) ; *tear-tricked* eyes (30) ; *Christ-done* deed (39).

(3) The 'locative' compound : *heaven-flung*, *heart-fleshed*, *maiden-furled* (4.34) ; *froliclavish* (72).

(4) The 'similative' compound : *moth-soft* Milky Way (4.27) ; *tool-smooth* . . . light (32) ; *foam-fallow* hanks (63).

(5) The 'parasynthetic' compound : *water-wattled* . . . sands (5) ; *silver-surfèd* cherry (18) ; *clearest-selvèd* spark (=Man—48). (A combination of Types 2 or 4 and Type 5 is common : *frost-furred* . . . ivies (83) ; *beak-leaved* boughs (32).)

(6) The compound 'of the adverbial adjective' : *blue-beating* . . . height (4.27) ; *hoar-hallowèd* shrines (17) ; *shining-shot* furls (43).

(7) The compound 'of the qualified noun' : *hoary-glow* height ; *The-last-breath* penitent spirits (4.27 and 33) ; *fresh-firecoal* chestnut-falls (13).

(8) The compound 'of the adjectival noun' : *hell-rook* ranks (23) ; *foam-tuft* fumitory (64).

(9) The 'bi-adjectival' compound : *blue-bleak* embers (12) ; *wilful-wavier* . . . meal-drift (14) ; *airy-grey* eye (24).

(10) The 'adjectival phrase' : *dappled-with-damson* west (4.5) ; *brown-as-dawning-skinned* (17) ; *not-by-morning-matchèd* face (36).

(11) The 'modified adjective or adverb' : *much-thick* . . . air (10) ; *very-violet-sweet* . . . hills (14) ; *black-about* air (4.24).

(12) The 'verb and object' : *fall-gold* mercies (4.23) ; *blear-all* black (26) ; *rollrock* highroad (33) ; *wring-world* right foot (40).

(13) The 'participle and adverb' : *lingering-out* skill (4.10) ; *hung-heavenward* boughs (54) ; *come-back-again* things (58).

(14) The 'appositional phrase' : *womb-of-all*, *home-of-all*, *hearse-of-all* night (32).

(15) The 'asyntactic' compound : *feel-of-primrose* hands (3) ; *rope-over* thigh (43) ; *forth-and-flaunting* sun (63) ; *fault-not-found-with* good (67).

APPENDIX D

(See Chapter VI)

The following reconstruction, by Fr. Geoffrey Bliss, of Hopkins's fragmentary poem No. 67, is based on a close examination of the two manuscript copies in "H"; his sensitive textual criticism should, of course, be read in full:

On a Piece of Music

Who shaped these walls has shewn
The music of his mind,
Made known, though thick through stone,
What beauty beat behind.

[How all is one way wrought!
How all things suit and sit!
Then ah the tune that thought
Trod to that fancied it!].

Not free in this because
His powers seemed free to play:
He swept what scope he was
To sweep and must obey.

Though down his being's bent
Like air he changed in choice,
That was an instrument
Which overvaulted voice.

Nor angel insight can
Learn how the heart is hence:
Since all the make of man
Is law's indifference.

Therefore this masterhood,
This piece of perfect song,
This fault-not-found-with good
Is neither right nor wrong.

No more than red and blue,
No more than Re and Mi,
Or sweet the golden glue
That's built for by the bee.

For good grows wild and wide,
Has shades, is nowhere none ;
But right must seek a side
And choose for chieftain one.

[What makes the man and what
The man within that makes :
Ask whom he serves or not
Serves and what side he takes.]

Who built these walls made known
The music of his mind,
Yet here he has but shewn
His ruder-rounded rind.
His brightest blooms lie there unblown,
His sweetest nectar hides behind. [1]

In introducing his rearrangement of the nine separated passages of *The Woodlark* (No. 64), Fr. Bliss says :

> " It will be seen that for the three missing lines (I do not know what will be thought of me !) I have supplied lines of my own, enclosing them in rather unnecessary square brackets. The excuse for this impiety is a pious one : I would have the effect of a lovely piece of verse to be, at least for a moment, not interrupted by gaps in its strain."

Teevo cheevo cheevio chee :
O where, what can thát be ?
Weedio-weedio : there again !
So tiny a trickle of sóng-strain ;
And al' round not to be found
For brier, bough, furrow, or gréen ground [2]
Before or behind or fár or at hand
Either left either right
Anywhere in the súnlight.

Well, after all ! Ah but hark—
' I am the little wóodlark.
The skylark is my cousin and he
Is known to men more than me.
Round a ring, around a ring
And while I sail (must listen) I sing.

---

[1] *The Month*, Feb., 1936, pp. 160–7. Stanzas 2 and 9 (in square brackets) would according to Fr. Bliss, be better omitted. In *The Month* stanzas 8 and 9 appear in reverse order. The change is an afterthought communicated to me by Fr. Bliss on Nov. 18, 1943.

[2] Fr. Bliss says, in the same letter : " If I were doing it now I should suggest another line after ' ground ' : ' If I sit, if I stand '. It is a dry, light line, but suits, I think, the tune."

To-day the sky is two and two
With white strokes and strains of the blue.
The blue wheat-acre is underneath
And the braided ear breaks out of the sheath,
The ear in milk, lush the sash,
And crush-silk poppies aflash,
The blood-gush blade-gash
Flame-rash rudred
Bud shelling or broad-shed
Tatter-tassel-tangled and dingle-a-dangled
Dandy-hung dainty head.

And down the furrow dry
Sunspurge and oxeye
And lace-leaved lovely
Foam-tuft fumitory.[1]

I am so véry, O só very glad
That I dó thínk there is not to be had
[Anywhere any more joy to be in.
Cheevio :] when the cry within
Says Go on then I go on
Till the longing is less and the good gone.
But down drop, if it says Stop,
To the all-a-leaf of the treétop.
And after that off the bough
[Hover-float to the hedge brow.]

Through the velvety wind V-winged
[Where shake shadow is sun's-eye-ringed]
To the nest's nook I balance and buoy
With a sweet joy of a sweet joy,
Sweet, of a sweet, of a sweet joy
Of a sweet—a sweet—sweet—joy.' [2]

---

[1] Of the metre of these four lines Fr. Bliss says : " It is a deliberate slow-down after the excitement of the previous passage, and is to be read in a dainty mincing manner. But I think it was intended to preserve the four-beat of the rest of the poem". This is true ; though the first of these lines has, in the MS., a gap between " down " and " the ". The variety of the sprung rhythm is bounded by the four syllables of " Fláme-rásh rúdréd " and the twelve of " Tátter-tassel-tángled and díngle-a-dángled ".

[2] *The Month,* June 1936, pp. 528–35.

BIBLIOGRAPHY

(Chronological)

A. *The Posthumous Works of Gerard Manley Hopkins.*

(1) Poems printed in Anthologies :

1893. *Robert Bridges and Contemporary Poets* (vol. vii. of " Poets and Poetry of the Nineteenth Century ", edited by A. H. Miles. Second Impression, 1906 ; pp. 179–88).

The poems, selected and introduced by Robert Bridges, are : Nos. 3, 8, 9, 26, 31, 33, 51, parts of 44, 50, 73, 77.

1895. *Lyra Sacra*, edited by H. C. Beeching. The poems are : Nos. 78, 7, 2, 24.

A Book of Christmas Verse, edited by H. C. Beeching. One poem : No. 37.

1915. *The Spirit of Man*, edited by Robert Bridges. (Fourteenth Impression, 1934.)

The poems are : Nos. 26, 31, 51, part of 3, first stanza of 4, 16, 27.

---

(2) Collected Verse and Prose, etc.

1918. *Poems of Gerard Manley Hopkins*, edited with Notes by Robert Bridges. (Portrait and MS. facsimile of No. 67 ; pp. 124.)

1929. *A Vision of Mermaids* : Prize Poem dated Christmas, 1862, and for the first time printed in full, etc. (See *Poems*, No. 77.)

1930. *Poems of G. M. H.* (Second Edition), edited, as before, by Robert Bridges, but with an Appendix of Additional Poems, and a Critical Introduction by Charles Williams ; pp. xvi. and 159.

1935. *The Letters of G. M. H. to Robert Bridges*, edited with Notes and an Introduction by Claude Colleer Abbott. (With portraits, two songs by Hopkins, and MS. facsimile of *Harry Ploughman*) ; pp. xlvii. and 322.

The Correspondence of G. M. H. and R. W. Dixon, edited with Notes and an Introduction by C. C. Abbott. (With portraits and facsimiles) ; pp. xxxi. and 192.

Early Poems and Extracts from the Note-books and Papers of G. M. H. (*The Criterion*, October ; pp. 1–17.)

All included later in the next item.

1937. *The Note-books and Papers of G. M. H.*, edited with Notes and a Preface by Humphry House. (With fourteen reproductions of drawings by G. M. H.) ; pp. xxxvi. and 473.

1938. *Further Letters of G. M. H., including his Correspondence with Coventry Patmore*, edited with Notes and an Introduction by C. C. Abbott. (With photographs and drawings) ; pp. xxxviii. and 297.

B. *Books, Essays, Articles, etc. on, or referring to, Gerard Manley Hopkins.*

1893. *Critical Memoir*, by Robert Bridges, in *Poets of the Century* (see above); pp. 179–82.

1909. *Impressions of G. M. H., S.J.*, by Joseph Keating, S.J. *The Month*: July (pp. 59–62); (ii) Aug. (pp. 151–60); (iii) Sept. (pp. 246–58).

1912. *Gerard Hopkins*, by Katherine Brégy. (*The Poets' Chantry*; pp. 70–88.)

1919. *Gerard Manley Hopkins*, by George O'Neill, S.J. (*Essays on Poetry*; pp. 117–38.)

Gerard Hopkins: A recovered Poet, by L. I. Guiney. *The Month*, March; pp. 205–14.

The Poetry of G. M. H., by J. Middleton Murry. *The Athenaeum*, June 6; reprinted in *Aspects of Literature* (1920), pp. 52–61.

Other selected reviews of *Poems* (1918), all containing excellent criticism, are:

Times Literary Supplement, January 9.

Improper Editing—A Counter-Blast (A Defence of R. Bridges, by L. I. Guiney, against an attack made by another writer in the same paper). (*The Universe*, March 21.)

The Tablet, April 5.

The Irish Rosary (Peter McBrien), June.

(1)

1920. *Father Gerard Hopkins, his poetry, his character, his prose*, by Frederick Page, "Plures", etc. *Dublin Review*, July; pp. 40–66.

The Essentials of Mysticism, by Evelyn Underhill. "The Mystic as Creative Artist"; pp. 71–2.

1921. *The Poetry of Gerard Hopkins*, by A. J. Kilmer. (*The Circus and Other Essays*; pp. 180–5.)

English Metrists, by T. S. Omond; *Postscript*; p. 263.

G. M. Hopkins (A Study), by Edward Sapir. *Poetry*, September.[1]

1922. *Poetry and Three Poets*, by G. N. Shuster. (*The Catholic Spirit in Modern Literature*; pp. 115–21.) The poets are Patmore, Hopkins, and Aubrey de Vere.

1923. *Difficult Poetry*, by Alan Porter. *The Spectator*, Jan. 13; p. 66.

1924. *G. M. Hopkins* (A Study), by Sam. Putnam. *Chicago Post*,[1] May 30.

1926. *Gerard Hopkins* (A study, mainly of *The Windhover*), by I. A. Richards. *The Dial* (Chicago), September 19; pp. 195–206.

G. M. Hopkins (A Study), by I. A. Richards. *Cambridge Review*, October 28; pp. 49–51.

1927. *A Survey of Modernist Poetry*, by Laura Riding and Robert Graves; pp. 90–4.

1928. *G. M. Hopkins and Associative Form*, by Alec Brown. *Dublin Magazine*, April; pp. 6–20.

---

[1] Read, with other cuttings, at the Oxford University Press, by the courtesy of Mr. Gerard Hopkins.

1930. *Gerard Manley Hopkins* (A critical biography), by G. F. Lahey, S.J.; pp. viii. and 172.

Critical Introduction (to *Poems*, Second Edition, 1930), by Charles Williams; pp. ix.–xvi.

Seven Types of Ambiguity (in Poetry), by William Empson ; Chapter VII. Contains a highly interesting study of *The Windhover*.

Poetry as Experiment and Unity, by M. D. Zabel. *Poetry*, December ; pp. 151–61.

Hopkins and Newman, by G. F. Lahey. *Commonweal*, June 25 ; pp. 211–13.

Practical Criticism, by I. A. Richards. Poem VI. (*Spring and Fall*, No. 31 in *Poems*) ; pp. 81–90.

Review of *Poems* (Second Edition)—*Times Lit. Supplnt.*,[1] December 25.

1931. *Some Modern Poetry*, by W. J. Turner. *Nineteenth Century*, February ; pp. 243–52.

Gerard Manley Hopkins, by Alan Pryce-Jones. *London Mercury*, May ; pp. 45–52.

The Poetry of G. M. Hopkins, by Harman Grisewood. *Dublin Review*, October ; pp. 213–26.

1932. *Form in Modern Poetry*, by Herbert Read ; pp. 45–54.

Gerard Manley Hopkins, by F. R. Leavis (Chapter V. of *New Bearings in English Poetry* ; pp. 159–93).

G. M. Hopkins, Poet and Prosodist, by Muriel Kent. *The Bookman*, March ; pp. 312–3.

1933. *Poetry and Belief in G. M. H.*, by Herbert Read. *New Verse*, No. 1 January ; pp. 11–15.

The Poetry of G. M. H., by Herbert Read. (*English Critical Essays* Twentieth Century, edited by P. M. Jones ; pp. 351–74.

N.B.—These two essays by Mr. Read must be read with the greatest caution. His classification of Hopkins's poems according to the presence or absence of " belief " is now entirely discredited.[2]

Gerard Manley Hopkins, by G. W. Stonier. (*Gog Magog and Other Essays* ; pp. 43–63.

English Poetry in the Later 19th Century, by B. Ifor Evans ; pp. 210–18 and *passim*.

Modern English Poetry (1882–1932), by R. L. Mégroz. " Anti-Decadence " ; pp. 61–3. " Technical Developments " ; pp. 235–7.[3]

The Poetry of G. M. H., by E. E. Phare ; pp. viii. and 149.

Discovering Poetry, by Elizabeth Drew ; pp. 82 *et seqq.*, 110, 157.

---

[1] See the collection of press cuttings at the O.U.P.

[2] In a letter to the present writer, dated Sept. 18, 1935, Mr. Read says : " In so far as I have, in my essay on Hopkins, implied that there was an open conflict between the poetic impulse and the theological faith in Hopkins, I confess I was wrong ".

[3] This section contains a rhythmical reading of *The Loss of the Eurydice* which is quite contrary to the poet's intention.

1934. *The Poetry of G. M. H.*, by D. P. McGuire. English Association—Adelaide Branch, Pamphlet No. 2 ; pp. 31.

La Poésie Naive et Savante de Gerard Hopkins, by André Bremond, S.J. *Études*, Oct. 5 ; pp. 23–49.

Contains translations of certain poems into French.

A Hope for Poetry, by Cecil Day Lewis ; pp. 2–12 ; 63–4.

Aspects of Modern Poetry, by Edith Sitwell ; pp. 51–70.

After Strange Gods, by T. S. Eliot ; pp. 47–8.

English Poetry and the English Language, by F. W. Bateson ; pp. 117–8.

The Trend of Modern Poetry, by Geoffrey Bullough ; pp. 23–25, 165–6 and *passim*.

1935. *The Mind and Poetry of G. M. Hopkins, S.J.*, by B. W. Kelly ; pp. 44.

Gerard Manley Hopkins, by Daniel Sargent. (*Four Independents* ; pp. 117–83.

New Verse, No. 14—The " Hopkins Number ". The contents are :

(i) *Hopkins's Religious Life*, by Humphry House ; pp. 3–5.
(ii) *Art and Inspiration*, by André Bremond, S.J. ; pp. 5–12.
(iii) *Hopkins and Duns Scotus*, by Christopher Devlin, S.J. ; pp. 12–17.
(iv) *What is all this juice ?*, by Charles Madge ; pp. 17–21.
(v) *Blood or Bran*, by Geoffrey Grigson ; pp. 21–23.
(vi) *Hopkins and Hopkinese*, by Geoffrey Grigson ; pp. 24–26.
(vii) *A Comment*, by Louis MacNeice ; pp. 26–27.
(viii) *The Welsh Influence*, by Ll. Wyn Griffith ; pp. 27–29.
(ix) *A Short Bibliography* ; p. 30.

Select Reviews of *Letters*, Vols. I. and II. :

Osbert Burdett in *Nineteenth Century*, February ; pp. 234–41.
Priest and Poet, by Joseph Keating. *The Month*, February ; pp. 125–36.
Max Plowman in *The Adelphi*, March ; pp. 356–61.
Herbert Read in *The Criterion*, April ; pp. 478–82.
Dom Wulfstan Phillipson in *The Downside Review* ; April ; pp. 210–28.
M. D. Zabel in *Poetry*, July ; pp. 210–19.

1936. *Gerard Hopkins : Jesuit*, by Egerton Clarke. *Dublin Review*, January ; pp. 127–41.

G. M. H., Poet or Priest ?, by J. Gould Fletcher. *American Review*, January ; pp. 331–46.

In a Poet's Workshop. An Unfinished Poem (No. 67) by *G. M. H.*, by Geoffrey Bliss. *The Month*, Feb. ; pp. 160–7.

In a Poet's Workshop. II. The Woodlark (*No.* 64), by Geoffrey Bliss. *The Month*, June ; pp. 528–35.

These two articles contain well reasoned recensions, based on a study of the MSS.

The Wreck of the Deutschland, by W. H. Gardner. *Essays and Studies* (Eng. Assocn.),Vol. XXI. (1935) ; pp. 124–52.

1936. *Hopkins and Duns Scotus*, by W. H. Gardner. *Scrutiny*, June ; pp. 61–70.

G. M. H. and Modern Poets, by David Daiches. *New Literary Values* ; pp. 23–51.

This Modern Poetry, by Babette Deutsch ; pp. 185–98 and *passim*.

Gerard Hopkins : A Study of Influences, by H. Downey. *Southern Review* (Louisiana State Univ.), Vol. I. No. 4 ; pp. 837–45.

The Wreck of the Deutschland (Review of W. H. Gardner's essay), by Christopher Morley. *Sat. Rev. of Lit.*, Aug. 15 ; p. 12.

Fr. G. Hopkins in His Letters, by Hugh Kelly. *Studies*, June ; pp. 239–52.

Forty Years of Verse, by G. M. Young. *London Mercury*, December ; pp. 112–22.

1937. *The Religious Problem in G. M. H.*, by W. H. Gardner. *Scrutiny*, June ; pp. 32–42.

G. M. H. and Music, by J. F. Waterhouse. *Music and Letters*, July ; pp. 227–35.

Editorial to *Psyche* (The Orthological Institute), Vol. XVI., by C. K. Ogden ; pp. 10–50.

A valuable discussion of sprung rhythm ; marred, as scholarship, by a certain flippancy.

The Formation and Use of Compound Epithets in English Poetry from 1579, by B. Groom. S.P.E. Tract XLIX. ; pp. 318–20.

Daylight and Champaign (Essays), by G. M. Young ; pp. 201–5.

1938. *Introduction to the Poetry of G. M. H.*, by R. S. Walker. *Aberdeen Univ. Review*, July ; pp. 232–43.

Patmore and Hopkins : Sense and Nonsense in English Prosody, by D. S. MacColl. *London Mercury*, July ; pp. 217–24.

Gerard Manley Hopkins, S.J., by Martin D'Arcy, S.J. (*Great Catholics*, edited by Claude Williamson ; pp. 438–46.)

1939. *Gerard Hopkins and His Influence*, by Laurence Binyon. *Univ. of Toronto Quarterly*, April ; pp. 264–70.

On Approaching Hopkins, by Terence Heywood. *Poetry Review*, May ; pp. 185–8.

Hopkins and Welsh Prosody, by Glyn Jones. *Life and Letters To-day*, June ; pp. 50–4.

The Poet and Society : Chapter IV. on G. M. H., by Philip Henderson.

Poet and Priest, by Ida Finlay. *Cornhill*, April ; pp. 467–78.

1940. *G. M. H.—His Literary Ancestry*, by Terence Heywood. *English* (Vol. III. No. 13) ; pp. 16–24.

1941. *G. Manley Hopkins as a Cywyddwr*, by W. H. Gardner. *Transactions of the Honourable Society of Cymmrodorion* (1940) ; pp. 184–8.

1942. *Dafydd ap Gwilym* : Introductory essay, " *The Problem of Translation* ", by David Bell. (*Y Cymmrodor*, Vol. XLVIII., May 1942 ; pp. 77–91. See especially page 85.)

Gerard Manley Hopkins, Poet and Priest, by John Pick ; pp. x and 169.

INDEX

Note.—All references to the prose works and poems of Hopkins are indexed under 'Hopkins, Gerard Manley'.

All matters relating to the technique of poetry are indexed under 'Versification'.